The Kādambarīnāṭaka
of
Narasiṁha

The Kādambarīnāṭaka of Narasiṁha

A Dramatic Version of Bāṇa's Classic *Kādambarī*

Translated into English with a critical introduction
by
Hideaki Sato

D.K. Printworld (P) Ltd.
NEW DELHI-110015

Catalogue in Publication Data — DK

Sato, Hideaki, 1955 –
The *Kādambarīnāṭaka* of Narasiṁha
Includes bibliographical references (p.).

1. Narasiṁha, 14th cent. Kādambarīnāṭaka. 2. Sanskrit drama — History and criticism. 3. Sanskrit drama — Translations into English. 4. English drama — Translations from Sanskrit. I. Title.

ISBN 81-246-0064-3

First Published in India in 1997

Published by:
D.K. Printworld (P) Ltd.
Regd. office: '*Sri Kunj*', F-52, Bali Nagar, New Delhi-110015
Phones: (011) 545-3975, 546-6019; *Fax:* (011) 546-5926

Typesetted at: Suneha Computer Systems, New Delhi. *Ph.:* 5504283

Printed by: DP's Impressive Impressions, New Delhi.

AVALOKITEŚVARABODHISATTVĀYA CA,

ACALANĀTHĀYA CA

NAMAḤ

Foreword

NARASIMHA'S only known play is a brilliant rearrangement of Bāṇa's unfinished novel *Kādambarī* with his son Bhūṣaṇa's completion. The matter is kept intact in almost every essential, but cutting out long descriptions and narrative and substituting action. In the successive acts this rises through a series of dramatic crises. The opening finds Candrāpīḍa already hunting in the northern mountains and carried by his horse to Mahāśvetā (who will introduce him to Kādambarī), which comes near the middle of the original narrative. Mahāśvetā's history is moved from there to Act V, where Narasiṃha has *kinnara* actors show it as a play within the play to Vaiśampāyana, her lover Puṇḍarīka transformed but thus reminded of his past. This resolution of the sub-plot has disastrous immediate consequences for Vaiśampāyana, but brings Candrāpīḍa back from his father to the mountains, thus renewing the main action. Yet as Kādambarī arrives to meet him, Candrāpīḍa is struck lifeless by Mahāśvetā's curse instigated by Vaiśampāyana's impetuous behaviour. This is the obstacle conjunction. Narasiṃha has here altered a detail in Bhūṣaṇa, who has Candrāpīḍa's heart fail on hearing what had happened to Vaiśampāyana. This change is surely an improvement, since hearts in this story do not fail even when seeing a lover apparently dead. In the final act (VIII) Narasiṃha has what is almost another play within the play when Rohiṇī by her divine power shows Candrāpīḍa living as Śūdraka listening to the parrot Vaiśampāyana at the very beginning of the original novel. The parrot's revelation brings about their restoration and the conclusion of the action. Dr. Sato in his Introduction has commented on several smaller changes by Narasiṃha which reinforce the action or modify the characterization, making Candrāpīḍa bolder as a lover than Bāṇa's cool and hesitant hero. This may make the play easier for an audience, but it spoils Bāṇa's psychological study of a different young lover, contrasting with his impulsive and undisciplined Puṇḍarīka.

Dr. Sato's translation is unusually straightforward and natural. It reads easily but brings out all the details of meaning without substituting simplified or vaguely 'equivalent' ideas.

The notes supply a new, critical text of the play, with corrections, restoration of omitted passages and elimination of unnecessary insertions. V. Krishnamacharya was a heroic editor, given the materials available, but he was not critical, does not let the reader see what he did or what readings were in the manuscripts. Now we have a full critical apparatus and a greatly improved text, which is here translated.

This excellent play shows the theatre tradition of India flourishing in the south (Āndhra) in the 14th century, when the north, ravaged by fanatics, lay in ruins, its literature in ashes. It gives the lie to the widespread prejudice that Indian culture was 'decadent' in the middle ages, the implication that conquerors were invited. But nothing is harder to eradicate than a prejudice rooted in many time-worn secondary and tertiary 'sources'. Here is an authentic and lively drama to exorcise it.

Toronto **A.K. Warder**
Nov, 1995

Preface

THE *Kādambarīnāṭaka* by the fourteenth-century Andhra playwright Narasiṁha is an eight-act Sanskrit-Prakrit dramatic version of the very well-known Sanskrit novel *Kādambarī* by Bāṇa and his son Bhūṣaṇa in the seventh century. Among the numerous innovations Narasiṁha introduces into the *Kādambarīnāṭaka* is the *garbhāṅka*, or the play within a play, in Act V, whose primary purpose is to remind its main spectator, Vaiśampāyana, of his former life as Puṇḍarīka and his unfulfilled love for Mahāśvetā. Narasiṁha is a maternal nephew of the renowned poet Agastyapaṇḍita, the author of the *Kṛṣṇacarita*, the *Nalakīrtikaumudī* and other works. Though the *Kādambarīnāṭaka* is obviously an excellent work, it has not yet received any appropriate treatment from scholars sine the only printed edition of it was published in 1936. It has never been thoroughly studied or translated into any modern language. This long neglect of the study of the play seems to be at least in part due to the popular theory that the Sanskrit-Prakrit dramatic literature after the tenth century or so is decadent, therefore unworthy of any special attention. The present researcher, however, has decided to undertake the task of introducing the *Kādambarīnāṭaka* to the world because he believes it is high time this fine *kāvya* work was properly treated by a specialist unbiased towards later Sanskrit-Prakrit plays.

This book consists of two parts. Part one is an introduction to the *Kādambarīnāṭaka*: it carefully examines the play in the light of its source story, that is, the novel *Kādambarī*; other Sanskrit-Prakrit plays; the *Nāṭyaśāstra* of Bharata and several later theoretical works on classical Indian dramaturgy and poetics, and the like. Part Two provides the first and complete English translation of the *Kādambarīnāṭaka* made directly from the only manuscripts of it now available, on which the printed edition of it is based, with detailed textual notes.

This book is a revised version of the researcher's doctoral dissertation, for which he was awarded the degree by the University of Toronto, Canada in 1991. The researcher must here express his gratitude to those who have helped him to accomplish this task. His deepest gratitude is due to his dissertation supervisor, Prof. A.K. Warder, who has always been the greatest inspiration for his studies. The researcher is also indebted to Dr. K.K. Raja and Mrs. R. Burnier in the Adyar Library and Research Centre, Madras; Mr. C.N. Ramesh in the Government Oriental Manuscripts Library, Madras; and Mr. S. Dasarathi in the Telugu Academy Library, Kakinada, who all assisted him on his visits to their institutions. He is also grateful to Prof. P. Sriramamurti in Andhra University, Waltair, who kindly provided him with some information by correspondence, and to Mr. G. Venu and his troupe in Irinjalakuda, Kerala, who delighted him with a Kutiyattam performance during his stay there. His gratitude is also due to Prof. N.K. Wagle in the University of Toronto and Prof. L. Rocher in the University of Pennsylvania for their constant encouragement and advice. Last but not least, his thanks are due to his family, friends and many others.

Hideaki Sato

Contents

PART ONE
AN INTRODUCTION TO THE *KĀDAMBARĪNĀṬAKA* OF NARASIṀHA

PART TWO
A COMPLETE ENGLISH TRANSLATION OF THE *KĀDAMBARĪNĀṬAKA* OF NARASIṀHA WITH DETAILED TEXTUAL NOTES

Abbreviations

The following abbreviations are used mainly in notes for the translation of the *Kādambarīnāṭaka* in Part Two.

H.S.	A Sanskrit or Prakrit reading given by the researcher, Hideaki Sato, for the improvement of the text of the *Kādambarīnāṭaka*.
H.S.Ch.	A Sanskrit *chāyā* reading given by the researcher, Hideaki Sato, for the improvement of the text of the *Kādambarīnāṭaka*.
K.N.	The *Kādambarīnāṭaka* of Narasiṁha; quotations from it given in Part One are the readings of them adopted by the researcher in Part Two, unless otherwise indicated.
M.Ch.M.	The Sanskrit *chāyā* manuscript of the *Kādambarīnāṭaka* preserved in the Government Oriental Manuscripts Library, Madras (Reference Number 4423), or its reading.
M.M.	The Sanskrit-Prakrit manuscript of the *Kādambarīnāṭaka* preserved in the Government Oriental Manuscripts Library, Madras (Reference Number 2484), or its Sanskrit or Prakrit reading.
M.M.V.1.	A variant Sanskrit or Prakrit reading given in a clear handwriting in the *M.M.* according to one of the two other manuscripts of the *Kādambarīnāṭaka*.
M.M.V.2.	A variant Sanskrit or Prakrit reading given in a faint handwriting in the *M.M.* according to the other of the two other manuscripts of the *Kādambarīnāṭaka*.
V.K.	V. Krishnamacharya's printed edition of the *Kādambarīnāṭaka* [He calls it the *Kādambarīkalyāṇa (Nāṭaka)*], or its Sanskrit or Prakrit reading.

V.K.Ch. A Sanskrit *chāyā* reading given by V. Krishnamacharya in his printed edition of the *Kādambarīnāṭaka*.

In addition to the above, certain English words in notes are abbreviated, but they are easily recognizable. E.g. "chap." for "chapter", "vs." for "verse" and "comm." for "commentary".

Moreover, in notes for Part Two, the researcher uses "(?)" to indicate a lacuna in a manuscript reading. E.g. *śaśva* (?) *ṇodayas*. Also, he uses "-" to indicate that the reading in question is part of a compounded word, or simply to avoid unnecessary repetition (In notes in Part One, ". . ." is used for the same purpose). E.g. *kumudinī-*, *-mitraḥ*, *nāṭaka-* and *-ka-*. Radings given for clarity's sake together with the reading in question are, as a rule, put into "( )". E.g. *(tarū)n yaugapadyā(d anekā)n*.

PART ONE

An Introduction to the *Kādambarīnāṭaka* of Narasiṁha

1

Preliminary

THE *Kādambarīnāṭaka*[1] is an excellent eight-act Sanskrit-Prakrit play[2] by the fourteenth-century[3] Andhra author Narasiṁha. It is a dramatic version of the very well-known Sanskrit novel *Kādambarī* by Bāṇa and his son Bhūṣaṇa[4] in the seventh century. The *Kādambarīnāṭaka* was edited by V. Krishnamacharya and published in 1936.[5] But since then, it has not received the kind of attention that it deserves. Only a few scholars have made brief surveys and mentions of it.[6] But why is this so? One of the reasons for this long neglect of the study of the *Kādambarīnāṭaka* seems to be that even specialists are subject to the impression that this relatively late play must be far inferior to those composed in earlier periods. Now arises this question: Is the *Kādambarīnāṭaka* really an inferior play unworthy of any special study?

The golden age of the Sanskrit-Prakrit drama virtually ended with Bhavabhūti in the eighth century, and a long age of gradual decadence started[7] — Such a theory is still readily accepted among many scholars in the field. Oft-cited causes of what they call the decadence of the Sanskrit-Prakrit drama are poets' lack of originality, the appearance of vernacular literature, Muslim invasion, and the like.[8] It is true that many of the post-Bhavabhūti, or later plays, already introduced to us lack the beauties found in Bhavabhūti's and pre-Bhavabhūti, or earlier plays, but it is utterly unscholarly to dismiss all later plays as decadent. Supporters of the above-mentioned theory tend to overgeneralize the so-called decadent nature of later plays; in fact, they appear to have simply copied the idea from their irresponsible predecessors without even examining for themselves a sufficient number of such works. This is indeed a case of "a blind man following another blind man".[9]

In spite of this regrettable fact, however, there are fortunately some sober scholars unaffected by the above misleading theory.[10] They do not resort to prejudiced modern secondary sources for the examination and evaluation of later dramatic literature; instead, they seek guidance directly from its authors and traditional Indian dramatic and poetic criticism.[11] They do not carelessly stigmatize every later play as decadent. They analyze the merits and demerits of such works in the light of the *Nāṭyaśāstra* of Bharata, numerous later treatises on classical Indian dramaturgy and poetics, and the like. This alone is the proper method of understanding later Sanskrit-Prakrit plays such as the *Kādambarīnāṭaka*.

Now, the researcher is not interested in scholars like "a frog in a well"[12] satisfied with only earlier plays universally recognized as excellent but averse to exploring the great ocean of lesser-known later ones. Since the *Kādambarīnāṭaka* is a later play, it may possess some tendencies peculiar — not necessarily decadent — to many such plays. Yet it should not be overlooked any longer. It is high time that it received a proper treatment from some unbiased specialist. Kālidāsa says:

Not every dramatic text is excellent
    Merely because it is old;
It is not unworthy of praise
    Because it is recent.
The learned favour one or the other
    After examining them;
Fools only have the wit to be
    Led by others' judgement.[13]

The researcher sincerely hopes that this introduction to the *Kādambarīnāṭaka* carefully prepared in the above-mentioned method, together with his translation of it, will secure the play some recognized position in the field of the Sanskrit-Prakrit dramatic literature.

Notes

1. To the best of the researcher's knowledge, this play is invariably referred to as the *Kādambarīkalyāṇa* (*Nāṭaka*) in all the secondary sources that mention it with the exception of this book and some articles by the researcher; *vide infra*, n. 5.
2. The researcher prefers to call classical Indian plays composed in Sanskrit and Prakrits "Sanskrit-Prakrit plays" rather than simply "Sanskrit plays", for it seems more accurate to do so.
3. Dates given in this book are all of the Christian era (= A.D.), unless otherwise indicated.
4. P. Peterson, ed., *Kādambarī by Bāṇa & His Son* (Bombay: Government Central Book Depot, 1885).
5. V. Krishnamacharya, ed., *Kādambarīkalyāṇaṁ Nāṭakam: A Drama by Narasiṁhakavi* (Madras: The Educational Publishing Co., 1936); *vide* also Intro., chaps. II & V.
6. For instance, P. Sriramamurti, *Contribution of Andhra to Sanskrit Literature* (Waltair: Andhra University, 1972), pp. 50-53, & *passim*.
7. S.K. De, *A History of Sanskrit Literature: Classical Period*, vol. I, ed. by S.N. Dasgupta (Calcutta: Calcutta University Press, 1947), p. 441.
8. *Ibid.*, pp. 441-49; A. B. Keith, *The Sanskrit Drama* (London: Oxford University Press, 1964), pp. 242-44; I. Shekhar, *Sanskrit Drama* (Leiden: E.J. Brill, 1960), chaps. VIII-IX. Shekhar sees symptoms of decadence even in the plays of Śrīharṣa (6th-7th cc.), Bhaṭṭanārāyaṇa (7th c.;

Shekhar gives *cir.* 800) and Bhavabhūti (7th-8th cc.); *vide op. cit.*, chap. X.

9. *Andhaparamparānyāya*; *vide* G.A. Jacob, *Laukikanyāyāñjaliḥ*, pt. I (Bombay: Tukārām Jāvajī, 1907), pp. 4-5.
10. For instance, A.K. Warder; *vide* his *Indian Kāvya Literature,* vol. I (Delhi: Motilal Banarsidass, 1972), Preface, pp. vii-viii.
11. *Ibid.*, p. viii: . . . the literature studied should be presented on its own terms . . . No literature, least of all a highly sophisticated movement such as *kāvya*, can be understood unless we know what its creators were trying to achieve and what sort of contemporary criticism they may have hoped to satisfy.
12. *Kūpamaṇḍūkanyāya*; *vide* Jacob, *op. cit.*, pp. 19-20.
13. *Mālavikāgnimitram of Kālidāsa*, ed. by C.R. Devadhar (Delhi: Motilal Banarsidass, 1977), Prologue, vs. 2:

    purāṇam ity eva na sādhu sarvaṁ, na cāpi kāvyaṁ navam ity avadyam ।
    santaḥ parīkṣyānyatarad bhajante, mūḍhaḥ parapratyayaneyabuddhiḥ ।।

    The above translation of the verse is the researcher's own.

2

The Critical Apparatus for the Study of the Kādambarīnāṭaka

V. KRISHNAMACHARYA, in his printed edition of the *Kādambarīnāṭaka,* fails to report exactly which manuscripts he made use of for editing the text; he merely mentions that the source of it was a catalogue in the Government Oriental Manuscripts Library, Madras, and expresses his gratitude to Kuppuswami Sastri, then curator of the library.[1] *A Triennial Catalogue of Manuscripts* of the library, edited by S. Kuppuswami Sastri, registers one Sanskrit-Prakrit manuscript[2] and one Sanskrit *chāyā* manuscript[3] of the play. Apart from these two, however, there do not seem to be any other manuscripts of the work registerd in catalogues; even *New Catalogus Catalogorum*, for instance, registers only the same two.[4] P. Sriramamurti, in his *Contribution of Andhra to Sanskrit Literature*, mentions another *chāyā* manuscript of the play preserved in the Telugu Academy Library, Kakinada,[5] but in fact, no such manuscript has been discovered yet.[6] Thus it is clear that V. Krishnamacharya's edition of the play is based on only the above-mentioned two manuscripts. No commentary on the play has been discovered; in fact, none seems to have existed, for the play is a relatively late one and its story, a well-known one. Therefore the primary materials used for the study of the *Kādambarīnāṭaka* in this book are namely: the Sanskrit-Prakrit manuscript and the Sanskrit *chāyā* manuscript preserved in the Government Oriental Manuscript Library, Madras,[7] and V. Krishnamacharya's printed edition based on these two manuscripts.

The Madras Sanskrit-Prakrit Manuscript

The Sanskrit-Prakrit manuscript of the *Kādambarīnaṭaka* preserved in the Government Oriental Manuscripts Library, Madras (reference number 2484; hereafter cited as the *M.M.*), is a recent paper Devanāgarī transcript manuscript. The size of the paper used for it is approximately 11 inches by 9.5 inches. The *M.M.* contains 163 pages of text,[8] and as a rule, each page contains 20 lines. The transcription was first made from 1917 to 1918 from a manuscript owned by P.K. Manavedan Anujan, Raja of Calicut.[9] But this manuscript is incomplete: it breaks off just before the end of the play.[10] In 1922 two other scribes compared the *M.M.* with two different manuscripts and completed it with their help.[11] It is not known where these two manuscripts used for the completion of the *M.M.* were from, or where they and the manuscript from Calicut are preserved now.

The title of the play on the first page of the *M.M.* is the *Kādambarīnāṭaka*; the same title appears on the top margins of four subsequent pages as well.[12] But at the end of the *M.M.*, which was completed in 1922, the play is called the *Kādambarīkalyāṇa*.[13] The play's title on the first page is preceded by an auspicious word and two salutations to Divinities: *śrīḥ, śrīgaṇeśāya maṅgalam* and *śrīśāradāyai namaḥ*. The two salutations, which are, strictly speaking, not part of the play, seem to have been added by some scribe in course of the copying of the text.

On the whole, the *M.M.* is a fairly legible Devanāgarī transcript, though in some places it is either faint or blurred. The *M.M.* has three different handwritings. The first, that of the scribe who transcribed the Calicut manuscript, is very clear. The second, that of the scribe who completed the *M.M.*, is equally clear. But the third, which probably belongs to either of the two scribes who compared the *M.M.* with two other manuscripts, filled out lacunae, provided variant readings and so on, is, though generally uniform, clear in some places and faint in others.[14] It may be conjectured that this scribe intentionally employed two levels of clearness in order to distinguish readings from one mansucript from those from the other. The first two handwritings constantly exaggerate the Devanāgarī signs for non-initial vowels; this seems to be a common practice in South India. As is often the case with Indian manuscripts, the *M.M.* does not always take a proper space between words. Also, it does not number its verses but usually provides a separate line for each *pāda* (lit. foot, or quarter) of a verse. As a general rule, the *M.M.* abbreviates speakers' names from the second time onwards in each act. Moreover, the *M.M.*, which is a recent transcript manuscript, occasionally uses modern European punctuation marks such as quotation marks, exclamation points, commas and parentheses.

One of the most important characteristics of the *M.M.* is the use of a very small circle called *nolli*.[15] It is an orthographic sign employed throughout the Prakrit passages of the manuscript. The function of the *nolli* is to indicate that the consonant following it is to be doubled. It is placed above the letter preceding a consonant to be doubled; as a result, it is often indistinguishable from the *anusvāra*. The *nolli* is frequently used when Prakrit is written in the Malayālam, Grantha, Kannaḍa and Telugu scripts. The *M.M.*, though a Devanāgarī transcript, has retained this South Indian orthographic sign from the Calicut manuscript. For instance, the *M.M.* almost invariably gives *e°va*[16] for *evva*, and *ta°sa*[17] for *tassa*. The scribe who gives different readings from two other manuscripts, however, places the *nolli* between the letter containing a consonant to be doubled and its preceding letter.[18] The *M.M.*

occasionally spells a double consonant in the usual way: for example, *takkemi*[19] and *bhaṭṭidāriā*.[20] For *ajja* whose Sanskrit equivalent is *ārya*, the *M.M.* gives *a°a*,[21] which seems closer in sound to *ayya* (Māgadhī) rather than to *ajja* (Śaurasenī).[22] But for *ajja* whose Sanskrit equivalent is *adya*, the *M.M.* gives *a°ja*,[23] not *a°a*. The *nolli* is employed also when an aspirated consonant is doubled. For instance, *haddhi* is spelled *ha°dhi*,[24] in which case it is appropriate to understand that only the unaspirated /d/ is doubled.

Another characteristic of the *M.M.* is a special use of the numeral 2 in its Prakrit passages. It is used to indicate that the word preceding it is to be repeated. For example, *haddhi2*[25] means *haddhi haddhi*. The numeral 2 used for this purpose is found in other Indian manuscripts as well. The *M.M.* uses this device in roughly its second half. In its first half, the *M.M.* uses instead *nna*, a Devanāgarī letter in which two n's are horizontally doubled. For instance, *idonna*[26] is equal to *ido ido*. Once used for the same purpose, probably through carelessness, are *nna* of which the two n's are vertically doubled,[27] *na*,[28] and *ja*.[29]

The M.M. contains a variety of scribal errors, particularly in its Prakrit passages: the confusion of letters, the unnecessary repetition of letters and words, the omission of necessary letters and words, and the like. The *M.M.* very frequently confuses the following consonants: /p/ and /v/ as in *avarokṣyate*[30] for *aparokṣyate*, and in *vāremi*[31] for *pāremi*; /ch/ and /h/ as in *pu°hīadu*[32] for *pucchīadu*, and in *a°hoda*[33] for *acchoda*; /v/ and /kh/ as in *khidyate*[34] for *vidyate*, and in *khelā*[35] for *velā*; and also /th/ and /dh/ as in *midhuna*[36] for *mithuna*, and in *vṛdhā*[37] for *vṛthā*. Moreover, the *M.M.* sometimes confuses, among others, /t/ and /k/ as in *kulūkeśvara*[38] for *kulūteśvara*, and /n/ and /t/ as in *jāte*[39] for *jāne*. The *M.M.* frequently confuses vowels as well: /a/ and /ā/, /i/and /ī/, /a/ and /i/, /e/ and /ai/, and so on. For instance, *kahaṁ* and *kahiṁ* are often confused,[40] and *nepathya* is frequently spelled *naipathya*.[41] The *M.M.* often confuses /l/ and /i/ as well. For example, frequently enough, *alaṁ* is spelled *aiṁ*;[42] and occasionally *vaṭṭai* is spelled *vaṭṭala*.[43] Sometimes /l/ or /ḷ/ and /u/ are confused as in *kāuṇādo*[44] for *kāl(ḷ)aṇādo*. Single consonants are sometimes substituted for double consonants as in *satva*[45] for *sattva*, and in *ujvala*[46] for *ujjvala*. The *anusvāra* is often added superfluously.[47] These problems concerning the confusion of letters and the like seem to originate in not only the scribe's carelessness but also the Calicut manuscript itself, which was either already corrupt or in which certain letters looked very much alike.[48] The Prakrit passages of the *M.M.* present various other problems such as the confusion of different Prakrits.[49]

The Madras Sanskrit Chāyā Manuscript

The Sanskrit *chāyā* manuscript of the *Kādambarīnāṭaka* preserved in the Government Oriental Manuscripts Library, Madras (reference number 4423; hereafter cited as the *M.Ch.M.*), is a recent paper Devanāgarī transcript manuscript like the *M.M.* The size of the paper used for it is about 10.5 inches by 9.5 inches. The *M.Ch.M.* contains 34 pages of text,[50] and as a rule, each page contains 20 lines. The *M.Ch.M.* was transcribed from 1924 to 1925 from a manuscript owned by Narayanasastri, Calicut.[51] The *M.Ch.M.* is incomplete: it breaks off in Act VI of the play.[52] The name of the *M.Ch.M.*, which appears on its first page alone, is the *Kādambarīnāṭakacchāyā*, preceded by *śrīḥ* above it. The *M.Ch.M.* does not provide speakers' names. With regard to its legibility, the *M.Ch.M.* is virtually free from difficulties.

Carefully collated with the *M.M.*, the *M.Ch.M.* presents several problems. One of them is that the *M.Ch.M.* often gives a *chāyā* for a Prakrit word, sentence or speech that the *M.M.* does not have. For instance, the *M.Ch.M.* gives *jayatu jayatu*[53] for *jedu jedu*, which the *M.M.* actually does not have.[54] The *M.Ch.M.* frequently does the reverse as well: it omits a *chāyā* for what the *M.M.* does have in Prakrit. For example, the *M.Ch.M.* does not give *etad vanaviharaṇopakaraṇam*[55] for *edaṁ vaṇaviharaṇo-vaaraṇaṁ*,[56] which is in the *M.M.* Sometimes the *M.Ch.M.* gives a synonym of, or a word slightly different from, the Sanskrit equivalent of a Prakrit word in the *M.M.* Moreover, the word order of a Sanskrit *chāyā* sentence in the *M.Ch.M.* often differs from that of its corresponding Prakrit sentence in the *M.M.* The following example illustrates all the above-mentioned problems but the first: the *M.Ch.M.* gives *bho anyathā na mantrayitavyam*[57] for *bho ṇa ya (= a)ºṇahā kiṁ vi maṇṇidaºvaṁ (vaṁ* given later) in the *M.M.*[58] It is quite evident from the above that the Calicut *chāyā* manuscript of the *Kādambarīnāṭaka* of which the *M.Ch.M.* is a transcript was based on a Sanskrit-Prakrit manuscript of the play other than the Calicut manuscript of which the *M.M.* is a transcript.

V. Krishnamacharya's Printed Edition

On the whole, V. Krishnamacharya's printed edition of the *Kādambarīnāṭaka*[59] is a fine piece of work; yet it has one major defect not to be overlooked. Like many Indian editors, Krishnamacharya provides no notes for variants, corrections, lacunae filled out, additions, omissions, changes and the like. In order to improve the text, he often adds what is not in the *M.M.* or the *M.Ch.M.* For instance, he supplies *yāvad aham api parisamāpitaniyamāṁ mahāśvetāṁ jñātvā āgacchāmi* |,[60] which is not in the *M.M.*[61] Also, Krishnamacharya often omits what is in the manuscripts; an omission is made particularly when a Prakrit passage in the *M.M.* appears incomprehensible and the *M.Ch.M.* does not provide any *chāyā* for it. For example, he omits in his edition[62] "*mada*" *janāntikaṁ, sahi kāambari ṇaº bhaṇiº jasiº caariº davāiº kameaº khiº ja iti* | in the *M.M.*,[63] for which the *M.Ch.M.* does not provide a *chāyā*.[64] Moreover, he often changes the word order of a sentence. For instance, he changes *aye vismṛta ivaiṣa vṛttānta(ḥ) smaryate mayā sarvaḥ* | in the *M.M.*[65] into *aye vismṛtaḥ sarvopyeṣa vṛttāntodya mayā smaryata iva* |,[66] in which he also supplies *api* and *adya*. In the case of a Prakrit passage, he often combines an *M.M.* reading with its corresponding *M.Ch.M.* *chāyā* reading, and if such a combined reading still appears unsatisfactory, he makes additional emendations. Also, since the incomplete *M.Ch.M.* does not provide any *chāyā* for the Prakrit passages in roughly the last third of the *M.M.*, Krishnamacharya performs the task himself. He makes various other emendations for the improvement of the text, but he never provides notes for them.

While the primary materials used for the translation of the *Kādambarīnāṭaka* in this book are the *M.M.* and the *M.Ch.M.*, V. Krishnamacharya's printed edition is also constantly consulted. But since the main purpose of this book is not to collate in detail the two manuscripts and Krishnamacharya's edition, the researcher confines himself to providing textual notes in Part Two, as a general rule, only for readings that seem to affect the translation: the manuscripts' readings and Krishnamacharya's emendations of them, and occasionally the researcher's own emendations as well when all the other readings appear unsatisfactory. The reading which the researcher follows is given first and then the others. If no note is given, it simply indicates that he follows the manuscripts' readings, and that Krishnamacharya gives them unchanged in his edition. The researcher, however, does not provide notes for what appear to be simple scribal errors of various sorts already discussed above. Also, no notes are given for the *M.M.*'s readings part of which is properly corrected by the scribes who afterwards compared the manuscript with two others, and adopted by Krishnamacharya. Furthermore, minor emendations such as slight changes in word order made by Krishnamacharya are given in notes, only if they seem to affect the translation.

Notes

1. V. Krishnamacharya, ed., *Kādambarīkalyāṇaṁ Nāṭakam*, editor's Skt. intro., p. 7: *etanmudraṇe madrapurarājakīyalikhitapustakaśālāsthaḥ kośa eva mātṛkā samajāyateti tatpustakaśālādhikāriṣu . . . kuppusvāmiśāstrimahāśayeṣu nitarāṁ kārtajñyam udvahāmaḥ* |
2. S. Kuppuswami Sastri, ed., *A Triennial Catalogue of Manuscripts* (Collected During the Triennium 1916-17 to 1918-19 for the Government Oriental Manuscripts Library, Madras), vol. III, pt. I, Sanskrit B (Madras: Government Press, 1922), pp. 3489-92, Reference No. 2484.
3. *Ibid.* (1922-23 to 1924-25), vol. I, pt. I, Sanskrit C (1932), pp. 6486-87, Reference No. 4423.
4. V. Raghavan, ed., *New Catalogus Catalogorum (An Alphabetical Register of Sanskrit and Allied Works and Authors)* (Madras: University of Madras, 1967), vol. III, p. 337-38.
5. P. Sriramamurti, *Contribution of Andhra to Sanskrit Literature*, pp. 53, fn. 5.
6. During the researcher's visit (May, 1986) to the Telugu Academy Library, Kakinada (now known as the Andhra Sahitya Parisat and operated by the Department of Archaeology & Museums, Government of Andhra Pradesh), Mr. S. Dasarathi, then curator in charge, carefully went through the two catalogues of the manuscripts preserved there (one prepared in Telugu in 1962; the other, in English in 1973), but did not find any manuscript of the *Kādambarīnāṭaka*. If such a manuscript was once preserved there, a possible reason

for its loss, according to Mr. Dasarathi, is that someone borrowed it and never returned it, or that someone bought it when the library was still a private institution before 1973. Also, P. Sriramamurti, in his reply (dated August 14, 1986) to the researcher's letter, kindly informed him that he mentioned the manuscript in his book on the grounds of some oral information about it, but that when he tried to find it himself in the library, he could not.

7. During his visit to the library (May, 1986), the researcher obtained a xerox copy of each of these two manuscripts.
8. 82 sheets of paper are used, and the second side of the last of them is left blank.
9. *M.M.*, p. 161. According to it, the scribe's name is K. Venkatasubhasastri. It also has the following: P.V., 3.2.18, which seem to be a supervisor's initials and the date of his inspection of the transcribing work respectively. The same initials, together with dates of inspection, appear on two preceding pages as well: pp. 48, & 152. Also, R.R., probably the initials of another supervisor, are on p. 96, with a date of inspection.
10. *Ibid.*: *tārāpīḍaḥ: kumāra candrāpīḍa divyātmā sukṛtair mama tvam udabhūḥ putraṁ kalāsu* [cf. V. Krishnamacharya's ed., p. 235 (Act VIII, vs. 42 & before)] . . . *asāmāptoyaṁ granthaḥ.*
11. *Ibid.*, p. 163. It says as follows: Compared with the mss of 16/469, T.S./27.3.22., M.A.J./ 27.3.22.; Compared with the mss of 6/469, T.S./19.4.22., M.A.J./19.4.22. The two sets of initials seem to be those of the scribes, and the dates, those of the completion of the comparison and transcription. The abbreviation "mss" used here does not seem to refer to manuscripts but only to pages of a manuscript, as is often the case in India according to A.K. Warder.; cf. *M.M.*, p. 161, "ms" used properly to refer to only one manuscript. *A Triennial Catalogue* (p. 3490; *vide supra*, n. 2) says that *M.M.* breaks off in Act VIII; *M.M.* was completed after the inspection of it by the editor of the catalogue.
12. *Ibid.*, pp. 41, 49, 97 & 145.
13. *Ibid.*, p. 163: *samāptaṁ caitat kādambarīkalyāṇaṁ nāma nāṭakam.*
14. Some of these readings in a faint hand look very different in shape; they may belong to the first or the second hand, or more probably to V. Krishnamacharya, for his readings often agree with them. But since it is not absolutely certain which hand they belong to, the researcher treats them as belonging to the third hand.
15. A.N. Upadhye, among others, calls a small circle employed for the same purpose by the name *nolli*; *vide* his *Rāma Pāṇivāda's Kaṁsavaho*, ed. (Delhi: Motilal Banarsidass, 1968), Intro., ix-xi.
16. *M.M.*, p. 7, line 15, & *passim*. This is the best that the researcher can do to show the position of a *nolli*; in *M.M.*, however, it is above a letter, not beside it.
17. *Ibid.*, p. 21, line 4, & *passim.*
18. *Ibid.*, p. 26, line 13, & *passim.*
19. *Ibid.*, p. 10, line 5, & *passim.*
20. *Ibid.*, p. 30, line 19, & *passim.*
21. *Ibid.*, p. 20, lines 4 & 19, & *passim.*
22. Cf. R. Pischel, *A Grammar of the Prakrit Language*, trans. from German into English by S. Jhā (Delhi: Motilal Banarsidass, 1981), p. 230: The spelling *yya* is found only sometimes in

South Indian MSS. Mostly they write, however, in place of the ligature a small circle: *a°a* = *ārya* . . . an orthographic device which may either permit of a choice between the pronunciations *jja* and *yya* or express an intermediate sound between the two sound-groups.

23. *M.M.*, p. 20, line 19; p. 129, line 5, & *passim.*
24. *Ibid.*, p. 8, line 13, & *passim.*
25. *Ibid.*, p. 124, line 16, & *passim.*
26. *Ibid.*, p. 76, line 3, & *passim.*
27. *Ibid.*, p. 41, line 11.
28. *Ibid.*, p. 20, line 10.
29. *Ibid.*, p. 8, line 3.
30. *Ibid.*, p. 11, line 1.
31. *Ibid.*, p. 7, line 18.
32. *Ibid.*, p. 54, line 13.
33. *Ibid.*, p. 82, line 16.
34. *Ibid.*, p. 42, line 11.
35. *Ibid.*, p. 48, line 12.
36. *Ibid.*, p. 11, line 1.
37. *Ibid.*, p. 97, line 2.
38. *Ibid.*, p. 79, line 12.
39. *Ibid.*, p. 117, line 6.
40. *Ibid.*, p. 134, line 8; p. 101, line 12, & *passim.*
41. *Ibid.*, p. 47, line 1.
42. *Ibid.*, p. 16, line 16.
43. *Ibid.*, p. 28, line 3.
44. *Ibid.*, p. 16, line 10.
45. *Ibid.*, p. 11, line 1.
46. *Ibid.*, p. 2, line 4.
47. *Ibid.*, p. 2, line 6.
48. In the Malayālam script, in which the Calicut manuscript was most probably written, certain letters look confusingly alike: those representing /v/, /p/ and /kh/; /ch/ and /h/; /t/ and /n/; and so on.
49. *Vide* Intro., chap. V.
50. 18 sheets of paper are used, and both sides of the last of them are left blank.
51. *M.Ch.M.*, p. 34. It also says: P.S. 16/7/25, which are probably the scribe's initials and the date of the completion of his transcribing work.

52. *Ibid.*, p. 34: . . . *tat kim* (*ataḥ paraṁ* crossed out) *avaśiṣṭam ataḥ paraṁ likhitavyasya* (cf. *M.M.*, p. 108 & V. Krishnamacharya's edn., p. 157).
53. *Ibid.*, p. 1, line 12.
54. Cf. *M.M.*, p. 8, line 6.
55. Cf. *M.Ch.M.*, p. 2, line 2.
56. *M.M.*, p. 8, line 17.
57. *M.Ch.M.*, p. 2, line 7.
58. *M.M.*, p. 9, line 14.
59. The researcher uses "*V.K.*" in notes as the abbreviation of his edition of the play; *vide* also the list of abbreviations.
60. *V.K.*, p. 97, lines 2-3.
61. Cf. *M.M.*, p. 68, lines 9-10.
62. Cf. *V.K.*, p. 37, lines 2-3.
63. *M.M.*, p. 28, line 20 & p. 29, line 1.
64. Cf. *M.Ch.M.*, p. 8, lines 3-4.
65. *M.M.*, p. 87, line 12.
66. *V.K.*, p. 126, lines 15-16.

3

The Poet Narasiṁha and His Works

THE purpose of this chapter is to obtain information about the poet Narasiṁha's country, times, genealogy, other literary works, royal patronage and the like from his *Kādambarīnāṭaka*, works that appear to belong to him and other authors' works.

Narasiṁha's Country, Times and Genealogy

In the *Kādambarīnāṭaka* Narasiṁha does not mention his country, nor does he give the name of the king under whose reign or patronage he composed the play. The only clue to his country seems to be that the play was intended for a festival of the Lord of some Mt. Śoṇa,[1] though its exact location is not known.[2] It is possible, however, to obtain sufficient information about Narasiṁha from his play and other poets' works. In the Prologue (*prastāvanā*) to the *Kādambarīnāṭaka*, Narasiṁha explicitly states that his father, Gaṅgādhara, born as Siddhanātha's son in a respectable family in which the goddess of speech was always present, was a renowned pundit who lived for the sake of literature.[3] Narasiṁha continues that he, the author of the play, is Gaṅgādhara's middle son,[4] and that his elder brother, Viśvanātha, is a great poet whose speech is like nectar and who is the leader of men of taste.[5] It is not known which religious school Narasiṁha's family followed, but at least Narasiṁha himself seems to have been a Śaiva, for he wishes for people's exclusive devotion to Śiva in the final benediction (*bharatavākya*) of his play.[6]

Narasiṁha's elder brother, Viśvanātha, mentioned above, is in all probability identical with the author of the *Saugandhikāharaṇa*, a one-act heroic play (*vyāyoga*) on the *Mahābhārata* episode of Bhīma's bringing a *saugandhika* flower for his wife Draupadī.[7] In the Prologue to this play, Viśvanātha makes it clear that the king under whose patronage he composed the play is Pratāparudra.[8] He is Pratāparudra II (reigned 1295-1326),[9] the last king of the Kākatīya dynasty (1000-1326),[10] which ruled in the beginning a part of and later the whole of the Andhra country from Warangal (Ekaśilānagara). King Pratāparudra was a very generous patron of scholars and poets. According to Ekāmranātha's *Pratāpacaritamu* in Telugu, Pratāparudra's royal court had as many as 200 poets of whom the most eminent were Vidyānātha,

Viśvanātha and Śākalyamallubhaṭṭa.[11] Narasiṁha might have been one of these court poets of Pratāparudra. Viśvanātha continues in the Prologue that his maternal uncle is the celebrated Agastya.[12] In other words, his father, Gaṅgādhara, was married to Agastya's sister. This Agastya is undoubtedly identical with the author of the *Bālabhārata*, an epic in verse (*mahākāvya*) in twenty cantos on the *Mahābhārata*;[13] the *Kṛṣṇacarita*, a prose poem (*gadyakāvya*) on the life of the Lord Kṛṣṇa;[14] and the *Nalakīrtikaumudī*, a short *mahākāvya* in four cantos on the episode of Nala and Damayantī in the *Mahābhārata*.[15] It seems fair enough to assume that Narasiṁha, who dramatized the novel *Kādambarī*, was to some extent influenced by his uncle Agastya, who himself was probably a great admirer of Bāṇa and composed the *Kṛṣṇacarita*, comparable in many respects to his two prose works: the *Kādambarī* and the *Harṣacarita*.[16] Some scholars have equated this Agastya with Vidyānātha, the author of the *Pratāparudrayaśobhūṣaṇa*, a treatise on poetics and dramaturgy, merely on the grounds of one verse in the treatise in which Vidyānātha refers to himself as Agastya.[17] Vidyānātha, according to them, was simply Agastya's title.[18] This assumption, however, does not seem tenable because Vidyānātha never calls himself Agastya elsewhere in his work, nor does Agastya ever refer to himself as Vidyānātha in his poems.[19] The *Pratāparudrayaśobhūṣaṇa*, or simply the *Pratāparudrīya*, of Vidyānātha is a work dedicated to King Pratāparudra as its title clearly indicates. The author even includes in it his own model play entitled the *Pratāparudrakalyāṇa* to illustrate various dramatic devices.[20] Agastya, on the other hand, never mentions the king as his patron in any of his above-mentioned three works.

The royal poetess Gaṅgādevī composed a *mahākāvya* entitled the *Madhurāvijaya* or the *Vīrakamparāyacarita* on the conquest of the Madurai sultanate (1365-70)[21] by her husband, Prince Kampaṇa or Kamparāya of the Vijayanagar Empire.[22] In its first canto Gaṅgādevī pays a tribute of admiration to Agastya, Gaṅgādhara and Viśvanātha, mentioned above,[23] together with more ancient poets. Agastya, according to her, is the author of as many as 74 poetic compositions (vs. 14). Gaṅgādhara, whom she calls another Vyāsa, composed a play on the story of the *Mahābhārata* (vs. 15). Gaṅgādevī seems to mean that Viśvanātha is her teacher when she says that by his grace omniscience kindles even in people like herself; moreover, he seems to have been still alive when she composed the poem, for she wishes for his long victory (vs. 16). It is most strange that while Gaṅgādevī extols Narasiṁha's father, elder brother and maternal uncle, she should not even briefly mention Narasiṁha himself, who must have been sufficiently famous in her times. The reason for this omission is not certain. Perhaps she simply did not admire him as a poet as much as she did his relatives; or she considered fiction too frivolous to admire, and preferred history or tradition (*itihāsa*). From all the above-mentioned scraps of information, Narasiṁha, like Viśvanātha, seems to have lived in Warangal or elsewhere in Andhra during the reign of the Kākatīya King Pratāparudra II, and most probably after the destruction of the dynasty as well, whether or not he ever received any royal patronage.

Narasiṁha's Works

In the Prologue to the *Kādambarīnāṭaka*, Narasiṁha describes himself as proficient in all the ten forms of dramatic composition.[24] In Warangal, there is a Kākatīya temple whose four gates have Sanskrit inscriptions in the Grantha script. The inscription on the eastern gate of it contains a verse from a prose novel called the *Malayavatī* which describes its author, Narasiṁha, as adept in the ten forms of dramatic composition.[25] This makes it highly possible that the two Narasiṁhas are the same author. According to the inscription on the northern gate of the temple, an author named Nṛsiṁha wrote a commentary on the *Ṛgveda* and works on philosophy; moreover, he composed a work entitled the *Kākatīyacarita* in just one day.[26] The inscription on another gate describes some prosodic beats (*gaṇa*s) spoken of by one Nṛsiṁha.[27] The last of the four inscriptions is a verse by one Nṛsiṁha in praise of the grandeur of the greatest Kākatīya king, Pratāparudra II.[28] These three Nṛsiṁhas are most probably one and the same author, for their inscriptions are found in the same location. They may be identical with Narasiṁha,[29] the author of the *Malayavatī*, and also with that of the *Kādambarīnāṭaka*, but there is not sufficient evidence to prove so. If they are identical with them, Narasiṁha of the *Kādambarīnāṭaka* did have some connections with the royal court of King Pratāparudra, and was more than an expert in dramatic composition, although he does not say so in his play.

There are two Sanskrit poems inscribed on large rocks, one on each side of a hillock called Urs Gutta near Warangal. One is in the Devanāgarī script; the other, in the Telugu script. The former is incomplete and damaged, while the latter is complete and well-preserved except for a few lines. Neither of them has a title. The poem inscribed in Devanāgarī characters gives, in the colophon at the end of its first canto,[30] its author's name, Narasiṁhamaharṣi, a son of a daughter of Viśveśvara, a royal preceptor.[31] The poem in Telugu characters depicts the love story of a couple of semi-divine beings called *siddha*s in about sixty verses.[32] At the end of it is found its author's name, Narasiṁharṣi, a son or grandson of Viśveśvara.[33] These two poems seem to belong to the same author. "*Ṛṣi*" and "*maharṣi*" in his name were probably attached to it by others out of respect. Viśveśvara, who is either his father or grandfather, seems identical with Viśveśvaraśāmbhu,[34] also called Viśveśvaraśivācārya,[36] of the Malkapuram inscription (1261), who was the preceptor of the Kākatīya King Gaṇapatideva[36] (reigned 1199-1262)[37] or of his daughter and successor, Queen Rudrāmbā[38] (reigned 1262-96).[39] If the author of these two inscribed poems is identical with that of the *Kādambarīnāṭaka*, Viśveśvara is Narasiṁha's maternal grandfather, not his father, for Narasiṁha explicitly states in his play that his father is Gaṅgādhara.[40] And if this is the case, Viśveśvara is also the father of Agastya,

Narasiṁha's maternal uncle. All this conjecture seems highly possible chronologically and otherwise, though there is no definite evidence to prove it.

Narasiṁha's Royal Patronage and the Kādambarīnāṭaka's Date

On the supposition that Narasiṁha of the *Kādambarīnāṭaka* is identical with the authors of the above-mentioned six inscribed works, it can be further conjectured as follows. When Narasiṁha was younger, he either was a court poet of the Kākatīya King Pratāparudra as his elder brother, Viśvanātha, was, or at least received his patronage in some other way. But after the death of Pratāparudra, or the fall of his dynasty (1326), Narasiṁha did not receive any royal patronage while Viśvanātha did by becoming Gaṅgādevī's teacher as mentioned above. This conjecture can explain why Narasiṁha does not mention in the *Kādambarīnāṭaka* any royal patron for whom he composed the play, while he describes the glory of the Kākatīya dynasty or of King Pratāparudra in some of his inscribed works. It seems reasonable enough to suppose from the above and considering his age that Narasiṁha composed the *Kādambarīnāṭaka* after Pratāparudra's death, that is, in the second or third quarter of the fourteenth century. Three verses from the play are quoted by the Reḍḍi King Peda Komaṭi Vema (15th c.), also known as Vemabhūpāla or Vīranārāyaṇa, of Kondavidu in the post-Kākatīya Andhra country in his treatise on poetics entitled the *Sāhityacintāmaṇi*.[41]

Notes

1. *K.N.*, Prologue, after vs. 2: . . . *śoṇācalanāthayātrāyām* . . .
2. P. Sriramamurti has informed the researcher in a lertter that Śoṇācala is probably the name of a temple (or a mountain where there is a temple?) near Warangal, Andhra Pradesh.
3. *K.N.*, Prologue, vs. 5:

   jānāty eva hi tadbhavān kavikulaṁ sabhyair yad abhyarhitaṁ,
   nityaṁ saṁnidadhāti sā bhagavatī yasmin girāṁ devatā |
   tatrāsīd kila siddhanāthatanayo gaṅgādharaḥ paṇḍito,
   bāhuśrutyaviśeṣaviśrutayaśāḥ sāhityasauhityabhūḥ ||
4. *Ibid.*, vs. 6:

   tasyaiṣa madhyamaḥ putro narasiṁha itīritaḥ |
   viśrutaḥ sa tu kartāsyāḥ kṛter ity avadhāraya ||
5. *Ibid.*, vs. 7, 2nd half:

   sudhārasataraṅgiṇīsurabhisūktir asyāgrajaḥ, kṣitau sahṛdayāgraṇīr jayati viśvanāthaḥ kaviḥ ||
6. *K.N.*, Act VIII, vs. 45, 4th *pāda*:

   svāntaṁ caitat parimṛśatu naḥ śāmbhavīm eva bhaktim ||
7. The author calls his play a *prekṣaṇaka*, probably in the sense of a show or spectacle in

general; *vide* his *The Saugandhikāharaṇa of Viśvanātha*, ed. M.P. Śivadatta *et al.* (Bombay: Nirṇaya Sāgar Press, 1934), p. 2. Viśvanātha the critic and theoretician in Orissa (15th c.) quotes in his *Sāhityadarpaṇa* the *Saugandhikāharaṇa* as an example of the *vyāyoga*; *vide* his *Sāhityadarpaṇa*, ed. by Ś. Śāstrī (Delhi: Motilal Banarsidass, 1982), chap. VI, vss. 231-33 & prose (p. 215).

8. Viśvanātha, *Saugandhikāharaṇa*, pp. 1-2:

   sūtradhāra: . . . *rājñā pratāparudreṇa. . . ādiṣṭo smi: . . . bhavati yaḥ saṁvananaṁ sāmājikahṛdayānām . . . viśvanātha iti khyātaḥ kavir asti yaduktayaḥ* |

   akāñcanam aratnaṁ ca viduṣām karṇabhūṣaṇam || 3 ||

9. K.A. Nilakanta Sastri, *A History of South India* (London: Oxford University Press, 1958), p. 217.
10. *Ibid.*
11. P. Sriramamurti, *Contribution of Andhra to Sanskrit Literature*, pp. 38-40.
12. Viśvanātha, *Saugandhikāharaṇa*, vs. 4:

    vācas tasya kaver udāramadhurā ity atra citraṁ kimu,
    prakhyātaḥ sakalāsu dikṣu guṇiṣu śreyān agastyaḥ sudhīḥ |

    vedhaś candramukhīkarāṅgulidalāsaṅgakvaṇadvallakī —
    vācoyuktisahoktidarśitasudhājanmā sa yanmātulaḥ ||

13. *New Catalogus Catalogorum*, vol. I (1949), ed. by V. Raghavan, p. 19; Sriramamurti, *op. cit.*, p. 45.
14. *The Kṛṣṇacarita of Agastyapaṇḍita,* ed. by T. Venkatacharya (Thanjavur: Sarasvati Mahal Library, 1975).
15. *The Nalakīrtikaumudī of Agastyapaṇḍita,* ed. by T. Venkatacharya (Delhi: D.K. Publishing House, 1975). Only the second and fourth cantos of the poem are available.
16. Venkatacharya assumes that Agastya must have written some verses or words in praise of Bāṇa in the beginning portion of the *Kṛṣṇacarita*, which is not available yet; *vide* his *The Kṛṣṇacarita of Agastyapaṇḍita*, ed., pp. ii-iii & xxi-xxii.
17. *Pratāparudrīya of Vidyānātha*, ed. by V. Raghavan (Madras: The Sanskrit Education Society, 1979), *kāvyaprakaraṇa*, vs. 60 (p. 64):

    aunnatyaṁ yadi varṇyate śikhariṇaḥ kra(u)dhyanti nīcaiḥ kṛtā,
    gāmbhīryaṁ yadi kīrttyate jaladhayaḥ kṣubhyanti gādhīkṛtāḥ |
    tat tvāṁ varṇayitum bibhemi yadi vā jātosmy agastyaḥ sthitas,
    tvatpārśve guṇaratnarohaṇagire śrīvīrarudraprabho ||

    But here Vidyānātha seems to be simply comparing himself to the great sage Agastya in Hindu mythology; *vide* Venkatacharya, ed., *The Kṛṣṇacarita of Agastyapaṇḍita*, p. x.

18. Venkatacharya, ed., *The Kṛṣṇacarita of Agastyapaṇḍita*, p. ix.
19. *Ibid.*, pp. ix-xiv; Venkatacharya enumerates many other reasons to believe that the two authors are different.
20. *Pratāparudrīya of Vidyānātha*, ed. by Raghavan, pp. 92-154, *nāṭakodāharaṇa.*

21. Nilakanta Sastri, *op. cit.*, p. 256.
22. *Madhurāvijayam of Gaṅgādevī*, ed. by S. Thiruvenkatachari (Annamalainagar: Annamalai University, 1957).
23. *Ibid.*, p. 74, canto 1, vss. 14-16:

    catussaptatikāvyoktivyaktavaiduṣyasaṁpade |
    agastyāya jagaty asmin spṛhayet ko na kovidaḥ ||

    stumas tam aparaṁ vyāsaṁ gaṅgādharamahākavim |
    nāṭakacchadmanā dṛṣṭāṁ yaś cakre bhāratīṁ kathām ||

    ciraṁ sa vijayībhūyād viśvanāthaḥ kavīśvaraḥ |
    yasya prasādāt sārvajñyaṁ samindhe mādṛśeṣv api ||

24. *K.N.*, Prologue, vs. 7, 1st half:

    ayaṁ daśasu rūpakeṣv api nirūḍhim āḍhaukituṁ,
    paraṁ prabhavatīti no manasi maiva bhūd adbhutam |

25. *Nṛttaratnāvalī of Jāya Senāpati,* ed. by V. Raghavan (Madras: Government Oriental Manuscripts Library, 1965), pp. 15-16; according to the editor, the following four verses are from the Mackenzie Mss. in the Madras Govt. Oriental Mss. Library (Local Records vol. 45, pp. 34-35).

    aprāpa(pta)sabhāstambo(mbho) pyu(pya) vipannahiraṇyakaśipur api |
    avikṛra(ta)mukho ṣi(pi) laśasu (daśasu) pragalbhate rūpakeśaḥ(ṣu) narasiṁhaḥ ||
    malayavatīnāmni gadyakāvye ||

    This is a punning (*śleṣa*) verse on the poet Narasiṁha and the god Viṣṇu in his fourth incarnation as Narasiṁha.

26. *Ibid.*:

    ṛkchāyā racitā nirargalagirā yenādhikuḍe(?) yasī śāstragūḍha (grantha)kṛtā nṛsiṁhakṛtinā hṛdgranthigaḍha(?) cchidā |

    ahnaikena hi kākatīyacarite tena dviśiṣṭā kṛtāḥ(?) kāṣṭhādhā . . . niha . . . ni (rmi?) tayaśaḥ . . . ṇḍha . . . sa . . . kṛtāḥ(?) ||

27. Sriramamurti, *op. cit.*, pp. 50-51; he calls the Kākatīya temple in question the Warangal fort.

    kṣmātī(dhī)śa bhītajāḍyā kharājiriṣyota |
    sajagādivāsā nṛsiṁhoktā gaṇāḥ ||

28. *(Siddhodvāha) of Nṛsiṁha*, ed. by Sri P. V. Parabrahma Sastri (Hyderabad: The Government of Andhra Pradesh, 1968), pp. 1-2; the editor calls the temple in question Warangal Fort.

    avyād urvīm udadhi raśanām agraṇīḥ kākatīnāṁ, vidyāśālī viditavinayo vīrarudrābhidhānaḥ |
    yātrākāle vijitaharito yasya senā gajānāṁ, madhye kaś cin malayaśikharī mālyavān mandaro vā ||
    nṛsiṁha(ṛṣiḥ)

29. The two names, Narasiṁha and Nṛsiṁha, are synonymous.
30. Parabrahma Sastri, ed., *op. cit.*, p. 2.

31. Sriramamurti, *op. cit.*, p. 51; this information is from the *Andhra Patrika Annual* (1960-61), p. 38:
iti rājaguruviśveśvaraduhitṛsūnor narasiṁhamaharṣeḥ kṛtau . . .

32. Parabrahma Sastri, ed., *op. cit.*, pp. 2-3; the editor tentatively entitles the poem *Siddhodvāha.*

33. *Ibid.*, p. 21 (lines 154-55): *viśveśvarasūno(r) narasiṁha-rṣeḥ kṛti(ḥ).* Here the word *sūnu* seems to mean a grandson, not a son, and specifically a daughter's son; cf. n. 31.

34. Sriramamurti, *op. cit.*, p. 51.

35. Parabrahma Sastri, ed., *op. cit.*, p. 2.

36. Sriramamurti, *op. cit.*, p. 51.

37. Nilakanta Sastri, *op. cit.*, p. 217.

38. Parabrahma Sastri, ed., *op. cit.*, p. 2.

39. Nilkanta Sastri, *op. cit.*, p. 217.

40. *K.N.*, Prologue, vss. 5-6.

41. Sriramamurti, *op. cit.*, pp. 52-53 & 66-67; *vide* also Intro., chap. V.

4

The Kādambarīnāṭaka's Source Story and Its Originality

In the Prologue to the *Kādambarīnāṭaka*, Narasiṁha explicitly states that the play is based on the prose novel *Kādambarī* by Bāṇa.[1] Narasiṁha, however, does not mention Bāṇa's son Bhūṣaṇa, who composed the second half of the novel, as if all of it had been composed by Bāṇa alone.[2] Bāṇa calls his novel *Kādambarī* a *kathā*.[3] But what exactly is a *kathā?* Poets and critics are not unanimous about the definitions of the two kinds of prose composition: the *ākhyāyikā* and the *kathā*. For instance, the lexicographer Amarasiṁha (5th c.), who lived before Bāṇa (7th c.), clearly contrasts the *ākhyāyikā* as factual with the *kathā* as imaginary.[4] His commentator Kṣīrasvāmin (12th c.) further explains the former as the narration of what has happened, and the latter as invented. He quotes Bāṇa's *Harṣacarita* as an example for the former, and his and his son's *Kādambarī* as an example for the latter.[5] Now, it seems almost universally believed that the source of the *Kādambarī* is a story in Guṇāḍhya's now lost Paiśācī Prakrit novel *Bṛhatkathā* (*ca.* 100 BC).[6] But if the *Kādambarī* is thus based on another story and not invented by its authors themselves, it does not fulfill the above-mentioned definition of the *kathā*. Now arises the question: Is the *Kādambarī* a genuinely original work of Bāṇa and Bhūṣaṇa, or simply their elaborately embellished version of a story in the *Bṛhatkathā?*

The Three Versions of the Story of Kādambarī

It has been stated that the novel *Kādambarī* is widely believed to be based on a story in Guṇāḍhya's novel *Bṛhatkathā*, but the story of Kādambarī is found in one other work: Daṇḍin's novel *Avantisundarī* (7th c.)[7] as well. In other words, there are three versions of the same story. Except for some insignificant differences, they agree with one another down to the point where Bāṇa's portion of the novel *Kādambarī* breaks off; with regard to the rest of the story, however, they somewhat differ from one another.

THE KĀDAMBARĪ VERSION

Bāṇa is the author of many works of which the best-known are the *Harṣacarita*, a prose biography of his patron, the Puṣyabhūti Emperor Harṣa;[8] the first half of the prose novel *Kādambarī* as mentioned; and the *Caṇḍīśataka*, a hymn in 100 verses in praise of the goddess Caṇḍī.[9] Also attributed to Bāṇa are the fragmentarily known *Mukuṭatāḍita*, a play on the main action of *Mahābhārata*;[10] and the *Śāradacandrikā*, most probably a play on Candrāpīḍa, the main hero in the *Kādambarī*.[11] Bāṇa's last work is obviously the *Kādambarī*, which was interrupted by his death but completed by his son Bhūṣaṇa.[12] Bhūṣaṇa states at the beginning of his sequel to the *Kādambarī* that the novel was created by his father,[13] but it is not absolutely clear whether he means by it that the novel was wholly created or invented in his father's mind, or that it was simply re-created by him out of a story in the *Bṛhatkathā*. On the supposition that the *Kādambarī* was truly Bāṇa's own creation, did Bhūṣaṇa know his father's plan of its unfinished portion? It is known that Bāṇa, in his *Śāradacandrikā*, arranged Candrāpīḍa's death on account of a divine being with his resurrection at the end,[14] and this is precisely what happens in Bhūṣaṇa's sequel to the *Kādambarī*. From this it seems highly probable that Bāṇa first wrote the *Śāradacandrikā* and then started the novel *Kādambarī* on the same story, and that Bhūṣaṇa used the *Śāradacandrikā* as a source to complete the novel.[15] The Kashmirian Kṣemendra (10th-11th cc.) quotes in his treatise *Aucityavicāracarcā* a verse attributed to Bāṇa which he explains as descriptive of Kādambarī's grief in separation from her lover.[16] This verse seems to have originally belonged to the *Śāradacandrikā*.[17] The Kashmirian Abhinanda (9th c.) wrote a concise yet readable summary of Bāṇa's and Bhūṣaṇa's *Kādambarī* it is in about 900 verses, mainly in the *vaktra* meter, in eight cantos.[18]

THE SO-CALLED BṚHATKATHĀ VERSION

Although the novel *Bṛhatkathā* is not extant in its original form, several paraphrases of it are available. The earliest of them seems to be the Jaina Māhārāṣṭrī Prakrit abridgment incorporated by Saṅghadāsa into his novel *Vasudevahiṇḍi* (*ca.* 5th c.).[19] The Sanskrit epitome *Bṛhatkathāślokasaṅgraha* by Buddhasvāmin (8th/9th c.?)[20] and the Tamil *Perungadai* by Kongu-Veḷir[21] are both incomplete. The *Bṛhatkathāmañjarī* by Kṣemendra[22] and the *Kathāsaritsāgara* by Somadeva (11th c.)[23] are Sanskrit epitomes of what is often referred to as the Kashmirian recension of the *Bṛhatkathā*.[24] Only the last two works contain a summary of a story supposed to be the model of the novel *Kādambarī*.[25] Kṣemendra and Somadeva summarize the story in about 70 and 160 verses respectively, mainly in the *vaktra* meter. In these summaries, the characters and places in the *Kādambarī* are called by totally different names, and the latter half of the story is somewhat different from Bhūṣaṇa's sequel to the novel. The heroine Kādambarī and the hero Candrāpīḍa are called Makarandikā and Somaprabha. The parrot is not Vaiśampāyana but Kādambarī's or Makarandikā's father reborn after cursing his daughter to become an Untouchable girl. King Śūdraka is called Sumānasa in Kṣemendra's summary and Sumanas in Somadeva's, and his soul is not that of Candrāpīḍa or Somaprabha but that of Puṇḍarīka, here called Raśmimant.

THE AVANTISUNDARĪ VERSION

The story of Kādambarī is also found in the novel *Avantisundarī* of Daṇḍin, who lived slightly after Bāṇa.[26] The *Avantisundarī*[27] as available at present is not complete; in fact, it breaks off in the story of Kādambarī.[28] But fortunately, it is possible to find out more about Daṇḍin's version of the story of Kādambarī from the *Avantisundarīkathāsāra*, an anonymous summary of his novel.[29] The first half of this summary[30] corresponds to Bāṇa's portion of the novel *Kādambarī*; the names of the characters and places in it are also, with one exception, identical with those in the novel. The rest of the summary,[31] however, differs considerably from Bhūṣaṇa's sequel to the *Kādambarī*. It seems that while Daṇḍin simply abridged Bāṇa's portion of the *Kādambarī*, which was already being circulated at his times, and grafted it onto his *Avantisundarī*, he had to provide his own conclusion of the story in order to make it fit into the frame story of his novel, whether or not he knew about Bhūṣaṇa's continuation of the story. In the *Avantisundarī*, it is Mahāśvetā who is cursed by her father to become an Untouchable girl, and King Śūdraka is not Candrāpīḍa but the god Śiva's attendant Nandikeśvara cursed by Śiva's consort, Bhavānī.

The Originality of the Novel *Kādambarī*

The three versions of the story of Kādambarī, briefly examined above, do not seem to provide any definite evidence either to prove that the novel *Kādambarī* is Bāṇa's own creation, or to refute the popular supposition of many scholars that it is based on a story in the *Bṛhatkathā*. As was mentioned earlier, the very imaginative poet Bāṇa calls his novel a *kathā*, and his son Bhūṣaṇa states that it was invented by his father. Moreover, the major discrepancies among the three versions of the story begin precisely where Bāṇa's portion of the novel breaks off. If all this does not convince the doubtful minds of the originality of the novel *Kādambarī*, what appears conclusive against their supposition is that in both Kṣemendra's and Somadeva's epitomes of the *Bṛhatkathā*, the story of Kādambarī is immediately followed by an abridgment of the *Pañcatantra*.[32] It is almost certain that the original *Bṛhatkathā* did not contain any version of the *Pañcatantra*.[33] In other words, the now lost Kashmirian recension of the *Bṛhatkathā*, which Kṣemendra and Somadeva epitomized, had already lost much of the original text of the novel, retaining only its frame story, and had been transformed into a kind of anthology of popular stories.[34] It seems reasonable enough to suppose, then, that the novel *Kādambarī*, created by Bāṇa himself, started being circulated independent of Bhūṣaṇa's conclusion to it, then in course of time acquired a conclusion different from Bhūṣaṇa's, and then like many other popular stories, was interpolated into the so-called Kashmirian recension of the *Bṛhatkathā*.

Notes

1. *K.N.*, Prologue, prose after vs. 2 & vs. 3, 2nd half:

   . . . nanu śrāvya evaiṣa kādambarīnāmā bhaṭṭabāṇasya gadyamayaḥ sūktiniṣyandaḥ . . . kenāpi nāṭakanibhāt kavinā tad eva, kāvyāmṛtaṁ nayanayoḥ kṛtam ātitheyam | | 3 | |

2. Among poets and critics, only Dhanapāla (10th c.), in his novel *Tilakamañjarī,* seems to mention Bhūṣaṇa, also known as Pulindhra, as having completed Bāṇa's novel *Kādambarī*, *vide The Tilakamañjarī of Dhanapāla*, ed. by P.B. Śāstrī & K.P. Parab, Kāvyamālā, 85 (Bombay: Nirṇaya Sāgar Press, 1938), vs. 26:

   kevalo pi sphuran bāṇaḥ karoti vimadān kavīn |
   kiṁ punaḥ klptasaṁdhānapulindhrakṛtasaṁnidhiḥ | |

3. *Kādambarī* (*Pūrvārddha*), ed. with Bhānucandra's & Siddhacandra's comm. by M. Pant (Delhi: Motilal Banarsidass, 1976), vs. 20:

   dvijena tenākṣatakaṇṭhakauṇṭhyayā, mahāmanomohamalīmasāndhayā |
   alabdhavaidagdhyavilāsamugdhayā, dhiyā nibaddheyam atidvayī kathā | |

4. *The Nāmaliṅgānuśāsana* (*Amarakoṣa*) *of Amarasiṁha*, ed. with Kṣīrasvāmin's comm. *Amarakośodghāṭana* by K.G. Oka (Poona: Law Printing Press, 1913), pt. 1, gp. 5, vs. 5, 3rd *pāda* & vs. 6, 1st *pāda* (p. 28):

   ākhyāyikopalabdhārthā; prabandhakalpanā kathā.

5. *Ibid*., p. 28:

   ācaṣṭe ākhyāyikā vṛttārthakathanād harṣacaritādiḥ;
   prabandhasya kalpanā kathā kādambaryādir utpādyatvāt.

6. For instance, A.B. Keith; *vide* his *A History of Sanskrit Literature* (Delhi: Oxford University Press, 1973), pp. 319-20 & 324; and M. Pant, ed., *op. cit*., Hindi intro., pp. 20-22.
7. *Avantisundarī*, (incomplete), ed. by S.K. Pilla (Trivandrum: Bhāskaramudrālaya, 1954).
8. *The Harshacarita of Bāṇabhaṭṭa*, ed. by P.V. Kane (Delhi: Motilal Banarsidass, 1986); *vide* also E.B. Cowell & F.W. Thomas, trans., *Harṣacarita* (Delhi: Motilal Banarsidass, 1961).
9. *Caṇḍīśataka*, ed. by P. Durgāprasād & K.P. Parab, Kāvyamālā, pt. 4 (Bombay: Nirṇaya Sāgar Press, 1937), pp. 1-46; *vide* also G.P. Quackenbos, ed. & trans., *The Sanskrit Poems of Mayūra with the Caṇḍīśataka of Bāṇa* (New York: Ams Press Inc., 1965).
10. A.K. Warder, *Indian Kāvya Literature*, vol. IV (1983), pp. 24-25.
11. *Ibid*., pp. 25-26.
12. *Kādambarī* (*Uttarārddha*), ed. by M. Pant (Delhi: Motilal Banarsidass, 1977), *upodghāta*, vs. 2:

    yāte divaṁ pitari tadvacasaiva sārdhaṁ, vicchedam āpa bhuvi yas tu kathāprabandhaḥ |
    duḥkhaṁ satāṁ yadasamāptikṛtaṁ vilokya, prārabdha eva sa mayā na kavitvadarpāt | |

13. *Ibid.*, vs. 1:

    āryaṁ yam arcati gṛhe gṛha eva lokaḥ, puṇyaiḥ kṛtaś ca yata eva mamātmalābhaḥ |
    sṛṣṭaiva yena ca katheyam ananyaśaktyā, vāgīśvaraṁ pitaram eva tam ānato smi ||

14. Śāradātanaya, *Bhāvaprakāśana of Śāradātanaya*, ed. by Y. Yatiraja & K. S.R. Sastri (Baroda: Oriental Institute, 1930), p. 252, lines 10-12 (chap. 8, *utsṛṣṭikāṅkalakṣaṇa*):

    candrāpīḍasya maraṇaṁ yatpratyujjīvanāntimam ||
    kalpitaṁ bhaṭṭabāṇena yathā śāradacandrikā |
    divyena martyasya vadhaḥ kāvyasyāvaśyabhāvataḥ ||

15. Warder, *op. cit.*, vol. IV, p. 25.

16. *Aucityavicāracarcā*, ed. by P. Durgāprasād & K.P. Parab, Kāvyamālā, pt. 1, pp. 115-60 (Bombay: Nirṇaya Sāgar Press, 1929), p. 121:

    yathā vā bhaṭṭabāṇasya, hāro jalārdravasanaṁ nalinīdalāni, prāleyaśīkaramucas tuhināṁśubhāsaḥ |
    yasyendhanāni sarasāni ca candanāni, nirvāṇam eṣyati kathaṁ sa manobhavāgniḥ ||
    atra vipralambhabharabhagnadhairyāyāḥ kādambaryā virahavyathāvarṇanā mādhuryasaukumāryādiguṇayogena pūrṇenduvadanena priyaṁvadatvena hṛdayānandadāyiniṁ dayitatamatām ātanoti.

17. In the *Kavikaṇṭhābharaṇa*, however, Kṣemendra cites several verses which he claims belong to his own versified version of the *Kādambarī*, the *Padyakādambarī; vide* his *Kavikaṇṭhābharaṇa*, ed. by P. Durgāprasād & P.K. Parab, Kāvyamālā, pt. 4, pp. 149-69 (Bombay: Nirṇaya Sāgar Press, 1937).

18. *The Kādambarīkathāsāra of Abhinanda*, ed. by P. Durgāprasād & K. P. Parab, Kāvyamālā, 11 (Bombay: Nirṇaya Sāgar Press, 1925); *vide* also Warder, *op. cit.*, vol. V (1988), pp. 311-21. There are many other summaries of Bāṇa's and Bhūṣaṇa's *Kādambarī*; *vide* V. Raghavan, ed., *New Catalogus Catalogorum*, vol. III, pp. 337-38; and M. Krishnamachariar, *History of Classical Sanskrit Literature* (Delhi: Motilal Banarsidass, 1974), pp. 450-51.

19. *The Vasudevahiṇḍi: An Authentic Jain Version of the Bṛhatkathā* (Ahmedabad: L.D. Institute of Indology, 1977).

20. *Bṛhatkathāślokasaṁgraha*, ed. & trans. into Friench by F. Lacote (Paris: Imprimerie Nationale, 1908-29).

21. Warder, *op. cit.*, vol. II (1974), p. 117.

22. *The Brihatkathāmañjarī of Kshemendra*, ed. by M. P. Śivadatta & K.P. Parab, Kāvyamālā, 69 (Bombay: NIrṇaya Sāgar Press, 1931).

23. *Kathāsaritsāgara*, ed. by J. Śāstrī (Delhi: Motilal Banarsidass, 1977).

24. F. Lacote, *Essai sur Guṇāḍhya et la Bṛhatkathā* (Paris: Ernest Leroux, 1908), pp. 122-45.

25. *Bṛhatkathāmañjarī, śaktiyaśolambaka* (chap. 16), vss. 183-248 (pp. 555-60); *Kathāsaritsāgara, śaktiyaśolambaka* (chap. 10), *taraṅga* 3, vss. 22-178 (pp. 304-8). An English translation of the latter is available in *The Ocean of Story (Being C.H. Tawney's Translation of Somadeva's Kathāsaritsāgara)*, ed. by N.M. Penzer (Delhi: Motilal Banarsidass, 1968), vol. V, pp. 27-38. The Kāvyamālā edition of the *Bṛhatkathāmañjarī* also gives in an appendix a faithful summary of Bāṇa's and Bhūṣaṇa's *Kādambarī*; it is in about 80 *vaktra* verses, and reads as one of the riddless in the *Vetālapañcaviṁśati* interpolated in the *Bṛhatkathāmañjarī*.

26. Daṇḍin praises Bāṇa in his novel; *vide Avantisundarī*, intro. vs. 19 (p. 3):

    bhinnas tīkṣṇamukhenāpi citraṁ bāṇena nirvyathaḥ |
    vyāhāreṣu jahau līlāṁ na mayūraḥ . . . ||

27. A substantial middle part of this novel has been independently circulated under the title *Daśakumāracarita; vide Daśakumāracarita of Daṇḍin*, ed. by M.R. Kale (Delhi: Motilal Banarsidass, 1979).
28. Only the middle part of the story is preserved; *vide Avantisundarī*, pp. 243-46.
29. *Avantisundarīkathāsāra*, ed. by G. Harihara Sastri (Madras: Kuppuswami Sastri Research Institute, 1957), canto V, vss. 112-49.
30. *Ibid.*, vss. 112-28.
31. *Ibid.*, vss. 129-49.
32. *Bṛhatkathāmañjarī, śaktiyaśolambaka* (chap. 16), approx. vss. 252-567 (pp. 561-87); *Kathāsaritsāgara, śaktiyaśolambaka* (chap. 10), *taraṅgas* 4-8. Somadeva's summary of the *Pañcatantra*, here called the *Prājñakathā*, or stories of the intelligent, is mingled with a collection of stories of fools under the title *Mugdhakathā*; Kṣemendra's is followed by stories of fools under the title *Mūrkhākhyāyikā*. These two epitomes of the *Bṛhatkathā* also contain, among other collections of stories, the *Vetālapañcaviṁśati*; *vide Kathāsaritsāgara, śaśāṅkavatīlambaka* (chap. 12), *taraṅgas* 8-32 (pp. 405-67); *Bṛhatkathāmañjarī, śaśāṅkavatīlambaka* (chap. 9), *guccha* 2, vss. 19-1221 (pp. 289-385).
33. F. Edgerton, *The Panchatantra Reconstructed*, vol. 2 (New Haven: American Oriental Society, 1924), p. 23.
34. Warder, *op. cit.*, vol. IV, pp. 48-49.

5

Some Basic Problems Concerning Narasiṁha's Dramatization of the Novel Kādambarī

THIS chapter will discuss some basic problems that arise from Narasiṁha's dramatization of the novel *Kādambarī*: the type and the title of the play, the use of Sanskrit and Prakrit languages, versification and the like.

The Title and the Type of the Play

As was mentioned earlier, both the *M.M.* and the *M.Ch.M.* call Narasiṁha's play the *Kādambarīnāṭaka* (Kādambarī Play).[1] Vemabhūpāla also calls it by the same title each time he quotes a verse from it in his *Sāhityacintāmaṇi*.[2] It seems possible, however, that the play was also circulated as the *Kādambarīkalyāṇa* (Good Fortune of Kādambarī), for it is once called by this title at the end of the *M.M.*, which portion is based on manuscripts other than those on which the greater part of the *M.M.* is based.[3] Now, the title *Kādambarīnāṭaka* appears a little too straightforward or commonplace, but immediately reminds one of the famous novel *Kādambarī* of Bāṇa and his son Bhūṣaṇa, on which the play is actually based; and it clearly indicates that it is a *nāṭaka*, a full-length play on a well-known story.[4] The title *Kādambarīkalyāṇa*, on the other hand, indicates the play's denouement, the good fortune (*kalyāṇa*)[5] of the heroine, Kādambarī, instead of rather unnecessarily mentioning the type of the play.

The oldest extant treatise on ancient Indian dramaturgy, the *Nāṭyaśāstra* of Bharata (2nd c. BC?-1st c. AD?)[6] is silent on the entitling of a play. But Sāgaranandin, in his *Nāṭakalakṣaṇaratnakośa* (11th c.), quotes the view of some authority and explains it as follows: one should entitle a *nāṭaka* and the like by referring to their plots and/or chief characters. He gives as examples the *Jānakīrāghava*, the *Rāmānanda*, the *Kundamālā*, the *Mālatīmādhava* and the *Mṛcchakaṭika*.[7] Similarly, Śāradātanaya holds in his *Bhāvaprakāśana* (13th c.) that the title of a *nāṭaka* should mention its hero and others, and/or its central theme; he gives the *Rāmābhyudaya* as an example.[8] Kuntaka states in his *Vakroktijīvita* (11th c.) that the titles of literary works should possess *vakriman* (lit. crookedness) by means of referring to their central themes in unusual, 'crooked' but intriguing words. To illustrate this point, he cites the *Abhijñānaśākuntala*, the

Mudrārākṣasa, the *Kṛtyārāvaṇa*, the *Chalitarāma*, the *Puṣpadūṣitaka* and the like. According to Kuntaka, straightforward titles such as the *Hayagrīvavadha*, the *Pāṇḍavābhyudaya* and the *Rāmānanda* are not good enough.[9] It is interesting to note that the *Rāmānanda*, cited by Sāgaranandin as a title that indicates both the plot and the cheif character of a play, is too simple, therefore a bad example to Kuntaka. It is unfortunate that Narasiṁha failed to give his play a little more impressive title, for instance, the *Titikṣukādambarīya* (Patient Kādambarī) or the *Śaptacandrāpīḍa* (Candrāpīḍa Cursed).[10]

The *Kādambarīnāṭaka* is a *nāṭaka*[11] as its title indicates and its author, Narasiṁha, states in its Prologue.[12] But one might wonder why it cannot be considered a *prakaraṇa*, since it is based on a *kathā* (imaginary or invented story), not on an *ākhyāyikā* (factual story, or history).[13] A *nāṭaka*, according to the *Nāṭyaśāstra*, has to have a well-known (*prakhyāta*) plot and a well-known and noble hero, for instance, a royal sage,[14] while a *prakaraṇa* has to have an invented (*autpattika*) plot and an invented hero, for instance, a Brahmin, a minister or a merchant, but not a king or a god.[15] Thus in the light of the *Nāṭyaśāstra*, the *Kādambarīnāṭaka* is without doubt a *nāṭaka*: its plot is well-known and its hero, a prince, is well-known and noble, though they are naturally fictitious, being based on the novel *Kādambarī*.[16]

Now, it seem possible to consider the *Kādambarīnāṭaka* a *toṭaka* (or *troṭaka*) as well, a secondary type of play (*uparūpaka*) not mentioned by Bharata and omitted by many later theorists. According to Sāgaranandin, the *toṭaka* is only a sub-variety of the *nāṭaka* whose main feature is the meeting of a celestial maiden with a male human being, and whose minor feature is the entry of a jester (*vidūṣaka*) in every act. His first example, Kālidāsa's *Vikramorvaśīya*, has the main feature but lacks such a jester as described in the minor feature. His second example, the now lost *Menakānahuṣa*, however, is described as possessing both features.[17] The *Kādambarīnāṭaka* lacks the minor feature: its Jester enters in only five of its eight acts (I, IV, VI, VII & VIII). Moreover, it does not have any songs or dances which delineate the hero's emotions; this feature is found in Act IV of the *Vikramorvaśīya*, though it does not seem to be mentioned by any ancient theorist on dramaturgy. The *Kādambarīnāṭaka*, however, fulfills the main requirement: it has the union of Kādambarī, an *apsaras* (strictly speaking, half *gandharva*), with Candrāpīḍa, a male human being (in fact, the moon reborn on the earth).[18] It does not seem inconsistent to consider the *Kādambarīnāṭaka* to be a *toṭaka* as well as a *nāṭaka*, for the former is only a sub-variety of the latter.[19]

The Languages and the Style

The *Kādambarīnāṭaka* is composed in two languages: Sanskrit and Prakrit. It employs three kinds of Prakrit: Śaurasenī Māhārāṣṭrī and Māgadhī.[20] Sanskrit is spoken by all the male characters except the Jester Dramiḍadhārmika, the hunter Mātaṅga and some menservants.[21] Śaurasenī is the language of all the female characters with the exception of the sylvan deity, who speaks Sanskrit (Prelude to Act VII).[22] Śaurasenī is the language of the Jester as well.[23] But these Śaurasenī-speaking characters use Māhārāṣṭrī for their verses.[24] The hunter Mātaṅga speaks Māgadhī in both prose and verse (Prelude to Act VIII).[25]

There is rather frequent confusion of Śaurasenī with Māhārāṣṭrī in the play, but this is often the case with Prakrit works and the Prakrit passages of Sanskrit-Prakrit plays. It is not certain whether the confusion is due simply to the scribes' negligence or the playwright Narasiṁha's incompetence to differentiate the two Prakrits accurately or some other cause.[26] There is also occasional confusion of Māgadhī with Śaurasenī in the play's Māgadhī passages.

With regard to Narasiṁha's grammer, a few peculiarities exist. He frequently confuses some demonstrative pronouns, or rather uses them according to his own rules. For instance, Candrāpīḍa is made to say *ayam* (sing., masc., nom. of *idam*) instead of *saḥ* (sing., masc., nom. of *tad*) when he refers to his friend not present on the scene.[27] This usage of *idaṁ* is unusual, if not wrong, because *idam* is, as a general rule, used for a person or object perceived or present, while *tad* is used for those not perceived, or absent. Narasiṁha's reason for this strange usage of *idam*, however, seems to be that Candrāpīḍa is referring to the same person that he has mentioned in the same speech.[28] Another peculiarity is a semantic one. Narasiṁha occasionally uses the passive past participle of a verb for an immediate future action. For instance, (*eṣo smi*) . . . *nivṛttaḥ* . . . is undoubtedly intended to mean "(I am) coming back. . .", not the expected "(I have) come back. . ."[29] This usage of a passive past participle seems very rare, though not non-existent, in other works.[30]

It seems reasonable to describe Narasiṁha's style as generally comparable to that of his better-known predecessors such as Kālidāsa and Bhavabhūti, though, of course, it requires a detailed study to draw any definite conclusion. His style is not particularly complicated or simple; yet it is highly refined. In his flowing style Narasiṁha confines himself to using very long compounds (*samāsa*s) only moderately.[31] He employs a great variety of figures of speech or *alaṅkāra*s without indulging in them. His favorite *alaṅkāra*s are the *upamā* (simile),[32] the *rūpaka* (metaphor),[33] the *utprekṣā* (fancy),[34] the *dīpaka* (lamp),[35] the *anuprāsa* (alliteration),[36] and the like. He does not seem very interested in the *śleṣa* (pun),[37] which is one of the favorite *alaṅkāra*s of Bāṇa, and of Bhūṣaṇa to a lesser extent.

Vemabhūpāla, the Reḍḍi (Rāṣṭrakūṭa) King Peda Komaṭi Vema (reigned 1403-20), also known as Vīranārāyaṇa, quotes three verses from the *Kādambarīnāṭaka* in his treatise on poetics, the *Sāhityacintāmaṇi*,[38] to illustrate *alaṅkāra*s. He cites Act VII, verse 19[39] to illustrate the *raśanopamā* (rope simile), in which the subject of comparison of the first simile is identical with the object of comparison of the following and so on. In this verse Candrāpīḍa separated from his friend Vaiśampāyana is compared to Spring separated from Gentle Breeze, to Love separated from Spring, and then to Youth separated from Love. Act VI, verse 26[40] is cited to illustrate the *vyājokti* (pretext), in which a clever excuse is made to cover up an embarrassing or unpleasant situation. In this verse Kādambarī, embarrassed at her mynahs repeating what she has spoken about her love for Prince Candrāpīḍa in a dream, gives the excuse that it was all about the god Śūlapāṇi (Candrāpīḍa and Śūlapāṇi are both epithets of the god Śiva). Vemabhūpāla also cites Act 1, verse 20[41] as an exapmple for the *tiryagāśrayasvabhāva* (= *-svabhāvokti*), that is, the naturalistic description of an animal. In this verse, the manner in which the horse Indrāyudha invites Candrāpīḍa to mount him is described simply but beautifully without the addition of any specific *alaṅkāra*.

The Verses and the Meters

The *Kādambarīnāṭaka* has a total of 341 verses.[42] Its Prologue has 9 verses; Act I, 40; Act II, 30; Act III, 50; Act IV, 34; Act V, 59; Act VI, 42; Act VII, 32; and Act VIII, 45. The *Kādambarīnāṭaka* is a relatively long play in respect of the number of its verses. For Bhāsa's *Pratimānāṭaka* (2nd c.), for instance, has only about 160 verses; Kālidāsa's *Abhijñānaśākuntala* (5th c.), about 190; his *Vikromorvaśīya*, about 160; Viśākhadatta's *Mudrārākṣasa* (6th c.), about 170; Bhavabhūti's *Uttararāmacarita* (8th c.), about 250; and his *Mālatīmādhava*, about 230, though Śūdraka's *Mṛcchakaṭika* (3rd c.) has about 390; and the longest Sanskrit-Prakrit play, Rājaśekhara's *Bālarāmāyaṇa* (10th c.) has about 780.[43]

Narasiṁha employs about twenty different meters for the verses of the *Kādambarīnāṭaka*, though they are all familiar ones. His most favorite meter is the *Śārdūlavikrīḍita*; he uses it in 81 verses. The *āryā* and its variants, the *gīti* and the *upagīti*, are also his favorite meters; they are used 43 times, 32 times and 6 times respectively. The *vasantatilakā* and the *vaktra* are also used frequently: 34 times and 25 times respectively. The other meters that Narasiṁha uses are: in order of frequency, the *hariṇī* and the *mandākrāntā* 16 times each; the *mālinī* 14 times; the *śikhariṇī* 13 times; the *upajāti* and the *aupacchandasika* 11 times each; the *pṛthvī* 10 times; the *sragdharā* and the *puṣpitāgrā* 8 times each; the *indravajrā* and the *rathoddhatā* 3 times each; the *vaṁśastha* twice; and the *śālinī*, the *drutavilambita*, the *praharṣiṇī*, the *mañjubhāṣiṇī* and the *aparavaktra* only once each.[44]

As was mentioned earlier, three verses are quoted by Vemabhūpāla in his *Sāhityacintāmaṇi*; they are in the *upagīti* (VII, 19), the *mandākrāntā* (VI, 26) and the *aupacchandasika* (I, 20). Two verses in the *āryā* meter are directly borrowed from Bāṇa's portion of the novel *Kādambarī* (V, 36 and VIII, 16). Ten verses are composed in Prakrit, all of them in the *āryā* or its variants (I, 23 & 38; II, 19; V, 10 & 23; VI, 13, 14 & 15; VII, 31; and VIII, 4). Kādambarī, who is a regular Prakrit-speaking character, resorts to Sanskrit in one verse in the *śārdūlavikrīḍita* (VII, 21). One verse in the *puṣpitāgrā* is repeated (VI, 40). And one in the *mālinī* is a split verse interrupted by prose (IV, 27). Narasiṁha seems particularly fond of and skillful in composing in the *āryā* and its variants; in fact, many of his verses composed in those meters appear good enough to be considered equal to verses of the best poets in the Sanskrit-Prakrit literature.[45]

Notes

1. *Vide* Intro., chap. II.
2. *Vide* Intro., chap. III & *infra*.
3. *Vide* Intro., chap. II; V. Krishnamacharya adopts this title in his edition of the play.
4. Cf. the *Pratimānāṭaka* and the *Abhiṣekanāṭaka* of Bhāsa, the *Mahānāṭaka* or *Hanumannāṭaka* (anthology) of Dāmodara or Madhusūdana, &c.
5. There are several other similarly entitled *nāṭakas*, all of which are later than the tenth c., such as the *Jāmbavatīkalyāṇa* and the *Candrakalākalyāṇa* (also known as the *Candrakalāpariṇaya*); *vide* S. Konow, *The Indian Drama*, trans. S. N. Ghosal (Calcutta: General Printers & Publishers, 1969), pp. 161, 171, &c. The word *kalyāṇa* in these titles seems to be used synonymously with the word *pariṇaya* (marriage).
6. A.K. Warder, *Indian Kāvya Literature*, vol. I, p. 21.
7. *The Nāṭakalakṣaṇaratnakośa of Sāgaranandin*, ed. by M. Dillon, vol. I (London: Oxford University Press, 1937), lines 383-87 (p. 17):

   pradhānavastunirdeśād bhavati hi nāṭakādīnāṁ nāmeti | pradhānasya nirdeśād vastunirdeśād vā nāṭakādīnāṁ nāma kartavyam | yathā jānakīrāghavaṁ nāma nāṭakam | rāmānandam | vastunirdeśāt kundamālā nāma nāṭakam | prakaraṇam api mālatīmādhavaṁ nāma | vastunirdeśān mṛcchakaṭikā nāma prakaraṇam |
8. *Bhāvaprakāśana of Śāradātanaya*, p. 200, lines 3-4:

   tan nāma nāṭakādyantargarbhitārthopasūcakam |
   yadā hi rāmābhyudayaṁ nāma nāṭakam ity ataḥ |

   The researcher adopts the emendation *nāyakādyantyar-* made by S. Chattopadhyaya; *vide Nāṭakalakṣaṇaratnakośa*: In *the Perspective of Ancient Drama and Dramaturgy* (Calcutta: Punthi Pustak, 1974), p. 192.
9. The *Vakroktijīvita of Kuntaka*, ed. by K. Krishnamoorthy (Dharwad: Karnatak University, 1977), p. 281:

   adbhutaṁ punar idaṁ yat sāratarasaṁvidhānakanibandhalakṣaṇā (yojitasara) sākṣareṇa nāmnāpi sā niveśyate | yathābhijñānaśākuntalamudrārākṣasapratimāniruddhamāyāpuṣpakakṛtyārāvaṇachalitarāmapuṣpadūṣitakādīni nāmān | evaṁvidhāni kāvyabandhānāṁ nāmadheyāny api nirupamollekhāni (vilakṣaṇavakratāsarasā)kṣarāṇi niveditāntargataviśiṣṭasaṁbandhatayā nibadhnanty eva vakrimāṇam, na punar hayagrīvavadhaśiśupālavadhapāṇḍavābhyudayarāmānandāmacaritaprāyāṇi saralasvarūpāṇi |
10. Possible titles of the play thought out by the researcher. For Candrāpīḍa's death from a curse, which is Narasiṁha's innovation, *vide* Intro., chap. VI.
11. The *nāṭaka* is one of the ten major types of plays (*rūpakas*); *vide* Bharata, *Nāṭyaśāstra*, ed. with Abhinavagupta's comm. *Abhinavabhāratī* (10th c.) by M.R. Kavi, K.S. Rāmaswāmin & J.S. Pade (Baroda: Oriental Institute, 1926-64), chap. 18 (vol. II), vss. 2-3:

nāṭakaṁ sapraka(ra, supplied by *H.S.)ṇaṁ aṅko vyāyoga eva ca |*
bhāṇaḥ samavakāraś ca vīthī prahasanaṁ ḍimaḥ || 2 ||
īhāmṛgaś ca vijñeyo daśamo nāṭyalakṣaṇe | . . . || 3 ||

12. *K.N.*, Prologue, vs. 3.
13. *Vide* Intro., chap. IV.
14. *Nāṭyaśāstra*, chap. 18, vs. 10:

    prakhyātavastuviṣayaṁ prakhyātodāttanāyakaṁ caiva |
    rājarṣivaṁśyacaritaṁ tathaiva divyāśrayopetam ||

15. *Ibid.*, vss. 45-46, & 48-49:

    yatra kavir ātmaśaktyā vastu śarīraṁ ca nāyakaṁ caiva ||
    autpattikaṁ prakurute prakaraṇam iti tadbudhair jñeyam || 45 ||

    yad anārṣam athāhāryaṁ kāvyaṁ prakaroty abhūtaguṇayuktam(*adbhuta-*, variant adopted by *H.S.*) |
    utpannabījavastu prakaraṇam iti tad api vijñeyam || 46 ||

    vipravaṇiksacivānāṁ purohitāmātyasārthavāhānām |
    caritaṁ yan naikavidhaṁ jñeyaṁ tat prakaraṇaṁ nāma || 48 ||

    nodāttanāyakakṛtaṁ na divyacaritaṁ na rājasambhogam |
    bāhyajanasaṁprayuktaṁ taj jñeyaṁ prakaraṇaṁ tajjñaiḥ || 49 ||

16. Such literary works as the *Mahābhārata* and the *Rāmāyaṇa*, and episodes in them, on which the plots and the characters of many *nāṭaka*s are based, are not only well-known but also historical — not fictitious — to the minds of ancient Indians. Also, it may be of some interest to note in passing that according to the *Nāṭyadarpaṇa* of Rāmacandra and Guṇacandra (12th c.), there are 21 sub-varieties of the *prakaraṇa* on the basis of the "inventedness" of their plots, heros and denouements (*phala*s); or even more on the basis of their heroines; *vide Nāṭyadarpaṇa*, ed. by G.K. Shrigondekar & L.B. Gandhi (Baroda: Oriental Institute, 1959), pp. 104-105. *K.N.* cannot be considered to be any of the 21 sub-varieties of the *prakaraṇa* because it does not satisfy even one of the three criteria, in addition to the fact that its hero is a prince. Abhinavagupta also mentions 21 kinds of *prakaraṇas*; *vide* his comm. on the *Nāṭyaśāstra*, vol. II, p. 433.
17. *Nāṭakalakṣaṇaratnakośa*, lines 2766-75 (pp. 114-15):

    toṭakaṁ nāṭakasyaiva prabhedaḥ | *āhāśmakuṭṭaḥ* | *divyamānuṣasaṁyogo py aṅke py aṅke vidūṣakaḥ nakhakuṭṭas tv āha* | *divyamānuṣasaṁyogas toṭakaṁ nāṭakārtham* | *bādarāyaṇo py evaṁ āha* | *toṭakaṁ taddhi vijñeyaṁ divyāmānavasaṁgamam* | *tad eṣāṁ divyāyā mānuṣeṇa saha saṁgamo yas tad eva mahallakṣaṇam* | *pratyaṅkavidūṣakapraveśas tūpalakṣaṇam* | *yathā vikramorvaśītoṭakaṁ na tathābhūtavidūṣakam* | *mena* (*vide Bhāvaprakāśana*) *pyuṣat tv asti vidūṣakatvāt* | *aśmakuṭṭanamatānugamāt siddham iti* || *vide* also *Bhāvaprakāśana*, p. 238, lines 4-14.
18. *Vide* Intro., chap. VI.
19. In the case of the *Vikramorvaśīya*, some manuscripts of it have such songs and dances as mentioned above and call it a *toṭaka*, while others omit them altogether and simply call it a *nāṭaka*. These songs (and dances) are probably not original, for none of them seems to be quoted by any ancient critic; *vide* Warder, *op. cit.*, vol. III (1977), pp. 138-39.
20. The *Nāṭyaśāstra* enumerates the following dramatic Prakrits, but Māhārāṣṭrī is not included in them; chap. 17 (vol. II), vss. 49-50:

    māgadhyavantijā prācyā śaurasenyardhamāgadhī |

bāhlikā dākṣiṇātyā ca sapta bhāṣāḥ prakīrtitāḥ || 49 ||

śakārābhīracaṇḍālaśabaradramilānghrajāḥ |
hīnā vanecarāṇāṁ ca vibhāṣā nāṭake smṛtā (*ḥ, H.S.*) ||50||

The *Mṛcchakaṭika* of Śūdraka (3rd c.) employs eight kinds of Prakrit: Śaurasenī, Avantikā, Prācyā, Māgadhī, Śakārī, Cāṇḍālī, Ḍhakkī, and Māhārāṣṭrī, i.e., the language of the Prakrit anthology *Gāhāsattasaī* of Hāla (2nd c.); *vide* Pṛthvīdhara's comm. on the play, ed. by M.R. Kale (Delhi: Motilal Banarsidass, 1972), text & comm. pp. 6-7.

21. For *K.N.*'s Sanskrit- and Prakrit-speaking characters, *vide* also Part Two, Dramatis Personae.

22. Kādambarī also speaks Sanskrit once; *vide infra*.

23. According to the *Nāṭyaśāstra*, Śaurasenī is the language of heroines and their female companions; the language of the jester is Prācyā, very close to Śaurasenī; *vide* chap. 17, vs. 52:

prācyā vidūṣakādīnāṁ. . . |
nāyikānāṁ sakhīnāṁ ca śūrasenyavirodhinī ||

According to Pṛthvīdhara, the Jester of the *Mṛcchakaṭika* speaks Prācyā; *vide* his comm. on the play, p. 7.

24. *Vide* Viśvanātha, *Sāhityadarpaṇa*, ed. by Ś. Śāstrī (Delhi: Motilal Banarsidass, 1982), chap. VI, vs. 159 (p. 204):

saurasenī prayoktavyā tādṛśīnāṁ ca yoṣitām |
āsām eva tu gāthāsu mahārāṣṭrīṁ prayojayet ||

This use of Māhārāṣṭrī may be an innovation by Śūdraka, for it does not seem to be found in any play earlier than his *Mṛcchakaṭika; vide* Warder, *op. cit.*, vol. III, p. 21.

25. The *Nāṭyaśāstra* assigns Māgadhī to guards of royal inner-citadels for women; *vide* chap. 17, vs. 51, 1st half: *māgadhī tu narendrāṇām antaḥpurasamāśrayā* | But it assigns Śakārī, Śābarī or Drāmiḍī to hunters, foresters and the like; *vide ibid.*, vss. 55-56:

. . . *vyādha* . . . | *yojyā śakāra* (*śabara*, variant) *bhāṣā tu kiṁ cid vānaukasī tathā* || 55 || . . . |
. . . *drāmiḍī vanacāriṣu* || 56 ||

In the Prelude to Act VI of the *Abhijñānaśākuntala*, the fisherman speaks Māgadhī.

26. As a rule, the researcher does not emend Śaurasenī forms to their Māhārāṣṭrī equivalents, and *vice versa*; but if *V.K.* makes such an emendation, he leaves it as it is. Konow, for instance, makes a considerable number of such emendations in his edition of a Prakrit play (*saṭṭaka*), and concludes that its author has a poor knowledge of the two Prakrits, while Upadhye, who does not make such emendations, holds that original readings must be retained, and that Prakrit plays are in only one language, that is, Prakrit, not in a mixture of Śaurasenī and Māhārāṣṭrī. *Vide Rājaśekhara's Karpūramañjarī*, ed. by S. Konow & trans. by C. R. Lanman (Delhi: Motilal Banarsidass, 1963), pp. 202-3; and *Rudradāsa's Candralekhā*, ed. by A. N. Upadhye (Bombay: Bharatiya Vidya Bhavan, 1967), pp. 5-9 & 63. Warder agrees with Upadhye's view; *vide op. cit.*, vol. V, p. 423. The researcher's conjecture is that poets — not theorists — considered a certain degree of the above-mentioned confusion to be natural and normal.

27. *K.N.*, Act VII, prose after vs. 10: *yāvad aham . . . suhṛdam anveṣayāmi* | . . . *ayam . . . anyato pasaret* |

28. *Etad* is also used for the same purpose; e.g. Act VII, vs. 12, 1st half:

    vayasyo na . . . nayanayor eti viṣayaṁ . . . etasya kva . . . mārgaṇam api |

    Similar examples can be found throughout the play.

29. *K.N.*, Act VI, vs. 42, 1st half. Similar examples are found, among others, in the Prelude to Act I, vs. 12, 2nd half: . . . *yaṁ śāpam . . . nītaḥ so pi . . . nirvāhyatām* ||; and in Act I, prose after vs. 19: *ayam aham āpatita eva.*

30. Cf. *ayam aham āgato smi; vide the Abhijñānaśākuntala of Kālidāsa*, ed. by S.K. Belvalkar (New Delhi: Sahitya Akademi, 1965), end of Act III (p. 53). Similarly, *ayam aham āgata eva;* same play, ed. by K. Śāstrī (Varanasi: Chowkhamba Sanskrit Series Office, 1960), same place (p. 232). Cf. *ayam aham āgacchāmi*; same play, ed. by M.R. Kale (Delhi: Motilal Banarsidass, 1977), same place (p. 118). Furthermore, cf. *maiṁ āgayā hūṁ*, Hindi used for the same purpose.

31. For instance, Madalekhā's Prakrit speech (Act IV, before vs. 23) has compounds consisting of ten to twenty words.

32. E.g. Act II, vs. 9; Act III, vs. 34; & *passim.*

33. E.g. Act II, vs. 23; Act III, vs. 46; & *passim.*

34. E.g. Act I, vss. 27 & 29; Act V, vs. 23; & *passim.*

35. E.g. Act V, vs. 27 & Act VIII, vs. 7.

36. E.g. *virahaveaṇāvihuravaravahū-*; *vide* Act IV, menservants' Prakrit speech before vs. 8.

37. E.g. Act III, vs. 36, and Act IV, vs. 27 & prose interrupting it.

38. "The Devanāgarī Transcript Manuscript of the *Sāhityacintāmaṇi* of Vemabhūpāla Preserved in the Adyar Library, Madras (Adyar Ms. Fol. 175)"; hereafter cited as *S.C.* Vemabhūpāla is also known as the author of the *Saṅgītacintāmaṇi*, a treatise on music; the *Śṛṅgāradīpikā*, a commentary on the *Amaruśataka* of Amaruka, and one other work. Moreover, he is the hero of the *Vemabhūpālacarita* or *Vīranārāyanacarita* of Vāmana-bhaṭṭabāṇa, patronized by Vemabhūpāla; *vide* M. Krishnamachariar, *History of Classical Sanskrit Literature*, pp. 478-79 & 778-80.

39. *S.C.*, pp. 174-75:

    maṁdānilena madhunīva madhuneva viyuktapān madanaḥ |
    madananaiva taruṇīvanāṁtare vihaṁgahastā suhṛdānurūpeṇa ||

    This manuscript is corrupt; for variant readings and translation, *vide* Part Two.

40. *S.C.*, pp. 282-83:

    caṁdrāpīḍa prakaṭaya dayāṁ dehi me dṛṣṭisaukhyaṁ, jānīṣe māṁ manasi nivasan baṁdhabhāvā tvam eva |
    itthaṁ svapne nigaditam anuvyāvṛtā śārikābhir, vrīlālola prathayati janāyānvitaṁ śūlapāṇau ||

    For vars. & trans., *vide* Part Two & *V.K.*, Act VI, vs. 25 (not 26).

41. *S.C.*, p. 288:

    namitonnamitānanena mūrdhnā, likhatā bhūtalam agrataḥ khanata |

madhureṇa ca vīkṣitena veṣāṁ, mukharasvām anumanyate dhiroddhuṁ ||

For vars. & trans., *vide* Part Two.

42. These include Act VI, vs. 15 (Prakrit), omitted by *V.K.* but retained by the researcher; count as one Act VI, vs. 40, repeated after Act VIII, vs. 9; and exclude a verse before Act VIII, vs. 22, omitted by *V.K.* and the researcher.

43. For the editions of these plays used here, *vide* Bibliography. Shekhar believes that a great numer of verses in a play is a sign of decadence; *vide* I. Shekhar, *Sanskrit Drama*, pp. 140-42.

44. For a detailed study of these meters, *vide*, among others, Kedārabhaṭṭa, *Vṛttaratnākara*, ed. by M. Shastri (Varanasi: Krishnadas Academy, 1982), and A. Mukherji, *Sanskrit Prosody: Its Evolution* (Calcutta: Saraswat Library, 1976).

45. E.g. I, 42 & 45; IV, 31 & 34; V, 6 & 29; &c.

6

Narasiṁha's Treatment of the Novel Kādambarī's Plot in His Kādambarīnāṭaka

As was discussed earlier, the source story of the *Kādambarīnāṭaka* is the novel *Kādambarī* of Bāṇa and his son Bhūṣaṇa.[1] The novel, however, has an extremely intricate plot, and this makes it a very difficult task to dramatize the novel. Nevertheless, Narasiṁha has succeeded in producing an excellent dramatic version of the novel by introducing various innovations into its plot.

Different Views on Innovations in a Nāṭaka's Plot

Śāradātanaya quotes in his *Bhāvaprakāśana* the view of Mātṛgupta (*cir.* 400)[2] that the plot of a *nāṭaka* may be to some extent invented even if it is taken from an old story.[3] Ānandavardhana (10th c.) also states in his *Dhvanyāloka* that the plot of a source story may be altered for the sake of the full development of *rasa*. But he insists that source stories such as the *Rāmāyaṇa*, in which the *rasa* is well-established, must not be altered at will, contrary to that *rasa*.[4] In the prologue to the Rāma play *Rāmābhyudaya*, Yaśovarman (8th c.) emphasizes that the course of the source story must not be violated.[5] In spite of this, many authors of Rāma plays — to name a few, Bhavabhūti (8th c.), Mātrarāja (or Māyurāja, 8th c.) and Rājaśekhara (10th c.) — have freely made alterations in the plots of their plays.[6] Kuntaka (11th c.) states in discussing *prakaraṇavakratā* (contextual crookedness or figurativeness) in his *vakroktijīvita* that a poet can make his work very beautiful by putting a little originality into its plot even if it is taken from a well-known work like the *Mahābhārata*.[7] He illustrates this with the Rāma play *Udāttarāghava*, in which the author Mātrarāja rearranges the incident of Mārīca's illusory deer by making Lakṣmaṇa instead of Rāma go after the deer and Rāma go to help him.[8] Narasiṁha also displays originality in his dramatic version of the novel *Kādambarī* by introducing a number of innovations into its plot.

The Altered Sequence of Incidents

There seems to be no need here to go into the details of the intricate but well-known plot of the novel *Kādambarī*, but it would be some help to give succinctly its major incidents.[9] An Untouchable girl comes to King Śūdraka's palace in Vidiśā and presents him with a parrot named Vaiśampāyana. Then the parrot tells the King of his birth as a parrot, the ascetic Jābāli's story, his recollection of his previous lives owing to it, and so on. The ascetic Jābāli's story consists of King Tārāpīḍa of Ujjayinī wishing for a son; his son, Prince Candrāpīḍa's birth, education and world conquest; his pursuit of *kinnaras* (mythical creatures like centaurs), which leads to his meeting with Mahāśvetā by Lake Acchoda; her story of separation from Puṇḍarīka; Candrāpīḍa's visit to Mt. Hemakūṭa with Mahāśvetā; his and Kādambarī's love at first sight; his return to Ujjayinī (Here Bāṇa's portion breaks off due to his death.); his return to Lake Acchoda to fetch his friend Vaiśampāyana but only to learn his death on account of Mahāśvetā's curse; Candrāpīḍa's death as a result of this; Kādambarī's preservation of his body according to a divine man's advice; Kapiñjala's appearance and his story of Puṇḍarīka's and the moon's curses at each other, and so on. Owing to this story by Jābāli, the parrot Vaiśampāyana recollects his previous lives as Puṇḍarīka and Candrāpīḍa's friend Vaiśampāyana, and tries to go to see Mahāśvetā. But a hunter captures him, and an Untouchable girl presents him to King Śūdraka. When the parrot finishes telling this much to the King, the Untouchable girl, who is, in fact, none other than the goddess Lakṣmī and Puṇḍarīka's mother, reminds the King of his previous lives as the moon and Candrāpīḍa. On hearing this, Śūdraka dies, and Candrāpīḍa immediately regains consciousness and gets reunited with Kādamabrī; likewise, Puṇḍarīka and Mahāśvetā get reunited. It is important to note here that almost the whole story is narrated by the parrot, and that the incidents in it do not take place in chronological order. Now, how does Narasiṁha tackle the task of dramatizing this complicated plot of the novel?

Narasiṁha begins the plot of the *Kādambarīnāṭaka* with Candrāpīḍa, who has already completed his world conquest; in other words, the playwright starts around the middle of Bāṇa's portion of the novel *Kādambarī*. While hunting, Candrāpīḍa finds *Kinnaras* who lead him to Lake Acchoda. There he meets Mahāśvetā and hears her story (Act I). They go to Mt. Hemakūṭa to see Kādambarī. Candrāpīḍa and Kādambarī fall in love with each other (Acts II-IV). But Candrāpīḍa goes back to Ujjayinī. Vaiśampāyana, staying by Lake Acchoda, sees a play which reminds him of his previous life as Puṇḍarīka, who loved Mahāśvetā (Act V).[10] Candrāpīḍa in Ujjayinī hears of Kādambarī's lovesickness, and waits for Vaiśampāyana to come home (Act VI). Vaiśampāyana dies as a result of Mahāśvetā's curse that he must be born a parrot. Candrāpīḍa comes back to Lake Acchoda to take Vaiśampāyana home, but dies on account of Mahāśvetā's other curse (Act VII).[11] Kādambarī preserves Candrāpīḍa's body for sixteen years. Then Vaiśampāyana in the form of a parrot is captured by a hunter and brought to King Śūdraka by the goddess Lakṣmī in the form of an Untouchable girl. Reminded of their previous lives by Lakṣmī, Śūdraka and the parrot die; then Candrāpīḍa and Puṇḍarīka immediately come to life and get reunited with their beloveds (Act VIII). Thus the sequence of incidents is ingeniously altered in the play. The novel makes Puṇḍarīka in the form of a parrot talk first of his present or third life, then of his and the moon's immediate past or second lives, and then of their original ones, and so on. The play, however, starts with their second lives, then proceeds to their third ones, and their first ones are dealt with by means of a play within a play, preludes and reports. This appears to be a far better choice than starting with their first or third lives because the denouement of the play is Kādambarī's union with Candrāpīḍa, the moon's first human existence. It is also interesting to note that because of this rearrangement of the plot, the action takes place in slightly over sixteen years in the play[12] instead of only one day in the novel, where nearly the whole story is put into the parrot's mouth.

Innovated Incidents

Apart from the altered sequence of incidents discussed above, the most significant innovation Narasiṁha introduces into the plot of the *Kādambarīnāṭaka* is the play within a play (*garbhāṅka*) in Act V. Entitled the *Mahāśvetāpuṇḍarīka*, it deals with the unfulfilled love of Puṇḍarīka and Mahāśvetā, the hero and heroine of the main play's sub-plot (*patākā*), which ends with the couple's happy union. This important innovation will be discussed in detail separately in a subsequent chapter.[13]

Another very important innovation by Narasiṁha is the cause and manner of Candrāpīḍa's death. According to Bhūṣaṇa's sequel to Bāṇa's unfinished novel *Kādambarī*, Candrāpīḍa dies on hearing from Mahāśvetā of his friend Vaiśampāyana's death on account of her curse.[14] In the play, however, his death is due to her other curse laid when she was harassed by Vaiśampāyana: "Any lover of a woman who enters this place again must instantly become equal to an immobile object."[15] It is also interesting to note that in the play Candrāpīḍa dies on his horse Indrāyudha's back immediately after entering Mahāśvetā's hermitage,[16] while in the novel he dies on the ground after dismounting from his horse in her hermitage.[17] His death, however, is not acted out on the stage but only reported by the Jester. This appears to be acceptable though it is not entirely conformable to what the *Nāṭyaśāstra* prescribes: incidents such as death should not be visually presented but only dealt with by means of preludes.[18] In any case, why is this innovation necessary? Perhaps Narasiṁha did not consider hearing of Vaiśampāyana's death to be calamitous enough to cause death to the generally self-composed Candrāpīḍa,[19] and introduced another curse by Mahāśvetā more powerful and covincing as a cause of his death.

In this connection, a few minor changes made in other curses in the story may also be mentioned. Both in the novel and the play, the direct cause of Vaiśampāyana's death is Mahāśvetā's curse that he must be born a parrot;[20] but prior to this incident, his hot-tempered father, Śukanāsa, also lays a curse on him. While in the novel Śukanāsa curses his son to be born as some beast,[21] in the play he curses him to be born specifically as a parrot.[22] Similarly, small changes are made in the curse laid on Puṇḍarīka's friend, Kapiñjala. In the novel some heavenly chariot rider's curse that Kapiñjala must become a horse is later modified by the curser himself so that the cursed may complete it when the rider of the horse, that is, Candrāpīḍa dies; Kapiñjala plunges into the ocean and rises as a horse; and in due course, he, of his own free will, leads Candrāpīḍa in pursuit of *kinnaras* to Lake Acchoda.[23] But in the play Kapiñjala under the curse goes to see the divine ascetic Śvetaketu, Puṇḍarīka's father, who orders him to lead Candrāpīḍa to the Caitraratha forest, where Lake Acchoda is located; then he jumps into the lake and waits for an opportunity to carry out the order; and the curse is later ended with the help of Śvetaketu.[24]

An interesting innovation is also found in the incident in which Kādambarī presents Candrāpīḍa with the necklace *śeṣahāra*. In the novel it is Kādambarī's friend Madalekhā who puts the necklace on Candrāpīḍa's neck,[25] but in the play Kādambarī is made by her friends at the last moment to undertake the task herself.[26] It goes without saying that this makes Candrāpīḍa even happier.[27] Perhaps more important as well as interesting is the spectacle in the last Act, VIII, made possible through the supernatural power of the moon's wife Rohiṇī, who has come down to the earth for the second time to serve her lord though he prevented her from doing so.[28] In the spectacle Rohiṇī shows Candrāpīḍa's father, or King Tārāpīḍa, and others, who now live in a forest, what is happening to King Śūdraka of Vidiśā, that is, Candrāpīḍa reborn.[29] This magic spectacle is not found in the novel; it is an innovation by Narasiṁha. It is presented by means of a series of the dramatic device *nepathye* (off stage); therefore, the spectators on the stage act seeing it and comment on it, but the real audience only imagine it. Thus in the play Rohiṇī is more actively engaged in her effort to unite Candrāpīḍa with Kādambarī. Mahāśvetā is also described as more consciously engaged in acting as a kind of go-between (*dūtī*) for the two. In the novel, after hearing of the firmness of Kādambarī's vow never to marry until she herself gets reunited with Puṇḍarīka, Mahāśvetā ponders long[30] — Bāṇa does not say exactly what she ponders here — and takes Candrāpīḍa to Mt. Hemakūṭa. But in the play she takes him there primarily according to Kādambarī's mother's, that is, Queen Madirā's plan to break her daughter's vow by showing him to her,[31] and makes efforts towards this goal.

The lovers' quarrel between Kādambarī's parrot Parihāsa (-ka in the play) and her mynah Kālindī is employed in a different context in the play. In the novel Bāṇa places it immediately after the incident of Kādambarī giving Candrāpīḍa betel on his first visit to Mt. Hemakūṭa,[32] but in the play Narasiṁha introduces it just after his other innovation in which Candrāpīḍa tries to ascertain Kādambarī's love for him by means of an ambiguous dialogue with her friends.[33] In both cases, the purpose of this incident is that of comic relief, that is, to provide temporary relief from tension.[34] In the play the Jester is made to speak what Candrāpīḍa does in the novel: how well-known this gossip of the parrot and the mynah is. The Jester's name, Dramiḍa-dhārmika, is undoubtedly derived from the Dravidian religious bigot (*draviḍadhārmika*, not a proper name) in the novel. Narasiṁha omits altogether the incident in which Candrāpīḍa encounters this irascible but comic character on the way back to

Ujjayinī,[35] for it is not essential to the development of the plot of the play; instead he introduces a jester named Dramiḍadhārmika as Candrāpīḍa's comic companion.

Narasiṁha makes many other minor changes, but they hardly affect the development of the plot. For instance, when Candrāpīḍa dies, the play sends his Jester, an added character here, to Ujjayinī to inform his elders of his death in place of his servant Tvaritaka, not mentioned here.[36] The author also omits or abridges incidents unessential to the plot of the play such as Candrāpīḍa's education, coronation and world conquest. He omits altogether Minister Śukanāsa's lengthy lecture on youth, fortune and so on given to Candrāpīḍa;[37] in exchange, he introduces a riddle verse on how the Prince should rule the earth.[38]

Innovations in the Characters

The psychology of the four major characters of the novel *Kādambarī* seems to be due at least in part to their supernatural origins. Candrāpīḍa and Mahāśvetā are generally cool or composed and rather hesitant because they owe their origins to the Moon (*Candra*). The former is the Moon himself reborn on the earth, and the latter is of the *apsaras* family sprung from the Moon's beams (*somaraśmis*). Puṇḍarīka and Kādambarī, on the other hand, are extremely susceptible because they are connected with Fortune (*Lakṣmī*) and nectar (*amṛta*) respectively, which appeared together when the ocean was churned by the gods and the demons.[39] In the *Kādambarīnāṭaka*, Kādambarī, Puṇḍarīka and Mahāśvetā are characterized as in the novel, but Candrāpīḍa is characterized as more confident and passionate. For instance, he boldly describes Kādambarī's physical beauty in front of herself,[40] and even tries to embrace her when they are left alone.[41] Another interesting innovation is found in Vaiśampāyana's parents, Śukanāsa and Manoramā. In the play they are described as partial incarnations (*aṁśāvatāras*) of Puṇḍarīka's divine parents, the ascetic Śvetaketu and the goddess Lakṣmī respectively.[42]

Notes

1. *Vide* intro., chap. IV.
2. A.K. Warder, *Indian Kāvya Literature*, Vol. I, p. 41. Mātṛgupta's works are known only from quotations by later theorists and the like.
3. *Bhāvaprakāśana of Śāradātanaya*, p. 234, lines 21-22:

   pūrvavṛttāśrayam api kiñ cid utpādyavastu ca |
   vidheyaṁ nāṭakam iti mātṛguptena bhāṣitam ||

4. Ānandavardhana, *Dhvanyāloka*, ed. with Abhinavagupta's comm. *Locana* by M.P. Durgāprasād & K.P. Parab; rev. by W.L. Ś. Paṇśikar, Kāvyamālā, No. 25; reper. (Delhi: Munshiram Manoharlal, 1983), p. 182, *kārikās*:

   kathāśarīram utpādyavastu kāryaṁ tathā tathā |
   yathā rasamayaṁ sarvam evaitat pratibhāsate ||

. . . santi siddharasaprakhyā ye ca rāmāyaṇādayaḥ |
kathāśrayā na tair yojyā svecchā rasavirodhinī ||

5. *Ibid.*, p. 183, *Dhvanyāloka, vṛtti: yad uktam, kathāmārge na cātikramaḥ*; and *Locana: yad uktam iti, rāmābhyudaye yaśovarmaṇā*. The whole verse whose part the above phrase forms is quoted by Bhoja in his *Śṛṅgāraprakāśa*; *vide op. cit.*, ed. by G.R. Josyer, vol. II (Mysore: Coronation Press, 1963), p. 461 (chap. XI). V. Raghavan believes that this verse cannot appear anywhere but in the Prologue of the play, which is known only from quotations; *vide* his *Some Old Lost Rāma Plays* (Annāmalainagar: Annāmalai University, 1961), p. 7.
6. *Vide* also Raghavan, *op. cit.*
7. *The Vakroktijīvita of Kuntaka*, pp. 248-49, *kārikā* 3 & *vṛtti:*

   itivṛttaprayukte pi kathāvaicitryavartmani |
   utpādyalavalāvaṇyād anyā lasati vakratā |

   . . . itivṛttaprayukte pi, itihāsaparigrahe pi . . . mahābhāratādau . . .
8. *Ibid.*, pp. 37 & 252.
9. For a detailed outline of the novel, *vide*, among others, M.R. Kale, ed. & trans., *Kādambarī* (*Pūrvabhāga*) (Delhi: Motilal Banarsidass, 1968), Intro., pp. 1-28.
10. *Vide infra.*
11. *Vide Infra.*
12. Between Acts VII and VIII, a period of 16 years is supposed to have elapsed; *vide* Act VIII, vs. 8.
13. *Vide* Intro., chap. VIII.
14. Bhūṣaṇa, *Kādambarī* (*Uttarārddha*), pp. 173-74: *. . . candrāpīḍasya tu tad ākarṇya . . . hṛdayam asphuṭat. Vide* also Intro., chap. IV; Candrāpīḍa does not die in the other two versions of the story of Kādambarī.
15. *K.N.*, Act VII, after vs. 22.
16. *K.N.*, Act VII, Jester's speech before vs. 20.
17. Bhūṣaṇa, *op. cit.*, p. 161:

    . . . indrāyudham āruhya mahāśvetāśramam upajagāma |
    tatra ca praviśann evāvatīrya . . .
18. Bharata, *Nāṭyaśāstra*, ed. by B. Śarman & B. Upādhyāya, Kāshī Sanskrit Series, 60 (Benares: Chowkhamba Sanskrit Series Office, 1929), chap. XX, vs. 21:

    yuddhaṁ rājyabhraṁśo maraṇaṁ nagararodhanañ caiva |
    apratyakṣakṛtāni praveśakaiḥ saṁvidheyāni ||
19. *Vide infra.*
20. Bhūṣaṇa, *op. cit.*, pp. 172-73: *. . . śuka iva . . . kimu tasyām eva jātau na nikṣipto si . . . madudīritāyām eva jātau patatu; K.N.*, just before the end of the Prelude to Act VII.
21. Bhūṣaṇa, *op. cit.*, p. 119: *. . . tena . . . kasyāṁ cit tiryagyonau patitavyaṁ . . .*

22. *K.N.*, Act VI, just after vs. 39. This situation seems to be a kind of *patākāsthānaka; vide* Intro., chap. VII.
23. Bhūṣaṇa, *op. cit.*, pp. 191-93.
24. *K.N.*, Prelude to Act I.
25. Bāṇa, *Kādambarī* (*Pūrvārddha*), pp. 656-61:

    . . . candrāpīḍaś . . . samucitopacārakrameṇa madalekhām āpatantīṁ jagrāha | sā tu . . . taṁ hāram ādāya candrāpīḍam uvāca . . . ayam . . . śeṣanāmā hāro . . . ity uktvā . . . taṁ tasya vakṣaḥsthale babandha |
26. *K.N.*, Act III, between vss. 39 & 40. This situation also seems to be a kind of *patākāsthānaka*; *vide* Intro., chap. VII.
27. *K.N.*, Act III, vs. 40 & prose before.
28. *K.N.*, Act VIII, after vs. 11.
29. The spectacle starts just before vs. 12.
30. Bāṇa, *op. cit.*, p. 597.
31. *K.N.*, Act I, between vss. 46 & 47.
32. Bāṇa, *op. cit.*, pp. 636-40.
33. *K.N.*, Act IV, vs. 27 & prose splitting it.
34. *Vide* also Intro., chap. IX on the *rasas* of the play.
35. Bāṇa, *op. cit.*, pp. 731-34.
36. *K.N.*, end of Act VII; Bhūṣaṇa, *op. cit.*, p. 213.
37. Bāṇa, *op. cit.*, pp. 348-75.
38. *K.N.*, Act VIII, vs. 43.
39. Warder, *op. cit.*, vol. IV, p. 45.
40. *K.N.*, Act III, vs. 31.
41. *K.N.*, Act IV, after vs. 29.
42. *K.N.*, Act VIII, vs. 39 & prose after. It may be interesting to note in this connection that Arjunapaṇḍita (*cir.* 1000) equates six characters of the novel *Kādambarī* with deities as follows: Puṇḍarīka with Brahmā; Mahāśvetā with Sarasvatī; Śvetaketu with Viṣṇu; Lakṣmī with herself; Candrāpīḍa with the moon, and the moon with Śiva; and Kādambarī with Pārvatī. *Vide* "An Edition of Arjunapaṇḍita's Commentary on the *Kādambarī* (*Uttarabhāga*)," U. Srivastava, Ph.D. Dissertation (Toronto: University of Toronto, 1979), Text & notes, pp. 6-11 & 208.

7

A Further Analysis of the Plot Structure of the Kādambarīnāṭaka

THE purpose of this chapter is to discuss various important elements which constitute the plot (*vastu, itivṛtta*), or the body (*śarīra*),[1] of the *Kādambarīnāṭaka* of Narasiṁha in the light of the *Nāṭyaśāstra* of Bharata and several other theoretical works on classical Indian dramaturgy.

The Arthaprakṛtis

The *arthaprakṛtis*, which Abhinavagupta interprets as instruments of gaining the fruit,[2] are the following five: the *bīja*, the *bindu*, the *patākā*, the *prakarī*, and the *kārya*.[3] The most important of these is the *kārya*, or the objective of the main (*ādhikārika*) action, towards which all the efforts in a play are directed.[4] The *kārya* of the *Kādambarīnāṭaka* is, no doubt, Kādambarī's union or marriage with Candrāpīḍa at the end, which purpose everything in the play serves directly or indirectly. The *bīja* (lit. seed) is a very small beginning which later ramifies and bears fruit at the end;[5] in short, it is the seed or potential of the *kārya*. The *bīja* of the *Kādambarīnāṭaka* is found in the Prelude to Act I, where Kapiñjala recalls Śvetaketu's order to enter into the horse Indryāyudha and lead Candrāpīḍa to the Caitraratha forest for the purpose of his union with Kādambarī.[6] The *bindu* (lit. drop) is an element which helps the main action to continue even when it appears to be interrupted or suspended for a while. The *bindu* prevades the main action up to the completion of it.[7] Abhinavagupta explains that the *bindu* is present everywhere (in a play) like a drop of oil (on the surface of water).[8] Siṁhabhūpāla also compares the *bindu* to drops of water which keep moistening the roots of a tree until the tree eventually bears fruit.[9] The example given by Abhinavagupta to illustrate the *bindu* is King Udayana's love for Vāsavadattā expressed by himself in every act of the *Tāpasavatsarāja*.[10] Similarly, the *bindu* of the *Kādambarīnāṭaka* is Candrāpīḍa's invariable love for Kādambarī, hers for him and their strong desire to get united with each other, which are expressed by themselves or other characters throughout the play.

The remaining two *arthaprakṛtis*, the *patākā* and the *prakarī*, are subsidiary (*prāsaṅgika* or *ānuṣaṅgika*)[11] actions or stories in a play. The *patākā* is a sub-plot which assists the main plot and is composed like it.[12] Siṁhabhūpāla states that the *patākā* achieves its own objective through assisting the main action. He illustrates it with the action of Sugrīvạ in Rāma plays and that of Makaranda and Madayantikā in the *Mālatīmādhava* of Bhavabhūti.[13] The *pātākā* of the *Kādambarīnāṭala* appears to be the action of Puṇḍarīka and Mahāśvetā, which achieves its objective, that is, their union through assisting the main action to achieve its objective, that is, Kādambarī's union with Candrāpīḍa.[14] But these two unions are accomplished at the same time at the end of the play. Bharata prescribes that the *patākā* has to come to an end in or before the third or fourth of the five *saṁdhi*s (conjunctions)[15] because its purpose is to assist another, that is, the main action.[16] Abhinavagupta explains that if the *patākā* extends up to the last *saṁdhi*, the fruit of the main action and that of the *patākā* will be almost simultaneously accomplished, and as a result, the distinction between the two actions will be lost.[17] Sāgaranandin, however, holds that the above-mentioned rule of Bharata should not be taken to be absolute or universal;[18] in other words, he permits the *patākā* to continue further to the last *saṁdhi* of the main action. This makes it acceptable to consider the action of Puṇḍarīkā and Mahāśvetā to be the *patākā* of the play.

Lastly, the *prakarī* is a subsidiary action the result of which is solely for the sake of the main action, and which does not develop as the *patākā* does.[19] Abhinavagupta illustrates the *prakarī* with the action of Kulapati in the *Kṛtyārāvaṇa* and that of Vāsudeva (Kṛṣṇa) in the *Veṇīsaṁhāra* of Bhaṭṭanārāyaṇa, the heroes of which act with complete disregard for their own objectives (*prakarṣeṇa svārthānapekṣayā*).[20] Another well-known *prakarī*, cited by Śāradātanaya, is the role of Jaṭāyu in Rāma plays.[21] The *Kādambarīnāṭaka* does not seem to have any subsidiary actions which strictly conform to Bharata's rule of the *prakarī*. Even the role of Kapiñjala in the form of Indrāyudha, and the action of Rohiṇī, who comes down to the earth for the second time to assist her lord, the moon, are so closely connected with the main action, in effect, part of it, that they can hardly be considered to be *prakarī*s. According to the *Nāṭyadarpaṇa* of Rāmacandra and Guṇacandra, the *patākā* and the *prakarī* are not absolutely necessary but optional; they are employed only if the main hero of a play needs assistance from other characters to achieve his objective.[22] Thus the *Kādambarīnāṭaka* has a *patākā* as discussed earlier, but lacks *prakarī*s.

The Opening Benediction and the Prologue

The opening benedictory verse (*nāndī*) of the *Kādambarīnāṭaka* may be considered particularly auspicious because it is dedicated to the moon god. Sāgaranandin, among others, states that if the *nāndī* of a play is properly performed, the substratum of *rasa* (aesthetic experience), that is, the moon becomes pleased, and as a result, a whole performance of the play becomes full of *rasa*.[23] This *nāndī* is also appropriately suggestive of the main hero of the play, Candrāpīḍa, who is the moon god himself in a human form. It somewhat resembles one of the *nāndī* verses of the *nāṭikā*[24] *Kanakalekhākalyāṇa*, but the latter play is by another Andhra author, Vāmanabhaṭṭabāṇa (14th c.).[25]

After the *nāndī* the Director (*sūtradhāra*) enters and introduces with the help of his Assistant (*pāripārśvaka*) the play about to be staged, its author, the occasion of its performance, and so on. Then he orders his Assistant to prepare for his role in the play, and prepares himself for the role of Kapiñjala, the first character to be introduced in the play. This device for leading into the play proper from the prologue (*prastāvanā*) does not seem to be any of the five such devices listed and defined by Bharata and variously interpreted and illustrated by later theorists.[26] The same device, however, is employed, for instance, by Bhavabhūti at the end of the Prologue to his *Mālatīmādhava*, where the Director and the Actor (*naṭa*) take up the role of the Buddhist nun Kāmandakī and that of her disciple Avalokitā respectively in order to start the play proper in the Prelude to Act I.[27]

The Acts

Though Bharata prescribes that a *nāṭaka* or *prakaraṇa* play may have five to ten acts (*aṅka*s),[28] there is a strong tendency among the extant plays of these types to have five to seven or ten acts, and those in eight or nine acts seem to be extremely rare.[29] Narasiṁha composed the *Kādambarīnāṭaka* in eight acts, but he could have had it in seven if he had arranged for the *garbhāṅka* (play within a play) and its effect on Vaiśampāyana in Act V to be simply reported, for instance, in the Prelude to Act VII instead of providing it a separate act. Sāgaranandin states that the acts of a *nāṭaka* or the like should be entitled in the same way as such plays.[30] For example, Bhavabhūti's *Mālatīmādhava* and Śūdraka's *Mṛcchakaṭika*, both *prakaraṇa* plays, have a title for each of their acts. Narasiṁha does not give separate titles to the acts of his play, but they would be unnecessary if the acts were not intended to be presented separately. As was discussed earlier, Candrāpīḍa's death in Act VII is not visually presented but only reported by the Jester; thus it does not violate Bharata's rule which prohibits the presentation of certain kinds of incidents.[31] Moreover, Narasiṁha closely follows Bharata's rule that the acts proper of a play should contain only incidents which take place in the course of a single day.[32] Acts II and III of the *Kādambarīnāṭaka* treat the incidents on the same day, but this does not violate the above-mentioned rule.[33]

The Preludes

Incidents unfit to be included in acts proper for a variety of reasons are dealt with in preludes or introductory scenes (*arthopakṣepaka*s). Bharata lists and defines five such devices: the *viṣkambha(ka)*, the *praveśaka*, the *cūlikā*, the *aṅkamukha* (or *aṅkāsya*) and the *aṅkāvatāra*.[34] Only the first three of them are frequently employed, the other two being quite rare. Narasiṁha uses four of them in seven acts of his play. The reason why Act II has no prelude attached to it is obvious: no significant incidents take place between Acts I and II. The *viṣkambhaka* is used four times. The *viṣkambhaka* to Act I is of the *śuddha* (pure) type because the only character in it, Kapiñjala, is a Sanskrit-speaking middle (*madhyama*) male character, while those to Acts IV, VII and VIII are of the *saṅkīrṇa* (or *miśra*, mixed) type because they have both a Sanskrit-speaking middle character and a Prakrit-speaking low (*nīca*) character. The Prelude to Act III is a *praveśaka* with two Prakrit-speaking low characters. The Prelude to Act V is a *cūlikā* in which only a voice briefly informs something significant from behind the curtain at the back of the stage (*nepathye*). Both the *M.M.* and the *V.K.* call the Prelude to Act VI a *viṣkambhaka*, but this is obviously wrong. It cannot be a *viṣkambhaka* because the only character in it, the Jester, is a Prakrit-speaking low character, nor can it be a *praveśaka* because it has no conversation between servants (*parijanakathānubandha*).[35] In fact, it appears to be an *aṅkamukha* in which only one character briefly introduces the Act proper.[36] Bharata states that a long period of time up to a year, but never more than that, may elapse between two acts of a play, and that incidents during such a period are treated in some *arthopakṣepaka* between the acts.[37] Between Acts VII and VIII of the *Kādambarīnāṭaka*, however, a long period of 16 years elapses. This apparently does not conform to Bharata's rule. But the elapse of the time is merely mentioned by Tārāpīḍa in Act VIII proper (vs. 8), and the Prelude to it treats only the incident that a hunter captures Vaiśampāyana in the form of a parrot, which takes place one day at the end of that period. Thus Narasiṁha does not seem to quite violate the above-mentioned rule of Bharata.

The Saṁdhis

The main plot of a *nāṭaka* or *prakaraṇa* play is developed with the five *saṁdhis*, which Abhinavagupta interprets as the conjunctions of different parts of the main plot with each other.[38] They are the *mukha*, the *pratimukha*, the *garbha*, the *avamarśa* or *vimarśa* and the *nirvahaṇa*.[39] The first *saṁdhi* is the *mukha* (opening), where the *bīja* is produced or sown, and *rasas* arise from various matters introduced.[40] The *mukha saṁdhi* of the *Kādambarīnāṭaka* is in Act I, where Kapiñjala in the Prelude summarizes what has happened and gives the *bīja* as discussed above, and in the Act proper Candrāpīḍa becomes curious about Kādambarī on account of a song by a pair of *kinnaras* (vs. 23) and encounters Mahāśvetā, from whom he obtains a chance to see Kādambarī. The second *saṁdhi* is the *pratimukha* (re-opening), where the *bīja* starts sprouting but it is as if it were now seen and now lost.[41] The *pratimukha saṁdhi* of the play is in Acts II and III, where Candrāpīḍa sees Kādambarī and falls in love with her, and he feels that she has also fallen in love with him, but is not certain of it. The third *saṁdhi*, the *garbha* (embryo), is where the *bīja* has germinated more fully, and there are both success and lack of it with a further search for some means to attain the fruit.[42] The *garbha saṁdhi* of the play starts in Act IV and ends before the point in Act VII where Candrāpīḍa dies. Strictly speaking, Act V is not part of the *garbha saṁdhi* because it is a play within a play (*garbhāṅka*) and its effect on Vaiśampāyana, the hero of the *patākā*. In these Acts Candrāpīḍa ascertains that Kādambarī, too, is deeply in love with him, but their union is hindered for a while by his return to Ujjayinī; his search for Vaiśampāyana, however, gives him a chance to see Kādambarī again. The fourth *saṁdhi*, the *avamarśa* (obstacle) or *vimarśa* (pause), is where the *bīja* germinated in the *garbha* is checked by or reconsidered because of a disaster or the like.[43] In the *Kādambarīnāṭaka*, this *saṁdhi* starts with Candrāpīḍa's death in Act VII and ends when he regains consciousness in Act VIII. The last of the five *saṁdhis* is the *nirvahaṇa* (conclusion), where the objective of the main plot is successfully accomplished.[44] The play's *nirvahaṇa saṁdhi* starts where Candrāpīḍa regains consciousness, and continues up to the end where his marital union with Kādambarī is achieved and all ends well.

The Saṁdhyaṅgas

Bharata prescribes for each of the five *saṁdhis* a dozen or more *aṅgas* (limbs) to make them complete.[45] He states that the total number of *saṁdhyaṅgas* is 64,[46] though in fact, he enumerates and defines more of them.[47] He is not clear on the order of the use of the *aṅgas*; he only suggests that they should be used in an appropriate order.[48] Abhinavagupta takes this to mean that they should be used in such an order that the objective of the main action may be attained, not in the order that they are enumerated.[49] But he states that such *aṅgas* as the *upakṣepa* must not be used in any other *saṁdhi* than that for which they are prescribed because of their nature.[50] Thus he admits the strict order of at least some *aṅgas*. According to him, however, *aṅgas* such as the *yukti* may be used in any *saṁdhi*;[51] some *aṅgas* may be used twice or three times in the *saṁdhi* for which they are prescribed;[52] and one *aṅga* may serve the purpose of two or three.[53] Moreover, Abhinavagupta holds that it is only a possibility, not a rule, to use all the 64 *aṅgas*.[54] Dhanañjaya does not consider the problem of the number of *saṁdhyaṅgas*, but his commentator Dhanika states that only five or six *aṅgas* in each *saṁdhi* are important (*pradhānas*) or indispensable (*avaśyaṁbhāvīs*), the rest being optional (*yathāsaṁbhavas*).[55] As for the definitions of the *saṁdhyaṅgas*, Bharata is most laconic; as a result, later theorists interpret them rather freely.

THE AṄGAS OF THE MUKHA SAṀDHI

The first *aṅga* of the *mukha saṁdhi*, the *upakṣepa* (hint) is defined by Bharata as the arising of the objective of a play; Abhinavagupta adds that it should hint at the objective in brief and indicate the main *rasa*.[56] The *upakṣepa* of the *Kādambarīnāṭaka* is found in the same place as the *bīja arthaprakṛti*, discussed earlier: in the Prelude to Act I, where Kapiñjala recalls Śvetaketu's order to lead Candrāpīḍa to Caitraratha for his union with Kādambarī.[57] The *parikara* (expansion) is the enlargement of the matter arisen in the *upakṣepa*; it is slightly expanded or more detailed than that.[58] The play has this *aṅga* at the end of the same Prelude (vs. 17), where Kapiñjala hopes that Kādambarī will fall in love with Candrāpīḍa. Bharata defines the *vilobhana* (temptation) simply as the description of good qualities, but Abhinavagupta explains further that it is praise, which is a cause of temptation.[59] The play has it where after hearing a song by *kinnaras* (Act I, vs. 23), Candrāpīḍa expresses that the word *kādambarī* has captured his heart whether or not it has a corresponding object (vs. 24). The *paribhāvanā* (surprise) is agitation or excitement accompanied by curiosity or mixed with a strong desire to know something.[60] The play has it where Candrāpīḍa decides to ask Mahāśvetā who she is and so on (Act I, after vs. 37). The *parinyāsa* (resolution), defined by Bharata simply as the completion of the *parikara*, is interpreted by Abhinavagupta as a situation in which the hero, whose mind is completely occupied with the main objective, decides to do something about it.[61] The play has it where Candrāpīḍa asks Mahāśvetā who Kādambarī is (Act I, before vs. 47). The *yukti* (judgement) is the consideration of matters; it is also the disclosure of what should be disclosed.[62] It is found where Mahāśvetā tells Candrāpīḍa about Kādambarī for the first time (Act I, before vs. 47). The *prāpti* (attainment), or the arrival of some delightful matter,[63] is found where Mahāśvetā delights Candrāpīḍa by requesting him to go to see Kādambarī with her (Act I, after vs. 47). The *karaṇa* (action) is the commencement of the matter under consideration;[64] in other words, it is the first concrete action towards the realization of the objective. It is found where Candrāpīḍa accepts Mahāśvetā's request to go to see Kādambarī (Act I, after vs. 48).

THE AṄGAS OF THE PRATIMUKHA SAṀDHI

The *vilāsa* (sport), which Bharata gives as the first *aṅga* of the *pratimukha saṁdhi*, is defined as a desire for the enjoyment of love. Abhinavagupta explains that it is a man's desire for a woman or a woman's for a man, and maintains that it must be used only in the *pratimukha saṁdhis* of plays whose objective is love.[65] This appears to be an *aṅga* which can be used more than once in the *saṁdhi* for which it is prescribed. The *Kādambarīnāṭaka* uses it several times; it is found, for instance, where before seeing Kādambarī, Candrāpīḍa hopes that she will be the same beautiful girl that he saw in a dream the previous night (Act II, vs. 1), and where after seeing her, he begs the goddess of sleep to let him see her in a dream (Act III, vs. 50). Narasiṁha employs some other *aṅgas* of this *saṁdhi* as well, but they are found in the two subsequent *saṁdhis*.

THE AṄGAS OF THE GARBHA SAṀDHI

The *narman* (joke), defined as laughter performed for the sake of sport,[66] is an *aṅga* prescribed primarily for the *pratimukha saṁdhi*, but Narasiṁha uses it in the *garbha saṁdhi* of the *Kādambarīnāṭaka*. It is found where Candrāpīḍa asks whatever dear man Kādambarī can be talking about, and the Jester jocularly answers that she must be talking about himself (Act IV, after vs. 22). The *mārga* and the *krama*, both of the *garbha saṁdhi*, are used in the same situation in the *Kādambarīnāṭaka*. The *mārga* (lit. search) is a speech that declares the truth.[67] The *krama* (progress) is the acquisition of the truth about someone's heart or love; it is the knowledge obtained through investigation of the truth of a matter which has been cherished.[68] They are found where Candrāpīḍa learns from Madalekhā that he himself is the cause of Kādambarī's illness, that is, her lovesickness (Act IV, prose split by vs. 27). The *ākṣipti* (exposure), an *aṅga* of the *garbha saṁdhi*, is the manifestation by some means of what is in someone's heart, that is, his or her desire.[69] Narasiṁha uses it where Candrāpīḍa shows his passion for Kādambarī by embracing her (Act IV, after vs. 29). The *vidhūta* (spurning), an *aṅga* of the *pratimukha saṁdhi*, is defined by Bharata as the rejection of some kindness offered; Abhinavagupta adds that the kindness is accepted afterwards.[70] It is found where Kādambarī rejects Candrāpīḍa trying to show his love for her by embracing her (Act IV, after vs. 29); of course, she requites his love later on. The *prārthanā* (wish), an *aṅga* of the *garbha saṁdhi*, is a very strong desire for the objective to be accomplished.[71] It is found where Candrāpīḍa expresses his strong determination to achieve his goal, union with Kādambarī, whatever it takes (Act VI, vs. 19). The *apavāda* (reproach), though it belongs primarily to the *avamarśa saṁdhi*, is used in the *garbha saṁdhi* of the play. It is defined as the declaration of a fault.[72] Narasiṁha uses it where Tārāpīḍa reproaches Candrāpīḍa for having come home without Vaiśampāyana, and Śuknāsas reproaches Vaiśampāyana for his ill nature (Act VI, vs. 39 and before and after).

THE AṄGAS OF THE AVAMARŚA SAṀDHI

In the *avamarśa saṁdhi* of his play, Narasiṁha uses the *tāpana* (helplessness), an *aṅga* of the *pratimukha saṁdhi*. Bharata defines it simply as seeing danger, and Abhinavagupta illustrates it with the verse in the *Ratnāvalī* where Sāgarikā (Ratnāvalī incognito) says death is the only refuge for her because she is in love with a man hard to obtain.[73] In the *Kādambarīnāṭaka*, this *aṅga* is found where Kādambarī decides to follow Candrāpīḍa in death (Act VII, before vs. 23). The following three *aṅga*s used in this *saṁdhi* of the play are all prescribed by Bharata for the *avamarśa saṁdhi*. The *kheda* (fatigue) is defined as mental or physical exhaustion.[74] Mental fatigue is seen where Tārāpīḍa says he has been afflicted with separation from his son, Candrāpīḍa, for sixteen years, but now even more so (Act VIII, vs. 8). Bharata defines the *drava* (deviation) as disrespect towards one's elder or superior, and Abhinavagupta illustrates it with the scene in the *Tāpasavatsarāja* where Vāsavadattā attemps suicide in spite of what Minister Yaugandharāyaṇa has told her.[75] Narasiṁha uses this *aṅga* where Vilāsavatī tells Tārāpīḍa that Kādambarī has resolved to kill herself by entering Lake Acchoda in spite of the words of the divine voice,[76] and that even Mahāśvetā has resolved likewise (Act VIII, after vs. 8 & after vs. 9). Bharata defines the *prarocanā* (anticipation), the last *aṅga* of this *saṁdhi* on his list, as a scene that shows the conclusion. Abhinavagupta explains that it shows the objective being accomplished. He illustrates it with the scene in the *Ratnāvalī* where King Udayana sees his palace in its usual state again, since the fire, which jeopardized Ratnāvalī's life, was nothing but another performance by the magician, and his union with her becomes attainable.[77] Narasiṁha uses this *aṅga* where Candrāpīḍa regains consciousness and the objective, his union with Kādambarī, becomes attainable in the near future (Act VIII, before vs. 28).

THE AṄGAS OF THE NIRVAHAṆA SAṀDHI

Bharata defines the *pūrvavākya* (reminding) as showing the objective mentioned before, and Abhinavagupta illustrates it with the scene in the *Ratnāvalī* where Yaugandharāyaṇa says his effort has at last borne fruit.[78] In the *Kādambarīnāṭaka* it is found where Citraratha and Haṁsa say to each other that the difficult task of choosing worthy suitors for their daughters has finally been accomplished (Act VIII, vs. 41). The *bhāṣaṇa* (conciliatory speech), or speech accompanied by conciliation, a gift and the like, is illustrated with the goddess Gaurī's speech in the *Nāgānanda* in which she says she is going to make Jīmūtavāhana Emperor of the *vidyādharas*.[79] In the *Kādambarīnāṭaka* it is found where Citraratha gives away Kādambarī to Candrāpīḍa, Haṁsa gives away Mahāśvetā to Puṇḍarīka, and Tārāpīḍa requests Candrāpīḍa to accept the sovereignty over Bhārata Varṣa, and so on (Act VIII, vs. 42 and before and after). The *kāvyasaṁhāra* (consummation of the *kāvya* or play) is defined as the granting and receiving of boons.[80] It is a dramatic convention in which towards the end of a play, some senior or noble character who has assisted the hero to accomplish his objective asks him what more he can do for him, and the hero expresses his complete satisfaction and often enumerates his acquisitions. In the *Kādambarīnāṭaka*. It is found towards the end where Kapiñjala asks Candrāpīḍa and Puṇḍarīka what more Tārāpīḍa and Śukanāsa can do for them, and they say there is nothing further to be done since all their elders, who shared their unhappiness, have become happy today (Act VIII, vs. 44 and before). The last *aṅga* of the *nirvahaṇa saṁdhi*, the *praśasti* (closing benediction) is defined as concerning a king, a country and peace.[81] It is another dramatic convention in which at the end of a play, the actor who has played the hero prays for peace, prosperity and the like in verse form as an actor on behalf of his troupe, not as the character he has played. Abhinavagupta quotes the view that the *praśasti* should not be considered an *aṅga* because it is not properly part of the plot of a play.[82] The *praśasti* of the *Kādambarīnāṭaka* is recited by the actors who have played the main hero, Candrāpīḍa and the secondary hero, Puṇḍarīka; in it they pray for, among others, their and the audience' exclusive devotion to the Lord Śiva (Act VIII, vs. 45).

The Saṁdhyantaras

Bharata lists twenty-one *saṁdhyantaras* (lit. other conjunctions) in the *Nāṭyaśāstra*.[83] They are not other *saṁdhi*s as their name suggests; in fact, they are similar to the *saṁdhyaṅga*s in nature.[84] Abhinavagupta quotes two views on them. According to one of them, the *saṁdhyantara*s fill out the gaps between *saṁdhyaṅga*s; therefore, they are closely related to them.[85] According to the other, however, they are of exactly the same nature as the *saṁdhyaṅgas*; they are only different varieties of them.[86] Siṁhabhūpāla clearly states that the *saṁdhyantaras*, unlike the *saṁdhyaṅgas*, can be freely employed in any of the five *saṁdhis*.[87] Neither Bharata nor the commentator Abhinavagupta defines or illustrates the *saṁdhyantaras*, but Sāgaranandin, who calls them *pradeśas*, does.[88] He defines one of them, the *svapna* (dream), as talking in one's sleep about some object on one's mind.[89] The *Kādambarīnāṭaka* has this *saṁdhyantara* where Kādambarī confesses her love for Candrāpīḍa in a dream (Act VI, vs. 26). It is also used where Vaiśampāyana in the form of a parrot tells in his sleep how much he loves Mahāśvetā (Prelude to Act VIII, vs. 1 and before). The *pradāna* (gift), which Sāgaranandin lists but does not define, is found where Kādambarī presents Candrāpīḍa with the necklace *śeṣahāra* (Act III, before vs. 40). The *lekha*, that is, a *saṁdeśa* (message) is not on Sāgaranandin's list; in place of it the *upadhi* (fraud) is given. The play has a love letter from Kādambarī to Candrāpīḍa (Act VI, vss. 13-15), and one from Puṇḍarīka to Mahāśvetā (Act V, vs. 36). In addition to these, it has a letter from Tārāpīḍa to Candrāpīḍa (Act V, Prelude), and two from Mahāśvetā to Candrāpīḍa (Act IV, vs. 8 and Act VI, vs. 30). Sāgaranandin defines the *citra* (painting) as a means of seeing one's beloved person.[90] It is found where Candrāpīḍa sees and even talks to Kādambarī painted in a picture (Act VI, vss. 7-11). The *dūta* (messenger) is defined simply as a message carrier.[91] The characters of the play who act as a messenger are Keyūraka, Taralikā, Patralekhā and others.

The Patākāsthānakas

Narasiṁha also employs small but charming dramatic devices called the *patākāsthānakas*.[92] They are not connected with the *patākā* (sub-plot) of a play though the term may suggest that; in fact, they somewhat resemble the *saṁdhyaṅgas* used for the main plot.[93] They are situations in which one thing is expected but another thing similar to that takes place through some accidental or unexpected cause.[94] Rāmacandra and Guṇacandra state that even one *patākāsthānaka* can make a play beautiful, to say nothing of more.[95] The most interesting of the four varieties of *patākāsthānakas* seems to be the third. It is a situation in which a person's statement which, on account of its ambiguous or equivocal nature, is accidentally taken as a reply to another person's statement foreshadows some significant future event in the main plot.[96] Abhinavagupta illustrates it with the situation in Act I of the *Mudrārākṣasa* where Cāṇakya, who has been pondering if it is ever possible to capture (*gṛhyeta*) Rākṣasa, takes Siddhārthaka's sudden and laconic statement 'Taken!' (*gaṇhido*) to mean that Rākṣasa has been captured (*gṛhīto*), though it, in reality, only means that Cāṇakya's message has been received.[97] Another good example of this *patākāsthānaka* is found in the situation in Act I of the *Uttararāmacarita* where the word 'separation' (*virahaḥ*) in Rāma's statement that separation from Sītā is unbearable to him gets accidentally connected with the portress' 'Arrived!' (*uvaṭṭhido*), which is, in fact, intended to mean that Rāma's spy Durmukha has arrived.[98] This *patākāsthānaka* is also used in the situation in Act III of the *Kādambarīnāṭaka* where the word *ukkaṇṭhā* (longing for or missing [Candrāpīḍa]) in Kādambarī's speech gets unintentionally connected with the portress Vijayā's *esā āgaā* (that has come!), by which she only means that Mahāśvetā has come.[99] Narasiṁha uses this *patākāsthānaka* once again in the situation in Act VII where the word *ahimaasamāame* (union with your beloved) in the Jester's speech gets by chance connected with Candrāpīḍa's *āstām* (Let it be! or Never mind that!), by which he really means, "My joy of seeing her surely *must be* near now."[100]

Narasiṁha also employs the second variety of *patākāsthānaka*. It is a poetically exaggerated speech which unintentionally foreshadows some important future event in the main plot as the third variety does.[101] Abhinavagupta illustrates it with the situation in Act III of the *Rāmābhyudaya* where the words in Sugrīva's message of encouragement to missing Sītā "Even if you are at the end of the ocean, (Rāma will soon get you back)" ominously hint her confinement by Rāvaṇa in Laṅkā, which will be found out only later on.[102] Another good example of this *patākāsthānaka* is found in the situation in Act I of the *Uttararāmacarita* where Rāma's exaggerated statement "I will give up even Sītā (to appease my subjects)" foreshadows his actual abandonment of her in the near future.[103] This *patākāsthānaka* is employed several times in the *Kādambarīnāṭaka*. It is found, for instance, in the situation in Act VI where the words in Candrāpīḍa's message to Kādambarī "(I will come to you right now,) if fate does not hinder us" foreshadow a future disaster: their union suspended for a long time by fate.[104] Here the imminent disaster is well hinted, though Candrāpīḍa does not even dream that fate is against their otherwise easily attainable near future union. Also, at the end of the same act, just before departing to search for Vaiśampāyana, Candrāpīḍa says that he will soon come back with his friend, unless fate assails him;[105] but of course, this is not to happen, for fate is against him. Similarly, Mahāśvetā says to herself in Act IV that Candrāpīḍa can marry Kādambarī when he returns from the camp, if fate does not interfere.[106] In the same act Candrāpīḍa declares that he will not live without realizing a meeting with Princess Kādambarī again,[107] but this only foreshadows his near future death without his fulfilling his wish. The same variety of *patākāsthānaka* is also found where *Kādambarī* says in her message to Candrāpīḍa in Act VI that she knows their union is not going to take place in this life of hers.[108] What she says here is not entirely true because she is not going to die herself, but it foreshadows the impending disaster which will hinder their union, that is, his death. In the same act Śukanāsa curses his son Vaiśampāyana to be reborn a parrot and suffer misery.[109] The hot-tempered Śukanāsa does this in spite of himself; he does not really wish it to happen. Nevertheless, it comes true as Tārāpīḍa fears.[110]

The first variety of *patākāsthānaka* is also used in the *Kādambarīnāṭaka*. It is a situation in which the objective is unexpectedly but richly attained through some form of help.[111] Abhinavagupta illustrates it with the scene in Act III of the *Ratnāvalī* where King Udayana accidentally saves the life of Sāgarikā, talking her for Queen Vāsavadattā. Here his purpose of preventing Vāsavadattā from committing suicide is not accomplished because the person saved is not she; instead another purpose, namely, gaining his beloved Sāgarikā, is quite unintentionally but opportunely fulfilled. Moreover, Sāgarikā, on her part, attains her objective, that is, Udayana; thus she plays a role similar to that of the hero of a *patākā*.[112] This *patākāsthānaka* is also found in the scene in Act III of the *Kādambarīnāṭaka* where Kādambarī is made by her friends at the last moment to hang the necklace *śeṣahāra* on Candrāpīḍa's neck herself.[113] When Tamālikā tells Madalekhā to give the necklace to Kādambarī so that she can hang it on Candrāpīḍa's neck herself, Taralikā equivocally says that it/he (*imo*) will not permit it to be otherwise. This is intended to be a kind of *śleṣa* (pun): the pronoun *imo* here refers to not only the *śeṣahāra* but also Candrāpīḍa. The *śleṣa*, however, does not play the major role in this situation. What is more significant here is that Candrāpīḍa gets the necklace hung on his neck by Kādambarī herself; needless to say, this is much more pleasurable to him than getting it hung by one of her friends. Most importantly, this action of hers can be taken to be equivalent to a maiden's choosing her future husband by hanging a garland on a suitor's neck in a *svayaṁvara* (self-choice ceremony). In fact, Candrāpīḍa says to himself that he is very happy because she herself has hung the necklace on his neck as if it were a bridegroom's garland (*varaṇasrag*).[114] Kādambarī, too, enjoys this unexpected opportunity of herself hanging the necklace on Candrāpīḍa's neck and choosing her future husband.[115]

In this chapter various important elements of the plot structure of the *Kādambarī-nāṭaka* have been discussed in the light of the *Nāṭyaśāstra* of Bharata and several other Indian treatises on dramaturgy. Narasiṁha employs still another dramatic device which deserves special attention, namely, the *garbhāṅka* (play within a play); this will be discussed separately in the next chapter.

Notes

1. Bharata, *Nāṭyaśāstra*, ed. with Abhinavagupta's comm. by M.R. Kavi *et al.*, chap. 19 (vol. III), vs. 1, 1st half.
2. *Ibid.*, comm. on vs. 20:

   yatrārthaḥ phalaṁ tasya prakṛtaya upāyāḥ phalahetava ity arthaḥ ।
3. *Ibid.*, vs. 21.
4. *Ibid.*, vs. 26:

   yad ādhikārikaṁ vastu samyak prājñaiḥ prayujyate ।
   tadartho yaḥ samārambhas tat kāryaṁ parikīrtitam ॥
5. *Ibid.*, vs. 22:

   svalpamātraṁ samutsṛṣṭaṁ bahudhā yad visarpati ।
   phalāvasānaṁ yac caiva bījaṁ tat parikīrtitam ॥
6. *K.N.*, Prelude to Act I, after vs. 12:

   bhavatā tu vājinam ayonijam indrāyudham evānupraviśya candrāpīḍamūrtiś candramāḥ kādambarīprasaṅgāya prāpaṇīyo vanaṁ caitraratham ।

When the Director says in the Prologue that the play about to be staged is a dramatic version of the famous novel *Kādambarī* (*vide* vs. 3 and before), the audience immediately understands what the play is about. This information, however, refers to the whole plot of the play, not specifically the *kārya* of it; therefore, it does not seem right to consider it to be the *bīja* of the play.

7. *Nāṭyaśāstra*, chap. 19, vs. 23:
prayojanānāṁ vicchede yad avicchedakāraṇam |
yāvat samāptir bandhasya sa binduḥ parikīrtitaḥ ||
8. *Ibid*., comm.: *tailabinduvat sarvavyāpakatvād api binduḥ*.
9. *The Rasārṇavasudhākara of Siṁhabhūpāla*, ed. T. Venkatacharya (Madras: The Adyar Library and Research Centre, 1979), chap. III, vs. 13:
jalabindur yathā siñcaṁs tarumūlaṁ phalāya hi |
tathaivāyam upakṣipto (var. *muhuḥ kṣipto*) *bindur ity abhidhīyate* ||
10. *Nāṭyaśāstra*, chap. 19, comm. on vs. 23.:
tathā hi tāpasavatsarāje vāsavadattāpremānusandhānaṁ rājamukhena pratyaṅkaṁ darśitam. . .
11. *Ibid*., vss. 2-4.
12. *Ibid*., vs. 24:
yad vṛttaṁ tu parārthaṁ syāt pradhānasyopakārakam |
pradhānavac ca kalpyate sā patāketi kīrtitā ||
13. *Rasārṇavasudhākara*, chap. III, vs. 14:
yat pradhānopakaraṇaprasaṅgāt svārtham ṛcchati |
sā syāt patākā sugrī vamakarandādivṛttavat ||
14. For the way this subsidiary action assists the main action, *vide* Intro., chap. VI, in which a summary of the play is given.
15. *Vide infra*.
16. *Nāṭyaśāstra*, chap. 19, vs. 29:
ā garbhād ā vimarśād vā patākā vinivartate |
kasmād yasmān nibandho syāḥ parārthaḥ parikīrtyate ||
17. *Ibid*., comm.: *nirvahaṇaparyante tatphale kriyamāṇe tulyakālayor upakāryopakārakatvābhāvāt tena pradhānopakāro* (*kārabhāvo*?) *na bhavet*.
18. *The Nāṭakalakṣaṇaratnakośa of Sāgaranandin*, lines 194-95:
sā (= *patākā*) *ca garbhe vamarśe ca nivartata iti nātyantikam etad avagantavyam* |
19. *Nāṭyaśāstra*, chap. 19, vs. 25:
phalaṁ prakalpyate yasyāḥ parārthāyaiva kevalam |
anubandhavihīnatvāt prakarīti vinirdiśet ||
20. *Ibid*., comm.
21. *Bhāvaprakāśana*, p. 202, line 1.
22. *Nāṭyadarpaṇa*, chap. I, comm. on vs. 29:
cet iti yadi phalasādhane sāhāyyāpekṣāṇāṁ nāyakānāṁ vṛttaṁ nibadhyate tadā patākā bhavati |
na tu svaparākramabahumāninām | *evaṁ prakarī* (*y*, *H.S.*) *api* |

23. *Nāṭakalakṣaṇaratnakośa*, lines 1120-22:

nāndīprayoge ca kṛte prīto bhavati candramāḥ |
kiṁ phalaṁ syād rasādhāratvāc candramasas tatprītisulabhā rasasaṁpattaya iti ||

24. A popular secondary type of Sanskrit-Prakrit play in four acts which resembles the *nāṭaka* and the *prakaraṇa*.

25. Ed. P. Sriramamurti (Waltair: Andhra University Press, 1978), *nāndī* 1:

sauhityaṁ vidadhāti yas sumanasāṁ śaśvat kalānāṁ nidhiḥ,
sarvāśāparipūraṇakṣamakaro yo rājaśabdāspadam |
jyotsnāsaṁvalitaḥ punaḥ kumudinīṁ yo rañjayaty añjasā,
bhūyād eṣa mude samastajagatām ānandanaś candramāḥ ||

26. *Nāṭyaśāstra*, chap. 20, vss. 33-37.

27. *Bhavabhūti's Mālatīmādhava*, ed. with Jagaddhara's comm. by M. R. Kale (Delhi: Motilal Banarsidass, 1967), pp. 10-12.

28. *Nāṭyaśāstra*, chap. 18, vs. 29, 1st half:

prakaraṇanāṭakaviṣaye pañcādyā daśaparā bhavanty aṅkāḥ |

29. Someśvara's *nāṭaka play Ullāgharāghava* (13th c.) has eight acts; *vide* A.K. Warder, *Indian Kāvya Literature*, vol. I, p. 65.

30. *Nāṭakalakṣaṇaratnakośa*, lines 383-88:

. . . pradhānasya nirdeśād vastunirdeśād vā nāṭakādīnāṁ nāma kartavyam |
. . . aṅko pi sugrīvāṅkaḥ | śaktir nāmāṅka iti |

Vide also Intro., chap. V for the titles of *nāṭaka* and *prakaraṇa* plays.

31. *Vide* Intro., chap. VI.

32. *Nāṭyaśāstra*, chap. 18, vs. 21, 1st half:

ekadivasapravṛttaṁ(-taḥ, H.S.) *kāryas tv aṅko. . . |*

33. In the *Uttararāmacarita*, for instance, Bhavabhūti spends as many as five acts (II-VI) on the incidents of a single day. It is also interesting to note that Sāgaranandin quotes the following two slightly different views that an act should contain incidents that last only half a day, or one day or one night (*Nāṭakalakṣaṇaratnakośa*, lines 298-99):

anyas tu vāsarārdhakṛto hy aṅka iti |
aparaś ca ekarātrīkṛtam ekavāsarakṛtam aṅke vaktavyam iti ||

34. *Nāṭyaśāstra*, chap. 19, vss. 110-16; chap. 18, vss. 26-39.

35. *Ibid*., chap. 18, vs. 28.

36. *Ibid*., chap. 19, vs. 116:

viśliṣṭamukham aṅkasya striyā vā puruṣeṇa vā |
yad upakṣipyate pūrvaṁ tad aṅkamukham ucyate ||

37. *Ibid*., chap. 18, vs. 31 and comm.:

aṅkacchedaṁ kṛtvā māsakṛtaṁ varṣasaṁcitaṁ vāpi |
tat sarvaṁ kartavyaṁ varṣād ūrdhvaṁ na tu kadā cit ||

yasmān māsakṛtaṁ varṣasaṁcitaṁ vā yac ca tat kāryaṁ sāmājikānāṁ hṛdayagataṁ tasmāt praveśakaviṣkambhakau kartavyau |

parimitan tu yad anusandheyaṁ tatrāṅkamukham alpānusandheye cūlikā, alpatame aṅkāvatāraḥ | . . .

38. *Ibid.*, chap. 19, comm. on vs. 37:

tenārthāvayavā sandhīyamānāḥ parasparam aṅgaiś ca sandhaya iti samākhyā niruktā |
tad eṣāṁ sāmānyalakṣaṇam |

39. *Ibid.*, vss. 37-44. Another pentad in the plot structure of a play is the five *avasthās* (stages): the *(pr)ārambha* (commencement), the *prayatna* (undertaking), the *prāptisambhava* (possibility of attainment), the *niyatā phalaprāpti* (certainty of attainment of the fruit) and the *phalayoga* (attainment of the fruit); *vide ibid.*, vss. 7-15. Dhanañjaya, among others, holds that the five *saṁdhis* are the combinations of the five *arthaprakṛtis* and the five *avasthās*; for instance, the *mukha saṁdhi* is the result of the *bīja arthaprakṛti* and the *prārambha avasthā* combined; *vide* his *Daśarūpaka*, ed. by T. Venkatacharya (Madras: The Adyar Library and Research Centre, 1969), chap. I, vss. 22-23. But this forced theory called *yathāsaṁkhya niyama* is rejected by Abhinavagupta, who gives various difficulties that arise from it; *vide Nāṭyaśāstra*, vol. III, p. 16, comm. The three pentads combined in the theory appear to have been quite independent doctrines in origin; *vide* Warder, *op. cit.*, vol. I, pp. 57-58.

40. *Nāṭyaśāstra*, chap. 19, vs. 39:

yatra bījasamutpattir nānārtharasasambhavā |
kāvye śarīrānugatā tan mukhaṁ parikīrtitam ||

41. *Ibid.*, vs. 40:

bījasyodghāṭanaṁ yatra dṛṣṭanaṣṭam iva kva cit |
mukhanyastasya sarvasya tad vai pratimukhaṁ smṛtam ||

42. *Ibid.*, vs. 41:

udbhedas tasya bījasya prāptir aprāptir eva |
punaś cānveṣaṇaṁ yatra sa garbha iti saṁjñitaḥ ||

43. *Ibid.*, vs. 42 and comm.:

garbhanirbhinnabījārtho vilobhanakṛto thavā |
krodhavyasanajo vāpi sa vimarśa iti smṛtaḥ ||

ke cid vimarśa iti paṭhanti, anye vamarśa iti |

44. *Ibid.*, vs. 43:

samānayanam arthānām mukhādyānāṁ sabījinām |
nānābhāvottarāṇāṁ yad bhaven nirvahaṇaṁ tu tat ||

45. The use of the *saṁdhyaṅgas* is said to serve the following sixfold purpose; *vide ibid.*, vss. 51-52:

iṣṭasyārthasya racanā vṛttāntasyānupakṣayaḥ |
rāgaprāptiḥ prayogasya guhyānāṁ caiva gūhanam ||

āścaryavad abhikhyānaṁ prakāśyānāṁ prakāśanam |
aṅgānāṁ ṣaḍvidhaṁ hy etad dṛṣṭaṁ śāstre prayojanam ||

46. *Ibid.*, vs. 67.

47. *Ibid.*, vss. 57 ff.

48. *Ibid*., vs. 50:
saṁdhīnāṁ yāni vṛttāni pradeśeṣv anupūrvaśaḥ |
svasampadguṇayuktāni tāny aṅgāny upadhārayet | |

49. *Ibid*., comm. on vs. 50:
anupūrvaśa iti mukhyaprayojanasaṁpādanabalopanatena krameṇa na tu lakṣaṇanirūpaṇaprasaṅgaparikalpitena. . .

50. *Ibid*., pp. 36-37:
kāni cit tv aṅgāni svarūpabalād eva niyamabhāñji yathopakṣepo mukhasaṁdhāv eva prathame |

51. *Ibid*., p. 36:
. . . saṁpradhāraṇam arthānāṁ yuktir ity abhidhīyate, iti yan mukhasandhau pañcamam aṅgaṁ vakṣyati tat sarveṣu sandhiṣu tāvan nibandhanayogyaṁ. . .

52. *Ibid*., p. 62:
tenaikam api sandhyaṅgaṁ tatraiva sandhau dvis trir yā(vā, H.S.) kartavyam |

53. *Ibid*., p. 63:
tathā dvayor yogo dvābhyām aṅgābhyāṁ saṁpādyaṁ tad ekenaiva ced ghaṭate tat kim apareṇa | *evaṁ triyogaḥ* |

54. *Ibid*., p. 37:
yat tūcyate catuḥṣaṣṭyaṅgasaṁyutam iti tena saṁbhavamātram eṣāṁ uktaṁ na tu niyamaḥ |

55. Dhanika's comm. *Avaloka* on the *Daśarūpaka*, pp. 28, 36, 45 & 55; he does not say which *aṅgas* are important in the *nirvahaṇa saṁdhi*.

56. *Nāṭyaśāstra*, chap. 19, vs. 69, 2nd half & comm.:
kāvyārthasya samutpattir upakṣepa iti smṛtaḥ |
kāvyārtha itivṛttaśarīralakṣaṇo bhidheyaḥ pradhānarasalakṣaṇaṁ ca prayojanasaṁkṣepeṇopakṣipyate |

Abhinavagupta uses mainly the *Ratnāvalī* of Harṣa and the *Veṇīsaṁhāra* of Bhaṭṭanārāyaṇa to illustrate the *saṁdhyaṅgas*; *vide ibid*., pp. 36 ff. For the same purpose the researcher has tried to find in the *Kādambarīnāṭaka* situations very close to those given by Abhinavagupta. Also, for a detailed study of the *saṁdhyaṅgas* that includes various other theorists' definitions and illustrations of them, *vide*, among others, T.G. Mainkar, *The Theory of the Saṁdhis and the Saṁdhyaṅgas* (Poona: M/s. Joshi & Lokhande, 1960).

57. *Vide supra* & n. 6.

58. *Nāṭyaśāstra*, chap. 19, vs. 70, 1st half & comm.:
yad utpannārthabāhulyaṁ jñeyaḥ parikaras tu saḥ | *tata īṣad vistāryate.*

59. *Ibid*., vs. 71, 1st half & comm.:
guṇanirvarṇanam caiva vilobhanam iti smṛtam |
tatas tad eva guṇavad iti ślāghyate ślāghaiva vilobhanahetutvād vilobhanam |

60. *Ibid*., vs. 73, 2nd half & comm.:
kutūhalottarāvego vijñeyā paribhāvanā |
kutuhaleti kautukena jijñāsātiśayena vyāmiśro ya āvegaḥ sā paribhāvanā kim etad iti |

61. *Ibid.*, vs. 70, 2nd half & comm.:

tanniṣpattiḥ parinyāso vijñeyaḥ kavibhiḥ sadā ||
tato pi niścayāpattirūpatayā parito hṛdaye so rtho nyasyate |

62. *Ibid.*, vs. 71, 2nd half & comm.:

saṁpradhāraṇam arthānāṁ yuktir ity abhidhīyate ||
asyāḥ prayojanaṁ prakāśyaprakāśanam api |

63. *Ibid.*, vs. 72, 1st half & comm.:

sukhārthasyābhigamanaṁ prāptir ity abhisaṁjñitā |
sukhayatītit sukhaṁ tādṛśasya vastunaḥ |

64. *Ibid.*, vs. 74, 2nd half:

prakṛtārthasamārambhaḥ karaṇaṁ nāma tad bhavet ||

65. *Ibid.*, vs. 76, 1st half & comm.:

samīhā ratibhogārthā vilāsa iti saṁjñitaḥ |
ratilakṣaṇasya bhāvasya hetubhūto yo bhogo viṣayaḥ pramadā puruṣo vā tadarthā yā samīhā sa vilāsaḥ | *kāmaphaleṣu rūpakeṣu pratimukha eva hy āsthāphalatvena ratirūpeṇa bhāvyam* |

66. *Ibid.*, vs. 78, 1st half:

krīḍārthaṁ vihitaṁ yat tu hāsyaṁ narmeti tat smṛtam |

67. *Ibid.*, vs. 83, 1st half:

tattvārthavacanaṁ caiva mārga ity abhidhīyate |

68. *Ibid.*, vs. 84, 2nd half & comm.:

bhāvatattvopalabdhis tu krama ity abhidhīyate ||

bhāvasya bhāvyamānasya vastuno bhāvanātiśaye saty ūhaṁ prati bhāvanādibalāt syāt yā paramārthopalabdhiḥ sā (sa, H.S.) kramaḥ |

69. *Ibid.*, vs. 86, 2nd half & comm.:

garbhasyodbhedanaṁ yat sākṣiptir ity abhidhīyate |

hṛdayāntaḥsthitaṁ (tasya) punaḥ pratiṣṭhāpitasyāpi yataḥ kutaś cin nimittād udbhedanam unapahnavanīyā yā sphuṭatāpattiḥ srā(sā, H.S.) ākṣiptiḥ, abhiprāyasya hi tatrākṣepo ḅahiḥ karṣaṇam |

70. *Ibid.*, vs. 77, 1st half & comm.:

kṛtasyānunayasyādau vidhūtaṁ hy aparigrahaḥ |
ādau prathamataḥ, kṛtasyānunayasya sāmavacaso nāṅgīkaraṇaṁ vidhūtaṁ, paścāt punar aṅgīkaraṇam iti |

71. *Ibid.*, vs. 86, 1st half & comm.:

ratiharṣotsavānāṁ tu prārthanā prārthanā bhavet |

etat sādhyaphalocitabhāvalakṣaṇaṁ, tatra sādhyaphale yaḥ prādhānyena samucito bhāvasthadviṣayā (- sthaviṣayā, H.S.) yā prakarṣeṇābhyarthanā sā prārthanākhyam aṅgam ||

72. *Ibid.*, vs. 89, 1st half:

doṣaprakhyāpanaṁ yat tu so pavāda iti smṛtaḥ |

73. *Ibid.*, vs. 77, 2nd half & comm.:

apāyadarśanaṁ yat tu tāpanaṁ nāma tad bhavet ।
yathā ratnāvalyām, dullahajaṇāṇurāo lajjāguruī paravaso appā piasahi visamaṁ pemmaṁ maraṇaṁ saraṇaṁ ṇu varaṁ ekkaṁ ॥

74. *Ibid.*, vs. 92, 2nd half & comm.:

manaśceṣṭāviniṣpannaḥ śramaḥ kheda udāhṛtaḥ ॥
mānasaḥ kāyīyaś cety ubhayo pi yāvat ।

75. *Ibid.*, vs. 90, 1st half & comm.:

guruvyatikramo yas tu sa dravaḥ parikīrtitaḥ ।

yathā vā tāpasavatsarāje ṣaṣṭhe ṅke vāsavadattāyā yaugandharāyaṇavacanātikrameṇa maraṇādhyavasāyaḥ ॥

76. K.N., Act VII, vss. 24 & 25.

77. *Nāṭyaśāstra,* chap. 19, vs. 95. 1st half & comm.:

prarocanā ca vijñeyā saṁhārārthapradarśinī ।
saṁhriyamāṇasya nirvāhyamāṇasyārthasya darśikā prakarṣeṇa rocata iti prarocanā ।
yathā "kvāsau jvalan hutavahas . . .

78. *Ibid.*, vs. 103, 1st half & comm.:

pūrvavākyaṁ tu vijñeyaṁ yathoktārthapradarśanam ।
yathā bābhravyaḥ, idānīṁ saphalapariśramo smi saṁpanna iti ।

This speech appears to be Yaugandharāyaṇa's, not Bābhravya's; *vide Ratnāvalī,* ed. by R. Mishra (Varanasi: Chaukhamba Amarabharati Prakashan, 1982), p. 206.

79. *Ibid.*, vs. 102, 2nd half & comm.:

sāmadānādisaṁpannaṁ bhāṣaṇaṁ samudāhṛtam ॥
sāmadānaṁ tu yathā bhagavatī jīmūtavāhanasya varaṁ dadāti,
tvāṁ vidyādharacakravartinam ahaṁ prītyā karomi kṣaṇāt ityādi ।

80. *Ibid.*, vs. 103, 2nd half:

varapradānasaṁprāptiḥ kāvyasaṁhāra iṣyate ॥

81. *Ibid.*, vs. 104, 1st half:

nṛpadeśapraśāntiś ca praśastir abhidhīyate ।

82. *Ibid.*, p. 56:

prasak(-śas, H.S.)ter itivṛttā(na inserted by *H.S.)ntarbhūtatvena gaṇanam anyāyyam . . .* The *praśasti* is commonly known as the *bharatavākya* (speech by an actor), though the term is not used by any ancient Indian theorist; it seems in origin a stage direction used before the *praśasti* in the text of a play; *vide* S. Chattopadhyaya, *Nāṭakalakṣaṇaratnakośa*, p. 121-22.

83. *Nāṭyaśāstra.*, chap. 19, vss. 107-109.

84. Bharata also discusses the *vīthyaṅgas*, the *lāsyāṅgas*, the *lakṣaṇas* and the like, which are of a similar nature to the *saṁdhyaṅgas* and the *saṁdhyantaras*, but they are not discussed here because of their relatively minor importance; *vide Nāṭyaśāstra*, chaps. 16 & 18.

85. *Ibid.*, vol. III, p. 63 (chap. 19):
tatra ke cid āhuḥ, antaraṁ chidraṁ sandhir iti |
tadaṅgamātraṁ tātsthyāc ca tatsthānyaṁ tena sandhyaṅgacchidravartitvāt sandhyantarāṇi, atra eva cāṅgānāṁ saṁbaddhāni ||

86. *Ibid.*:
anye manyante, ya evopakṣepādyā sāmānyā uktāḥ teṣām evaitad viśeṣā avāntarabhedāḥ |

87. *Rasārṇavasudhākara*, chap. III, vss. 93-95:
bhāgakalpanayāṅgānāṁ mukhapramukhasaṁdhiṣu ||
pratyekaṁ niyatatvena yojyā tatraiva kalpanā |
saṁdhyantarāṇāṁ vijñeyaḥ prayogas tv avibhāgataḥ ||
tathaiva darśanād eṣām anaiyatyena saṁdhiṣu |
Vide also *Nāṭyaśāstra*, vol. III, p. 36:
yat tu sandhinaiyatyenābhidhānaṁ tatra sandhāv avaśyaṁbhāvitvakhyāpanārthaṁ yuktir mukhe bhavaty eva | sandhyantarātāni (= -antarāṇi) tu nettham iti pṛthak tāni varṇayiṣyante |

88. *Nāṭakalakṣaṇaratnakośa*, lines 923 ff.

89. *Ibid.*, line 985: *svapnaḥ nidrāyāṁ cittagatārthālāpaḥ |*

90. *Ibid.*, line 987: *citram ālekhyābhimatajanadarśanopāyaḥ |*

91. *Ibid.*, line 983: *dūtaḥ saṁdeśahāraḥ |*

92. *Nāṭyaśāstra*, chap. 19, vss. 30-34.

93. *Nāṭyadarpaṇa*, chap. I, comm. on vs. 30:
. . . upakāriṇī pradhānaphalopakārikā tad itivṛttaṁ patākāsthānakam |
. . . kva cid ity antarāntarā, na tu patākāvan nirantaram |
ata eva patākāto bhidyate ||

94. *Nāṭyaśāstra*, chap. 19, vs. 30:
yatrārthe cintite nyasmiṁs talliṅgo nyaḥ prayujyate |
āgantukena bhāvena patākāsthānakaṁ tu tat ||

95. *Nāṭyadarpaṇa*, chap. I, comm. on vs. 30:
maṇḍanam iti ekam api patākāsthānakaṁ nāṭyakāvyasyālaṅkaraṇam, kiṁ punar dve trīṇi catvāri vā |

96. *Nāṭyaśāstra*, chap. 19, vs. 33:
arthopakṣepaṇaṁ yatra līnaṁ savinayaṁ bhavet |
śliṣṭapratyuttaropetaṁ tṛtīyam idam iṣyate ||

97. *Ibid.*, comm.:
yathā mudrārākṣase cāṇakyaḥ, api nāma rākṣaso durātmā gṛhyeta |
evam asphuṭe rthe upakṣipte, (praviśya) siddhārthakaḥ, a°a gaṇhido |
ity etat pratyuttaraṁ sandeśāśayena prayuktam aucityād viśeṣaniścayaṁ karoti |
tathā ca punaś cāṇakyaḥ (saharṣam ātmagatam) hanta gṛhīto durātmā rākṣasaḥ, iti |

98. *Uttararāmacarita*, ed. P.V. Kane (Delhi: Motilal Banarsidass, 1971), Act I, vs. 38 & after:

. . . kiṁ asyā na preyo yadi param asahyas tu virahaḥ | |
(praviśya)

Pratīharī: *deva uvaṭṭhido* |

Rāma: *ayi kaḥ* |

Pratīharī: *āsaṇṇapariārao devassa dummuho* |

99. *K.N.*, Act III, after vs. 47:

Kādambarī *(svagatam): . . . jai paccā ṇa tārisī ukkaṇṭhā* |

(praviśyāpaṭākṣepeṇa)

Vijayā: *esā āgaā* |

Kādambarī (*sāvegam*): *kā* |

Vijayā: *ayyā mahāsedā* |

100. *Ibid.*, Act VII, after vs. 7:

Vidūṣaka: *mā dāva dāṇiṁ ahimaasamāame khijjasu* |

Candrāpīḍa: *vayasya, āstāṁ tāvad anantarāvaśyaṁbhāvī devīsaṁdarśanotsavaḥ* |

The ambiguity here would disappear if *bhaviṣyati, bhavitā* or *bhavet* were used in place of *āstām*.

101. *Nāṭyaśāstra.*, chap. 19, vs. 32:

vacaḥ sātiśayaṁ śliṣṭaṁ kāvyabandhasamāśrayam |
patākāsthānakaṁ idaṁ dvitīyaṁ parikīrtitam | |

102. *Ibid.*, comm.:

yathā rāmābhyudaye tṛtīye ṅke sītāṁ prati sugrīvasya saṁdeśoktiḥ,
bahunātra kim uktena pāre pi jaladheḥ sthitām |
acirād eva devi tvām āhariṣyati rāghavaḥ | |

atrānyaprayojanenātiśaktyāśayena prayukte pi vacasi
pāre pīty ādi prakṛtopayogātiśayāt patākāsthānakam |

103. *Uttararāmacarita*, Act I, vs. 12:

snehaṁ dayāṁ ca saukhyaṁ ca yadi vā jānakīm api |
ārādhanāya lokānāṁ muñcato nāsti me vyathā | |

104. *K.N.*, Act VI, vs. 33, 2nd half:

tvatpādāntikam asmi sevituṁ asāv āyāta eva priye,
seyaṁ nau bhavitavyatā bhagavatī jāyeta cen nārgalā | |

105. *Ibid.*, Act VI, vs. 42:

eṣo smi bahubhir yatnair nivṛttaḥ suhṛdā saha |
niyateḥ prātikūlyāni yadi māṁ nābhiyuñjate | |

106. *Ibid.*, Act IV, after vs. 30:

(*svagatam*): *paccā vi khandhāvārādo ṇivaṭṭia sakko imiṇā sahīe pāṇiggaho kāduṁ,*
jai devvaṁ ṇāntarāo hodi |

107. *Ibid.*, Act IV, after vs. 33:

na tu jīvatāmunā punardevīdarśanam asaṁbhāvya sthīyata ity. . .

108. *Ibid.*, Act VI, vs. 15:

jāṇe ahaṁ imassiṁ jamme maha ṇaddhi āsaṅgo ।
tā suhaa sulahasaṁgamasokkho jammantare hohi ।।

109. *Ibid.*, Act VI, after vs. 39:

. . . śukeneva . . . । *tad ayaṁ tasyām eva tiryagjātau nipatya kva cic chūnyāraṇye duḥkhaśatabhājanaṁ bhūyāt* ।

110. *Ibid.*:

ārya maivaṁ tāvat ।
amarṣitasya hi gurujanasya pāruṣyaṁ garbharūpeṣu śāpatayā pariṇamaty eva ।

For this incident, *vide* also Intro., chap. VI.

111. *Nāṭyaśāstra*., chap. 19, vs. 31:

sahasaivārthasampattir guṇavaty upakārataḥ ।
patākāsthānakam idaṁ prathamaṁ parikīrtitam ।।

112. *Ibid.*, comm.:

yathā ratnāvalyāṁ sāgarikāyāṁ pāśāvalambanapravṛttāyāṁ vāsavadatteyam iti manyamāno yadā rājā pāśaṁ muñcati tadā taduktyā sāgarikāṁ pratyabhijñāya "hā kathaṁ priyā me sāgarikā, alam alam atimātram" ity ādi ।

atrānyatprayojanaṁ cintitaṁ tadvaicitryakāri ca prayojanāntaraṁ saṁpannam ।
tatra ca daivayogaḥ tathābhūtadeśakālayogo nāyakaḥ svātmaivānyābhisandhibalāt kalpitabhedaḥ sāgarikaiva vā maraṇam evocitam ity anyābhisandhānena vadatīti patākānāyakasadṛśatvaṁ bhajate ।

113. *K.N.*, Act III, between vss. 39 and 40:

Tamālikā: *maalehe devīe hatthammi dehi muttāvaliṁ* ।
saaṁ evva se kaṇṭhammi avalambijjadu esā ।

Taralikā: *ṇa khu aṇṇahā aṇumaṇṇai imo* ।

Madalekhā: *jujjai* ।

[*iti kādambarīhaste śeṣahāram arpayati*]

Kādambarī [*nāṭyenādāya tathā karoti*]

114. *Ibid.*, vs. 40 and before.

115. For this incident, *vide* also Intro., chap. VI.

8

The Garbhāṅka : A Special Feature of the Kādambarīnāṭaka

In Act V of the *Kādambarīnāṭaka*, Narasiṁha introduces a relatively rare dramatic device called the *garbhāṅka* (lit. embryo act; in effect, play within a play). Narasiṁha's *garbhāṅka*, entitled the *Mahāśvetāpuṇḍarīka*, treats the past history of the main play's *patākā* or sub-plot on the love and union of the secondary hero and heroine, Puṇḍarīka and Mahāśvetā.

The Garbhāṅka According to Theorists

The play within a play is a device the appearance of which implies a considerable previous dramatic development. It was unknown to the ancient Greek and Roman dramas, nor does it seem to have been employed in any other ancient drama except in the Sanskrit-Prakrit drama. Outside the ancient Indian drama, it was as late as the Elizabethan drama that the play within a play made its first appearance in a fully developed form, for instance, in *Mousetrap* of Shakespeare's *Hamlet* (1600-1), and its development can easily be traced back to the old interlude in the pre-Elizabethan drama.[1] In the ancient Indian drama, however, it is not possible to find out how the *garbhāṅka* was actually developed, for it is not employed in any of the extant plays before Harṣa's *Priyadarśikā* (7th c.), which has the oldest available example of it.

The *garbhāṅka* is not mentioned anywhere in Bharata's *Nāṭyaśāstra* (2nd c. B.C.?-1st c. A.D.),[2] the oldest extant treatise on ancient Indian dramaturgy. The commentator Abhinavagupta (10th-11th cc.), however, equates one of the two types of what is called the *nāṭyāyita* with the *garbhāṅka*. The *nāṭyāyita* is one of the six types of acting with the body (*śārīra abhinaya*).[3] Abhinavagupta comments that it is of two types: the *nāṭyarūpakaniṣṭha* and the *kāryāntaraniṣṭha*.[4] In the view of Śaṅkuka (9th c.) and others quoted by him, the former type is employed by the actor who enters first while he waits for another to enter, but he rejects this view.[5] According to Abhinavagupta, the *nāṭyarūpakaniṣṭha* is nothing but the *garbhāṅka*. He states that this is also of two types, namely, the *bahutaravyāpin* (prolonged) and the *parimitavyāpin* (limited). The former type is a play within a play which contains a play within a play like a dream within a dream which contains a dream within a dream, but the latter type is only one long play within a play like a long dream within a dream.[6] In order to illustrate the former type, Abhinavatupta cites the now lost *Vāsavadattānāṭyadhārā* of Subandhu (3rd c. B.C.).[7] As an example of the latter type, he mentiones the *garbhāṅka* entitled the *Sītāsvayaṁvara* in the *Bālarāmāyaṇa* of Rājaśekhara (9th-10th cc.).[8] In spite of this unique interpretation by Abinavagupta, the *nāṭyarūpakaniṣṭha* type of the *nāṭyāyita* mentioned in the *Nāṭyaśāstra* does not seem to have referred to anything like the *garbhāṅka* but probably to what Śaṅkuka and others described.

Dhanañjaya (10th c.) does not discuss the *garbhāṅka*, but his commentator Dhanika (10th-11th cc.) illustrates the *narmagarbha* (hidden sport), an *aṅga* in the *kaiśikī vṛtti* (tender mode of stage business), with the *garbhāṅka* of the *Priyadarśikā*, in which King Udayana himself substitutes for Manoramā in his costume.[9] Bhoja (11th c.) uses the *garbhāṅka* synonymously with the *aṅkāvatāra*, one of the five *arthopakṣepakas* (introductory scenes).[10] The *aṅkāvatāra*, according to the *Nāṭyaśāstra*, is an act, or rather a scene, at the end of an act, which contains the *bīja* (seed) and the *artha* (objective) of a play.[11] Bhoja, however, states in one place of his *Śṛṅgāraprakāśa* that it is placed within an act,[12] not necessarily at the end of it; and he states in another place of the same work that it is the act, among the acts of a play, which has the above characteristics.[13] Here again the *Sītāsvayaṁvara* of the *Bālarāmāyaṇa* is cited to illustrate the *garbhāṅka*, which Bhoja considers to be an ornament of a whole composition (*prabandhālaṅkāra*). He also mentions elsewhere that the *garbhanāṭaka*, that is, the *garbhāṅka* is a composition within a composition.[14] The view that the *garbhāṅka* and the *aṅkāvatāra* are identical was known to Rāmacandra and Guṇacandra (11th-12th cc.), and also to Śāradātanaya (12th-13th cc.).[15]

According to the *Vakroktijīvita* of Kuntaka (11th c.), the play within a play is a variety of *prakaraṇavakratā* (contextual figurativeness) which adorns a whole composition. When it is employed, some actors — expert in entertaining audiences — themselves play the role of its audience on the stage while other actors engage in acting in it.[16] It is also called the *garbha* (embryo) because it is placed like an embryo in an act.[17] It is extremely charming because it appears to have the essence of the main play.[18] The actors of the main play watching it provide the real audience with a variety of *camatkāra* (poetic charm), that is, *rasa* (aesthetic experience) by means of various forms of recollection and roundabout speech.[19] The play within a play is not found everywhere but only in plays composed by poets of genius.[20] The examples given by Kuntaka here are the *garbhāṅkas* in Rājaśekhara's *Bālarāmāyaṇa* and Bhavabhūti's *Uttararāmacarita* (7th-8th cc.).

It is the *Rasārṇavasudhākara* of Siṁhabhūpāla (14th c.) that provides the fullest definition of the *garbhāṅka* in terms of its structure.[21] According to it, the *garbhāṅka*, placed within an act, should have a *nāndī* (opening benediction) indicative of its plot and a compact *āmukha* (prologue). It should not have any *arthopakṣepaka* with the exception of the *cūlikā*. There should be only three or four characters in it. Its plot should not be too elaborate; and it should treat something connected with a matter already mentioned, not something irrelevant to such a matter. It adorns the portion of the act where it belongs. Its characters naturally should exit at the end of it. And it should not be employed in the first act of a play. The *garbhāṅka* enhances the main play's *rasa*, hero or plot. The *Uttararāmacarita*, for instance, has its predominant *rasa* enhanced by the use of a *garbhāṅka*; the *Bālarāmāyaṇa*, its hero; and the *Amogharāghava*, which is now lost, its plot. The *Sāhityadarpaṇa* of Viśvanātha (14th-15th cc.) briefly defines the *garbhāṅka* as follows. It is a secondary act incorporated into the body of an act. It has its own *raṅgadvāra* (item like the *nāndī* in the *pūrvaraṅga* "preliminaries of a play"), prologue and the like. And it has a *bīja* and a *phala* (objective) (of its own).[22] The example provided by Viśvanātha here is again the *Sītāsvayaṁvara* in the *Bālarāmāyaṇa*.

The Garbhāṅkas in Other Sanskrit-Prakrit Plays

Here the following four examples of the *garbhāṅka* will be briefly examined: those in the *Priyadarśikā* of Harṣa, the *Uttararāmacarita* of Bhavabhūti, the *Bālarāmāyaṇa* of Rājaśekhara and the *Naiṣadhānanda* of Kṣemīśvara (10th-11th cc.).[23] As was mentioned earlier, the *Priyadarśikā* is the oldest extant play that provides an example of the *garbhāṅka;* Harṣa's predecessors such as Bhāsa (2nd c.), Śūdraka (3rd c.) and Kālidāsa (5th c.) do not employ the device even in its crude form in their plays. The immediate function of the *garbhāṅka*, as will be seen in the examples given below, is to produce a strong effect on some major character of the main play watching it by hinting or revealing some important facts to him or her.

Harṣa's *garbhāṅka*, or *garbhanāṭaka* as he calls it, is found in Act III of the *nāṭikā Priyadarśikā*.[24] It is entitled the *Udayanacarita*, and compactly depicts the episode in which King Udayana won Princess Vāsavadattā's love during lute lessons. This *garbhāṅka* has no *nāndī* or *āmukha*, since the beginning part of it is supposed to have already been presented.[25] The role of Vāsavadattā is played by Āraṇyakā (Priyadarśikā incognito), with whom Udayana has fallen in love, but that of Udayana is played by Udayana himself through some cunning intrigue in spite of the prearrangement which made the maidservant Manoramā play it. Thus the King, acting himself, enjoys a very close meeting with Āraṇyakā. But this dramatic performance appears so real and vivid that Queen Vāsavadattā in the audience begins to suspect that something is wrong, though she is repeatedly reminded by the playlet's author, Sāṅkṛtyāyanī, that it is only a play. Soon the whole intrigue is revealed, and the performance ends abruptly. As is clear from the above, the purpose of this *garbhāṅka* is to give Udayana a chance to approach Priyadarśikā, his union with whom is the objective of the main play.

Bhavabhūti has his *garbhāṅka* in the last act of the seven-act *nāṭaka Uttararāmacarita*.[26] It does not have a *nāndī*, but a short prologue (*prastāvanā*) is attached to it. The Director in the Prologue announces that Vālmīki is the author of the play about to be staged, and that it is full of the *karuṇa* (pathetic) and the *adbhuta* (marvelous) *rasas*.[27] This *garbhāṅka* treats Sītā's pathetic life after her banishment by Rāma. During the performance of it, Rāma in the audience, though reminded by his brother Lakṣmaṇa that it is only a play, loses consciousness twice because it appears so real and unbearable to him. After his second swoon the real Sītā enters and helps him to regain consciousness. Thus Rāma's reunion with Sītā, the objective of the main play, is successfully accomplished.

Rājaśekhara's *garbhāṅka*, which is employed in Act III of the ten-act *nāṭaka Bālarāmāyaṇa*,[28] has a *nāndī* and a prologue. The *nāndī*, dedicated to Love, is recited by Kohala, who also acts as the Director in the following Prologue, where he announces Bharata's play *Sītāsvayaṁvara*. This playlet treats the episode in which Rāma, who bent Śiva's bow, was chosen for Sītā's husband from among many suitors in her *svayaṁvara* (self-choice ceremony). The chief spectator of this dramatic performance, Rāvaṇa himself could not bend the bow; so he made a vow to kill whoever married Sītā (Act I), but returned to Laṅkā without awaiting the result of the *svayaṁvara* (Act II). When the play reveals that Rāma has been chosen for Sītā's husband, Rāvaṇa gets enraged in spite of his general Prahasta's effort to convince him that it is a mere show. Needless to say, this effect of the *garbhāṅka* on Rāvaṇa plays a very important role in the plot of the main play, in which Rāvaṇa subsequently abducts Sītā, fights against Rāma and dies.

Kṣemīśvara's *garbhāṅka* is found in Act VI of the seven-act *nāṭaka Naiṣadhānanda*.[29] Damayantī in the main play has sent a troupe of actors to perform a play at King Ṛtuparṇa's palace, where Bāhuka (in fact, Nala in disguise) is serving him as a charioteer. This *garbhāṅka* has a *nāndī* and a prologue. The Director in the Prologue announces that the play about to be presented is called the *Svapnavañcita* (Deceived While Dreaming). It vividly describes Damayantī's endangered life after her desertion by Nala in the forest. Ṛtuparṇa and Bāhuka in the audience react quite differently to this dramatic presentation. While Ṛtuparṇa enjoys various *rasas* (aesthetic experiences), Bāhuka, that is, Nala only suffers their corresponding *bhāvas* (emotions)[30] because it shows his own beloved's sufferings. He gets excited and jumps up several times; so Ṛtuparṇa has to remind him each time that it is only a play. This overly emotional reaction of Bāhuka is good enough to convince the actress playing Damayantī that he is none other than Nala himself though his body is transformed. In fact, the ascertainment of his identity was the main task entrusted to her by Damayantī. After the performance the actress announces that Damayantī is going to hold her second *svayaṁvara*. This delights Ṛtuparṇa but naturally angers Nala. In the last act (VII) of the main play, they hurry to the *svayaṁvara* only to find out that the whole purpose of announcing it has been for Damayantī to find Nala. Now his original body restored, Nala gets happily reunited with Damayantī. Thus the objective of the main play is successfully accomplished.

The Garbhāṅka in the Kādambarīnāṭaka

Narasiṁha's *garbhāṅka* and its effect on the audience on the stage occupies the greater part of Act V, the longest act, of the *Kādambarīnāṭaka*.[31] This *garbhāṅka* is, no doubt, Narasiṁha's own innovation, but its plot closely follows the story of the unfulfilled love of the secondary hero and heroine, Puṇḍarīka and Mahāśvetā, which is narrated by the latter to Candrāpīḍa in their first meeting in Bāṇa's portion of the novel *Kādambarī*.[32] This unfortunate episode is also briefly treated in the same scene in Act I of the play.[33] The *garbhāṅka* forms the past history of the play's *patākā* or sub-plot, which ends with the couple's happy union.[34]

In the *cūlikā arthopakṣepaka* to Act V, a voice off stage, probably that of the Director of the *garbhāṅka*, tells the divine actors to give a faultless dramatic performance for Candrāpīḍa's best friend, Vaiśampāyana, who remained by Lake Acchoda with General Valāhaka to supervise the camp after Candrāpīḍa departed for Ujjayinī by order of his father, King Tārāpīḍa. After this, in the Act proper, Valāhaka enters and says that the divine actors are going to present a play in a theater built through their supernatural power (before vs. 3). Even before the performance begins, Vaiśampāyana (in fact, Puṇḍarīka reborn) already feels agitated as if the place, that is, Lake Acchoda, were the eyewitness of the moment of his first meeting with his beloved and he had not yet attained his object (vs. 6); moreover, he starts feeling stupefied (vs. 7). He wonders if this is due to his separation from Candrāpīḍa (after vs. 6), and Valāhaka tries to convince him that is exactly the case (after vs. 7).

Now the Director of the *garbhāṅka* enters and recites a *nāndī* dedicated to Love (vs. 8), and in the Prologue he announces that the play (*rūpaka*)[35] about to be staged is called the *Mahāśvetāpuṇḍarīka* composed by Kādambarī. Naturally, Vaiśampāyana gets surprised at the name Mahāśvetā (after vs. 9). Then a voice off stage is heard singing a Prakrit song suggestive of the unfulfilled love of Puṇḍarīka and Mahāśvetā (vs. 10). The Director, seeing his actress wife off stage already in Mahāśvetā's costume, exits to prepare himself for some part.

When the playlet proper begins and Mahāśvetā enters accompanied by Taralikā, Vaiśampāyana feels inexplicably attracted to her as if he had seen her somewhere before (vs. 11). Then with Kapiñjala enters Puṇḍarīka, whom Valāhaka describes as the common substratum of the *śṛṅgāra* (erotic) and the *śānta* (calmed) *rasa*s (vs. 14 and before).[36] Vaiśampāyana wonders why Puṇḍarīka looks exactly like himself and why Kapiñjala looks as if he were his childhood friend (vs. 15 and before). Valāhaka also gets surprised at the incredible likeness between Vaiśampāyana and Puṇḍarīka (vs. 18 and before). Vaiśampāyana begins to feel irresistible grief although he knows all this to be a mere play (vs. 19). He gradually comes to feel as if he remembered the whole incident (after vs. 23), but Valāhaka tells him that this is simply due to his feeling down with separation from Candrāpīḍa, and that his recollection of an intention denied in his previous life is being occasioned by the same object (vs. 24 and before). When Mahāśvetā reads aloud Puṇḍarīka's love letter to her, Vaiśampāyana gets greatly moved (vs. 36 and after), but Valāhaka again tries to convince him that this is nothing personal but art produced by a poet of genius (vs. 37 and before). The performance of the playlet moves on, and Puṇḍarīka off stage is heard cursing the moon; he is on the verge of dying of lovesickness (vs. 46 and before and after). In the meantime, Mahāśvetā hurries to save his life. Now Vaiśampāyana is extremely discomposed and about to lose consciousness (vs. 47) in spite of Valāhaka's effort to convince him that it is only natural for a man of poetic taste (*bhāvuka*) to feel this way watching the play, and that he is depressed because of separation from Candrāpīḍa (before and after vs. 48). Mahāśvetā arrives but learns of Puṇḍarīka's death and faints. When she regains consciousness, she decides to follow him in death (after vs. 51). Then a divine man descends from the sky and tells her to sustain her life because she will certainly be united with Puṇḍarīka some day (after vs. 52). After some thought she takes the divine man's advice and decides to wait for the day of her union with Puṇḍarīka by performing asceticism by Lake Acchoda. Then she exits with Taralikā. Now Valāhaka tries to wake up Vaiśampāyana, who has been unconscious all this time (before vs. 56). Vaiśampāyana regains consciousness with difficulty but still feels strange. He feels as if he remembered something that he has forgotten and as if he were someone else though he is himself (vs. 57 and before). Now Valāhaka tells the actors to stop acting and perform the rest of the playlet tomorrow (after vs. 58). Thus the performance is interrupted owing to Vaiśampāyana's overreaction to it. As for the rest of the playlet, it seems safe to conjecture that Kādambarī, the author and Mahāśvetā's best friend, must have given it a happy ending, that is, Mahāśvetā's union with Puṇḍarīka. Vaiśampāyana is still trying to figure out why his mind is so agitated. He somehow feels that seeing the dramatic performance is not the only cause of it; he keeps wondering if it is due to the excitement of everyone there or his desires or his memory of a previous life (vs. 59 and before and after).

As is clear from the above, the immediate purpose of this *garbhāṅka* is to remind Vaśampāyana of his previous life as Puṇḍarīka and of his unfulfilled love for Mahāśvetā. It is interesting to note here that while the chief spectators of the other *garbhāṅka*s examined earlier feel basically only *bhāva*s because what they see in the playlets is so personal to them, Vaiśampāyana seems to feel both *rasa*s and *bhāva*s because he does not realize that what he sees in the playlet is, in fact, nothing but an event in his own previous life. He does not know exactly what he feels; he gradually comes to feels as if he remembered the whole event but is not sure of it. In any case, owing to this powerful effect of the playlet on him, he subsequently approaches Mahāśvetā, gets cursed by her to become a parrot and dies (Act VII); then he is born a parrot and tells King Śūdraka (Candrāpīḍa reborn) all that he has recollected about his two previous lives as Puṇḍarīka and Vaiśampāyana (Act VIII). Needless to say, all this is necessary for the accomplishment of the objective of the main play, that is, Candrāpīḍa's union with Kādambarī, as well as for that of the objective of the *patākā*, that is, Puṇḍarīka's union with Mahāśvetā.

Overall, this *garbhāṅka* conforms to the above-mentioned relatively detailed rules for the device prescribed by Siṁhabhūpāla; there is, however, something that deserves attention here. When Siṁhabhūpāla says that the *garbhāṅka* should treat something connected with a matter already mentioned (*prastutārthānubandhī*), he may be referring to the objective of the main play. If this is the case, all the four examples of the *garbhāṅka* examined earlier conform to this rule; each of them treats only what is closely connected with the main objective of the play where it belongs. Or rather, Siṁhabhūpāla may have established the rule from these examples, for they were all available in his times. In either case, Narasiṁha must have been familiar with at least these examples of the *garbhāṅka*, though he probably did not know any established rules for the device. Now, there does not seem to be any good reason to believe why the *garbhāṅka* should not treat something not directly connected with the main play's objective. Narasiṁha seems to have made the right choice in arranging for his *garbhāṅka* the past history of the *patākā* instead of something more directly connected with the main play's objective, for the former appears to be the best possible incident in the novel *Kādambarī* to be arranged for a *garbhāṅka*. This *garbhāṅka* is undoubtedly the highlight of Narasiṁha's play; without it the *Kādambarīnāṭaka* would not be as charming.

Notes

1. A.V. Williams Jackson, Appendix "Notes on the Use of a Play Within a Play on the Sanskrit Stage," *Priyadarśikā: A Sanskrit Drama by Harṣa,* A.V. Williams Jackson *et al.* (New York: Ams Press Inc., 1965), pp. cv-cxi. This is a reprint with minor alterations of his article "Certain Dramatic Elements in Sanskrit Plays with Parallels in the English Drama" In *American Journal of Philology,* vol. 19 (1898), pp. 242-47.
2. A.K. Warder, *Indian Kāvya Literature,* vol. I, p. 21.
3. Bharata, *Nāṭyaśāstra,* ed. with Abhinavagupta's comm. by M.R. Kavi *et al.*, chap. 22 (vol. III), vss. 42-43.
4. *Ibid.*, comm. on vs. 48.
5. *Ibid.*, vs. 48 and comm.:

   nāṭyāyitam upacārair yaḥ kriyate bhinayasūcayā nāṭye |
   kālaprakarṣahetoḥ pravaiśakaiḥ saṁgamo yāvat ||

   pūrvapraviṣṭasya pātrasyāparapātraṁ praviśya tadrūpam udīkṣamāṇasya praveśo pi taddhruvāgāna-tatsūcāparikramaṇādikālena kiṁ cin nāṭyam astīti tatkāle pūrvapātreṇa ye samucitā upacārāḥ kriyante nāṭyāyitaṁ ityādy āryāyās tātparyam |

   . . . *śrīśaṅkukādyāḥ* | *tac cāyuktam* |
6. *Ibid.*, comm.:

   tathā yāvad iti svapne svapnāntaraṁ tatrāpy anyat svapnātaraṁ ityādinyāyena vā bhavatv eka(ghana)svapnāyitavṛttyā vā sarvathā tan nāṭyāyitaṁ |

7. *Ibid.*:

tatrāsya bahutaravyāpino bahugarbhasvapnāyitatulyasya nāṭyāyitasyodāharaṇaṁ mahākavisubandhu-nibaddho vāsavadattānāṭyadhārākhyaḥ samasta eva prayogaḥ I . . .

Warder discusses this play in further detail; *vide op. cit.*, vol. II, pp. 110-12.

8. *Nāṭyaśāstra*, chap. 22, comm. on vs. 48:

parimitavyāpino nirgarbhasya nāṭyāyitasyodāharaṇaṁ yathā bālarāmāyaṇe garbhāṅke sītāsvayaṁvare I

9. *The Daśarūpaka of Dhanañjaya*, ed. with Dhanika's comm. *Avaloka* and Bhaṭṭanṛsiṁha's sub-comm. *Laghuṭīkā*, chap. II, comm. on *kārikā* 52 (p. 126):

yathā priyadarśikāyāṁ garbhāṅke vatsarājaveṣamanoramāsthāne sākṣād vatsarājapraveśaḥ I

10. For the five *arthopakṣepakas*, *vide* Intro., chap. VII.

11. *Nāṭyaśāstra*, chap. 19, vs. 115:

aṅkānta eva cāṅko nipatati yasmin prayogam āsādya I
bījārthayuktiyukto jñeyo hy aṅkāvatāro sau I I

12. *Maharaja Bhojaraja's Shringara Prakasha*, vol. II, p. 463 (chap. XI):

aṅkāntare parāṅko nipatati yasmin prayogam āsādya I
bījārthayuktiyukto garbhāṅko nāma sa jñeyaḥ I I

13. *Ibid.*, p. 477:

bījārthayuktimān aṅko yo ṅkeṣv ekaḥ prayujyate I
sa nāṭakeṣu garbhāṅko ṅkāvatāraś ca kathyate I I

14. *Ibid.*, vol. I, p. 120 (chap. 3):

prabhandheṣv api prabandhā yathā, uttaracaritādau garbhanāṭakādīni I

15. *Nāṭyadarpaṇa of Rāmacandra and Guṇacandra*, pp. 36-37; *Bhāvaprakāśana of Śāradātanaya*, pp. 218-19.

16. *The Vakroktijīvita of Kuntaka*, chap. IV, *kārikā*s 12-13 (p. 270):

sāmājikajanāhlādanirmāṇanipuṇair naṭaiḥ I
tadbhūmikāṁ samāsthāya nirvartitanaṭāntaram I I
kva cit prakaraṇasyāntaḥ smṛtaṁ prakaraṇāntaram I
sarvaprabandhasarvasvakalpāṁ puṣṇāti vakratām I I

17. *Ibid.*, comm. (p. 271):

ekasya madhyavarty aṅkāntaragarbhīkṛtaṁ garbho vā nāmeti yāvat I

18. *Ibid.*:

. . . *prakṛtārthajīvita iva* . . . *taraṅgitavakratāmahimni* . . .

19. *Ibid.*:

. . . *kuśīlavāḥ* . . . *sāmājikībhavanto vividhābhir bhāvanābhaṅgībhiḥ sākṣātsāmājikānāṁ kim api cittacamatkāravaicitryam āsūtrayanti* I

20. *Ibid.* (p. 270):

kasmins cit kavikauśalonmeṣaśālini nāṭake, na sarvatra ।

21. *The Rasārṇavasudhākara of Siṁhabhūpāla*, chap. III, vs. 212, 2nd half — vs. 218, 1st half (pp. 419-20):

aṅkaprasaṅgād garbhāṅkalakṣaṇaṁ vakṣyate mayā ।।

rasanāyakavastūnāṁ mahotkarṣāya kovidaiḥ ।
aṅkasya madhye yo 'ṅkaḥ syād ayaṁ garbhāṅka īritaḥ ।।

vastusūcakanāndīko diṅmātrāmukhasaṅgataḥ ।
arthopakṣepakair hīnaś cūlikāparivarjitaiḥ ।।

aneṣyadvastuviṣayaḥ pātrais tricaturair yutaḥ ।
nātiprapañcetivṛttaḥ svādhārāṅkāṅgaśobhitaḥ ।।

prastutārthānubandhī ca pātraniṣkramaṇāvadhiḥ ।
prathamāṅke na kartavyaḥ so yaṁ kāvyaviśāradaiḥ ।।

so yaṁ uttararāme tu rasotkarṣāya kathyatām ।
netur utkarṣako jñeyo bālarāmāyaṇe tv ayam ।।
amogharāghave so yaṁ vastūtkarṣaikakāraṇam ।

22. *Sāhityadarpaṇa*, chap. VI, *kārikā* 20 (p. 172):

aṅkodarapraviṣṭo yo raṅgadvārāmukhādimān ।
aṅko paraḥ sa garbhāṅkaḥ sabījaḥ phalavān api ।।

23. K.K. Dutta discusses some lesser-known examples of the *garbhāṅka* as well: those in Ravivarmabhūpa's *Pradyumnābhyudaya* (13th c.), Rūpagosvāmin's *Lalitamādhava*, Kavikarṇapūra's *Caitanyacandrodaya* (16th c.) and Rāmabhadradīkṣita's *Jānakīpariṇaya* (17th c.); also, briefly discussed here are the magic shows in Jayadeva's *Prasannarāghava* and Mahādeva's *Adbhutadarpaṇa*, which somewhat resemble the *garbhāṅka* in form and effect; *vide* "*Garbhāṅka*: Its Genesis and Development in Sanskrit," *Our Heritage*, vol. VII, pt.1 (Calcutta: Calcutta Sanskrit College, 1959), pp. 37-58. Williams Jackson also discusses some devices similar to the *garbhāṅka* in form and/or effect to various extents: Mālavikā's dance and song performance in Kālidāsa's *Mālavikāgnimitra*, the magic shows in Harṣa's *Ratnāvalī* and Rājaśekhara's *Karpūramañjarī*, and Urvaśī's blunder in performing the play *Lakṣmīsvayaṁvara*, which is merely reported in a *viṣkambhaka* in Kālidāsa's *Vikramorvaśīya*; the last could have been arranged as a *garbhāṅka* with advantage; *vide op. cit.*

24. *Priyadarśikā of Śrī Harṣadeva*, ed. by M.R. Kale (Delhi: Motilal Banarsidass, 1977), Act III, after vs. 4 — after vs. 14.

25. *Ibid.*, Manoramā's speech before vs. 1:

ṇaccidavvaṁ amhehiṁ tassa evva ṇāḍaassa ṇaccidasesaṁ ।

26. *Uttararāmacarita of Bhavabhūti*, ed. with Ghanaśyāma's comm. by P.V. Kane (Delhi: Motilal Banarsidass, 1971), Act VII, after vs. 1 — between vss. 15 and 16 (The *garbhāṅka* proper seems to end here, where Sītā exits with the two goddesses, and then Rāma in the audience faints for the second time, and before the real Sītā enters after vs. 17).

Bhavabhūti does not call this playlet by any special term in the text, but the commentator Ghanaśyāma (18th c.) calls it a *garbhanāṭaka* and an *antarnāṭaka*; *vide* his comm. on the play, p. 144ff. *Vide* also Vīrarāghava's (*cir.* 1800) comm. on the play; *The Uttararāmacharita of Bhavabhūti*, ed. with his comm. by M.R. Kale (Bombay: Gopal Narayan & Co., 1911), pp. 177ff.

27. For the varieties of *rasas*, *vide* Intro., chap. IX.

28. *The Bālarāmāyaṇa: A Drama by Rājaśekhara*, ed. by G.D. Śāstrī (Benares: The Medical Hall Press, 1869), Act III, vs. 11 — vs. 88.

29. *Naiṣadhānanda of Kṣemīśvara*, ed. by A.K. Warder and K.K. Raja (Madras: The Adyar Library and Research Centre, 1986), Act VI, vs. 8 — vs. 29.

30. For the difference between the *rasas* and the *bhāvas*, *vide* Intro., chap. IX.

31. *K.N.*, Act V, vs. 8 — vs. 59.

32. *Kādambarī* (*Pūrvārddha*), ed. by M. Pant, pp. 473-572.

33. *K.N.*, Act I, between vss. 41-42.

34. For the *patākā*, *vide* also Intro., chap. VII.

35. Here the word *rūpaka* is used obviously in the sense of a play in general; *vide* after vs. 9. Elsewhere in the play, this playlet is referred to as a *pekkhaṇaa* (*prekṣaṇaka*) in the sense of a show or spectacle in general; *vide* Act II, after vs. 5.

36. For the varieties of *rasas*, *vide* Intro., chap. IX.

9

The Rasas of the Kādambarīnāṭaka

WHILE a plot is considered a play's body,[1] *rasa* or aesthetic experience[2] is considered its essence or soul, for without *rasa*, as Bharata states, no subject matter can be presented.[3] Bharata lists the following eight varieties of *rasas*: the *śṛṅgāra* (erotic), the *hāsya* (comic), the *karuṇa* (pathetic or compassionate), the *raudra* (furious), the *vīra* (heroic), the *bhayānaka* (apprehensive), the *bībhatsa* (horrific) and the *adbhuta* (marvelous).[4] To these eight *rasas* are added by later theoreticians many others the most important of which is the *śānta* (calmed).[5] The *Kādambarīnāṭaka* has the *śṛṅgāra* as its pre-dominant *rasa* as the novel *Kādambarī* does; the play, however, also gives some scope to many of the other *rasas* developed in the novel.[6]

Theories of Rasa

Before examining the *rasas* of the *Kādambarīnāṭaka*, it seems necessary to explain in a little more detail what *rasa* is and how it arises. Each variety of *rasa* has as its basis a corresponding *sthāyibhāva* or basic emotion; for instance, the *śṛṅgāra rasa* has the *rati* (love) *sthāyibhāva*.[7] According to Abhinavagupta's *rasa* theory, which is generally considered the highest achievement in the field, *rasa* is an experience on the aesthetic plane entirely different from *(sthāyi)bhāva* or mere emotion. *Rasa* is a non-individual or universalized perception which transcends all space, time, cognizing subjects and obstacles; it is neither worldly nor false nor ineffable; it is, in fact, nothing other than immersion in enjoyment and in one's own self. *Rasa* can be enjoyed only by people whose hearts possess a spotless intuitional understanding.[8]

Now, how does *rasa* arise? Bharata states in his famous *rasa sūtra* that *rasa* arises from the conjunction of *vibhāvas* (causes of emotion), *anubhāvas* (effects of emotion) and *vyabhicāribhāvas* (transient emotions).[9] Some later theoreticians further classify *vibhāvas* into *ālambanas* (lit. supports) and *uddīpanas* (lit. exciters).[10] For instance, a hero's beloved is an *ālambana vibhāva*, and her charming behaviour is an *uddīpana vibhāva*. *Anubhāvas* are effects shown by actors by means of speech, gestures and facial expressions. *Vyabhicāribhāvas* (or *sañcāribhāvas*) are also effects shown by actors. They are only transient as opposed to *sthāyibhāvas*, which are lasting. Among the thirty-three *vyabhicāribhāva* listed by Bharata are joy, eagerness, jealousy and sickness.[11] In addition to these three kinds of *bhāvas* or emotions, there are *sāttvika* (expressive) *bhāvas*, which are effects directly shown by actors. Among the eight *sāttvika bhāvas* listed by Bharata are horripilation, trembling, tears and fainting.[12] Now, the reason why *sthāyibhāvas* are not mentioned in the *rasa sūtra* seems obvious: they do not exist in the theater. As a rule, actors do not experience the emotions imagined to be present in the characters that they play; they only provide their audience various sorts of effects in relation to their causes. Spectators who are *rasikas* (connoisseurs), however, imagine the emotions thus suggested and enjoy their corresponding *rasas*.

The Rasas Developed in the Kādambarīnāṭaka

As was mentioned earlier, the predominant *rasa* of the *Kādambarīnāṭaka* is the *śṛṅgāra*, which has *rati* as its *sthāyibhāva*.[13] Bharata classifies the *śṛṅgāra* into the *sambhoga* (in union) and the *vipralambha* (in separation of frustration either before or after union), and some later theoreticians further classify these two main varieties of the *rasa* into many different sub-varieties.[14] While the *sambhoga śṛṅgāra* is found only briefly at the end of the play, where the two couples get happily united, different varieties of the *vipralambha śṛṅgāra* are seen to be developed in all the rest of it.

Viśvanātha describes the *karuṇa* (pathetic) variety of the *vipralambha śṛṅgāra* as arising in a situation in which a lover grieves at the death of his or her beloved though they will be reunited subsequently.[15] He illustrates it with the episode of Puṇḍarīka and Mahāśvetā in the novel *Kādambarī*, in which Mahāśvetā, practising asceticism, waits for the day of her union with Puṇḍarīka, whose dead body has been taken away by a divine man to another world.[16] No matter how pathetic this situation may appear, the *rasa* here is the *śṛṅgāra* because there are still hopes of the lovers' getting united; the divine man has assured Mahāśvetā of her future union with Puṇḍarīka. This applies to the play's sub-plot of the lovers as well. Between Puṇḍarīka's death and the divine man's assurance of their future union, however, the *rasa* is the *karuṇa*, which has *śoka* (grief) as its *sthāyibhāva*,[17] because then Mahāśvetā has no hope of getting united with Puṇḍarīka and even tries to follow him in death (Act V, before vs. 52). According to a view quoted by Viśvanātha, the *rasa* after the divine man's assurance is the *pravāsa* (in going abroad or traveling) variety of the *vipralambha śṛṅgāra*; but according to another, it is not because it is caused by death, not by mere traveling. In the case of the play's main plot of Candrāpīḍa and Kādambarī, the *rasa* is the *karuṇa* for a while between his death and the divine man's assurance of their future union (Act VII, before vs. 20 - before vs. 23), but it becomes the *karuṇa vipralambha śṛṅgāra* after the divine man's assurance (Act VII, vs. 24) and remains so until Candrāpīḍa regains consciousness towards the end of the play (Act VIII, before vs. 28).

Another variety of the *vipralambha śṛṅgāra*, the *pūrvarāga* (approx. in pre-union)[18] is also seen to be developed where Candrāpīḍa and Kādambarī get more and more attracted to each other by hearing of or seeing each other (Acts I-IV and VI-VII), and similarly where Puṇḍarīka and Mahāśvetā do the same (Act V). Moreover, the *pravāsa vipralambha śṛṅgāra*[19] proper is found where Kādambarī gets distressed at Candrāpīḍa's absence caused by going back to his camp sojourning by Lake Acchoda (Act IV) and to Ujjayinī by Tārāpīḍa's order (Acts V-VII).

A subsidiary but very important *rasa* throughout the play as well as the novel is the *adbhuta*, which has *vismaya* (astonishment) as its *sthāyibhāva*.[20] The play is full of supernatural elements. To begin with, many of its characters are either celestial beings or incarnations of such beings. Among its numerous incidents productive of the *adbhuta rasa* are the divine man's appearance and action (Act V, after vs. 52 & Act III, vss. 24-25) and Rohiṇī's magic spectacle (Act VIII, after vs. 11).[21]

The *hāsya rasa,* whose *sthāyibhāva* is *hāsa* (laughter),[22] is also given some scope in the play. The novel's incident of the irascible but comic Dravidian religious bigot is replaced by the appearance of a jester in the play.[23] This jester produces laughter, for instance, by saying jocularly that Kādambarī must be talking about himself when it is obviously Candrāpīḍa that is the topic of her talk (Act IV, after vs. 22).[24] The *hāsya rasa* is also found in the lovers' quarrel between Kādambarī's parrot Parihāsaka and her mynah Kālindī (Act IV, after vs. 27).[25]

The novel treats Candrāpīḍa's *digvijaya* or world conquest in detail,[26] but the play mentions it only briefly (e.g. Prelude to Act I, after vs. 15), for it is not essential to the play's objective.[27] As a result, the play has virtually no scope for the development of the *vīra rasa*, the *sthāyibhāva* of which is *utsāha* (energy).[28]

The *raudra rasa*, whose *sthāyibhāva* is *krodha* (anger),[29] has a few occasions for its development in the play as in the novel. It is developed, for instance, where the hot-tempered Śukanāsa unknowingly reproaches his son Vaiśampāyana (Puṇḍarīka reborn) for his ill conduct and curses him to be born a parrot (Act IV, after vs. 38),[30] and similarly where Mahāśvetā, angry at Vaiśampāyana's advances, curses him to become a parrot (end of the Prelude to Act VII).[31]

The *bhayānaka rasa*, whose *sthāyibhāva* is *bhaya* (fear),[32] is highly developed in the novel's incident in which the parrot Vaiśampāyana witnesses his father's death by a hunter and barely escapes his own in the Vindhya forest.[33] This incident is only succinctly mentioned in the play (Act VIII, vs. 20); as a result, there is hardly any scope for the *bhayānaka rasa* there. The *bhayānaka*, however, is seen somewhat developed in the scene where the parrot is captured and taken away by a hunter to his settlement (Prelude to Act VIII).[34] Part of the same scene is also highly productive of the *bībhatsa rasa*, whose *sthāyibhāva* is *jugupsā* (disgust).[35] The *bībhatsa* is briefly but intensely developed when the parrot grieves at his near future misfortune of living in the hunter's loathsome settlement (vs. 3) and describes how repulsive the settlement is (vs. 6).

The *śānta rasa*, which has *śama* (calm) as its *sthāyibhāva*,[36] is not mentioned by Bharata but recognized as a ninth *rasa* by Abhinavagupta and others. The novel gives full scope to this *rasa* where the parrot Vaiśampāyana describes in great detail the ascetics Hārīta and Jābāli and their hermitage,[37] but the play omits this description altogether, for it is unessential to its objective. The *śānta*, however, is slightly developed where Valāhaka in the audience for the playlet describes Puṇḍarīka as the common substratum of the *śānta* and the *śṛṅgāra rasa*s (Act V, vs. 14 and before).

Among many other *rasa*s not mentioned by Bharata but recognized by later theoreticians are the *preyas* and the *vatsala*. They are both *rasa*s of affection or non-sexual love distinguished from the *śṛṅgāra rasa* of sexual love. The *preyas*, which has *sneha* (affection) as its *sthāyibhāva*, is the *rasa* arising from friendship or love towards one's friends,[38] while the *vatsala*, whose *sthāyibhāva* is *vatsalatāsneha* (affection towards one's offspring), is the *rasa* arising from parental love.[39] The play as well as the novel gives great scope to these *rasa*s in numerous situations. The *preyas rasa* is seen to be developed in the friendship between Candrāpīḍa and Vaiśampāyana, that between Kādambarī and Mahāśvetā, that between Candrāpīḍa and Mahāśvetā, that between Puṇḍarīka and Kapiñjala, and so on. The *vatsala rasa* is developed in the parental love of Tārāpīḍa and Vilāsavatī towards Candrāpīḍa, that of Śvetaketu and Lakṣmī towards Puṇḍarīka, that of Citraratha and Madirā towards Kādambarī, and so on. In passing, the novel has one other situation most productive of the *vatsala rasa*, though the play omits it altogether. It is where the parrot Vaiśampāyana describes how his old father took care of him when he was a baby and how he tried to save him from a terrible hunter's hands.[40]

As is clear from the above, the *Kādambarīnāṭaka* has the *śṛṅgāra*, mainly its *vipralambha* variety, as its predominant *rasa* as the novel *Kādambarī* does. As for the various subsidiary *rasa*s relatively briefly but highly developed in the novel, however, some are given nearly as much scope but others are given little or no scope in the play, for certain incidents unessential to the play's objective are either only succinctly mentioned or totally omitted. But this way the *śṛṅgāra rasa* appears to secure its predominant position over the other *rasa*s in the play more thoroughly than in the novel.

Notes

1. Bharata, *Nāṭyaśāstra*, ed. with Abhinavagupta's comm. by M.R. Kavi *et al.*, chap. 19 (vol. III), vs. 1, 1st half:

   itivṛttaṁ tu nāṭyasya śarīraṁ parikīrtitam ।

2. R. Gnoli's "aesthetic experience" appears to be the best translation of the term *rasa*; *vide* his *The Aesthetic Experience According to Abhinavagupta* (Varanasi: The Chowkhamba Sanskrit Series Office, 1968). Other scholars call *rasa*, which literally means 'taste', by such names as 'relish', 'sentiment', 'mood' and 'beauty'.

3. *Nāṭyaśāstra*, chap. 6 (vol. I), prose after vs. 31:

   na hi rasād ṛte kaś cid arthaḥ pravartate ।

4. *Ibid.*, vs. 15.

5. V. Raghavan discusses many other *rasas*; *vide* his *The Number of Rasa*-s (Madras: The Adyar Library and Research Centre, 1975).

6. N. Sharma discusses the *rasas* of the *Kādambarī* together with those of the *Harṣacarita; vide* her *Bāṇabhaṭṭa: A Literary Study* (Delhi: Munshiram Manoharlal, 1968), pp. 128-49.

7. Bharata lists the corresponding *sthāyibhāvas* of the above-mentioned eight *rasas*; *vide Nāṭyaśāstra*, chap. 6, vs. 17, and *infra*.

8. *Ibid.*, comm. on prose after vs. 31 (pp. 272 ff.). Here Abhinavagupta introduces and refutes entirely or partly various other theories of *rasa* before introducing his own. *Vide* also Gnoli, *op. cit.*

9. *Ibid.*, prose after vs. 31:

   vibhāvānubhāvavyabhicārisaṁyogād rasaniṣpattiḥ ।

10. It seems to be Dhanañjaya who first introduced this classification of *vibhāvas*, which is not found in the *Nāṭyaśāstra; vide The Daśarūpaka of Dhanañjaya*, chap. IV, *kārikā*. 2; also *Viśvanātha, Sāhityadarpaṇa*, chap. III, *kārikās* 29 and 131, 2nd half — 132, 1st half.

11. *Nāṭyaśāstra*, chap. 6, vss. 18-21.

12. *Ibid.*, vs. 22.

13. *Ibid.*, after vs. 45; here Bharata starts expounding the *śṛṅgāra* and the other seven *rasas*, and various sorts of *bhāvas* necessary for their appearance. The *śṛṅgāra*, which is usually translated as 'erotic', 'amorous', 'romantic', and the like, is described as having flaming apparel as its soul (*ujjvalaveṣātmakaḥ*); therefore, it seems possible to call it, for instance, 'brilliant' or 'flamboyant'.

14. For instance, Vemabhūpāla; *vide Amaruśatakam*, ed. with his comm. *Śṛṅgāradīpikā* by C.R. Devadhar (Poona: Oriental Book Agency, 1959), comm. on vs. 7. Also Viśvanạtha; *vide Sāhityadarpaṇa*, chap. III, vss. 186-213.

15. *Sāhityadarpaṇa*, chap. III, vs. 209 and comm.:

    yūnor ekatarasmin gatavati lokāntaraṁ punar labhye ।
    vimanāyate yadaikas tadā bhavet karuṇavipralambhākhyaḥ ।।

    yathā kādambaryām puṇḍarīkamahāśvetāvṛttānte ।
    punar alabhye śarīrāntareṇa vā labhye tu karuṇākhya eva rasaḥ ।
    kiṁ cātrākāśasarasvatībhāṣānantaram eva śṛṅgāraḥ saṁgamapratyāśayā rater udva(udha, H.S.)vāt ।
    prathamaṁ tu karuṇa eva ity abhiyuktā manyante ।
    yac cātra 'saṁgamapratyāśānantaram api bhavato vipralambhaśṛṅgārasya pravāsākhyo bheda eva' iti ke cid āhuḥ, tad anye 'maraṇarūpaviśeṣasaṁbhavāt tadbhinnam eva' iti manyante ।

16. For this episode, whose past history is arranged by Narasiṁha as a *garbhāṅka*, *vide* also Intro., chap. VIII.

17. For this *rasa*'s *vibhāvas* &c., *vide Nāṭyaśāstra*, chap. 6, prose after vs. 61 — vs. 63.

18. *Sāhityadarpaṇa*, chap. III, vss. 188-97.

19. *Ibid.*, vss 204-208.

20. For this *rasa*'s *vibhāvas* &c., *vide Nāṭyaśāstra*, chap. 6, prose after vs. 74 — vs. 76.

21. The latter is Narasiṁha's innovation; *vide* Intro., chap. VI.

22. For this *rasa*'s *vibhāvas* &c., *vide Nāṭyaśāstra*, chap. 6, prose after vs. 48 — vs. 61.
23. *Vide* also Intro., chap. VI.
24. This situation can also be considered an example of the *narma* (joke), one of the *saṁdhyaṅgas*; *vide* Intro., chap. VII.
25. For this incident, *vide* also Intro., chap. VI.
26. Bāṇa, *Kādambarī (Pūrvārddha)*, ed. by M. Pant, pp. 382-406.
27. For Narasiṁha's treatment of Candrāpīḍa's *digvijaya*; *vide* Intro., chap. VI.
28. For this *rasa*'s *vibhāvas* &c., *vide Nāṭyaśāstra*, chap. 6, prose after vs. 66 — vs. 68.
29. For this *rasa*'s *vibhāvas* &c., *vide Nāṭyaśāstra*, chap. 6, prose after vs. 63 — vs. 66.
30. Narasiṁha makes a small but interesting change in this incident in order to make it a *patākāsthānaka*; *vide* Intro., chap., VI & VII.
31. *Vide* also Intro., chap. VI.
32. For this *rasa*'s *vibhāvas* &c., *vide Nāṭyaśāstra*, chap. 6, prose after vs. 68 — vs. 72.
33. Bāṇa, *op. cit.*, pp. 93-119.
34. For this incident in the novel, *vide* Bhūṣaṇa, *Kādambarī* (*Uttarārddha*), ed. by M. Pant, pp. 262-69.
35. For this *rasa*'s *vibhāvas* &c., *vide Nāṭyaśāstra*, chap, 6, prose after vs. 72 — vs. 74.
36. For this *rasa*'s *vibhāvas* &c., *vide Nāṭyaśāstra*, chap. 6, after vs. 82; Abhinavagupta uses a manuscript of the *Nāṭyaśāstra* which includes this *rasa*, but it is obviously a later interpolation.
37. Bāṇa, *op. cit.*, pp. 123-68.
38. Rudraṭa seems to be the first known theoretician to recognize this *rasa*; *vide The Kāvyālaṅkāra of Rudraṭa*, ed. with Namisādhu's comm. by M.P. Durgāprasād and W.L. Ś. Paṇśikar (Bombay: Nirṇaya Sāgar Press, 1928), chap. 16, vss. 17-19.
39. Viśvanātha, *op. cit.*, chap., III, vss. 251-53.
40. *Vide supra*, n. 33.

10

Concluding Remarks

In this introduction the *Kādambarīnāṭaka* of Narasiṁha has been examined in the light of its source story, that is, the novel *Kādambarī* of Bāṇa and Bhūṣaṇa; the *Nāṭyaśāstra* of Bharata and several later theoretical works on classical Indian dramaturgy and poetics, and the like. As the study has clearly demonstrated, the *Kādambarīnāṭaka* is by no means a work of decadence, though it is a relatively late product from the fourteenth century.[1] In fact, it seems fair to say that the play is a very fine piece of *kāvya* comparable to those of great authors such as Śūdraka, Kālidāsa, Bhavabhūti and Rājaśekhara. Among Narasiṁha's numerous impressive innovations introduced into his dramatic version of the famous novel are the ingeniously altered sequence of incidents,[2] and the *garbhāṅka* or play within a play[3] in Act V, which seems to add a special enjoyment to his whole work. It is strongly hoped that this introduction to the *Kādambarīnāṭaka* prepared in the light of traditional Indian dramatic and poetic criticism, together with the translation of it, will help the play to secure a recognized position in the field of the Sanskrit-Prakrit dramatic literature, and that this volume will encourage scholars in the field to explore the great ocean of later Sanskrit-Prakrit plays in the same unprejudiced manner.

Notes

1. *Vide* Intro., chap. I.
2. *Vide* Intro., chap. VI.
3. *Vide* Intro., chap. VIII.

PART TWO

A Complete English Translation of the *Kādambarīnāṭaka* of Narasiṁha with Detailed Textual Notes

Note on the Translation

THE researcher cannot agree more with the late Dr. M. Coulson, who said:

> Translators from all languages have a difficult and thankless task: in the end there are no degrees of success, only degrees of failure. But translators of Sanskrit *kāvya* have more to complain about than most. To translate a Sanskrit stanza so that it merely bores rather than bewilders the reader can be an achievement in itself. . .[1]

Now, this English translation of the *Kādambarīnāṭaka* may be nothing other than a good specimen of a high degree of failure. Nevertheless, the researcher strongly hopes that it will be of some use since, to the best of his knowledge, it is at least the only translation of the play now available in a modern language.

The researcher has tried his best to make his translation as close to the original as he can; in other words, it is not intended to be a free and readable translation, but rather a literal but accurate one. It should be noted here, however, that he has made no special effort to distinguish the play's Sanskrit and Prakrit; as a result, virtually the same level of English is used for both. Similarly, the play's verses are not versified but put into normally four to eight lines of prose English with a slight difference. A versified translation of a Sanskrit or Prakrit verse does not necessarily convey the spirit of the original better. Among other problems in translating the play, the researcher has consistently translated the two oft-used stage directions *svagatam* and *ātmagatam* not as 'aside' but as 'to oneself' in order to avoid confusion with *janāntikam, apavāritam* and *apavārya* used indiscriminately in the play to mean "aside (to someone else)." Moreover, he has translated the indeclinable participles in stage directions in such a way as to clearly show that the action expressed by an indeclinable participle is completed before the next action. For instance, *parikramya* is translated as 'having walked around,' 'after walking around' or 'walks around and . . .,' but never simply 'walking around,' which almost all other translators adopt, but which appears quite inaccurate to the researcher. This method of translating indeclinable participles is helpful in distinguishing them from a relatively small number of present participles used in the play's stage directions such as *parikrāman*, which is strictly 'walking around,' or 'as he walks around.' Lastly, since this translation is primarily intended for the reader sufficiently familiar with Sanskrit-Prakrit literature, the researcher confines himself to explaining in notes, as a general rule, only things that appear peculiar to the *Kādambarīnāṭaka*, not those that appear familiar enough from other works: mythological episodes, deities' names and epithets, plants' and animals' names, customs, poetic and dramatic conventions, and the like.

Note

1. M. Coulson, *Three Sanskrit Plays* (Harmondsworth, England: Penguin Books Ltd., 1981), Intro., pp. 15-16.

Dramatis Personae

ALL the major characters and most of the minor ones in the *Kādambarīnāṭaka* are given below in alphabetical order with some comments on them; the Sanskrit speakers among them are marked with an asterisk.

ASSISTANT*:	[*Pāripārśvaka*]; appears in the Prologue with Director (1).
BARDS*:	[*Vaitālika*s]; serve in the royal palaces.
CANDRĀPĪḌA*:	The main hero of the play; the moon reborn on the earth; the son of Tārāpīḍa and Vilāsavatī; the Crown Prince of India; the lover of Kādambarī.
CHAMBERLAIN(1)*:	[*Kañcukin*]; serves in the royal palace of Tārāpīḍa.
CHAMBERLAIN(2)*:	[*Kañcukin*]; named Kṣīroda; serves in the royal palace of Citraratha.
CITRARATHA*:	The Supreme *gandharva* King on Mt. Hemakūṭa; the father of Kādambarī.
DHĀRĀDHARA*:	The groom of Candrāpīḍa.
DIRECTOR(1)*:	[*Sūtradhāra*]; appears in the Prologue with his Assistant.
DIRECTOR(2)*:	[*Sūtradhāra*]; appears in the Prologue of the *garbhāṅka*.
DIVINE MAN*:	[*Divyapuruṣa*]; the spirit of the moon.
GAURĪ:	The Queen of Haṁsa; an *apsaras*; the mother of Mahāśvetā.
HAṀSA*:	The second *gandharva* king; the father of Mahāśvetā.
HĀRĪTA*:	A young ascetic; the son of Jābāli; saves Parrot (1) from exhaustion; only mentioned.
INDRĀYUDHA:	The horse of Candrāpīḍa; Kapiñjala reborn; never speaks.
IRĀVATĪ:	The chowrie bearer [*cāmaragrāhiṇī*] of Kādambarī.

JĀBĀLI*:	A sage; the father of Hārīta; tells Parrot (1) of his past; only mentioned.
JESTER:	[*Vidūṣaka*]; named Dramiḍadhārmika; the comic companion of Candrāpīḍa.
KĀDAMBARĪ:	The main heroine of the play; an *apsaras*; the daughter of Citraratha and Madirā; the beloved of Candrāpīḍa.
KAPIÑJALA*:	A divine ascetic youth; the friend of Puṇḍarīka.
KEYŪRAKA*:	A *gandharva* youth; the messenger of Kādambarī.
KINNARAS:	Animals similar to centaurs; allure Candrāpīḍa into the hermitage of Mahāśvetā.
LAKṢMĪ:	A goddess; the mother of Puṇḍarīka; appears on the earth in the form of an Untouchable girl.
MADALEKHĀ:	A female companion of Kādambarī.
MADIRĀ:	The Queen of Citraratha; the mother of Kādambarī.
MAHĀŚVETĀ:	The secondary heroine of the play; an *apsaras*; the daughter of Haṁsa and Gaurī; the best friend of Kādambarī; the beloved of Puṇḍarīka.
MANORAMĀ:	The wife of Śukanāsa; the mother of Vaiśampāyana; a partial incarnation of Lakṣmī.
MĀTAṄGA:	A hunter; catches Parrot (1).
MEGHANĀDA*:	The son of Valāhaka.
MYNAH:	[*Śārikā*]; named Kālindī; a female pet bird of Kādambarī; the wife of Parrot (2); quarrels with him.
PARROT (1)*:	[*Śuka*]; Vaiśampāyana reborn.
PARROT (2)*:	[*Śuka*]; named Prahāsaka; a male pet bird of Kādambarī; the husband of the Mynah; quarrels with her.
PATRALEKHĀ:	The female companion and betel box bearer [*tāmbūlakaraṅkavāhinī*] of Candrāpīḍa; the moon's favorite wife, Rohiṇī, born on the earth as a daughter of the King of the Kulūtas.
PUṆḌARĪKA*:	A divine ascetic youth; the son of Śvetaketu and Lakṣmī; the lover of Mahāśvetā.
ROHIṆĪ:	The favorite wife of the moon; *vide* also PATRALEKHĀ.
SAUDĀMINĪ:	A portress [*pratihārī*]; serves Candrāpīḍa.

ŚŪDRAKA*:	The King of Vidiśā; Candrāpīḍa reborn.
ŚUKANĀSA*:	A minister of King Tārāpīḍa; the father of Vaiśampāyana; a partial incarnation of Śvetaketu.
ŚVETAKETU*:	A divine sage; the father of Puṇḍarīka; only mentioned.
SYLVAN DEITY*:	[*Vanadevatā*] of the Caitraratha forest; named Navamālikā; a friend of Taralikā.
TAMĀLIKĀ:	A female companion of Kādambarī.
TARALIKĀ:	The betel box bearer [*tāmbūlakaraṅkavāhinī*] of Mahāśvetā.
TĀRĀPĪḌA*:	The King of India; the father of Candrāpīḍa.
UNTOUCHABLE GIRL:	[*Caṇḍālakanyakā*]; Lakṣmī in a temporary human form on the earth.
VAIŚAMPĀYANA:	The secondary hero of the play; the son of Śukanāsa and Manoramā; Puṇḍarīka reborn; the best friend of Candrāpīḍa.
VALĀHAKA*:	The general of Candrāpīḍa's army.
VIJAYĀ:	A portress [*pratihārī*]; serves Kādambarī.
VILĀSAVATĪ:	The Queen of Tārāpīḍa; the mother of Candrāpīḍa.

In addition to these characters, there are various kinds of both male* and female servants, divine actors* and actresses who perform the *garbhāṅka*, and the like.

The *Kādambarīnāṭaka* of *Narasiṁha*[1]

OPENING BENEDICTION

Who bestows benefit upon the right-minded
With his ever-gracious risings,[2]
Whom the virtuous declare to be
Another body of the great[3] god,[4]
Who repeatedly expels a flood of darkness[5]
And goes united with moonlight —
May the friend of white water lilies,[6]
The abode of digits,[7] bring you good fortune! [1][8]

PROLOGUE

[*Enter the* DIRECTOR *after the Opening Benediction.*]

DIRECTOR [*Joyfully*]:

We have a poet of taste,
A wonderful story,
A charming arrangement of words,
Rasa manifested, and
An audience appreciative of merits;
Moreover, we are proficient.
Now, what other than these[9]
Would be dear to us? [2]

[*After turning around towards the dressing room*] Friend, aren't[10] the actors ready yet? How long does our assembly of people of taste here have to wait, impatient[11] to see Kādambarī in a festival for the Lord of Mt. Śoṇa?[12]

[*Having entered*]

ASSISTANT: What are you talking about, sir? Indeed worthy to be heard is the stream of excellent speech in prose[13] called the *Kādambarī*[14] of Bāṇabhaṭṭa. But then, how do you wish to act it out, sir?

DIRECTOR: You surely haven't heard of this. Listen now!

Brilliantly arranged,
  Productive of *bhāva*s and *rasa*s,
That nectar of literature
  Is an elixir of life
To the ears of the learned;
  A certain author[15] has made that
Into a hospitality to their eyes
  Under the guise of a *nāṭaka*.[16] [3]

ASSISTANT [*delightedly*]: Sir, if so,

Now people of taste[17] could[18]
  Directly experience the fragrance
Of sandal trees' blossoms, and
  Even taste the juice of red sugar cane's fruit. [4][19]

Now you should favor me by announcing the name of this author who has control over speech.

DIRECTOR: All right, I'll tell you.

You know that family of poets honored by the refined,
  Where the glorious goddess of speech is ever present;
There was born Gaṅgādhara, a son of Siddhanātha,
  A scholar whose glory was widely known
Especially for his great scholarship, and who lived
  For the benefit of literary composition.[20] [5]

He has this middle son
  Who is called Narasiṁha —
Know him to be the celebrated author
  Of this literary work. [6][21]

ASSISTANT [*recollecting*]: That's right, sir.[22]

Since he is quite capable of attaining proficiency[23]
  In all the ten forms of drama,
There should not be any surprise in our minds;
  His elder brother is the poet Viśvanātha,
Whose beautiful speech[24] is like the fragrance
  Of a river of nectar,

And who is preeminent on the earth
As the leader of people of taste. [7]

DIRECTOR: Now get ready[25] for your part.

ASSISTANT: As my master directs. [*Exit.*]

DIRECTOR: Now I'll worship the ṣtage. [*After walking around*]

O Mother, victory to you!
Victory to you, entertainer of the world!
Moon's digit to the ocean
Of the joy of performance!
Giver of good fortune to actors' families!
Venerable tutelary goddess of the stage! [8]

[*After looking[26] around, scattering[27] handfuls of flowers*]

Why! a group of actors have started acting. For

Some are ingeniously flourishing their hands[28]
In their perfect performance of gesticulation;[29]
Others are preparing literary compositions here
With *rāgas*[30] conformable to their *rasas*.
Some are, as I am, putting on their costumes
Along with crowns, necklaces and the like;[31]
Others are striving[32] to express *bhāvas*
With their minds dutiful. [9]

Now I'll play the part of Kapiñjala, a divine ascetic to be introduced before all of these who are in special costumes. [*After going near the dressing room and turning around with a gesture*][33] Now I've become Kapiñjala by the power of contrivance! [*Exit.*][34]

END OF THE PROLOGUE

Notes

1. Before the title *Kādambarīnāṭakam*, the *M.M.* has *śrīḥ, śrīgaṇeśāya maṅgalam* and *śrīśāradāyai namaḥ*; *vide* Intro., chap. II.
2. *V.K.: śaśvatprasannodayaḥ; M.M.: śaśva(?)nodayas; M.M.V.2.:(-)tprasanno(-).*
3. *M.M.V.1.* and *V.K.*: *nahato*; *M.M.*: *mahito*.
4. Śiva. The moon is said to be one of the eight visible forms of the god Śiva; *vide* the opening benediction of Kālidāsa's *Abhijñānaśākuntala*.

5. *M.M.V.2.* and *V.K.: tamasaḥ; M.M.: tamas.*
6. *Kumudinīmitraḥ* here seems to be used in place of *kumudinīpatiḥ* (lord of-) for a metrical reason.
7. *M.M.V.2.* and *V.K.: kalānāṁ; M.M.: kalanāṁ.*
8. This opening benedictory verse somewhat resembles the first of the two of Vāmanabhaṭṭabāṇa's *Kanakalekhākalyāṇa; vide* Intro., chap. VII.
9. *V.K.: ato; M.M.: ito.*
10. *M.M.V.2.* supplies *na*; *V.K.* follows.
11. *M.M.V.1.* and *V.K.: -utsukaḥ sahṛdayasamājaḥ; M.M.: -utsukasahṛdayasamājaṁ.*
12. Probably Śiva; *vide* Intro., chap. III.
13. *H.S.: gadyamayasūktiniṣyandaḥ; M.M.: gadyakṣayasūkti-; M.M.V.2.: gadyakṣayah sūkti-; V.K.: gadyamayaḥ sūkti-.*
14. *M.M.V.2.* and *V.K.: kādambarīnāmā; M.M.: -nāma.*
15. *M.M.* and *V.K.: kavinā; M.M.V.2.: kavitā.*
16. *Vide* Intro., chap. V.
17. *M.M.V.2.* and *V.K.: rasikaiḥ; M.M.: (?)sikaiḥ.*
18. *M.M.V.2.* and *V.K.: pāryeta; M.M.: cceta.*
19. The point here seems to be that the absent or long-past is made perceivable as if it were actually present.
20. Or: whose satisfaction arose from literary composition (*sāhityasauhityabhūḥ*).
21. *M.M.V.1.* and *V.K.*:
    tasyaiṣa madhyamaḥ putro narasiṁha itīritaḥ |
    viśrutaḥ sa tu kartāsyāḥ kṛter ity avadhāraya ||
    M.M. gives only the incomplete and corrupt
    tasyaiṣa madhyamaḥ putraḥ narasiṁha iti kṛti(tī, M.M. V.2.)kartā kṛter asyāḥ ||
22. *V.K.: bhāva; M.M.: vas; M.M.V.1.: bhāvas.*
23. *M.M.* and *V.K.: nirūḍhim āḍhaukitum; M.M.V.1.; -ācoda(kate).*
24. *M.M. V.2. and V.K.: (-surabhi)sūktir (asyāgrajaḥ); M.M.; (- -) (?) (rasyāgraja); M.M. V.1.; (- -) rāśir (asyāgrajaḥ).*
25. *M.M.: -parigrahāya; V.K.: -parigrahaṇāya.*
26. *M.M.V.1.* and *V.K.: vilokya; M.M.: (-to) valokya.*
27. *V.K.: vikiran; M.M.: vikaran.*
28. *V.K.: hastān; M.M.: hastaiḥ.*
29. *V.K.: (prauḍhāṅga)hāra-; M.M.: (-)bhāra-.*
30. Modes.
31. *V.K.: -hārādikam; M.M.: -bhārādhikam; M.M.V.1.: -bhārādikam.*
32. *Samujjṛmbhate* is substituted here for *-jṛmbhante* for a metrical reason.
33. He acts as if he had just come out of the dressing room.
34. *V.K.* supplies (*iti*) *niṣkrāntaḥ.*

Śuddhaviṣkambhaka
Prelude to Act One

[Enter KAPIÑJALA.]

KAPIÑJALA: Oh, a long time has passed indeed!

The moon and that Puṇḍarīka of Lakṣmī
Were born here at the same time;[1]
The two youths were brought into existence on the earth
Owing to suffering each other's curse. [10]

[*Having reflected*] Ah![2] the venerable Śvetaketu with a name auspicious to utter, though devoted[3] to the eternal *brahman*, has extremely great affection for his son. For[4]

Since he heard the news I told him about his son,
Which was obstructive to his asceticism,[5]
He has been performing some rite to preserve his son's life,
His anger well-restrained.[6] [11]

Moreover, that great, merciful sage[7] who shows kindness to his disciple

Is going to put an end[8]
Today by a quick means
To the curse[9] laid in anger upon me
With the words "You, become a horse!"
By some rider of a heavenly vehicle
Kicked by my foot in the sky[10]
When I was returning from the moon's presence
After abandoning my friend. [12]

[*Having acted recollecting*] Just now my preceptor directed me with the words "Dear Kapiñjala, Puṇḍarīka's mother, Lakṣmī, now stays without wearing any ornaments at all in order that his fate may have a fortunate end.[11] Now you must enter into Indrāyudha, a horse not born from a womb, and lead the moon in the form of Candrāpīḍa to the Caitraratha forest for his meeting with Kādambarī. After that, by means of that Mahāśvetā, your friend — his attendant in the form of Vaiśampāyana — will depart from his human form." Now I'll act[12] accordingly. [*Acting descent from the sky*] Oh,[13] how hard it is to take out arrows sunk deeply in the hearts of living beings!

Though constantly consoled by the great sage
    With words flowing like nectar,
I have passed all this time
    With difficulty;
Now this fire of grief[14]
    Born of separation from my friend,
Obtaining scope,
    Gives even more torment to my heart. [13]

[*Having sighed*] Oh, it's impossible to escape the play[15] of accursed fate!

For that friend of mine
    At once fell in love with her.[16]
Which man does not get bewitched
    By girls' naturally charming emotions?[17]
Still, this is not right:
    Angry at the curse laid upon himself,[18]
The moon immediately laid[19] upon him
    A curse for separation in two lives. [14]

[*Having pondered*] Or rather, this is the greatest wonder. For the moon himself, who has remembered his relationship with Mahāśvetā, is preserving my friend's body[20] uninjured though his consciousness is yoked to another body. [*After walking and looking around*] Why! now the sun,[21] which has appeared from behind Mt. Śaṅkaraśarāsana, is beginning to illuminate India.

Beautiful with corals on the coast of the sky-ocean,
    A few rays of the hot sun participating in its rising
Are breaking the darkness, letting lotus forests bloom
    And setting ruddy geese free from sorrow. [15]

[*with a glance*] Oh! here near Suvarṇapura is the camp of Ujjayinī's King, relieved of its fatigue due to the world conquest by sojourning for three or four days. And here in the middle of it is Candrāpīḍa staying in his tent, his morning duties performed.

He — who has ascended the throne,
    Surrounded by princes with folded hands —
Stays absolutely unagitated,
    All his enemies vanquished,
His silken upper garment's hems shaking
    With the wind from the chowries
In choice women's[22] hands, and
    Looking up at prancing Indrāyuddha held by a groom. [16]

[*Having pondered*] Since I'm engaged[23] in another matter, it's not quite proper for me to console Mahāśvetā, though she's staying nearby, with the words "The moon will surely[24] revive the lord of your life." Now,

Let the *gandharva* Princess,
    Who[25] disregarded in her self-choice ceremony
Even the sons of the guardians of the regions,
    Fall in love with Tārāpīḍa's son!
Let Haṁsa's daughter disturb
    Her friend's state of firmness[26] even more!
Then I will console the two
    By telling them of their future happiness. [17]

All right. Now I'll deposit my body in that nectarous Acchoda lake not too far from here, and undertake my preceptor's directions at the right time. [*Exit.*]

END OF THE *ŚUDDHAVIṢKAMBHAKA*
PRELUDE TO ACT ONE

Notes

1. *V.K.: sahajāv iha; M.M.: sahajanmajau; M.M. V.2.: -janmanau* (instead of *-janmānau* for a metrical reason).
2. *M.M.: aho; M.M.V.1.* and *V.K.: aye.*
3. *M.M.* and *V.K.: niṣṭhita-; M.M.V.1.: pariniṣṭhita-.*
4. *M.M.V.1.* and *V.K.: (putravātsalya)ṁ yataḥ; M.M.: (-)layatā.*
5. *V.K.: putrasya tattaporodhi; M.M.: tapo viruddham api; M.M.VI.: putrasya tattitorodhi.*
6. *M.M.V.1.* and *V.K.: (-ṁ) susaṁhṛtā-; M.M.: (-m) upasaṁhṛtā-.*
7. *Maharṣiṇā-* in the last *pāda* of the following verse.
8. *Nirvāhyatām.*
9. *M.M.: yaṁ (śāpaṁ); V.K.* gives *ya* with both a *visarga* and an *anusvāra* (misprint).
10. *M.M.V.1.* and *V.K.: (kilā)bhra(saraṇau); M.M.: (-)bhi(-).*

11. *H.S.*: *asya vidheḥ śubhodarkasaṁvidhāne (a)lam abhṛtakaṅkaṇāste; M.M.*: *alam asya vidheḥ rasya(abhyu, M.M.V.2.) racitopakaraṇasambhṛtiṣu; M.M.V.1.*: . . . *śubhodarkasaṁvidhāne bhṛtakaṅkaṇāste*; V.K. follows *M.M.V.1.* but omits *alam*. This portion also means "she stays wearing (*bhṛta-*) only her marriage thread (*kaṅkaṇa, -ṇam*)."
12. *M.M.* and *V.K.*: *kartavyam*; *M.M.V.1.*: *anuṣṭhātavyam*.
13. *M.M.* and *V.K.*: *hanta*; *M.M.V.1.* repeats.
14. *M.M.V.2.* and *V.K.*: *śokavahniḥ (saṁtāpam)*; *M.M.*: *-vahni(saṁ-)*.
15. *M.M.*: *vilāsānām*; *V.K.*: *vilasitānām*.
16. *V.K.*: *yad abhavad ayaṁ raktas tasyāṁ suhṛn mama sāṁpratam*; *M.M.*: *labhata suhṛdas tasyā(?)te vaśīkriyate na kaḥ*; *M.M.V.1.* gives the reading adopted by *V.K.* except that it has *mana* instead of *mama*.
17. *V.K.*: *prakṛtisubhagair bhāvaiḥ strīṇāṁ vaśīkriyate na kaḥ*; *M.M.*: *-bhāvair dhairyoparodhini manmadhe*; *M.M.V.1.* gives the reading adopted by *V.K.* except that it has *bhāvaistrīṇām*, not *bhāvaiḥ strīṇām*.
18. *V.K.*: *svaśāpakṛtakrudhā*; *M.M.*: *(?)dhṛtakrudhā*; *M.M.V.2.*: *svaśāpa(dhṛta-)*.
19. *M.M.* and *V.K.*: *vihitaḥ*; *M.M.V.1.*: *nihitaḥ*.
20. *V.K.*: *suhṛccharīram*; *M.M.*: *-charīram api*; *M.M.V.1.*: *-charīraṁ vaiśaṃpāyanasya hitam*.
21. *M.M.*: *aruṇasārathiḥ*; *M.M.V.2.* and *V.K.*: *anūrusārathiḥ*.
22. *Vārastrī-*. It seems more appropriate here to take this word in its Vedic sense of a choice woman or beautiful woman instead of in its later sense of a courtesan or prostitute. Cf. *vārayoṣit*, which seems to be used in the same sense by Bhavabhūti; *vide Bhavabhūti's Mālatīmādhava*, ed. with Jagaddhara's comm. by M.R. Kale, Act I, after vs. 32; but the commentator takes it in its later sense of a prostitute (*gaṇikā*); *vide* also A.K. Warder, *Indian Kāvya Literature*, vol. IV, p. 283.
23. *V.K.*: *-vyāpṛta-*; *M.M.*: *-vyāvṛta-*.
24. *H.S.*: *(pratyāsannām apy) avaśyam (oṣadhīpatir - mahāśvetām)*; *M.M.*: *(- api) vaśyam (- - -)*; *M.M.V.1.*: *(pratyāsannāmahāśvetām) (oṣadhī-)*; *VK.*: *(pratyāsannām api mahāśvetām) (oṣadhī-)*.
25. *M.M.*: *yā*; *V.K.*: *sā*.
26. *V.K.*: *dhairyasthitim*; *M.M.*: *dhairye sthitim*.

Act One

[Off stage]

BARD: Prince, let this[1] Fortune of summer congratulate[2] you on your completion of the ceremony of consecration after your world conquest!

Revered for your splendor hard to resist
  And possessed of virtues spoken of,
You and the sun, two among the powerful,
  Have reached the northern region;
Through one of you, enemies' fame
  Has attained complete destruction,[3]
And through the other, a mass of snow[4]
  Causing numbness to people has disappeared. [18]

[Enter CANDRĀPĪḌA *as described, his* JESTER *and betel box bearer.]*

CANDRĀPĪḌA: Ah! the passage of spring is not honored even if it is greatly engaged in its devotion to the desire to conquer. *[Longingly]* For at this time especially in Ujjayinī,[5]

The Siprā[6] River must have her water
  Gentle with a host of tall-stalked lotuses;
The gardens on her banks must be[7] charming[8]
  With the scent of jasmine flowers;
Mālava women's faces must be shining
  Sweetly with honey wine —
What ever belonging to Rati's husband
  Could not conquer the world? [19]

JESTER: Friend, it's quite appropriate you remember[9] the long-familiar Avanti country from time to time. For even I still can't forget the forests of the Vindhya region,[10] which were our dwelling places.[11] There anger and laughter were easily obtained from a herd of monkeys whose dwellings were burnt in a forest fire,[12] and jokes were made by a group of travelers deceived and bewitched by going after a mirage.

PATRALEKHĀ *[with a smile]*:[13] This preoccupation fits your foresterhood and mercilessness.

CANDRĀPĪḌA: Friend Dramiḍadhārmika, don't you really miss[14] sporting in the Vindhya forest?

JESTER: Surely not! Surely not! For the goddess residing in the Vindhya forest has shown me a kindness for a long time by granting me your positive[15] friendship with me.

[*Having entered*]

PORTRESS [*with a bow*]: May the Crown Prince be victorious! May he be victorious! Here's the leader of a hunters' army, Nirghātaka,[16] roaming nearby, who informs you that his huntsmen roving in a forest adjacent to a north-western foot of Mt. Kailāsa called Candrapatha have found a wood abundant in tigers, lions, boars and rhinoceroses, and so suitable for hunting.

CANDRĀPĪḌA [*eagerly and energetically*]: Saudāminī, tell Nirghātaka to go ahead and surround the forest with screens, and that I'm coming soon.

PORTRESS: As the Crown Prince commands. [*Exit.*]

JESTER: Tut tut! The rain has ceased, but a flood of mist won't stop;[17] that is, his conquest of kingdoms on the earth has been accomplished, but[18] he's still amusing himself by slaughtering wild deer.

CANDRĀPĪḌA: Patralekhā, make preparations for hunting.

PATRALEKHĀ: Here's the paraphernalia for roaming about forests.

CANDRĀPĪḌA: [*having acted taking it, acting holding it*]: Patralekhā, you go inside. I'm now attracted by the desire to hunt[19] in the divine forest.

PATRALEKHĀ: Prince, please travel carefully in the forests full of beasts of prey. [*Exit.*]

CANDRĀPĪḌA: Friend, do you want[20] to see the hunting, too?

JESTER: Our[21] ancestors, fearing impurity, have avoided entering even a sacrificial enclosure where there's a mass of wild beasts cut up. So how can I, a calf-killer,[22] possibly approach the region evil with abundant slaughtering?[23]

CANDRĀPĪḌA [*after smiling*]: This Brahminhood of yours, thus handed down by succession, shouldn't be violated. [*Towards the dressing room*] Dear Dhārādhara, bring Indrāyudha quickly!

[*Having entered with* INDRĀYUDHA, *a whip tied up*[24] *and his hands folded*]

DHĀRĀDHARA[25] [*having bowed*]: Master, listen! This saddled[26] royal horse,

His head and face bent up and down,
    His hoof[27] scratching the ground in front
And neighing loudly with a sweet glance,

Permits you to mount[28] him. (20)

[*Exit after giving him.*]

CANDRĀPĪḌA [*having observed him*]: Why! he looks as if he had ascended another class by being possessed by some special, unsurpassed being.

JESTER: Sir, you should never think[29] otherwise. He's really quick[30] at the times of activities for excellent horses.

CANDRĀPĪḌA [*recollecting*]: Ah! when I completed my studies,[31] Father showed his greatest affection to me by granting me this horse-gem sprung from the water of the ocean, with which he had been presented by the King of Persia. Is he

The chief of birds, who has left them
    And descended[32] to the surface of the earth,
Thinking, "Would an arrow, though unconscious, not fly
    Because of the existence of its wings?[33] Or is he
The god of wind become a horse, or rather its mind,
    Because of his affection[34] for a mare?
He attains[35] visibility when in a solid state
    In order to demonstrate he is the lightest. [21]

[*Having acted mounting him*] Friend,[36] please tell Minister Vaiśampāyana to supervise the camp carefully until our return.

JESTER: Sir, as you said, I think you'll get married right there and live in a divine mansion.

CANDRĀPĪḌA: Friend, that's surely not impossible.[37] Look!

Which man will attain happiness or unhappiness?
    And when and where?
Who ever[38] can ascertain that?
    For it is a sport of fate. [22]

JESTER: All right. Now I'll approach the Minister's presence. Hurry up[39] for the attainment of your object. [*Exit.*]

CANDRĀPĪḌA [*urging on* INDRĀYUDHA]: Ah, how fast[40] this excellent horse[41] is! For I have instantly entered this very remote hunting forest.

[*Sung in the air*]

On the earth, there may be women[42]
    Possessed of youthfulness, beauty and charm;

Even so, Kādambarī[43] is a princess
Endowed with beauty of an uncommon kind. [23]

CANDRĀPĪḌA [*having heard*]: The meaning of the song is heartstirring. Moreover,

The word *Kādambarī* has captured my heart,
Whether it has its corresponding object or not;
If not,[44] oh! the flower-bowed Love's[45] action
Would be without its support. [24]

Now, where's the source[46] of this? [*Having looked with his eyes turned*[47] *on all sides, in astonishment*] Oh! what are these paired animals seen with wonderful forms? [*Having reflected*] They surely must be a pair of *kinnara*s I've heard of before in stories of tradition.

For they possess bodies indistinguishable from men's,
Resemble a horse by the face alone,
Allure with the sound of a sweet song
And oh! cannot be found anywhere.[48] [25]

I should learn accurately[49] from them the story of the girl-gem. Now I'll capture them alive. [*Having observed them as he tries to urge on* INDRĀYUDHA, *in astonishment*][50]

Indrāyudha is running after them
Thus by himself;
First through my effort,
But now what is the cause?
Is it his jealously born of another's speed?
Or his desire for the song?
Or his affection for his species?
Or something else? [26]

[*Having acted traveling fast*]

Raising his neck and erecting his ear-sheaths,
The horse is indeed drinking[51] in the way;
The mountains seem to retreat by themselves
For fear of kicks by his hooves;
This unique large forest, I imagine,
Shows many trees at the same time,[52]
For he seems to stand still right in front of them[53]
With his body become motionless. [27][54]

[*After looking ahead*] Oh, how strange this is! The pair of *kinnaras* are already a great distance away from the horse-gem in spite of his extreme swiftness.[55] That is, they —

Repeatedly casting a frightened glance this way,
    Their necks turned around,
And covering each other with their bodies
    In order to protect them out of affection —
For a moment seem catchable by the hand
    But at the next moment[56] seem to traverse a path
Almost impossible to perceive with the eyes
    On account of its very great distance.[57] [28][58]

[*Having observed them, agitatedly*] Oh, why! they are climbing to the peak of a mountain in front of me[59] while I'm watching them. [*After pondering*] This region is unsuitable for a horse to go in,[60] for it's beset with crores of peaks of large rocks. [*Stopping the whip*] Oh, what a pity! The sprout of the desire in my heart for the story of Kādambarī seems to have been cut off. And my hunting retinue are remotely separated. Moreover, another difficulty has befallen me: the sun is scorching my forehead now. For thus

The sovereign of the sky,
    The glorious leader of the planets,
Who was raising the gem *kaustubha* at the start,
    Has reached midday and is blazing;
Unable to endure his own heat,
    He is surrounded on all sides
By hundreds of rays drinking up
    Round shades under trees. [29]

[*Having looked at* INDRĀYUDHA] He's really very tired. But where can I refresh him? [*Having looked around anxiously, with a glance*] I've found a sign of a reservoir of water. For here's

Some path where lotus fibers are mixed
    with the shoots of *śaivala* weeds,
And which is scattered with half[61]-destroyed hosts
    Of white water lilies and lotuses
And is muddy with the very fresh footprints
    Of wild elephants that passed here not too long ago. [30]

All right. Then I'll go along this path[62] immersed in an avenue of *tamāla* trees.

[*After going a small distance*] One born with sense organs has obtained a unique delight now. For

Here in front is some[63] beautiful lake
  Full of cold, sweet, pure water
Where *kalahaṁsa* and *mallikākṣa* geese are melodious
  And red[64] and blue lotuses are diffusing their scents. [31]

Friend Indrāyudha, from now on I won't consider you, whose subtle[65] mental function is thus ascertainable, to be common with other horses.

You are exhausted from traversing the long forest paths.
  Relieve your fatigue under the umbrageous trees![66]
Sport in the lake as you please!
  And take[67] a walk on the grounds of its bank
Green with the shoots of *dūrvā* grass! [32]

Now I'll sit down on this shady, cool slab of the crystal stairs and enjoy the breeze from the waves. [*Having done so*] Ah! even in desolate forests, fortunate people easily find suitable cushions. For

The sandy beach is covered
  With wild creepers' flowers trickling honey;
Geese approach the honey
  With gagglings charming to the ears;
This wind from the billows
  Brings[68] me very cold water drops;
And the delightful fragrance of lotuses
  Drinks up my fatigue born of the heat. [33[

[*Having observed* INDRĀYUDHA] Luckily, he's regaining his usual condition. [*Having observed him again*] Why! now he appears to be listening to something, his head put down, ears erected and eyes half-closed.[69] [*Having given ear*] Oh! where in this uninhabited forest does this come from — a very charming song mixed with the pluckings of the lute? Here's great scope for my curiosity. [*Having mounted* INDRĀYUDHA *and observed*] I can pursue the sound of this song without any effort. For

Their necks raised[70] and ears pricked up towards it,
  Walking with their mouths dropping mouthfuls of grass
And their eyes' corners closed tremulously with tears,
  These deer are telling me the way. [34]

[*After walking around and looking*] Oh! this almost deserted temple looks very much like one of Śiva. [*Having seen as he dismounts from his horse*] Luckily, Dhārādhara has arrived here, following me very fast. Dhārādhara, take Indrāyudha now.

[DHĀRĀDHARA *enters, takes* INDRĀYUDHA *and exits.*]

[*With a gesture of going inside*] Ah! this is the holy four-faced god: an icon of his phallus made of pure pearl stones and worshiped[71] with fresh golden lotuses. [*Having looked elsewhere with folded hands*]But who's this girl?

She is beautiful with a calm, white, bright body,[72]
    And playing the lute[73] for Śiva;
She looks like Rati practising asceticism
    For her beloved, who has done wrong. [35]

Through the power of fate, various unexpected events inevitably happen to those who are born. For thus

On one hand is the hunting;
    On the other are the pair of *kinnaras*.[74]
On one hand we are;
    On the other is this divine lake.
On one hand is the song;
    On the other is this beautiful maiden.
Oh, what is fate trying to accomplish? [36]

This asceticism does not befit
    Her youth and beauty.

[*Having observed her*]

Besides, I do not find anything
    Inauspicious about her. [37]

Then I'll wait quietly until she completes the song, and ask her.[75] [*Waits thus.*]

[*Enter* MAHĀŚVETĀ *as described.*]

MAHĀŚVETĀ [*sings*]:

O moon-crested one,
    Quickly do[76] me[77] as well
That favor by which Rati was united[78]
    With her beloved[79] once again! [38]

CANDRĀPĪḌA [*in admiration*]: Ah, what a perfect knowledge of music!

The sweetness of nectar's taste
May touch the arrangements of the notes;
This wave of the notes
May attain loveliness in its own ways;
And if the measures assume clearness,
And the scales flash[80] —
Yet where possibly[81] is this mixture of sounds
Arisen from the lute's throat? [39]

MAHĀŚVETĀ [*after putting down the lute in front, to herself*]: Oh, who's this glorious one possessed of a body that appears gentle and profound as if it were decorum itself?

CANDRĀPĪḌA [*with folded hands*]: Lady,[82] Candrāpīḍa, the son of India's sovereign Tārāpīḍa, salutes you!

MAHĀŚVETĀ [*to herself*]: Why! this is the Prince of the middle world, whose beauty, virtue, knowledge and prowess are described[83] by pairs of bards in Father's presence. [*Aloud*] May your desires be without obstacles! [*Stands up and offers appropriate hospitality.*]

CANDRĀPĪḌA [*to himself*]: This is indeed a result of her asceticism.

The trees spontaneously grant[84] flowers and fruit,
Their best branches bent down whenever appropriate;
The water deities with invisible bodies offer water
Deposited in the folds of lotus petals. [40]

[*Aloud*] Lady, you have taken this great trouble for a person expecting only a favor.

MAHĀŚVETĀ: Glorious one, what ever is the reason that you are protecting this place?

CANDRĀPĪḌA [*tells her exactly.*]

MAHĀŚVETĀ: There's no need to talk much. The pair of *kinnaras* have done us a service.

CANDRĀPĪḌĀ [*to himself*]: I should learn her story, too. And[85] I think this is the right time to ask her. But modesty very much confuses me with a double policy whether it's a good plan or not.[86] [*Looks at* MAHĀŚVETĀ.]

MAHĀŚVETĀ [*having observed him*]: Glorious one, that's enough. I've developed friendship for you. So ask me privately and confidently now.[87] I regard you as a worshiper of Śiva.[88] Do you want to ask about my unfortunate life?

CANDRĀPĪḌĀ [*to himself*]:[89] The Lady has a great skill to find out internal thoughts accurately. [*Aloud*][90] Yes, I do, indeed.

MAHĀŚVETĀ [*with a sigh*]: Why am I going to make your[91] flower-tender heart sad with my personal story unbearable because of my encounter with thousands of miseries? [*Sheds tears.*]

CANDRĀPĪḌA [*to himself*]: This shock surely must be due to separation from her beloved. For

She is weeping agitatedly with a voice
Choked in her throat pressed by hardship,
Sprinkling her upper garment with tears
Which for a moment look like pearls
Concealed in her eye-oysters,
Then unite[92] into larger and larger drops,
Heap up throughout the edges of her eyelashes
And fall like a stream down her cheek-walls. [41]

[*Aloud*] Lady! I think I've given you offense[93] by thus opening up your great mental anguish due to a past misfortune.

MAHĀŚVETĀ [*after wiping her eyes with her bark garment's edge*]: Glorious one, please don't talk like that! For the burden of misery, when told to a friend, surely becomes lighter as if divided. So listen!

CANDRĀPĪḌA: As you command.

MAHĀŚVETĀ: There's a lot to tell.[94] Glorious one, you'll hear the story[95] in detail[96] when you're relaxed later on. Now I'll tell it briefly.

CANDRĀPĪḌA: The best course to take.

MAHĀŚVETĀ: Citraratha is known to be the ruler of the *kinnara* land, to possess an independent army of all *gandharvas* and to be Indra's friend.

CANDRĀPĪḌA: That much[97] is well-known on the earth.

MAHĀŚVETĀ: I'm his youngest brother Haṁsa's ill-fated daughter called Mahāśvetā.[98]

CANDRĀPĪḌA: Oh! you're dissatisfied with your noble birth as the second *gandharva* king's daughter.

MAHĀŚVETĀ: I'm such an unfortunate girl. Because of me,[99] the shameless[100] and merciless Love[101] brought a certain indescribably strange state[102] on my lord, Puṇḍarīka, a divine sage's son with a name auspicious to utter.

CANDRĀPĪḌA [*to himself*]: I'm appropriately propitiated.

MAHĀŚVETĀ: In order that I may get united with him, who has been taken away to another world by some divine man because of an old cause, even today[103] I'm pitilessly[104] staying here in the vicinity of Acchoda, keeping[105] my accursed body by practising mere austerities. [*Weeps.*]

CANDRĀPĪḌA [*to himself*]: The sudden attacks of a calamity are certainly irresistible even to those endowed with excellent bodies. [*Aloud*] Lady!

The sorrows of those dwelling in bodies
Do not break their hearts
So badly when experienced
As when separated by time and remembered. [42]

Even so,[106] enough of grief. For you[107] have told what should be told.

MAHĀŚVETĀ: I don't know how long I have to keep my body in separation.[108]

CANDRĀPĪḌA:

Abandon despair and take[109] courage,
And tenderly restore your beloved to life![110]
Did not Kṛṣṇa revive Sāṁdīpani's son
Though under confinement? [43]

MAHĀŚVETĀ [*having given ear as she barely restrains*[111] *her agitation due to grief*]: Oh, that sounds like a footstep! Surely Taralikā must have come back from Hemakūṭa. [*After looking*[Why! Keyūraka in charge of the ladies' inner-citadel is following her.

CANDRĀPĪḌA: Lady,[112] who's that called Taralikā?

MAHĀŚVETĀ: She's my friend, the sole eyewitness of all my miseries.

[*Enter* TARALIKĀ *and* KEYŪRAKA.]

TARALIKĀ: Oh, who's that glorious one whose beauty surpasses[113] that of Jayanta or of Nalakūbara?

KEYŪRAKA:

This man with such an excellent body as this,
It is judged,
Has been created by Brahmā, who has created
The Princess of such excessive beauty as that. [44]

TARALIKĀ: I surely don't known him, but my friend is treating[114] him as if he were long-familiar to her with eyes full of affection and kindness.

KEYŪRAKA: He's probably the Prince of India. He came on the world conquest, and when he was hunting nearby, a pair of *kinnaras* brought him to Caitraratha — thus the *gandharva* King's Chief Queen,[115] Madirā, told me in private through a messenger's mouth.[116]

TARALIKĀ [*with a smile*]: That's a delightful happening for the right time.

[*Both approach.*]

KEYŪRAKA: May our Mistress[117] be victorious!

TARALIKĀ: May our Princess be victorious!

MAHĀŚVETĀ: Taralikā, did my dear friend Kādambarī assent to my advice?[118]

CANDRĀPĪḌA [*to himself*]: Can she be that Kādambarī?

My ears are delighted by hearing of her;
    My eyes are afflicted by not seeing her;
And[119] this heart of mine is swinging[120]
    With passion between them.[121] [45]

TARALIKĀ: Friend, I told her everything the way you directed me. But the Princess looked surprised at her friend,[122] wept long sitting, and then told something to this honorable Keyūraka. So he should tell it to Your Highness himself.

MAHĀŚVETĀ: Sir, tell me now.

KEYŪRAKA: The Princess requests Your Highness[123] thus: "Dear friend, what you have directed me to do is equal to cleverly reproaching me[124] for committing an offense[125] by staying home. I need not talk much.

If you have regard for my life,
    Please do not think in this manner.[126]
I will not give up what I have woved —
    I swear it by your friendship with me." [46]

MAHĀŚVETĀ: My dear friend is greatly intent on that obstinacy.[127] In any case, I'm unfortunate. I've given grief to the whole *gandharva* family again and again.

CANDRĀPĪḌA [*to himself*]: What could be her vow so painful to her? All right, I'll ask her when I have a chance.

KEYŪRAKA [*to himself*]: Now I'll give her the message[128] sent by Chief Queen Madirā. [*Says so-and-so in* MĀHĀŚVETĀ's *ear.*]

MAHĀŚVETĀ [*to herself*]: Mother has rightly acquired a means of accomplishing her aim[129] in bringing him. She has decided to undo the knot of my friend's vow by showing him to her. However,[130] the moon has come out at last, and the white water lilies are giving up sealing their buds. [*Aloud*] Honorable Keyūraka, day has just come to an end today. I'll come tomorrow and remove that obstinacy of hers. So go ahead and tell my friend[131] we're coming.

KEYŪRAKA: As the Lady commands. [*Exit.*]

CANDRĀPĪḌA: Lady, who's that called Kādambarī?

MAHĀŚVETĀ: Kādambarī is the daughter of the *gandharva* King, Citraratha. She distresses the *gandharva* royal family with her vow that as long as I am thus unhappy, she will not get married, either.[132]

CANDRĀPĪḌA: That's a great misfortune; or rather, it befits friendship.

Even people temporarily acquainted with you,
  Observing your condition, get distressed;
How much more, your dear friends —
  Very precious friends from childhood?[133] [47]

MAHĀŚVETĀ: Then I wish to request[134] the Prince to see Kādambarī with me at daybreak.

CANDRĀPĪḌA [*to himself*]:

I have only heard her name, Kādambarī,
  But my heart is excited;
I do not know what ever will happen
  If I see her. [48]

[*Aloud*] Lady, you can order me. I'll obey you.

MAHĀŚVETĀ:[135] That befits your magnanimity.[136] [*To* TARALIKĀ][137] Now friend, show the Crown Prince to the place for rest, and make all the arrangements.

TARALIKĀ:[138] Glorious one, this way, this way.

CANDRĀPĪḌA [*after standing up, looking around*]:

His passion grown, he is zealous
  To approach a lotus pool
Accessible with his daytime glory and love,
  And serving the western region[139]
Furnished with a darkness-destroying tie —
  Now the sun is entering Mt. Mandara's cave. [49]

[*Exeunt omnes.*]

END OF ACT ONE

Notes

1. *M.M.: iyaṁ; V.K.: ayaṁ.*
2. *M.M.V.1.: diṣṭyā (vṛddhaye) stu; M.M.: dṛṣṭyā (-) -; M.M.V.2.: diṣṭi (-) -; V.K.: diṣṭyā (-) bhavatu.*
3. *M.M.V.1.* and *V.K.: niḥśeṣatām; M.M.: naśśeṣitām.*
4. *M.M.V.2.* and *VK.: himānī; M.M.L hitānir.*
5. *V.K.: ujjayinyām; M.M.: -nyāḥ.*
6. *V.K. supplies siprā.*
7. *M.M.V.1.* and *V.K.: syāt ta(syā-); M.M.: jāyeta.*
8. *V.K.: (parimalai)r hṛdyā (taṭo-); M.M.: (-)(?) tyā (- -).*
9. *H.S.: sumarīadi; H.S.Ch.: smaryate; M.M.: sumañjadī; V.M.: sumajjadi; M.Ch.M.* and *V.K.Ch.: smartavyaḥ.*
10. *H.S.: viñjhāadaṇakānanāiṁ; M.Ch.M.: vindhyāyatanakānanāni; M.M.: atapaṇḍi atannāparitakānnālan; V.K.: viñjhāṭavikānanāiṁ; V.K.Ch.: vindhyāṭavikānanāni.*
11. *V.K.: samāvāsabhūdāiṁ; M.M.: pusāvāsadāi; M.Ch.M.* and *V.K.Ch.: samāvāsabhūtāni.*
12. *H.S.: dāvaggidaddhaṁtara-; M.Ch.M.* and *V.K.Ch.: dāvāgnidaghāntara-; M.M.: bhāva°gī(?) (sa°jaṁ, M.M.V.1.)tara-; V.K.: dāvaṇhidakkhaṁtara-.*
13. *M.M.: sasmitam; VK.* omits.
14. *V.K.: smarati (bhavān); M.M.: smarasi (-).*
15. *M.M.V.2.* and *V.K.: ṇiccidaṁ; V.K.Ch.: niścitaṁ; M.M.: (maen) nī°cidaṁ; M.Ch.M.; cintitaṁ.*
16. *V.K.: ṇigghāao; M.M.: raṇṇa°bāa°; M.Ch.M.* and *V.K.Ch.: nirghātako.* This passage in *M.M.* is blurred and very corrupt; *V.K.* seems to follow mainly *M.Ch.M.*
17. *V.K.: ṇa pasammai sīarappasaro; V.K.Ch.: na praśāmyati śīkaraprasaraḥ; M.M.: ṇa vaṁsamai sīhara°vasaro; M.Ch.M.: punar api śyāmalābhradhārāprasaraḥ.*
18. *V.K.: vi; V.K.Ch.: (-te) pi; M.M.: kahaṁ vi; M.Ch.M.: (-te) pi katham api.*
19. *M.M.: -mṛgavya-; V.K.: -mṛgayā-.*
20. *M.M.V.2.: kutūhalī; M.M.: kutra(?); V.K.: kutuhalī.*
21. *M.M.* and *V.K.: ahmāṇaṁ; M.Ch.M.: asmādṛśaiḥ (puruṣaiḥ); V.K.Ch.: asmākam.*
22. *V.K.: taṇṇakavaheṇa; M.M.: tāṇakuvānu; M.M.V.1.: tāṇakurūṇa; M.Ch.M.* and *V.K.Ch.: tarṇakavadhena.*
23. *V.K.: pahūdasūṇādoso; M.M.: bhaveṇasūṇāvāo; M.Ch.M.: prasūtāpāyadoṣaḥ; V.K.Ch.: prabhūtasūnādoṣa.*
24. *M.M.* and *V.K.: paribaddhakaśo; M.M.V.2.: paribandhakakaśā.*
25. *V.K.* supplies.
26. *V.K.: paryāṇito; M.M.: paryānīto.*
27. This verse is quoted by Vemabhūpāla in his *Sāhityacintāmaṇi* (hereafter cited as *S.C.*); *vide* Intro., chàp. V. *M.M.* and *V.K.: khureṇa; S.C.: khanata.*
28. *M.M.* and *V.K.: - heṣāmukharas tvām (anumanyate) dhiroḍhum; S.C.: - veṣāṁmukharasvām (-) dhiroddhum.*

29. *V.K.: maṇṇidavvaṁ; M.M.: maṇṇida°(vaṁ, M.M.V.2.); M.Ch.M.: mantrayitavyam; V.K.Ch.: mantavyam.*
30. *V.K.: cauro; M.M.: (?); M.M.V.2.: paadaṁ; M.Ch.M.* and *V.K.Ch.: caturaḥ.*
31. *V.K.: vidyā(nirgatasya); M.M.: vindhyān(-).*
32. *V.K.: avatīrṇavān; M.M.: -kīrṇa-.*
33. The point here seems to be that he has come down to the earth, thinking that flight is rather a contemptible thing because even an arrow can fly with its wings, or the feathers of a bird it has.
34. *V.K.: -sauhṛdāt; M.M.: -sauhṛdān.*
35. *M.M.V.2.* and *V̈.K.: aśnute; M.M.: aśvake.*
36. *M.M.V.2.* and *V.K.: sakhe; M.M.: sarve.*
37. *V.K.: nopapannam; M.M.: nopavanam.*
38. *M.M.: (ka) iva; V.K.: (-) iha.*
39. *M.M.: tuvaresu; V.K.: tuvaredu; M.Ch.M.* and *V.K.Ch.: tvarasva.*
40. *M.M.V.2.* and *V.K.: raṁhasvitā; M.M.: -sthitā.*
41. *M.M.V.2.: turaṅgavaryasya; M.M.: turagāḥ vayasya; V.K.: turagavaryasya.*
42. *H.S.: mahilā a; M.M.: mahilāo* (the *o* here is, in fact, an *a* with a *visarga* and the Devanāgarī diacritical sign for an *o* that appears to have been added afterwards.); *V.K.: mahilāo; M.Ch.M.: mahilāś ca; V.K.Ch.: mahilā(ḥ).* In the Prakrit, *H.S.* is the best reading for a metrical reason.
43. *M.M.: kāaṁbari(devī): V.K.: kāaṁ barī (-); M.Ch.M.* and *V.K.Ch.: kādambarī (-).* In the Prakrit, *M.M.* seems to be the right reading for a metrical reason though grammatically wrong.
44. *Athavā.*
45. *V.K.: prasūnadhanuṣaḥ; M.M.: -dhanuṣā.*
46. *M.M.V.2.* and *V.K.: prabhavaḥ; M.M.: prabhāvaḥ.*
47. *M.M.V.2.* and *V.K.: vitīrṇa-; M.M.: vikīrṇa-.*
48. *Labhate - na kutra cit pratiṣṭhānam.* The point here seems to be that they are extremely rare or never to be obtained, or so elusive that their habitation can never be found.
49. *M.M.: samyag avagantavyaḥ; V.K.: samavagantavyaḥ.*
50. *V.K.: sāścaryam; M.M.: āścaryam.*
51. *V.K.: prapibati; M.M.: praviśati.*
52. *M.M.V.2.* and *V.K.: (tarū)n yaugapadyā(d anekā)n; M.M.: (-) (?) (- -) (?).*
53. *V.K.: yat tatraivāgrabhāge sthita (iva); M.M.V.2.: - -āgraśe - (-); M.M.: (?) ka iva.*
54. This verse somewhat resembles one of Kālidāsa's; *vide The abhijñānaśākuntalam of Kālidāsa*, ed. M.R. Kale, Act I, vs. 8.
55. *V.K.: tīvravega-; M.M.: tīvrakṛṣṭavega-; M.M.V. 2.: aptiprakṛṣṭavega.*
56. *M.M.V.2.* and *V.K.: bhūyo: M.M.: (?).*
57. *M.M.V.2.* and *V.K.: davīya(stayā); M.M.: (?) (-).*

58. Cf. Kālidāsa, *op. cit.*, Act I, vs. 7.
59. *M.M.V.2.* and V.K.: *me sammukhīnam; M.M.: sakhīnam.*
60. *M.M.V.2.* and *V.K.: aśvacārasya; M.M.: aśvaratnasya.*
61. *V.K.: (khaṇḍitā)rdhair; M.M.: (-)rthair.*
62. *V.K.* supplies *pathā.*
63. *M.M.V.1.* and *V.K.: kim api; M.M.: kavi; M.M.V.2.; kim a(vi).*
64. *V.K.: -halla(kā-); M.M.: -(?) (- -); M.M.V.2.: -ha (?) (- -).*
65. *M.M.V.2.* supplies *(unneya)nipuṇa(dhīvṛttir); V.K.* follows.
66. *M.M.V.2.* and *V.K.: (chāyā)drumeṣu; M.M.: (-)bhūmeṣu.*
67. *M.M.V.2.* and *V.K.: kriyatām (pracāro); M.M.: (?)ma(-).*
68. *Āharan* is given in place of *āharati* for a metrical reason.
69. *V.K.: āmukulite(kṣaṇaḥ); M.M.: āmukilitake(-); M.M.V.1.: āmukulitake(-); M.M.V.2.: āmukulīkṛta(-).*
70. *V.K.: vitīrṇa-; M.M.: vikīrṇa-.*
71. *M.M.V.1.* and *V.K.: -viracitārcanaś; M.M.: -racitāsanaś.*
72. *V.K.: -mūrtiramyā; M.M.: -mūrtīramyāramyā.*
73. *V.K.: upavīṇayantī; M.M.: upavīṇayanni.*
74. *V.K.: (turaṅga)mukha-; M.M.: (-)mṛga-.*
75. *M.M.V.2.* and *V.K.: mayānuyoktavyā; M.M.: mayā na yoktavyā.*
76. *V.K.: karehi; M.M.: karei; M.Ch.M.* and *V.K.Ch.: kuru.*
77. *M.M.: (jaṇe) ima°siṁ; V.K.: (-) imassaṁ; M.Ch.M.* and *V.K.Ch.: (jane) smin.*
78. *V.K.: laggā; M.M.: līnā; M.Ch.M.* and *V.K.Ch.: lagnā.*
79. *V.K.: daieṇa; M.M.: daiaṁ; M.Ch.M.: dayitaṁ; V.K.Ch.: dayitena.* In the Prakrit, *V.K.* is the right reading both grammatically and metrically.
80. *M.M.: dadhati (yadi) - sphuranti -; M.M.V.1.: dadhatu (-) - - -; V.K.: dadhatu (-) - sphurantu -.*
81. *M.M.: nu; V.K. omits.* This is metrically necessary.
82. *M.M.: bhavati; V.K.: bhagavati.*
83. *H.S.: vaṇṇīanti; M.M.: vaṇe(?); M.M.V.1.: vaṇṇedi; M.M.V.2.: vaṇetti; V.K.: vaṇṇīadi; M.Ch.M.* and *V.K.Ch.: varṇyante.*
84. *V.K.* supplies *(vitaranti) hi; M.M.V.1.: (?).* This is metrically necessary.
85. *M.M.V.2.: ca; M.M.: (?); V.K.* omits.
86. *V.K.* supplies *na (veti).*
87. *H.S.: vijaṇe a vīsahmeṇa puccha(su) dāva; M.M.: vijahevīsamaheṇa pu°līsu -; M.M.V.2.: vijaṇe - - pucchasu -; V.K.: - - vīsahmeṇa pucchīyadu -; M.Ch.M.: vijane idānīm eva savisrambheṇa pṛccha tāvat; V.K.Ch.: vijane ca visrambheṇa pṛcchjyatāṁ tāvat.*
88. *V.K.: lakkhido si girisārāhaattaṇeṇa (mae, H.S.); M.M.: i°viosi puriāhara°taṇeṇa; M.Ch.M.: lakṣito si giriśārādhakatvena mayā; V.K.Ch.: - - giriśā-tvena.*

89. *V.K.* supplies.
90. *V.K.* supplies.
91. *H.S.: de; M.Ch.M: tava; M.M.: kamala*^{o}*sa; V.K.: mahābhāassa; V.K. Ch.: mahābhāgasya.*
92. *V.K.: -nibaddha-; M.M.: -nibadya-.*
93. *V.K.* omits *(kṛtāgasaṁ) iva.*
94. *V.K.: atthi bahu vattavvaṁ; M.M.: a*^{o}*(?) oso; M.M.V.2.: (a*^{o}*)dhibadha (oso); M.Ch.M.* provides no *chāyā*; *V.K.Ch.: asti bahu vaktavyam.*
95. *M.M.: va (= pa)saṁgo; M.Ch.M.* provides no *chāyā*; *V.K.: pasaṁgo eso; V.K.Ch.: prasaṅga eṣa.*
96. *H.S.: vittharādo; V.K.* supplies *vittharado; V.K.Ch.: vistarāt.*
97. *M.M.: etāvat; V.K.: etat.*
98. *V.K.: - ṇandiṇī ahaṁ mahāsedā ṇāma mandabhāiṇī; M.M.: - ṇandiṇaṁ - mahāsaṇā - -; M.Ch.M.: - nandinīm mahāśvetāṁ nāma māṁ mandabhāgyām avagaccha; V.K.Ch.: - nandiny aham mahāśvetā nāma mandabhāginī.*
99. *V.K.: maha; M.M.: maha*^{o}*cia; M.Ch.M.* and *V.K.Ch.; mama.*
100. *V.K.: avilakkheṇa; M.M.: avila*^{o}*va*^{o}*ṇaṇa; M.M.V.2.: avila*^{o}*khaṇeṇe; M.Ch.M.: āvailakṣanyena; V.K.Ch.: avilakṣeṇa.*
101. *V.K.: maaṇeṇa; M.M.: rūvaiṇā; M.Ch.M.* and *V.K.Ch.: madanena.*
102. *M.M.* and *V.K.: dasaṁtaraṁ; M.Ch.M.: deśāntaram; V.K.Ch.: daśāntaraṁ.*
103. *H.S.: ajja vi; M.Ch.M.: adyāpi; M.M.: (ta*^{o}*sa)jjaajaṁkī; M.M.V.2.: (tassa) ajja ki; V.K.; ajja; V.K.Ch.: adya.*
104. *V.K.: akaluṇā; M.M.: akala*^{o}*aāeaṁ; M.Ch.M.: akaruṇā mandabhāgyā; V.K.Ch.: akaruṇā.*
105. *V.K.: parivattayantī; M.M.: variva*^{o}*tivaṁti (vva*^{o}*ṭāmi); M.Ch.M.: kṣapayantī; V.K.Ch.: parivartayantī.*
106. *M.M.V.2.: tad api; M.M.: tadavi; V.K.: tat.*
107. *V.K.: bhavatyāḥ; M.M.: (?).*
108. *H.S.: vippalaṁbhaa-; M.Ch.M.: vipralambhaka-; M.M.: ṇīpalaṁbhaa-; M.M.V.2.* and *V.K.: (edaṁ) ṇiccalahaa-; V.K.Ch.: (etat) niścalahata-.*
109. *V.K.: badhāna; M.M.: bandhāna.*
110. *V.K.: sañjīvaya - dayitaṁ; M.M.: sañjīvaye - dayitā.*
111. *V.K.: saṁsthāpayantī; M.M.: saṁsthāpayanti.*
112. *M.M.V.2.* supplies *ārye; V.K.* follows.
113. *M.M.: -adisaa-; M.M.V.2.* and *V.K.: -adisaia-; M.Ch.M.:- atiśaya-; V.K.Ch.: -atiśayita-.*
114. *V.K.: aṇugiṇhīadi; M.M.: aṇugihnaadi; M.M.V.2.: aṇugiṇṇīadi; M.Ch.M.: anugamyate; V.K.Ch.: anugrhyate.*
115. *M.M.V.2.* and *V.K.: (-rāja)mahiṣyā; M.M.: (- -)hi(?).*
116. *V.K.: (- iti) dūtamukhāt -; M.M.: (-rājasūnuḥ yo) dūtamukhād (digvijayāgato-).*
117. *V.K.: svāminī; M.M.: svāmī; M.M.V.2.: svāmini.*

118. *V.K.: ahmavaaṇā; M.M.: ahmaaṇā; M.Ch.M.: madājñā; V.K.Ch.: asmadvacanā.*

119. *V.K.: (ratyā) tu (madhya-); M.M.: (-) ti (- -).*

120. *V.K.: ca ḍolāyate; M.M.: tṛḍotyāyate; M.M.V.1.; tuḍotyāyate; M.M.V.2.: tu ḍolāyate.*

121. *Mahdyagocaraṁ*: between delight and affliction.

122. *H.S.: sahīviṁhaeṇa pekkhia; H.S.Ch.: sakhīvismayena prekṣya; M.M.: mahīvīmahaṇa ve°viaṁ; M.M.V.2.: - pekkhiaṁ; M.Ch.M.: madavismayaprekṣitaṁ; V.K.: madavīmaheṇa pekkhia; V.K.Ch.: madavismayena prekṣya.*

123. *V.K.: devīṁ; M.M.: devī.*

124. *V.K.: upālabdhāsmi; M.M.: upa(upā, M.M.V.1.)labdhosmi.*

125. *V.K.: -aparādhinī; M.M.: -aparādhini.*

126. *V.K.: iyaṁ; M.M.: ayaṁ.*

127. *V.K.: duraggahe; M.M.: duravaggahe; M.Ch.M.: duravagrahe; V.K.Ch.: durāgrahe.*

128. *M.M.V.2.* and *V.K.: arthaṁ; M.M.: ādhiṁ.*

129. *V.K.: paoaṇasiddhī; M.M.: payoasi°dhīe; M.Ch.M.: medhā; V.K.Ch.: prayojanasiddhiḥ.*

130. *H.S.: kiṁ uṇa; H.S.Ch.: kiṁ punaḥ; M.M.: keūra; V.K.: keūraa: M.Ch.M.* and *V.K.Ch.: keyūraka. Keūraa* seems out of place here; it is probably a scribal error.

131. *M.M.* and *V.K.: sahīe; M.Ch.M.: tābhyaḥ; V.K.Ch.: sakhyai.*

132. *M.M.* and *V.K.: mai evvaṁ dukkhiāe saaṁ vi pāṇiggahaṁ ṇa saṁbhāvemi tti kaapaḍiṇṇā āāsei daṁ gandhavvarāaulaṁ; M.Ch.M.: yayā mayy evaṁ duḥkhitāyām aham api pāṇigrahaṁ na sambhāvayeyam iti kṛtapratijñā tayā āyāsitaṁ gandharvarājakulaṁ; V.K.Ch.: mayy - - svayam api - - saṁbhāvayāmīti - āyāsayatīdaṁ gandharvarājakulam.*

133. *Sahapāṁsukrīḍādurlalitaḥ.*

134. *V.K.: abbhatthaiduṁ ahilasāmi; M.M.: a°bha°niu ṇa paremi; M.M.V.1.: a°bha°tiḍuduṁ - -; M.M.V.2.: a°bha°rattiu - -; M.Ch.M.: abhyarthitum na pārayāmi; V.K.Ch.: abhyarthayitum abhilaṣāmi.*

135. *M.M.* and *V.K.* assign this and the next speeches to Taralikā, and *M.Ch.M.* does not provide any speakers' names; but it seems clear enough from the context that this is Mahāśvetā's speech and only the next is Taralikā's.

136. *M.M.: mahāṇubhāvadāe; V.K.: - bhava-; M.Ch.M.* and *V.K.Ch.: mahānubhāvatāyāḥ.*

137. *H.S.* supplies *taralikām prati.*

138. *V.K.* supplies *candrāpīḍam prati; H.S.* omits.

139. *V.K.: vāruṇīṁ sevamānaḥ; M.M.: eva (?)śa.*

ACT TWO

[*Enter* CANDRĀPĪḌA *and* MAHĀŚVETĀ, *being shown the way by* TARALIKĀ.]

CANDRĀPĪḌA [*walking around, to himself*]:

This is the same path
That I saw in a dream last night;
I will be very happy
If the divine maiden is also the same. [1]

[*Aloud*] Lady,[1] is this golden mountain Hemakūṭa?[2]

MAHĀŚVETĀ: [3]Yes, it is.

TARALIKĀ: And here on its tableland is the royal city of the *gandharvas*.

CANDRĀPĪḌA: Ah! the beauty of Citraratha's capital is extraordinary indeed.

For those gardens possess the charms
Obtained in all the seasons;
The oblong pools give a feast to the eyes
With their full-blown golden lotuses;
The music with a scale in a special gamut
Sighs in the mansions;[4]
And all these genuinely lovely people
Sport joyfully everywhere. [2]

MAHĀŚVETĀ: This is Princess Kādambarī's palace.[5]

CANDRĀPĪḌA: Oh, how charming the girls' inner-citadel is! For here

With the banners' white cloths,
The celestial Ganges seems to descend from the sky;
With the masses[6] of luster from the gems on the portals,
Peacocks seem to fly up in all directions;
With the offerings of fresh flowers,
Stars seem scattered here and there;
And with the incense going up out of the windows,
Clouds seem to pervade everywhere. [3]

TARALIKĀ: This is the gate of the girls' inner-citadel.

MAHĀŚVETĀ: Glorious one, please enter.

CANDRĀPĪḌA [*to himself*]: This good-natured lady is taking me to the girls' inner-citadel out of kindness, but isn't my entry into it[7] unapproved?

[*All act entering it.*]

MAHĀŚVETĀ: Crown Prince, this way, this way. Look at the Princess' servants' skill[8] to carry out her instructions properly!

CANDRĀPĪḌA: Surely I see

One playing the lute with her nail tips,
Her breasts trembling,
Some talkative one[9] teaching[10]
A caged parrot lovely sounds here,
Another drawing Kāma very skillfully
Together with[11] Rati on a painting cloth,
Still another making a peacock dance[12]
By clapping her hands[13] with jingling bracelets. [4]

Moreover,

With the lovely girls' charmingly[14] moving
Eyes, hands, necklaces and breasts,
The sky looks as if it were decorated with
Lotuses, shoots, stars and bunches of flowers. [5]

[*All walk around.*]

TARALIKĀ [*towards the dressing room*]: Friends,[15] tell us! Where's the Princess? And what's she doing? Are you saying[16] she's examining[17] some play *gandharva* girls are performing in the temple of Lakṣmī?

MAHĀŚVETĀ [*to herself*]: That surely must be the poetic work my dear friend has composed on my ill-fated life.[18]

CANDRĀPĪḌA [*showing with his hand*]:

This is the Princess' temple of Lakṣmī
Furnished with a pearl-studded canopy.
And this is the path leading to it:
With a flood of rays from the gemmed ornaments
Of the girls standing on both its sides,
It looks as if it were navigable in front of us. [6]

MAHĀŚVETĀ [*wth a glance given at a window, having seen* KĀDAMBARĪ]: Glorious one, take a look this way where there's a window.

CANDRĀPĪḌA [*having done so, to himself*]:

This surely must be the girl
I have heard of;
This beauty of hers appears
Absolutely faultless to me. [7]

Even so, now,[19] [*Aloud*]

Who is this lotus-faced girl surrounded by her friends
Dressed to match herself?
She looks as if she were Lakṣmī entirely encircled
By her treasures' guardian deities. [8]

And she has

A face like a full moon,
Eyes moist and lovely as water lilies,
Arms delicate as young lotus fibers,
Breasts resembling jars,
A waist excessively slim as Love's bow,[20]
Buttocks like those of a ruddy goose
And feet pink as buds —
This uncommon beauty is extremely attractive.[21] [9]

MAHĀŚVETĀ: She's the *gandharva* family's jewel lamp, Rati's image, Kāma's friend,[22] and the limit of Brahmā's skill in creating women — she's my dear friend Kādambarī.

CANDRĀPĪḌA: Why! she's the daughter of Citraratha. [*To himself*]

Repeatedly driving away with her fingers
Bees flying around her face,[23]
Slowly fixing a loosened bud
Worn as her ear ornament,
Smilingly patting with a play lotus
Her friend who has started making jokes —
With charming gestures, she draws
A feathered arrow, a flower weapon.[24] [10]

MAHĀŚVETĀ: Taralikā, go and tell the Princess of the great fortune of seeing the Crown Prince for the first time.

TARALIKĀ: I'll do so. [*After going and observing*] Keyūraka is telling her something. He surely must be describing[25] the Crown Prince now.[26] Then I'll give her good news,[27] too. [*Approaches.*]

[*Enter* KĀDAMBARĪ, *accompanied by her attendants as described, her two friends and* KEYŪRAKA.]

KĀDAMBARĪ [*to herself*]: Why! my heart is beside itself because of his description of the Prince's such and such beauty, charms and virtues.[28] [*Aloud to* KEYŪRAKA] I hope my dear friend is bringing him here as well.

KEYŪRAKA: What doubt is there about that?[29]

If she is not going to show you[30]
    To the Prince fit for pleasure alone,
Who approached her abode through the power of fate,
    What other honor is she going to do him? [11]

TWO FRIENDS: Princess, why would the Lady deprive you of such a feast for the eyes?[31]

KEYŪRAKA [*to himself*]:

A complete description of his beauty
    Is impossible for me to give;
Nevertheless, extreme admiration for him
    Has arisen in her heart. [12]

TARALIKĀ [*having approached*]: May the Princess be victorious!

KĀDAMBARĪ [*excitedly*]: Did you see my dear friend?

TARALIKĀ: She has arrived at the gate.

TWO FRIENDS: With the Prince?

TARALIKĀ: Tamālikā, I've come ahead to tell the Princess he's arrived.

TAMĀLIKĀ: Madalekhā, such is the Lady's affection for her friend.

KĀDAMBARĪ [*as if jealously*]:[32] How?

TAMĀLIKĀ [*with a smile*]: I'm talking about her friendship she's showing by coming back from her hermitage like this, which she's never done before.[33]

KĀDAMBARĪ [*to herself*]: Ah! Tamālikā has taught me even the charm of clever speech. [*Aloud*] Keyūraka, inform the elders the Lady has arrived.

KEYŪRAKA [*to himself*]: I surely must tell the Chief Queen of Candrāpīḍa's arrival. [*Aloud*] As the Princess commands. [*Exit.*]

KĀDAMBARĪ: Now I'll go to greet her. [*Having stood up, walking around,*[34] *towards the dressing room*] Dancing girls, stop dancing[35] now.[36]

TWO FRIENDS: This way, this way, Princess.

ATTENDANTS: Princess, here're the parasol[37] and chowrie bearers.

MADALEKHĀ: Princess, this way, this way.

KĀDAMBARĪ [*to herself*]: Oh! because of my desire to see the glorious one, my heart seems to run forward as if it were cut off from my body.[38] [*Walks around.*]

CANDRĀPĪḌA: Oh! this special respectfulness of hers is conformable to her beauty and noble birth. For

Tying up with one hand a braid of hair
  Hanging down on her shoulders,
Holding with the other her loosened upper garment
  Fastened on her breasts,
Stumbling on the ground again and again,
  Her slow gait given up in a flurry,
The slender Kādambarī is approaching[39] here
  As if another girl, her attendants set aside. [13][40]

MAHĀŚVETĀ: Why! my friend is coming towards us all by herself.

KĀDAMBARĪ [*approaches and falls*[41] *at* MAHĀŚVETĀ's *feet.*]

[*The two hug each other.*]

CANDRĀPĪḌA [*with horripilation, to himself.*]

At the mere sight of her,
  Delight thus arises in me;
What good deed has my friend Mahāśvetā done
  In order to embrace her body? [14]

TARALIKĀ [*aside*]: Madalekhā, he's really worthy to be our dear friend's husband.

MADALEKHĀ [*aside*]: Everything will be fine if she gives up that stubbornness in her vow.

MAHĀŚVETĀ [*showing* CANDRĀPĪḌA *with great respect*]: Friend Kādambarī, this is the Prince of India, who has conquered the whole earth by the strength of his arms. In the course of hunting,[42] he has become a full moon to our eyes.[43] So you should be particularly kind[44] to him.

KĀDAMBARĪ [*to herself*]: Who am I to myself? I'm utterly[45] powerless at the sight of him.

TAMĀLIKĀ: Princess, did you hear what the Lady said? Honor[46] the Prince in such a manner.

KĀDAMBARĪ: How?

TAMĀLIKĀ: In such a manner as would please the Lady.[47]

KĀDAMBARĪ: I don't know how to be bold.[48]

CANDRĀPĪḌA [*after observing* KĀDAMBARĪ, *to himself*]: Surely her

Buttocks' plumpness cannot bear owing to her girdle[49]
  The quick gait[50] she has taken up;
Her eyes seem to forget and remember
  Their not long-accustomed straight courses;[51]
Her speech makes frequent visits
  To artlessness[52] and shrewdness in turn —
I think the moon-faced girl is on the unique border
  Between childhood and youth. [15][53]

KĀDAMBARĪ [*to herself*]: All right, I'll just perform the customary salutation: [*Folds her hands gracefully.*]

CANDRĀPĪḌA [*to himself*]: I've found the line for the limit of beautiful things. For

Her hand-lotuses reddened
  By the color of the gem on her hair's parting,
Her cheeks struck
  By the earrings slightly trembling,
Her breast-jars visible
  Owing to the pearl necklace somewhat gone up,
This slender girl has saluted me
  By folding her hands. [16]

[*With folded hands, aloud*] *Gandharva* Princess, what is wrong now?

MADALEKHĀ [*showing a gold seat*]: Honorable one,[54] please sit down here.

MAHĀŚVETĀ: Prince, please grace this seat.

CANDRĀPĪḌA [*sits down.*]

MAHĀŚVETĀ [*sits down and forces reluctant Kādambarī to sit down beside herself.*]

KĀDAMBARĪ [*casting a sidelong glance at* CANDRĀPĪḌA, *to herself*]: Alas! Alas! I made a vow in that manner, but now I've become a target of such[55] great excitement as I've never felt before.

CANDRĀPĪḌA [*to himself*]: Now I have indeed limitlessly great self-respect.[56] For this

Charming-eyed girl repeatedly intoxicates my heart

With the corners of her eyes —
For a moment accompanied by tremulously contracted brows,
For a moment gentle and slow,
For a moment attended by a studied false merriness,
For a moment only a little open as buds,
For a moment embraced by bending lashes
And for a moment closed. [17]

MAHĀŚVETĀ: Friend, are you happy?

KĀDAMBARĪ: To see you[57] now.

MAHĀŚVETĀ: Prince, is this course of conduct of the Princess agreeable to you?

CANDRĀPĪḌA: What are you talking about?

This is like the coolness of moonlight,
Or the sweetness of a stream of nectar;
I find something charming by nature
And very human about the Princess. [18]

KĀDAMBARĪ [*to herself*]: Oh, how quick the Prince is at compliments! But fallen into the power of shyness, I can't even look at him at will.[58] And again,

I could see him well
If I had
As many mental eyes
As he has limbs. [19]

[*Acts*[59] *timidity due to love.*]

TAMĀLIKĀ: Ah, this is a beautiful union!

MADALEKHĀ: Yes, indeed.

KĀDAMBARĪ [*looks with a frown.*]

MADALEKHĀ [*aside*]: Tamālikā, stop it. The Princess seems to be scowling in anger.

TAMĀLIKĀ [*to herself*]: Then I'll disguise[60] it this way. [*Aloud*] King Citraratha, the overlord of the whole land of *gandharvas* is a master praiseworthy in every way.[61] His daughter is going to do the honors. And this glorious son of the sole sovereign of the middle world is going to be honored. So why can't I celebrate this extremely noble, worthy[62] meeting?

CANDRĀPĪḌA [*having observed, to himself*]: Away with the misgivings[63] that my desires may not attain their objects!

Since she is checking
    With knit brow-creepers
Her friend telling something under a pretext
    In the presence of people,
And repeatedly revealing her charms
    Even though dissembling,
Now the fawn-eyed girl must bear
    Such a strong emotion as I do. [20]

MADALEKHĀ [*aside*]: Friend, honor properly the person worthy to be honored.

KĀDAMBARĪ: Friend Tamālikā, bring camphorated betel.

TAMĀLIKĀ [*takes it out of a small box and gives it.*]

KĀDAMBARĪ [*acts taking it.*]

CANDRĀPĪḌA [*to himself*]:

Upon her arm-creeper bearing ray-blossoms
    From her gently-moving nails,[64]
Wonderful shoots appear to come out
    Under the guise of betel leaves. [21]

KĀDAMBARĪ: Friend, take this back.

MAHĀŚVETĀ: We all[65] should entertain[66] the Crown Prince.

CANDRĀPĪḌA [*to himself*]:[67] This is a great effort to show respect.

KĀDAMBARĪ: Then do it yourself. I can't entertain like a clever girl.

MAHĀŚVETĀ: Friend, enough of shyness! Do it, believing he's long-familiar to you.[68]

TWO FRIENDS: Princess, enough of shyness! Follow the Lady's instructions.

CANDRĀPĪḌA [*having observed her and himself covered with horripilation,*[69] *to himself*]:

In order to suit itself well to the season's beauty,[70]
    Though it is full of honey,
A jasmine creeper desires to touch with its twig
    A red *pāṭala* bud brought near. [22]

KĀDAMBARĪ [*to herself*]: What can I do? I'm utterly overcome by fright, and my heart is throbbing. But my friends are watching.[71] If I don't act properly,[72] what will the Prince think?[73] [*Gives him the betel in her trembling hand without withdrawing her eyes from* MAHĀŚVETĀ's *face.*]

CANDRĀPĪḌA: Princess, is this the opening benediction of a *nāṭikā* play to honor me with? [*After acting taking it, to himself, trembling with horripilation*] This right hand of mine is extraordinarily fortunate indeed. For it[74]

Touched that hand-lotus[75] of hers[76]
With trembling finger-petals,
Hair-filaments erected for joy[77]
And drops of perspiration[78]-honey sprung up. [23]

[*Having observed*] Oh, why! even now I'm not satisfied.

Her gemmed[79] bracelet became loose and dropped
From her arm kept[80] trembling;
But the slender girl[81] did not notice it at all,
Her heart infatuated.
Wondering, "Is she lovesick as I am or not?"
My heart has now mounted the balance of doubt. [24]

TAMĀLIKĀ [*with a smile, aside*]: Madalekhā, look at the liberality of the *gandharva* Princess! She's offering the Prince even her gemmed bracelet.

KĀDAMBARĪ [*having observed, to herself*]: Why am I feeling this change in composure? I didn't even notice the bracelet falling[82] from my wrist. Didn't Mahāśvetā notice this blunder? [*Acting anger, her real feelings concealed*] Oh, foolish Tamālikā, go away! You've offended me now. You put the bracelet loosely on me. Bring it here now!

TAMĀLIKĀ: Take it yourself!

KĀDAMBARĪ: Oh, wicked-natured girl, bear that in mind![83] Friend Madalekhā, never mind this willful Tamālikā talking nonsense. You tie it on my wrist.

MADALEKHĀ [*smilingly takes the gemmed bracelet and ties it.*]

CANDRĀPĪḌA [*to himself*]:[84] Ah! it seems this[85] desire of mine can easily obtain an opportunity now.

She felt that[86] emotion arising
And became agitated;
She made some specious excuse
In order to conceal it;
And she showed anger to her friend
With words full of ambiguity[87] —
Love's arrows, I believe, found a place
In the fawn-eyed girl's heart. [25]

TAMĀLIKĀ[88] [*aside to* MAHĀŚVETĀ]: The Princess has betrayed several different states[89] of her confusion caused by the gemmed bracelet dropped in a flurry.

MAHĀŚVETĀ [*aside*]: The tree of passion has seen its buds come out.[90] Even so, we should remain as if we didn't know that until it bears fruit.

CANDRĀPĪḌA [*after observing himself, to himself*]: I can't possibly hide[91] this unusual state of mine. For

Sigh-winds are coming out[92] —
  My fatigue from the journey conceals that.
Sweat is coming forth excessively —
  There is the midday heat for that.
My body is richly covered with masses of erect hair
  Like Love's arrows planted inside it
With their feathers visible outside it —
  What can I do about that? [26]

[*Having entered without using a curtain*][93]

KEYŪRAKA: Lady Mahāśvetā, the elders wish to see you, who have returned from your hermitage after a long time.

MAHĀŚVETĀ: Here I am! [*After standing up*] Friend Kādambarī, where[94] should the Crown Prince take[95] a rest?

KĀDAMBARĪ [*to herself*]: Right in my heart![96] [*Aloud*] Why do you say that, dear friend? Let the Crown Prince amuse[97] himself everywhere here just as in his own palace!

MAHĀŚVETĀ: Keyūraka, take the glorious one to the Spring Sport Garden.[98] There let him take a rest on the Pleasure Mountain, where there are intoxicated peacocks.

KEYŪRAKA: As the Lady commands.

CANDRĀPĪḌA: The Princess is also[99] very tired from excessive midday heat. For

The hair's parting of the fawn-eyed girl
  Has been rubbed off by her forehead ornament;
Her eyes are only a little open;
  The *śirīṣa* flower on her ear is somewhat shriveled;
Her locks are disheveled from excessive sighing;
  Both her brows have stopped their devotion to dancing;
Her cheeks are perspiring, arm-creepers drooping
  And pair of breasts trembling. [27]

MAHĀŚVETĀ: Kādambarī, go inside now. [*Exit with* TARALIKĀ.]

KĀDAMBARĪ [*to herself*]: Why! my feet won't move from this place. [*Aloud*] Taralikā, show the Crown Prince the way.

TAMĀLIKĀ: Why shouldn't I carry out my friend's order? Crown Prince, this way, this way.

CANDRĀPĪḌA [*walks around, leaning on* KEYŪRAKA's *arm.*]

KĀDAMBARĪ: Madalekhā, show me the way to my bedroom. [*Exit with* MADALEKHĀ.]

CANDRĀPĪḌA [*to himself*]: I just can't make sure whether that peculiar behavior of hers was innate or[100] temporary. Whichever the case,[101] how irresistible lovesickness is!

I have kept this heart away from that object,
Considering it unsuitable;
It is still infatuated just as before,
Suffering torture as if by itself.[102] [28]

KEYŪRAKA: Prince,[103] here on the right hand is the path where peacocks are bathing themselves. And on the left is the bedroom of the Princess. And

A she-dove in a cage hanging near its window,
Her play checked, desirous to sport,
Is watching, her eyes bestowed[104] on a gold net,
Her beloved he-dove in a dovecot of the best gems. [29]

CANDRĀPĪḌA [*with a smile within,*[105] *to himself*]:

My heart, you have left your beloved;[106]
Why are you lovelorn unreasonably?[107]
Does a bee[108] in the human world
Long for a cluster of *pārijāta* flowers? [30]

[*Exeunt omnes.*]

END OF ACT TWO

Notes

1. *V.K.: ārye; M.M.V.1.: arye.*
2. *V.K.: kaccid; M.M.: kaś cid.*
3. *V.K.* supplies *ayya; H.S.* does not follow.

4. *M.M.V.2.* and *V.K.: saudheṣu (saṅgītakam); M.M.: saudheṣṭa(-).*
5. *M.M.* and *V.K.: bhavaṇaṁ; M.Ch.M.: mahābhavanam; V.K.Ch.: bhavanam.*
6. *V.K.: (chāyā)cayair; M.M.: (-)calair.*
7. *V.K.: kanyāntaḥpurapraveśaḥ; M.M.: kanyāvagamaḥ.*
8. *V.K.: -ṇeuṇaṁ ṇirūvei; M.M.: -ṇeuraṁ ṇirūpei; M.Ch.M.: (-nirvahaṇaṁ) nūpuraṁ nirūpyate; V.K.Ch.: -naipuṇaṁ nirūpaya.*
9. *H.S.: vāgminyā(tra): M.M.: vā(?)ny (atra); V.K.: paśyāmy (-). V.K.* seems redundant because *M.M.* has *paśyāmi* immediately before this verse.
10. *V.K.: pāṭhyate; M.M.: padyate.*
11. *V.K.: (ratyā) samaṁ (likhyate); M.M.: (-) samā(-).*
12. *M.M.V.2.* and *V.K.: (apy) ānartyate; M.M.: (avy)ānartate.*
13. *M.M.* and *V.K.: tālaiḥ; M.M.V.2.: nālaiḥ.*
14. *M.M.V.2.* and *V.K.: vibhrama-; M.M.: vidruma-.*
15. *M.M.* and *V.K.: halā; M.Ch.M.: sakhyaḥ; V.K.Ch.: halā.*
16. *M.M.* and *V.K.: bhaṇaha; M.Ch.M.: bhaṇatha; V.K.Ch.: bhaṇata.*
17. *V.K.: parikkhantī vaṭṭai; M.M.: parikhantīe khaṇṭai; M.Ch.M.: parīkṣantyāvartyata (iti); V.K.Ch.: parīkṣamāṇā vartata* (-).
18. *V.K.: ṇūṇaṁ taṁ evva bhave jaṁ piasahīe kaaṁ kavvabandhacariaṁ me mandabhāāe; M.M.: ā(nū, M.M.V.2.)ṇantaṁ ṇe°* (*ev, M.M.V.1.*)*va bhave jaṁ viasahīe raiaka°bala°(?)dhapariaṁ me mandabhāāe; M.Ch.M.: ānando naiva bhavet yat priyasakhīracitakāvyabandhaparikarmaṇi mandabhāgyāyāḥ; V.K.Ch.: nūnaṁ tad eva bhavet yat priyasakhyā kṛtaṁ kāvyabandhacaritam mama mandabhāgyāyāḥ.*
19. *M.M.: tad apy evaṁ tāvat; V.K.* omits.
20. *V.K.: -cāpavat; M.M.: -cāpalas.*
21. *H.S.: harahara (cchāyeyam); M.M.: harahara (-); V.K.: kim aparaṁ (chā-). Hararahā* also means "attractive to Śiva (Hara)." Candrāpīḍa is an incarnation of the moon, which in its turn is another body of Śiva; *vide K.N.*'s Opening Benediction. An alternative reading could be *hariharā*, which means "attractive to Viṣṇu (Hari)"; cf. the preceding verse (8), in which Kādambarī is compared to his consort, Lakṣmī.
22. *V.K.: paḍicchando radīe sahī aṇaṁgassa; M.M.: paḍiha(cha)ndo raṇṇā - -; M.Ch.M.: praticchandaḥ anaṅgasya ratyā sahitasya; V.K.Ch.: praticchando ratyāḥ sakhī anaṅgasya.*
23. *V.K.: mukhā(ntika)-; M.M.: dukhā*(-) -.
24. *Puṣpāyudhaṁ*; it also means Love.
25. *M.M.: kaṇi(ri, M.M.V.2.)°jaṁtaṁ (-vaṇṇaṇaṁ); M.Ch.M.: kriyamāṇaṁ; V.K.: karīadi; V.K.Ch.: kriyate.*
26. *M.M.V.2.* supplies *dāṇiṁ; V.K.* follows. After this *M.M.* has *visurā; M.Ch.M.* gives no *chāyā; V.K.* omits.
27. *V.K.: piaṇivedaittiā hommi; M.M.: pī(pa, M.M.V.1.) āpiāṇivedai°tiā homi; M.Ch.M.: priyam priyanivedayitṛkā bhaviṣyāmi; V.K.Ch.: priyanivedayitrī (= tṛkā) bhavāmi.*

28. *V.K.: rūvasohaggaguṇavaṇṇaṇeṇevva; M.M.: rūpasoha°gaguṇāa°ṇaṇaṇe°va; M.Ch.M.: rūpasaubhāgyaguṇāḥ tasmāt anyonyeneva; V.K.Ch.: rūpasaubhāgyaguṇavarṇanenaiva.*

29. *M.M.V.2.* and *V.K.: (ko) tra; M.M.: (-) nu.*

30. *V.K.: adarśayantī bhavatīm (athetarat); M.M.: adarśayanti bhavatī kim (-).*

31. *V.K.: bhaṭṭidārie kahaṁ vā tumaṁ tāriseṇa ṇaaṇuccaveṇa vañcedi ajjā; M.M.: - - - - - ṇaaṇā(ṇū, M.M.V.1.)saveṇa - a°a; M.Ch.M.: bhartṛdārike kathaṁ vā tvayā tādṛśe nayanotsave vañcyate āryaḥ keyūrakaḥ; V.K.Ch.: - - - tvāṁ tādṛśena nayanotsavena vañcayaty āryā.*

32. *Sāsūyam iva*: as if jealous of Mahāśvetā, who is with Candrāpīḍa.

33. *V.K.: jaṁ akaapuvveṇa evvaṁ assamapadādo āamaṇeṇa daṁsei sohaddaṁ tado(taṁ, H.S.) bhaṇāmi; M.M.: ja°to ja°to aviakaavu°veṇa evaṁ a°samavāādo - - - - -; M.Ch.M.: yad apriyakṛtapūrveṇa evam āśramapadād āgamanena sakhīsneho darśitaḥ tad bhaṇāmi; V.K.Ch.: -akṛtapūrveṇaivam - - darśitaṁ sauhārdaṁ tato -.*

34. *V.K.: parikrāmantī; M.M.: -krāmanti.*

35. *Saṅgītavyāpāram*: playing music, singing and dancing.

36. *M.M.: dāva; M.Ch.M.* and *V.K.* omit.

37. *V.K.: eso(edāo, H.S.) chaḍḍha-; M.M.: esa caddha-; M.Ch.M.: etāḥ svacchanda-; V.K.Ch.: etāḥ chatra-.*

38. *H.S.: aṁgādo khaṇḍiaṁ via -aggado dhāvai me hiaaṁ; M.M.* and *V.K.: ka(kha, V.K.)ṇḍaiṁ via - dhāvai me aṁgado hiaaṁ; M.Ch.M.: khaṇḍitam iva - dhāvatīva me hṛdayam agrataḥ; V.K.Ch.: - - - dhāvati meṅgāt hṛdayam.*

39. *M.M.V.1.* and *V.K.: abhyeti; M.M.: anyeti.*

40. After this verse *M.M.* has the following speech of Kādambarī: *kādam || candrāpīḍam avalokya, ātmagatam, su°pa°ta°mi imaṁ si°va°ṇaṇaveaṁḍīsa°ti āa ahaṁ diṭha°mi jeṇa kahia°taṁ (M.M.V.2.* inserts *kemiataṁ) aṇuntiṇe uṇiaṁ; V.K.* omits it because the Prakrit is incomprehensible and *M.Ch.M.* does not provide a *chāyā* for it.

41. *M.M.: patati; V.K.: praṇamati.*

42. *V.K.: miaāppasaṅgeṇa; M.M.: vitarāvabha viaa°vasaṁgeṇa; M.Ch.M.: mṛgayāpadavikāprasaṅgena; V.K.Ch.: mṛgayāprasaṅgena.*

43. After this *M.Ch.M.* has the following: *yad aham iva tvam api nirmāṇanaipuṇyam pitāmahasya pṛthivyāḥ saphalatāṁ ca mānuṣīlocanānām ajayyatāṁ ca manmathasya jānīhīti balād ānīta eṣaḥ*, which means: I have brought him by force, thinking that you as well as I should know Brahmā's skill in creation, the fruitfulness of the earth, and Love's unconquerability to women's eyes. *V.K.* omits this. It may have been in the original text of the play, but it seems a little too explicit in Candrāpīḍa's presence.

44. *M.M.* and *V.K.: sahiaāe; M.Ch.M.: sakhījanena: V.K.Ch.: sahṛdayayā.* Here Mahāśvetā seems to be suggesting that Kādambarī should appreciate (*sahṛdayā*) him, or even love him.

45. *M.M.V.2.* and *V.K.: savvassiṁ; M.M.: sakhī: M.Ch.M.: sarvasya: V.K.Ch.: sarvasmin.*

46. *M.M.* and *V.K.: saṁbhāvehi; M.Ch.M.: śabdāpaya; V.K.Ch.: sambhāvaya.*

47. After this speech *M.Ch.M.* has in a separate line: *kādambari anyathā na manyasva*, which means: Kādambarī, don't think otherwise! *V.K.* omits it. It seems best to assign this speech to Madalekhā.

48. *H.S.: ṇāhaṁ jāṇāmi poḍhaattaṇaṁ avagamiduṁ; M.M.: - - o (po, M.M.V.2.)ḍa°taṇāiva(pa, M.M.V.1.)ateḍaduṁ; V.K.: - sakkuṇomi de poḍhaattaṇaṁ avagamiduṁ; M.Ch.M.: nāhaṁ jāne (?); V.K.Ch.: - śaknomi te prauḍhatām avagantum.*

49. *M.M.: nīvyā; V.K.: navyā* (misprint?).

50. *M.M.V.2.* and *V.K.: drutacaṅkramaṁ; M.M.: (?)n.*

51. *V.K.: acirābhyastānarālakramān; M.M.V.2.: -ḷakramāt; M.M.: acirādvyastādarādutkramāt.*

52. *V.K.: maugdhya-; M.M.: mauḍhya-.*

53. After this verse *M.M.* has the following speech assigned to Madalekhā: *mada* || *janāntikam, sahi kāambari ṇaṁ bhaṇi°jasi°caari°davāi°kamea°khi°ja iti. V.K.* omits this because the Prakrit is too corrupt to make sense of, and *M.Ch.M.* provides no *chāyā* for it.

54. *V.K.: ajjo; M.M.: a°ā; M.Ch.M.* omits the whole line.

55. *V.K.: eārisassa; M.M.: ahī eārisassa; M.Ch.M.: taddhṛdayā etādṛśasya: V.K.Ch.: etādṛśasya.*

56. *H.S.: kāmaṁ khalu mamedānīm aparyantasvabahumānam; M.M.: - - - aparyāntasvabahumānam; M.M.V.2.: - - - aparyantasabahumānam; V.K.: kathaṁ - - aparyāptaṁ* | *(sabahumānaṁ).*

57. *M.M.* and *V.K.: tumhāṇaṁ; M.Ch.M.: bhavatām; V.K.Ch.: yuṣmākaṁ.*

58. *V.K.: - saccandado pekkhiduṁ vi na(= ṇa) pārīadhi; M.M.: - sa°vī (ba, M.M.V.2.)dado pulauṁ vi°ṇa tīrae eso; M.Ch.M.* provides no *chāyā* for the prose portion of this *svagata* speech; *V.K.Ch.: - svacchandataḥ prekṣitum api na pāryate.*

59. *M.M.: rūpayati; V.K.: nāṭayati.*

60. *V.K.: paccādaissaṁ; M.M.: va°hī (pucchi, M.M.V.2.) dai°saṁ; M.Ch.M.* and *V.K.Ch.: pracchādayiṣyāmi.*

61. *H.S.: saalappasassassa; M.Ch.M.: sakalapraśasyasya; M.M.: saamahasaha°sa; V.K.* omits.

62. *V.K.: - imaṁ sadia-; M.M.: -ima°sa ra°tua a-; M.Ch.M.: -asya rateś ca-; V.K.Ch.: -imaṁ sadṛśa-.*

63. *V.K.: -śaṅkayā; M.M.: -śaṅkā.*

64. *M.M.V.2.* and *V.K.: -nakha-; M.M.: -nava-.*

65. *V.K.: savvehiṁ; M.M.: savehi; M.Ch.M.: sarvair; V.K.Ch.: sarvābhir.*

66. *H.S.: abbhārāhidavvo; M.M.: a°bharā(ri, M.M.V.2.)hida°vo; M.Ch.M.: abhyārādhitavyaḥ; V.K.: uvaaridavvo; V.K.Ch.: upacaritavyaḥ.*

67. *H.S.* supplies *svagatam.*

68. *H.S.: sahi alaṁ lajjāe* | *imassiṁ ciraparïido tti hiae kadua paḍipaccehi; V.K.: - - -* | *- - tti paḍipaccehi samuidaṁ āāraṁ; M.M.: - du(alaṁ. M.M.V.2.) (?) sahi ae ima°sim ci(vi, M.M.V.1.) apario°ti paḍi°tie; M.Ch.M.: sakhi alaṁ lajjayā* | *hṛdaye āśaṅkya asminn aciraparicita iti kṛtvā kuru: V.K.Ch.: - - -* | *asmin cira - - pratipadyasva samucitam ācāram.*

69. *Saromāñcam ātmānaṁ tām ca -.*

70. *(Spraṣṭum - kāṅkṣati) svānuvṛttim ucitām ṛtuśriyaḥ.*

71. *H.S.: - vevadi hiaaṁ* | *pekkhanti a sahīo; V.K.: - - -* | *- sahīo; M.M.: - i°pe°khati hiaaduṁ kiṁ piasahī (?); M.Ch.M.:- vepate hṛdayam* | *paśyanti ca sakhyaḥ; V.K.Ch.: - - -* | *- sakhyaḥ.*

72. *V.K.: ahavā; M.M.: ahava; M.Ch.M.* and *V.K.Ch.: athavā.*
73. *M.M.: -kiṁ viārei; M.Ch.M.: -kiṁ vā vicārayati; V.K.: -kahaṁ maṇṇea; V.K.Ch.: -katham manyeta.*
74. *V.K.* supplies *yena hi.*
75. *M.M.V.2.* and *V.K.: karapaṅkajaṁ; M.M.: - pallavaṁ.*
76. *M.M.: tasyāḥ; M.M.V.2.* and *V.K.: tanvyāḥ.*
77. *M.M.V.2.* and *V.K.: -pulaka-; M.M.: -culaka-.*
78. *M.M.V.2.* and *V.K.: -gharmoda-; M.M.: -varmoda-.*
79. *M.M.V.2.* and *V.K.: ratna-; M.M.: rakta-.*
80. *V.K.: dhṛta-; M.M.: dhūta-.*
81. *M.M.V.2.* and *V.K.: tanvyā; M.M.: tasyāḥ.*
82. *V.K.: ṇivaḍantaṁ* (*u* given for *ḍa*, misprint); *M.M.; ṇipīḍantaṁ; M.Ch.M.: niṣpatad; V.K.Ch.: nipatantaṁ.*
83. *V.K.: hidae; M.M.: ṇadae; M.Ch.M.* omits; *V.K.Ch.: hṛdaye.*
84. *H.S.* supplies *svagatam.*
85. *V.K.: mama; M.M.: mām.*
86. *V.K.: imaṁ; M.M.: idaṁ.*
87. *M.M.V.2.* and *V.K.: vakrimagarbhayā; M.M.: (?)garhayā.*
88. *V.K.* assigns this speech to Tamālikā, though *M.M.* does to Taralikā. *V.K.* seems more appropriate, for Tamālikā has been participating in this conversation, while Taralikā has not.
89. *V.K.: avatthantarāi; M.M.: a°va°tarāiṁ; M.Ch.M.* omits the whole speech; *V.K.Ch.: avasthāntarāṇi.*
90. *V.K.: pallavubbhedo; M.M.: va°ipu (pallavu, M.M.V.2.)°bhedao; M.Ch.M.: pallavo nā(murāga-); V.K.Ch.: pallavodbhedaḥ.*
91. *M.M.V.2.* and *V.K.: apahnavanīyam; M.M.: evaṁ tapanīyam.*
92. *V.K.: udgacchanti; M.M.: utpaśyantu.*
93. *M.M.: praviśyāpaṭākṣepeṇa; V.K.: praviśya paṭākṣepeṇa.* Like most editions of Sanskrit-Prakrit plays, *V.K.* consistently gives *paṭākṣepeṇa* for *apaṭākṣepeṇa*. According to A.K. Warder, the stage direction *apaṭākṣepeṇa* is used when an actor enters suddenly without the use of a curtain; *vide* his *Indian Kāvya Literature*, vol. IV, p. 249 and *passim*, and Vol. V.
94. *V.K.: kahiṁ; M.M.: kahaṁ; M.Ch.M.: kathaṁ kasmin; V.K.Ch.: kutra.*
95. *V.K.: aṇuhodu; M.M.: āṇahodi; M.Ch.M.* and *V.K.Ch.: anubhavatu.*
96. *M.Ch.M.* does not have a *chāyā* for this, but instead gives the following: *kim evam bhanasi, yatosya darśanam āsīt tata ārabhya mama śarīrasyāpy eṣa eva prabhuḥ, kim punar bhavanasya vibhavasya parijanasya vā*, which means: Why do you talk like that? Since I saw him, he's been the master of even my body; how much more of my mansion, wealth and servants?
97. *V.K.: viharau; M.M.: viharai; M.Ch.M.* and *V.K.Ch.: viharatu.*

98. *V.K.: vasantavilāsojjāṇaṁ; M.M.: satavilasu°jāṇuṁ; M.Ch.M.: (?)vilāsodyānam; V.K.Ch.: vasanta-*

99. *V.K.: api; M.M.: iti.*

100. *V.K.: (kim) -uta; M.M.: (-) - vā.*

101. *Tathāpy.*

102. *H.S.: svayaṁ iva kadarthanasahaṁ yathāpuram eva tad iha mugdham* ||; *M.M.* and *V.K.: - - kadarthanāsahaṁ tad iha yathāpuram eva muhyati.* This change is metrically necessary.

103. *M.M.: deva; V.K. omits.*

104. *M.M.V.2.* and *V.K.: - vitīrṇa-; M.M.: -vikīrṇa-.*

105. *V.K.: sāntaḥsmitam; M.M.: sāntasmitam.*

106. *V.K.: virahayya dayitāṁ; M.M.: viraha(?); M.M.V.2.: virahayya.*

107. *V.K.: kimartham apade; M.M.: -artha(dha, M.M.V.2.)m pade.*

108. *M.M.V.2.* and *V.K.: (-loka)madhukaraḥ; M.M.: (- -)dhu-.*

Praveśaka
Prelude to Act Three

[*Enter* TARALIKĀ *and* TAMĀLIKĀ.]

TAMĀLIKĀ: Taralikā, why did you leave Lady Mahāśvetā and come here?

TARALIKĀ: Just now the Lady,[1] who was going[2] to see[3] the honorable Haṁsa and Gaurī after receiving a favor from the revered[4] Citraratha and Madirā, sent me to tell the Princess to entertain the Crown Prince properly.

TAMĀLIKĀ: Do so. But what incident has happened now?

TARALIKĀ: What event is there other than the vow the Princess has taken?

TAMĀLIKĀ: That's indeed unbearable mental anguish to the whole *gandharva* family.

TARALIKĀ: That's why Mahāśvetā has brought here the Prince of the middle world endowed with the wealth of beauty attainable by no one else[5] in order to enchant her, whose heart was not fascinated even by the sight[6] of the divine princes headed by Viśākha, Mammatha, Nalakūbara and Jayanta shown[7] in her picture self-choice.

TAMĀLIKĀ: Well done![8] Mahāśvetā has done a favor to the *gandharva* King's Chief Queen. She[9] attracted[10] him by means of a pair of *kinnaras*.

TARALIKĀ: Now I'll ask this. Friend, do you know our friend's heart? Does the Princess like him?

TAMĀLIKĀ: Didn't we all[11] notice then the Princess' heart was overcome by Love?[12]

TARALIKĀ: All right. Then what?

TAMĀLIKĀ: When I returned from the presence of the Crown Prince, I heard from Madalekhā's mouth, "After you left,[13] she gave up all her engagements, lay down on a gemmed couch[14] and stayed there with her eyes expanded[15] and her face fixed upward. Now as a result of our advice, she has taken a meal and is staying on a breezy bed in the moon[16] room."

TARALIKĀ: That seems[17] to be some lovesickness just[18] before the actual manifestation of passion.[19] Now, where's the thief of Kādambarī's heart?

TAMĀLIKĀ: The most fortunate one is amusing himself on the Moon[20] Stone Mountain by spending his time on the sixty-four arts with the clever girls the Princess has sent him — I can imagine his engagements of the whole day.

TARALIKĀ: Where are you going?

TAMĀLIKĀ: I've been ordered by the Princess to fetch the *śeṣahāra* from the treasure house.[21]

TARALIKĀ: Then go and carry out the order[22] of your Mistress. Now I'll hear from the Princess' own mouth about the arrangements she has made for the Crown Prince's comfort, and tell the Lady.

TAMĀLIKĀ: All right. [*Walks around towards the treasure house.*]

TARALIKĀ: I'm sure the Crown Prince is going to be honoured with that distinguished necklace.

[*Exeunt ambo.*]

END OF THE *PRAVEŚAKA*
PRELUDE TO ACT THREE

Notes

1. *V.K.*: supplies *ayyāe*.
2. *M.M.*: *ga°ha(cha, M.M.V.2.)ntīe*; *M.Ch.M.*: *gacchantyā*; *V.K.*: *gacchantī*; *V.K.Ch.*: *gacchantī*.
3. *M.M.*: *daṁsaṇa°sa*; *M.Ch.M.*: *darśanāya*: *V.K.*: *daṁsaṇaṇimittaṁ*; *V.K.Ch.*: *darśananimittaṁ*.
4. *Tāda- ambāe -*.
5. *M.M.* and *V.K.*: *aṇaṇṇa-*; *M.Ch.M.*: *anyonya-*; *V.K.Ch.*: *ananya-*.
6. *V.K.*: *daṁsaṇeṇa aṇakkhittahiaaṁ imaṁ*; *M.M.*: *-aṇa°* (*khit*, inserted by *M.M.V.2.*)*ta- -*; *M.Ch.M.*: *darśanenākṣiptahṛdayā imāḥ*; *V.K.Ch.*: *darśanenānākṣiptahṛdayām imāṁ*.
7. *M.M.*: *-paāsiāṇaṁ*; *M.Ch.M.*: *-prakāśitānāṁ*; *V.K.*: *-paaṁsiāṇaṁ*; *V.K.Ch.*: *-pradarśitānāṁ*.
8. *M.M.V.2.* and *V.K.*: *sāhu*; *M.M.*: *sahi*; *M.Ch.M.*: *sakhi*; *V.K.Ch.*: *sādhu*.
9. *M.M.* and *V.K.*: *tāe*; *M.Ch.M.*: *tasyāḥ*; *V.K.Ch.*: *tayā*.
10. *H.S.*: *āaṭṭho*; *M.M.* and *V.K.*: *āaddhio*; *M.Ch.M.*: *ākhyātaḥ*; *V.K.Ch.*: *ākṛṣṭaḥ*.
11. *M.M.*: *sa°vāhī(hiṁ, M.M.V.2.)*; *V.K.*: *savvehiṁ*; *M.Ch.M.* and *V.K.Ch.*: *sarvābhir*.
12. *V.K.*: *mammahaparavasaṁ*; *M.M.*: *hovi°jataṁ vammaha via*; *M.Ch.M.*: *bobhuvat manmathahṛtaṁ*; *V.K.Ch.*: *manmathaparavaśaṁ*.
13. *H.S.*: *gaāsu amhāsu*; *V.K.*: *gaesu amhesu*; *M.M.*: *-ki-*; *M.Ch.M.* and *V.K.Ch.*: *gatāsv asmāsu*.

14. *V.K.: raaṇapallaṅke ṇipaḍia; M.M.: raalava(pa, M.M.V.1.) °laṅke ṇipaḍi; M.Ch.M.: ratnaphalake nipatitā; V.K.Ch.: ratnaparyaṅke nipatya.*
15. *V.K.: ummīlida-; M.M.: uṁmii(mīḷi, M.M.V.1.)da-; M.Ch.M.: uccalita-; V.K.Ch.: unmīlita-.*
16. *M.M.V.2.* and *V.K.: canda-; M.M.: vaṁda-; M.Ch.M.: prānta-; V.K.Ch.: candra-.*
17. *M.Ch.M.: (-vikāra) iva; V.K.* omits.
18. *M.M.: (pamuhe) e°va; V.K.* omits.
19. After this *M.M.* has: *ahave ke°ciraṇa ṇīsaṁdai va°doa eyaṁ maṇisālabhaṁjiā,* for which *M.Ch.M.* provides: *athavā kiyacciraṁ(?). V.K.* skips this because it is very corrupt and *M.Ch.M.* does not provide a complete *chāyā* for it. *H.S.* provisionally reads: *ahavā keccireṇa ṇisīdadi mandā via iaṁ maṇisālabhaṁjiā; H.S.Ch.: athavā kiyacciréṇa niṣīdati mandeva iyaṁ maṇiśālabhañjikā.* A possible meaning of this is: But how long has she been unwell, sitting like a gemmed statue?
20. *V.K.: canda-; M.M.: caa-; M.Ch.M.* skips; *V.K.Ch.: candra-.*
21. *V.K.: kosagharādo; M.M.: kosasarāhi; M.Ch.M.* and *V.K.Ch.: kośagṛhād.*
22. *M.M.* and *V.K.: ṇiesaṁ; M.Ch.M.: niyogaṁ; V.K.Ch.: nideśaṁ.*

ACT THREE

[*Enter* CANDRĀPĪḌA, *seated on a slab of emerald, being served by* KEYŪRAKA.]

CANDRĀPĪḌA [*to himself*]: Oh, how intently devoted[1] the mind-born Love is to kindling a desire for an object hard to attain!

On one hand am I, and on the other is the lovely girl
A man of abundant merit may wish to be united with;
Nevertheless, even one of little merit
Does not cease longing for good fortune.[2] [1]

KEYŪRAKA [*to himself*]: Fortunately, it seems from this motionless sitting position that his heart is fixed on the Princess. After all, what[3] wonder is it that a cluster of mango blossoms attracts a bee?

CANDRĀPĪḌA [*hopefully, to himself*]: Can she be like me in this matter? [*After reflecting*]

She looked[4] with sidelong glances slow with shyness
But sweet with love[5] manifested;
She saw her smiling-faced friends[6] and reproached them
Covertly with a gesture of her brows[7];
And she pulled her breast-cloth
Though it was in its right place —
In all likelihood the flower-arrowed Love
Aimed[8] at the heart of the long-lashed girl. [2]

[*After stopping for a moment and sighing*] Or rather,[9] that's not the case at all.

Tell me, my heart, why are you dancing
With a mere treasure of imagination?
Do not become a butt of people's ridicule
By doing a frivolous thing! [3]

KEYŪRAKA [*having observed, to himself*]:

This deep love for the *gandharva* Princess,
Full of anxiety, surely tells something:
It suspects her, whose emotion is concealed, to be
Otherwise, and despairingly sighs in its desires. [4]

[*Aloud*] Crown Prince, do you long to see your[10] kinsmen?[11]

CANDRĀPĪḌA: All[12] encounters with blessed people who don't refuse intimacy[13] with me make me forget them. Moreover,

I saw that genuine affection
Offered by Mahāśvetā;
I beheld Kādambarī sweet with a favor
Rich in courtesy;
And I observed their dear friends
With hearts full of kindness —
At once I was made dependent on their friendship
As if I were one of you. [5]

KEYŪRAKA: I think that's the nature of the good-hearted. Now, is anything in the state affairs neglected because the Prince is a great distance away?

CANDRĀPĪḌA: I don't have to worry about anything[14] in the camp because my friend Vaiśampāyana is staying there.

Yet his heart overflowing with friendship[15]-nectar,
He does not know I am doing well.
On the contrary, suspecting I have had an accident,
He may be afflicted — This is my worry. [6]

KEYŪRAKA: Doesn't he know the might of the Prince's arms?

Roaming in mountains' impenetrable depths
Abundant in ferocious beasts, he has no companions —
Thus, oh! thinks the thoughtful one.
Tell me, whom should a lion be with? [7]

Now Prince,[16] entertain your eyes from here with the trees on the border of the Pleasure Mountain the Princess[17] has grown with her own hands.

CANDRĀPĪḌA: I surely see summer's riches, which has obtained scope especially in this grove though the youthfulness[18] of all the seasons is present in it. For

The *śirīṣa* flower has a swarm of bees clinging.
And that is inferable from their hummings;
The jasmine[19]-creeper possesses[20] sweat
Under the guise of opening buds;

This young mango tree is as if it were breaking,
Stooping with the burden of its fruit;
And the *pāṭala* tree is diffusing
Its abundant fragrance with its flowers. [8]

KEYŪRAKA [*after looking elsewhere*]: Why! that's the Princess with her friends in the moon room.

CANDRĀPĪḌA [*looking at her, to himself*]: This is the best encouragement I've received.

At the top of her mansion
She repeatedly attracts[21] me sporting
With the corners of her eyes
Gleaming with her trembling lovely brows
And variegated by the breaking of an abundance
Of her teeth's[22] luster arising from smiling,
As if with garlands of blue water lilies large with rows
Of white ones[23] and their leaves attached. [9]

KEYŪRAKA [*to himself*]:

For a young couple thus shy
But longing for each other,
The meeting of their eyes
Is surely sweeter than even union. [10]

CANDRĀPĪḌA: Oh, what is this?

The wide-eyed girl is looking, her flurry concealed, and
Smiling on a contrived pretext, her breasts trembling;
Or rather, beautiful girls naturally and easily acquire
Various sorts of gestures in the prime of their youth. [11]

[*Enter* KĀDAMBARĪ *as described, and her two friends.*][24]

KĀDAMBARĪ [*to herself*]: Oh, how hard it is to look without desire[25] at the moon of kings from the middle world! Dear me! Dear me! Where are my shyness and naivety[26] easy to attain in maidenhood?

TARALIKĀ:[27] The Prince is gracing an emerald slab in the jasmine arbor made to decorate the top of the Gem Mountain. There an offering is made with a heap of fresh *pāṭala* flowers falling, struck by a swarm of bees' wings.

CANDRĀPĪḌA [*observing, to himself*]:

For a moment she playfully winds
Her arm-creeper around her friend's neck;
For a moment she smells
A bunch of white water lilies in her hand;
And for a moment she tears
A betels leaf with the tips of her nails —
Surely they are very suggestive of her heart now. [12]

KEYŪRAKA [*to himself*]: Luckily, their excessive[28] love is indeed equal. For

The more of her emotion she betrays
With various charming gestures,
The more of his growing passion
Becomes manifested by itself. [13]

KĀDAMBARĪ [*to herself*]: Oh, my wretched heart, hide your boldness! You regard[29] a man you've never seen before as if he were long-familiar to you. What would you do if he should become adverse[30] to you by an unfavorable twist of fate?

MADALEKHĀ [*aside*]: Taralikā,[31] her heart must be still burning,[32] for she won't tell what's in her heart even to me because she's shy within.

TARALIKĀ:[33] That's all right. We'll know it in course of time.[34]

CANDRĀPĪḌA [*to himself*]: Oh, why is[35] Brahmā's creation[36] like this?

By firmly combining the moon, blue lotuses,
Conch-shells, sandalwood, creepers,
Ruddy sheldrakes, flights of bees,
Ruddy geese flying in the sky,
Royal deer, cranes, gems and sprouts,
He, I suspect, has created Kādambarī
As a sorceress at Śambara's command
In order to make[37] my heart powerless. [14]

Moreover,

Love knows whatever my heart feels for her
Touching the ground with her toes,
And after putting her face[38] obliquely
On her left hand decorated with a bracelet
Of a bunch of white water lilies,
Its fingers placed and stretched on her friend,[39]
Shaking a play lotus with her other hand,
Her eyelashes touched by perspiration. [15]

KEYŪRAKA [*to himself*]:

Will Brahmā successfully accomplish
The object of his creation
Before long by uniting this couple,[40]
Whose mutual love is thus growing? [16]

KĀDAMBARĪ [*to herself*]: Now even dullwitted people can surely tell my excitement; how much more can Mahāśvetā? She has thoroughly experienced a love affair. And after considering her friendship, I made a vow thus contrary to the action I've started. Besides, if Father or Mother,[41] whose request I disappointed[42] in that manner, hears[43] of this incident, what will they say?[44]

TARALIKĀ:[45] Princess, why are you flurried like this?

KĀDAMBARĪ [*acting*[46] *not hearing her, to herself*]: Who brought this prince, the violator of an innocent girl's heart? And why? Or rather, Love himself, who made an attack because of my heart's excitement, introduced him to me.

MADALEKHĀ: Friend, tell me the cause of your mind's agitation.[47] You don't even notice you're being asked something.

KĀDAMBARĪ [*to herself*]: I have nothing to say. Even my friends will make fun of me. What can I do?[48] And whom can I tell?[49] No doubt death alone is my refuge. What's the use of this obedience to the wretched Love's order?[50] It makes shame certain and conquers death.

TARALIKĀ[51] [*aside*]: Madalekhā, in this case,[52] you must show[53] something.

MADALEKHĀ [*aside*]:[54] Yes.

CANDRĀPĪḌA [*to himself*]:

If this curved-browed girl is suffering, as I am,
Being the wicked-arrowed Love's target,
Perhaps the banner of my good fortune's play
Has been hoisted once again. [17]

[*After observing her*]

Putting together[55] her locks
Scattered by the wind from a fan,[56]
Slowly tying up the front of her girdle
Loosened from walking for pleasure,
Placing her hand on her well-developed breasts
In order to adjust[57] her pearl necklace,

Whatever emotion can she not show?
    My heart is very[58] excited. [18]

KEYŪRAKA [*to himself*]:

Her passion for him concealed,
    She regrets having taken the vow;
Unable to ascertain her heart,
    He doubts[59] it. [19]

MADALEKHĀ: Isn't[60] your[61] heart oscillating again about whether the very noble-natured Prince will accept the necklace out of courtesy towards us or not?

KĀDAMBARĪ: [*to herself*]:[62] Let another wish be thus announced![63] I wish I could observe the Prince's love for me right now. [*Aloud*] Then, what do you think of this matter?

MADALEKHĀ: A reservoir of inexhaustible affection,[64] he surely won't disregard[65] the request of the Princess.

KĀDAMBARĪ: Taralikā,[66] tell me. How's that?

TARALIKĀ: He's truly the foremost of the sincere[67]-hearted; he'll fulfill[68] the wish of the Princess.

KĀDAMBARĪ: The Lady's dignity is indeed very great.[69] [*To herself*] I'll regale my eyes by watching him until Taralikā leaves. [*Watches him.*]

CANDRĀPĪḌA [*to himself*]:

My mind devoted to propriety alone,
    What I can do right now is, oh!
To enter[70] into the beautiful girl
    With my sense-organs not so hesitant;[71]
If I luckily attain the joy of experiencing
    Even that,[72] or becoming one with her,
What ever among desirable objects
    Can my eyes not make attainable now? [20]

[*Off stage*]

TWO BARDS: Prince Candrāpīḍa, may you be victorious! May you be victorious! May the evening be pleasant to you!

FIRST:

The reddish sun's disc falls from the sky[73]

As if a ripe fruit from a tree;
Its rays nourish the idea that they are vermilion[74]
In the heads of mountain elephants;[75]
The twilight's red color departs
As if the glory-fire of the king of love;
And the darkness forms a line of musk salve
On the faces of the sky's region-maidens. [21]

SECOND:

Surrounded by swarms of bees
Humming sweetly with intoxication
And by two or three unfolded leaves,
A nocturnal jasmine flower desires to open;
Moreover, the sound of bracelets,
Awaking the five-arrowed Love now and then,
Indicates the bathing of doe-eyed girls,
Sport to remove their fatigue from heat. [22]

KEYŪRAKA: These servants of the Princess are serving the Crown Prince by telling the time. Now,

Heaving a sigh-breeze at sunset,
Closing face-lotuses,
Lying down on a bed[76] of evening twilight buds,
As if perspiring with hosts of stars,
Covered[77] with a spread of darkness, and pathetic
With the lamentations of paired wailing ruddy geese,
This time looks like some lovely girl
Afflicted with separation. [23]

CANDRĀPĪḌA: Oh, why, day has withdrawn its light! [*To himself*][78] Alas! Now,

Pouring nectar[79] into these eyes
As if upon *cakora* birds,[80]
Some lovely digit of the moon called Kādambarī
Has gone out of sight. [24]

KEYŪRAKA: Now Prince, please grace the steps made of moonstones simply dropping from a mass[81] of moonbeams near the mansion's slope of white water lilies.

CANDRĀPĪḌA [*to himself*]: I'll divert myself there.

KEYŪRAKA: This way, this way, Crown Prince.

CANDRĀPĪḌA [*after standing up, walking around and looking*]: How delightful the host of white water lilies is! For

Filled with water pure as pieces of gems,
This host of full-blown white lotuses glitters;
Reflected in the mosaic pavement of crystals,
It looks as if it were a part of the sky marked with stars.[82] [25]

Now I'll perform my evening duties here. [*Exit.*]

KĀDAMBARĪ [*to herself*]: Oh, it's too dark to see the charming[83] man. [*Aloud*] How come Tamālikā is still tarrying[84] from the treasure house?

[*Having entered with a casket in her hand*]

TAMĀLIKĀ: I've brought the *śeṣahāra* here!

KĀDAMBARĪ [*after standing up*]: Now, where's the glorious one?

TARALIKĀ: I saw him in the arbor just now.

MADALEKHĀ: We'll find out from a servant's mouth[85] where[86] he is now.

KĀDAMBARĪ [*towards the dressing room*]: Which portress is there?

[*Having entered*]

VIJAYĀ: It's me!

KĀDAMBARĪ: Vijayā, go to find out where the Prince is and tell me.

VIJAYĀ: As the Princess commands. [*Having exited and reentered*] Princess, the glorious one is protecting the mansion's slope of white water lilies.

MADALEKHĀ: Princess, please stand up.[87]

[*All stand up and walk around.*]

VIJAYĀ: The torch bearers[88] have arrived here.

TARALIKĀ: Vijayā, show the Princess the way.

VIJAYĀ: Princess, this way, this way.

KĀDAMBARĪ [*acts descending from the mansion and climbing the Pleasure Mountain with her friends*]: Taralikā, you're the closest to Mahāśvetā; so you have power over this matter.

MADALEKHĀ: That's right. Tamālikā, give the *śeṣahāra* into Taralikā's hands.

TAMĀLIKĀ [*gives her the casket.*]

TARALIKĀ [*having acted receiving it*]: I'll surely get him to accept this.

MADALEKHĀ: Otherwise, the heart of the Princess will be[89] greatly disturbed.

TAMĀLIKĀ: Ah! these two among the noble[90] are both praiseworthy: one insists on giving such a jewel[91] as this worth the three worlds, and the other is trustworthy enough to receive it.

MADALEKHĀ: This is the vicinity of the slope of white water lilies. Both its sides are surrounded with camphor and banana trees, and its entrance is made loud with the buzzings of bees sitting on the fragrance of full-blown jasmine[92] flowers.

KĀDAMBARĪ: Vijayā, inform the Crown Prince of our arrival.

VIJAYĀ [*after going ahead*]: Here's the Prince sitting on a moonstone slab, accompanied by Keyūraka. [*Approaches him.*][93]

[*Enter* CANDRĀPĪḌA *as described, and* KEYŪRAKA.][94]

KEYŪRAKA: Prince, look here!

Their languor from amorous enjoyment[95] removed
By a breeze fragrant with white lotuses,
Couples of geese are sporting,
Their bodies embraced by each other's wings. [26]

CANDRĀPĪḌA:

Who would not fall in love with this time,[96]
Whose face is the clear moon's disc,
And garment, a host of star-pearls[97]
At the end of the enfeebled twilight? [27]

VIJAYĀ [*having approached him*]: Crown Prince, Princess Kādambarī has arrived here.

CANDRĀPĪḌA [*with joy and great respect*]: I'll get up to greet her right now. Show her in at once!

VIJAYĀ [*returns and makes* KĀDAMBARĪ *apporach*[98] *him.*]

CANDRĀPĪḌA: Keyūraka, why is the Princess acting inappropriately like this?

Does a lotus plant approach a goose for itself?
Or a creeper on a mango tree, a cuckoo?
Or a creeper on a *nīpa* tree, a peacock?
Or a jasmine flower, a bee? [28]

KEYŪRAKA: Thus he declares his noble birth.

VIJAYĀ [*having approached*]: Princess, approach, approach.

KĀDAMBARĪ: Now wait for Lady Mahāśvetā to return from the elders' presence and let me know.

VIJAYĀ: Certainly. [*Exit.*][99]

CANDRĀPĪḌA[100] [*after looking ahead*]:

Surrounded by beautiful girls
With glittering gem-lamps in their fingers,
She is glowing as if she were vernal beauty
Surrounded by creepers with pink buds. [29]

[*After observing*] Ah, how charming the *gandharva* Princess' leisure-dress is! For

Her body anointed with sandal paste
Of a moderate scent,
Supporting with her breasts' slopes
A very small moonlight-white silken cloth,[101]
Illuminating with her locks[102]
A garland of aromatic leaves
And wearing a girdle of lovely pearls,
This beautiful girl gives me joy. [30]

[*After standing up, his hand*[103] *supported by* KEYŪRAKA] Princess, this way, this way!

KĀDAMBARĪ [*acting embarrassment due to love,*[104] *to herself*]: Overwhelmed by his sight, I forget everything I wish to do[105] when I don't see him.

CANDRĀPĪḌA: Princess, what's this excess of respect for your servants?

This body is extremely slim;
Its waist is even slimmer;
These paired breasts are higher than mountains;[106]
And these buttocks are hard to bear.
Since you, I believe,
Are slow[107]-gaited by nature,
Walking in this manner
Surely does not befit you. [31]

KĀDAMBARĪ [*aside*]: Madalekhā, request the glorious one to grace the seat.

CANDRĀPĪḌA: I'll sit now. Princess, please sit down here.

[*All sit down duly.*]

CANDRĀPĪḌA: Taralikā, has Lady Mahāśvetā completed her daily services?

TARALIKĀ: Just[108] now by her mother's insistence, she was[109] taking a meal of fruit, roots and bulbs[110] brought from the Pleasure Garden in the presence of her father.

CANDRĀPĪḌA: Oh, dear! Oh, dear!

Love has thus made this passion of hers
    Ascend to its highest point;
When and how by the mercy of fate
    Will it attain a happy end? [32]

KEYŪRAKA: No doubt it will attain a beautiful end by a special favor of great men like you.

CANDRĀPĪḌA: Madalekhā, I've never before seen this excess of kindness of the Princess to her servant.[111]

She has bought this heart of mine
    Become tender through hundreds of favors
In such a way that it is impossible
    To be acquitted of the debt[112]
Even with uninterrupted series of services
    In thousands of lives. [33]

KEYŪRAKA: It's quite appropriate for the Princess to serve you with affection. Look!

Your fame is spotless as your family;
    Your glory is bright as your garment;
Your learning is great as your gift;
    And your conduct is exalted[113] as your speech. [34]

KĀDAMBARĪ [*looks at* MADALEKHĀ.]

MADALEKHĀ [*after standing up, to the servants*]: Girls, bring the boxes!

SERVANTS: Right now! [*Give them.*]

MADALEKHĀ[114] [*having acted receiving them*]: Crown Prince, we readily gained confidence in you at the very first sight. Please endure this sole troublesome request[115] of ours!

CANDRĀPĪḌA: Friend, what are you talking about? This is indeed a favour.

MADALEKHĀ [*gives him garlands, scented cosmetics and the like*]: Taralikā, show that here![116]

TARALIKĀ [*opens the casket.*]

CANDRĀPĪḌA [*acting astonishment with a glance cast at it*]:

Oh! is this moonlight
  Readily obtained at the right time?
Or dripping camphor resin[117]
  Scattered in the air?
Or rather the Ganges River
  Falling down from heaven?
Or possibly *ketaka* flowers'[118] pollen
  Spreading with the wind? [35]

[*After observing it carefully, to himself*] Why! this is a flood of light from some[119] pearl necklace[120] Taralikā is holding[121] in a sapphire casket — a necklace resembling a lotus fiber bracelet deposited in fresh lotus leaves.

TARALIKĀ: Surrounded with hosts of streaming rays, this pearl necklace looks as if it were covered[122] with masses of horripilation because of its desire to touch the Crown Prince's chest. [*Gives it to him.*]

CANDRĀPĪḌA: Madalekhā, what's this other resolve?

The Princess has captured me
  With her faultless,[123] pure[124] virtues alone;
What is she going to do[125] furthermore
  With this string[126] of pearls? [36]

MADALEKHĀ [*having acted taking the necklace, with a bow*]: Glorious one, the Princess requests you, because she has developed affection for you by reason of your virtuousness attainable by no one else, and not from her pride in wealth.

CANDRĀPĪḌA: What does she order me?

MADALEKHĀ: "Glorious one, you have for yourself forcibly taken possession of my body, heart and life — everything I have. So what else can I give you worthy of great respect? Even then, here is the necklace *śeṣa*. It is so called because it was the only one left of the gems taken out during the churning by the thirty-three gods. The ocean presented it to the *gandharva* King, and the latter made it my necklace. Now Prince, please show me a favor by gracing it."

CANDRĀPĪḌA [*to himself*]: I desire to touch this pearl necklace because the Princess has caressed it by embracing it with her body. [*Aloud*] In that case,

This necklace should never[127] leave the Princess

As a row of geese, the Ganges,
Or as a cluster of flowers,
A creeper on a *pārijāta* tree. [37]

KĀDAMBARĪ [*looks at* TARALIKĀ's *face.*]

TARALIKĀ: The Lady will be blamed[128] for this rejection of the flood of the Princess' own first love, for she was the cause[129] of her friendship with you. If you don't wish her to be distressed,[130] give up the cruelty of refusing it.

KĀDAMBARĪ [*to herself*]: Well done! Taralikā said[131] just what I wished to say.[132]

CANDRĀPĪḌA:

How can this[133] be otherwise here?
For the moon shines upon night with moonlight,
And a cloud adorns a *kadamba* tree's creeper[134]
With an uninterrupted series of buds. [38]

KEYŪRAKA: Oh, don't say that!

For even the lotus-eyed god,[135] who gave away
All the gems in the ocean to the gods and demons,
Wears the *kaustubha* on his chest — that should be indeed
Regarded as a sign of his courtesy for Lakṣmī. [39]

CANDRĀPĪḌA [*to himself*]: Clever Keyūraka!

TAMĀLIKĀ: Madalekhā, give the pearl necklace into the Princess' hands. Let her hang it on his neck herself!

TARALIKĀ: He[136] surely won't permit[137] it to be otherwise!

MADALEKHĀ: All right. [*Gives the śeṣahāra into* KĀDAMBARĪ's *hand.*]

KĀDAMBARĪ [*acts taking it and doing so.*]

CANDRĀPĪḌA [*to himself*]: My life has borne fruit. For

Her fingers glittering with horripilation,
Breasts trembling and armpits showing a little,
She has by herself tied on my neck the pearl necklace
As if it were a bridegroom's garland.[138] [40]

[*Aloud*] Masters indeed have power over honoring their servants!

MADALEKHĀ: The Princess has honored[139] us, too, now.

CANDRĀPĪḌA:

I have now become a slave of the Princess;
She has bought me at the price[140] of her friendship.
She can entrust me with duties;[141]
There is no need to speak. [41]

KEYŪRAKA: The Crown Prince is saying what we should be saying now.

CANDRĀPĪḌA [*to himself*]:[142] Oh, *śeṣahāra*, you are lucky[143] to clasp Kādambarī's neck!

All this time you have been
The most fortunate[144] in the three worlds.
What else among desirable things
Is there for you to seek after?
You have very long acted like an elephant's necklace
On the lovely-buttocked girl's breasts
Resembling the pair of jar-like seats
On the elephant of the god of love. [42]

KĀDAMBARĪ [*aside*]: Friend, ask the Prince if he misses[145] his dear people in Ujjayinī or the camp when he remembers them.

TAMĀLIKĀ [*with a smile*]: Ask him yourself!

KĀDAMBARĪ [*aside*]: Never mind, Tamālikā.[146] Friend Madalekhā, I thus fold my hands to you. Carry out this[147] sole order of mine.

TARALIKĀ: In that case, I'll tell the Lady the Princess[148] isn't entertaining the Prince at all.

KĀDAMBARĪ [*to herself*]: I've gotten into trouble! [*With courage*] Crown Prince — [*Acts embarrassment, her speech unfinished.*]

CANDRĀPĪḌA [*to himself*]: Daughters of good family really[149] do not resort to boldness on account of their modesty even when they are overpowered[150] by the bodiless Love.

Her heart overflowing with love,
She longs to see and speak to her beloved man;
Yet her shyness hinders her action
That has barely started to take place. [43]

[*Aloud*] Madalekhā, you shouldn't distress the Princess!

MADALEKHĀ: What kind of distress is there from a mere salutation?

KĀDAMBARĪ: I'm going now.

TAMĀLIKĀ: Where are you going without attaining what you have come for, thinking of it?

KĀDAMBARĪ [*angrily, aside*[151]]: What's my desire?

TAMĀLIKĀ: It's nothing other than the Crown Prince here.

CANDRĀPĪḌA: Princess, be confident! What other than these are you going to honor me with? Look!

In order to behold your face
    Lovely with sweet smiles,
To receive your favor
    Unfit to be enjoyed by others
And to feast upon this speech
    Resembling nectar,
What good deeds did I perform in my past lives?
    Thus thinking, I am amazed.[152] [44]

KĀDAMBARĪ [*aside to* MADALEKHĀ]: Friend, why do you act like this Tamālikā, who talks wickedly?

MADALEKHĀ: Prince, the Princess said now that the Crown Prince is very good at flattering his female friends with witty talks in which he attributes to them even virtues they don't possess.[153]

CANDRĀPĪḌA: Oh, don't say that!

Birth in the *gandharva* race, matchless riches of beauty,
    Proficiency in the arts, this very sweet youth,
Noble charm and naturally elegant affection —
    This complete set of excellences indeed exists in you. [45]

KĀDAMBARĪ [*stands still, her face bent down with embarrassment.*]

KEYŪRAKA [*to himself*]: The *gandharva* Princess is very much embarrassed. I should introduce another topic. [*Aloud*] Prince, listen!

This is a white sunshade for the flower-bowed Love,
    A conch-shell in the sky-ocean,
A round pinnacle at the top of an eastern king's palace,
    A looking glass for eastern women,

A cup from which an assembly of gods drink abundantly
    And a fruit of a moonlight creeper—
The moon's disk yields very great delights for the eyes. [46]

CANDRĀPĪḌA [*after observing*]: Devotion to the right object, I believe, is the nature of the pure-minded. For

The moon's beam-hands[154] are bestowing the splendor
    Of a pearl necklace on the Princess' neck,
The luster of sandal paste on her breasts,
    The elegance of a gentle smile on her lips,[155]
The impression of large earrings on her ears' vicinity,
    The beauty of a line of camphor on her hair's parting,
The charm of a jasmine flower's look on her braided hair
    And the semblance of *lodhra* powder on her cheeks. [47]

KĀDAMBARĪ [*to herself*]: My heart, it surely befits you to be delighted[156] at the mere sight and talk[157] of your beloved man if you're not going to miss him later on.

[*Having entered without using a curtain*][158]

VIJAYĀ: She has arrived!

KĀDAMBARĪ [*in a flurry*]: Who?

VIJAYĀ: Lady Mahāśvetā!

MADALEKHĀ: Where[159] is she?

VIJAYĀ: She's waiting for the Princess in the temple of Lakṣmī.

KEYŪRAKA: She probably wishes to see the Prince, thinking it's bedtime.

KĀDAMBARĪ [*to herself*]: Mahāśvetā surely wouldn't think[160] of anything else. She herself is the directress of his services.[161] But what can I do?[162] I'm an unfortunate girl. I have to suppress my desire in order to carry out a vow hard to keep. [*Aloud*] Madalekhā, we are leaving.

TAMĀLIKĀ: Shouldn't the Prince dismiss you?

KĀDAMBARĪ: Friend, tell the Prince I have to see Lady Mahāśvetā.

MADALEKHĀ: Crown Prince, permit the Princess to attend Lady Mahāśvetā.

CANDRĀPĪḌA: A white water lily should invite night!

KĀDAMBARĪ [*to herself*]: How can I leave him and go away? Or rather, he'll stay in my heart. [*Exit, accompanied by her friends.*]

CANDRĀPĪḌA [*to himself*]: Oh, alas! the intoxicatingly beautiful girl has gone out of sight. [*Having approached*]

The lovely-buttocked[163] girl is gone
Form my presence for my torment;
A shower that has not yet started is better[164]
Than one that has started but stopped soon.[165] [48]

[*Acts sorrow.*]

KEYŪRAKA: Now Prince, you should enjoy the comfort of sleep, too.

CANDRĀPĪḌA [*after standing up*]: [166]Show me the way to my bedroom.

KEYŪRAKA: This way, this way, Prince.

CANDRĀPĪḌA [*walks around.*]

KEYŪRAKA: Your bedroom is this way, this way. And now,

Adorned on all sides with rows of bursting gem-lamps,
Canopies of strings of glittering pearls,
Fans waving of their own accord,
Brilliant golden pitchers[167]
And fluttering silken cloths
Hanging from shaking gold[168] chains,
It looks almost like a swing
Bestrewn with hosts of flowers. [49]

CANDRĀPĪḌA [*to himself*]: Now I must say this.

O goddess of sleep, do me a favor!
Let me have a dream of her!
These eyes do not[169] despise that
Though their sole desire is to see her in person. [50]

[*Exeunt ambo.*]

END OF ACT THREE

Notes

1. *V.K.: (-sandhukṣaṇa)vyasanitā; M.M.: (- -)sya (?)tā.*
2. *V.K.: śriyaṁ na vi(ramaty); M.M.: śra(śri, M.M.V.2.)yan na pi(-).*
3. *V.K.: kiṁ; M.M.: kiyad.*
4. *M.M.V.2.* and *V.K.: dṛṣṭaṁ; M.M.: draṣṭuṁ.*
5. *M.M.* and *V.K.: -bhāva(bandha-); M.M.V.2.: -hāva(- -).*
6. *M.M.V.2.* and *V.K.: ālīḥ smeramukhīr; M.M.: ālī smeramukhī.*

7. *V.K.* supplies *-bhrū(saṁjñayā)*.
8. *M.M.*: *lakṣīkṛtaṁ*; *V.K.*: *lakṣyīkṛtaṁ*.
9. *V.K.* supplies *athavā*.
10. *M.M.V.2.* and *V.K.*: *sva-*; *M.M.*: *(utkaṇṭhate) sya (janadarśanāya yuvarājaḥ)*.
11. *V.K.*: *kim*; *M.M.*: *api kim*.
12. *M.M.*: *sarve*; *V.K.* omits.
13. *V.K.*: *saṁstavānuparodhinaḥ*; *M.M.*: *-stavanupa-*.
14. *M.M.*: *na kiñ cid api*; *V.K.*: *na kim api*.
15. *M.M.*: *sauhārda-* (*dra* later corrected as *da*); *V.K.*: *sauhārdra-*.
16. *M.M.*: *devena*; *V.K.* omits.
17. *M.M.*: *devyā*; *V.K.*: *devyāḥ*.
18. *M.M.V.2.* and *V.K.*: *(-ṛtu)yauvane*; *M.M.*: *(- -) (?)vane*.
19. *M.M.V.2.*: *vicakila(latā)*; *M.M.*: *vicakita(-)*; *V.K.*: *(svedāmbho) pi ca kila (-)*.
20. *V.K.*: *pratīṣṭe*; *M.M.*: *prakṛṣṭais*.
21. *V.K.*: *ākarṣaty*; *M.M.*: *ākṛṣyaty*.
22. *M.M.V.2.* and *V.K.*: *-danta-*; *M.M.*: *-antar-*.
23. *M.M.*: *-kumuda-*; *V.K.*: *-kusuma-*.
24. *M.M.* and *V.K.*: *sakhyau*. Kādambarī's two closest *sakhī*s are Tamālikā and Madalekhā. But here *sakhyau* seems to refer to Madalekhā, and Taralikā instead of Tamālikā. Tamālikā has gone to the treasure house to fetch the *śeṣahāra* necklace (*vide* the *praveśaka* prelude to this act) and has not returned yet; she will enter slightly after verse 25. And Taralikā has come to ask Kādambarī about the arrangements made for the Prince's enjoyment (*vide* the prelude).
25. *H.S.*: *avitaṇhapekkhaṇijjattaṇaṁ*; *V.K.*: *avitiṇha-*; *M.M.*: *aṇhapoodyaṇī°ja°taṇaṁ*; *M.M.V.2.*: *aviadhipekkhaṇ-*; *M.Ch.M.* and *V.K.Ch.*: *avitṛṣṇaprekṣaṇīyatvam*.
26. *V.K.*: *lajjāmuddhattaṇāiṁ*; *M.M.*: *i(la, M.M.V.2.)°jādu(mu, M.M.V.2.)°dha°taṇāiṁ*; *M.Ch.M.*: *(-sulabhāni) lajjāmugdhatvādīni*; *V.K.Ch.*: *(-) -tvāni*; *H.S.Ch.*: *(-sulabhe) -tve*.
27. *H.S.* assigns this speech to Taralikā, though *M.M.* and *V.K.* assign it to Tamālikā; *vide* n. 24.
28. *M.M.*: *-atiyogaḥ*; *V.K.*: *-abhiyogaḥ*.
29. *V.K.*: *viāresi*: *M.M.*: *viāraṁto*; *M.Ch.M.*: *vicārayat*; *V.K.Ch.*: *vicārayasi*.
30. *H.S.*: *(paccakkhāṇa)saṁmuho*; *M.Ch.M*: *(pratyākhyāna)saṁmukho*; *M.M.* and *V.K.*: *(-)paraṁmuho*; *V.K.Ch.*: *(-)parāṁmukho*.
31. *M.M.*: *taralie*; *M.Ch.M.*: *taralike*; *V.K.*: *tamālie*; *V.K.Ch.*: *tamālike*. *Vide* n. 24.
32. *V.K.*: *tatta-*; *M.M.*: *ta°tohu°ta-*; *M.Ch.M.*: *tavatībhūta-*; *V.K.Ch.*: *tapta-*.
33. *H.S.* assigns this speech to Taralikā, though *M.M.* and *V.K.* assign it to Tamālikā; *Vide* n. 24.
34. *V.K.*: *kamado*; *M.M.*: *kāmado*; *M.Ch.M.*: *kramāj (-)*; *V.K.Ch.*: *kramata (-)*.

35. *V.K.: vidyate; M.M.: khidyate* and *vi-*.
36. *M.M.V.2.* and *V.K.: sṛṣṭiḥ; M.M.: dṛṣṭiḥ.*
37. *M.M.V.2.* and *V.K.: netum; M.M.: netur.*
38. *M.M.V.2.* and *V.K.: vaktraṁ; M.M.: vakraṁ.*
39. *V.K.: adhisakhi sthāpitottānitāgre; M.M.: adhisakhīsthāpitokta (tā* for *kta, M.M.V.2.)nitāgre.*
40. *V.K.: (-praṇayaṁ) dvandvaṁ; M.M.: (-praṇaya) (?)ñcam.*
41. *V.K.: ambā tādo vā; M.M.: aṁbaṁ tāde vā; M.Ch.M.: ambā me tātaś ca; V.K.Ch.: ambā tāto vā.*
42. *V.K.: mohidabbhatthaṇā; M.M.: mohikaa°bha(t,* inserted by *M.M.V.2.)thaṇā; M.Ch.M.: mohitābhyarthanā; V.K.Ch.: modhitā-; H.S.Ch.: moghitā-.*
43. *V.K.: āaṇṇia; M.M.: dū(ā, M.M.V.2.)a°ṇia; M.Ch.M.: dūrād ākarṇya; V.K.Ch.: ākarṇya.*
44. *M.M.* and *V.K.: kahei; M.Ch.M.* and *V.K.Ch.: kathayet; H.S.Ch.: kathayati.*
45. *H.S.* assigns this speech to Taralikā, though *M.M.* and *V.K.* assign it to Tamālikā; *vide* n. 24.
46. *M.M.V.2.* and *V.K.: nāṭayantī; M.M.: nāṭayati.*
47. *V.K.: cittāvakkheva-; M.M.: vi(ce, M.M.V.1.)°tāva°kheva-; M.Ch.M.: cintopakṣepa-; V.K.Ch.: cittāvakṣepa-*
48. *V.K.: karemi; M.M.: karomi; M.Ch.M.: kuryām; V.K.Ch.: karomi.*
49. *M.M.* and *V.K.: ṇiveemi; M.Ch.M.: nivedayeyam; V.K.Ch.: nivedayāmi.*
50. *V.K.: ṇiesa-; M.M.: ṇī(ṇi, M.M.V.1.)esa-; M.Ch.M.: nijasāhasa-; V.K.Ch.: nideśa-.*
51. *H.S.* assigns this speech to Taralikā, though *M.M.* and *V.K.* assign it to Tamālikā; *vide* n. 24.
52. *M.M.: edāva; M.Ch.M.: etāvat; V.K.: ettha dāva; V.K.Ch.: atra tāvat.*
53. *H.S.: paaḍīkarehi; M.M.: vusīkarehi; M.M.V.2.* and *V.K.: puḍī-; M.Ch.M.* and *V.K.Ch.: prakaṭīkuru.*
54. *H.S.: apavārya; M.M.* and *V.K.: svagataṁ.*
55. *M.M.: saṁśleṣayantī; V.K.: saṁśoṣayantī.*
56. *M.M.V.2.* supplies *tāla(vṛnta-); V.K.* follows.
57. *V.K.: -samādhaye; M.M.: -(?)mādhaye.*
58. *H.S.: kiṁ apy (ākulam); M.M.: tadā vy(py, M.M.V.2.) (-); V.K.: tathāpy (-).*
59. *M.M.V.2.* and *V.K.: saṁśete; M.M.: saṁvete.*
60. *M.M.: ṇa; M.Ch.M.: na; V.K.: ṇaṁ; V.K.Ch.: nanu.*
61 *M.M.: de; M.Ch.M.* and *V.K.* omit.
62. *V.K.* supplies *svagatam.*
63. *M.M.V.2.* and *V.K.: -evvaṁ paā(yā, M.M.V.2.)sio hodu; M.M.: -eṣa savaāsao-; M.Ch.M.: -evaṁ prakāśito bhavati; V.K.Ch.: - - - bhavatu.*
64. *H.S.: akkhaasohaddaṇihī; M.M.: ya°khaasoha°daṇīhi; V.K.: akkhaasohaggaṇihī; M.Ch.M.: saubhāgyanidhiḥ; V.K.Ch.: akṣayasaubhāgyanidhir; H.S.: -sauhārda-.*

65. *V.K.: uvekkhai; M.M.: upekhai; M.Ch.M.: upekṣeta; V.K.Ch.: upekṣate.*
66. *M.M.* and *V.K.: taralie; M.Ch.M.: tamālike; V.K.Ch.: taralike.*
67. *M.M.* and *V.K. sarala-; M.Ch.M.: sarasa-; V.K.Ch.: sarala-.*
68. *M.M.* and *V.K.: pūrei; M.Ch.M.: pūrayed; V.K.Ch.: pūrayaty.*
69. *H.S.: mahantaṁ via; M.M.: va(ma, M.M.V.2.)haiva; V.K.: mahadiva; M.Ch.M.: vahati; V.K.Ch.: mahad iva.*
70. Or to enjoy or feel (*nirveṣṭuṁ*). After this *M.M.V.2.* fills out a lacuna with *yat; V.K.* follows.
71. *V.K.: śaṅkyamānair (na tāvat); M.M.: śakya- (- -).*
72. *V.K.: tasyāpy: M.M.: kasyāpy.*
73. *M.M.V.2.* and *V.K.: aho; M.M.: aho.*
74. *V.K.: sindūra-; M.M.: sindhūra-.*
75. *V.K.: -kariṇāṁ; M.M.: kiraṇo(ṇā, M.M.V.2.).*
76. *M.M.* and *V.K.: -talpam; M.M.V.2.: -kalpam.*
77. *V.K.: krāntā; M.M.: kāntā.*
78. *M.M.: svagatam; V.K.* omits.
79. *M.M.V.2.* and *V.K.: amṛtarasam; M.M.: ādṛta-.*
80. *V.K.: cakorayor iva hi; M.M.: cakarayor iva.*
81. *H.S.: -kandala-; M.M.* and *V.K.: -kandalī-.*
82. *M.M.V.2.* and *V.K.: tārakāṅkitaḥ; M.M.: tārakāḥ(?).*
83. *V.K.: -daṭṭuṁ ṇa pārīadi ahirūvo-; M.M.: -da°viṇṇa kiraehi aarūo-; M.Ch.M.: -draṣṭuṁ na pāryate eṣo bhyarhito-; V.K.Ch.: - - -pāryate abhirūpo-.*
84. *V.K.* unnecessarily adds *āgamiduṁ (-vilambai); V.K.Ch.: āgantuṁ (-vilambate); H.S.* omits.
85. *V.K.: parianaṇamuhādo; M.M.: vaaṇamuheṇa; M.Ch.M.: parijanamukhe; V.K.Ch.: parijana-mukhāj (-).*
86. *V.K.: kahiṁ; M.M.: kahaṁ; M.Ch.M.* and *V.K.Ch.: kutra.*
87. *M.M.V.2.* and *V.K.: uṭṭhedu devī; M.M.: i°ṭhedu-; M.Ch.M.: vayaṁ gacchāmaḥ; V.K.Ch.: uttiṣṭhatu devī.*
88. *V.K.: dīpiādhāriṇīo; M.M.: devī uva°di (dhāriṇī, M.M.V.2.)āo; M.Ch.M.* and *V.K.Ch.: dīpikādhāriṇya (upa-).*
89. *V.K.* supplies *bhave; V.K.Ch.: bhavet.*
90. *V.K.: (ahiṇandaṇijjā) udāresu; M.M.: (-) idāresu; M.Ch.M.: (abhinandyāv eva) dāreṣu; V.K.Ch.: (abhinandaniyāv) udāreṣu.*
91. *M.M.* and *V.K.: raaṇassa; M.Ch.M.: ratnahārasya; V.K.Ch.: ratnasya.*
92. *V.K.: paphullamallia(ā, H.S.)-; M.M.: va°pulama° (?)ā-; M.Ch.M.: pṛṣṭhamallikā-; V.K.Ch.: praphulla - -.*
93. *V.K.: upasarpati; M.M.: (rāautto) uvasappati.*
94. *M.M.: tataḥ praviśati yathānirdiṣṭaś candrāpīḍō(ḍaḥ, M.M.V.2.) keyūra(ka,* inserted by *M.M.V.2.)ś ca; V.K.* omits.

95. *M.M.V.2.* supplies *-rati-; V.K.* follows.
96. *M.M.V.2.* and *V.K.: velā; M.M.: khelā.*
97. *M.M.V.2.* and *V.K.: -mauktika-; M.M.: -(?)ka-.*
98. *V.K.: upasarpayati; M.M.: upasarpati.*
99. *M.M.V.2.* and *V.K.: vijayā, taha, iti niṣkrāntā; M.M.: vijayayā saha niṣkrāntā.*
100. *V.K.* supplies.
101. *M.M.: kṣauma(ṁ,* supplied by *V.K.) jyotsnāśuci; V.K.: - - chavi.*
102. *M.M.: kuntalai(r,* supplied by *V.K.) dyotayantī; V.K.: -mānayantī.*
103. *M.M.: -kara (utthāya); V.K.: -hasta (-).*
104. *Śṛṅgāralajjāṁ.* It primarily refers to Kādambarī's embarrassment due to her love for Candrāpīḍa, in which case *śṛṅgāra* (the erotic *rasa* or aesthetic experience) is simply a substitute for *rati* (the *sthāyibhāva* or basic human emotion of love) (for the difference between the two terms, *vide* Intro., chap. IX). But it also seems to refer to her embarrassment due to the way she is dressed, in which case *śṛṅgāra* is taken to mean a brilliant (*ujjvala*) dress suggestive of the *rasa* (*vide* Intro., chap. IX, n. 13), for in the preceding verses (29 and 30) and the prose between them, Candrāpīḍa vividly describes the way she is dressed and looks.
105. *V.K.: (adaṁsaṇe) kāuṁ (āsaṁsāmi); M.M.: (-) kāiṁ (āsaṁsemi); M.Ch.M.: (adarśana)kāle (āśaṁsāmi); V.K.Ch.: (-ne) kartum (-).*
106. *M.M.: atituṅgaṁ; V.K.: -kumbhaṁ.*
107. *V.K.: alasa-; M.M.: alasi-.*
108. *M.Ch.M.: (idānīm) eva.*
109. *M.M.* and *V.K.: āsi; M.Ch.M.: āsīt; V.K.Ch.: āste.*
110. *V.K.: phalamūlakandehiṁ; M.M.: -mūla^{o}dehi; M.Ch.M.: phalamūlaiḥ; V.K.Ch.: -mūlakandaiḥ.*
111. *V.K.: parijane; M.M.: parigṛhītajane.*
112. *M.M.V.2.* and *V.K.: nānṛṇyam; M.M.: (?)m.*
113. *M.M.V.2.* and *V.K.: ūrjitaṁ; M.M.: ū(?)taṁ.*
114. *V.K.* supplies.
115. *H.S.: uvarohaabbhatthaṇā; M.Ch.M.: uparodhābhyarthanā; M.M.: uvarohakaa^{o}dhāṇā; V.K.: -kaatthaṇā; V.K.Ch.: uparodhakadarthanā.*
116. *V.K.: ido; M.M.* repeats; *M.Ch.M.* and *V.K.Ch.: ito.*
117. *V.K.: ghanasāradravarasaḥ; M.M.: ghanasādravarasaḥ; M.M.V.2.: -dravabharaḥ.*
118. *M.M.* and *V.K.: kaitakam; M.M.V.2.: kaitavam.*
119. *M.M.: kasya cin (-); V.K.* omits.
120. *V.K.: muktāhārasya (prabhāprasaraḥ); M.M.: muktāhāra (-).*
121. *M.M.: taralikayā (-) dhāryamāṇasya; V.K.: (-) nikṣiptasya.*
122. *H.S.: āvaā dīsai; M.M.: āmaā dūsai; V.K.: pūriā dīsai; M.Ch.M.: ābhāti sarvatomukhaṁ; H.S.Ch.: āvṛtā dṛśyate; V.K.Ch.: pūritā -.*

123. *V.K.: anaghair; M.M.: ananyaiḥ; M.M.V.2.: anarghaiḥ.*

124. *V.K.: amalair; M.M.: kamalai (r,* supplied by *M.M.V.2.).*

125. *V.K.: kariṣyati; M.M.: kariṣyasi.*

126. *Guṇa* means both a string and a virtue.

127. *M.M.V.2.* and *V.K.: na kadāpi; M.M.: - -cid.*

128. *M.M.V.2.* and *V.K.: uvālambhijjai; M.M.: -jala; M.Ch.M.: upalabhyeta; V.K.Ch.: upālabhyate.*

129. *V.K.: -ṇimitta-; M.M.: -ṇi°ta-; M.Ch.M.: -mitra-; V.K.Ch.: -nimitta-.*

130. *M.M.* and *V.K.: akhedaṇijjaṁ; M.Ch.M.: avedanīyām; V.K.Ch.: akhedanīyām.*

131. *V.K.: ācakkhidaṁ; M.M.: ca°khitaṁ; M.Ch.M.: ācakṣitaṁ; V.K.Ch.: ākhyātaṁ.*

132. *V.K.: vivakkhidaṁ; M.M.: vica°khiaṁ; M.Ch.M.: ākhyātavyaṁ; V.K.Ch.: vivakṣitaṁ.*

133. *Iyam = ekāvalī = śeṣahāra.*

134. *M.M.: -vallīṁ; V.K.: -vallīr.*

135. Viṣṇu.

136. *Imo; ayam.* This is intended to refer to both the necklace *śeṣahāra* and Candrāpīḍa.

137. *V.K.: aṇumaṇṇai; M.M.: aṇama°ṇala(i, M.M.V.2.); M.Ch.M.: anumanyeta; V.K.Ch.: anumanyate.*

138. *V.K.: varaṇasrag iva; M.M.: -sragrīva.*

139. *V.K.: bahumadāo; M.M.: bahumalpā; M.Ch.M.: bahumatāḥ smaḥ; V.K.Ch.: bahumatāḥ.*

140. *V.K.: -mūlyena; M.M.: -mūlena.*

141. *M.M.: niyojanīyo devyā smi;* this is metrically acceptable. But *V.K.* unnecessarily rearranges it into *devyā niyojanīyo smi.*

142. *M.M.V.2.* supplies *svagatam; V.K.* follows.

143. *V.K.* supplies *-subhaga.*

144. *Dhanyas.*

145. *H.S.: kiṁ (-) payyussuo hoditti; V.K.: - (-) payyusio-; M.M.: (-) va(pa, M.M.V.2)°ūsidavā hohi°ti; M.Ch.M.: (-) paryutsuko bhavasīti; V.K.Ch.: kim (-) -bhavatīti.*

146. *V.K.: tamālie tumaṁ ciṭṭha; M.M.: tamāliā - evvatha; M.Ch.M.: taralike tvaṁ tiṣṭha; V.K.Ch.: tamālike - -.*

147. *H.S.: imaṁ; M.Ch.M.: idam; M.M.* and *V.K.: tumaṁ; V.K.Ch.: tvaṁ.*

148. *V.K.: ettha - ṇivedemi devīe; M.M.: e°* (?, blurred)*iṇivehemi-; M.Ch.M.: atra - nivedayiṣyāmi bhartṛdārikayā; V.K.Ch.: - - nivedayāmi devyā.*

149. *V.K.* unnecessarily adds *yat(satyam-).*

150. *V.K.: -balāt kṛtopi; M.M.: - - kṛtepi; M.M.V.2.: - - kṛtāpi.*

151. *M.M.V.2.* and *V.K.: apavārya; M.M.: avalokya.*

152. *V.K.: vismitaḥ; M.M.: vismṛtaḥ.*

153. *H.S.: abhūdaṁ; M.M.: ahotaṁ; V.K.: ahodaṁ; M.Ch.M.: abhavantam; V.K.Ch.: abhūtaṁ.*

154. *V.K.: (śaśikiraṇa)karo; M.M.: (-) haro.*

155. *V.K.: oṣṭhe; M.M.: oṣṭhaṁ.*

156. *H.S.: (-metteṇa) vi ṇaṁ suhaṁ; M.M.: (- -) - - puhaṁ; M.Ch.M.* skips; *V.K.: saṁmodo; V.K.Ch.: saṁmodaḥ; H.S.Ch.: (-mātreṇā)pi nanu sukham.*

157. *M.M.: -ālāpa-; M.Ch.M.: -ālāpa-; V.K.: -lāha-; V.K.Ch.: -lābha-.*

158. *H.S.: praviśyāpaṭākṣepeṇa; M.M.* and *V.K.: praviśya paṭākṣepeṇa. Vide* Trans., Act II, n. 93.

159. *V.K.: kahiṁ; M.M.: kiṁ; M.Ch.M.* and *V.K.Ch.: kutra.*

160. *H.S.: cintejjā; M.M.: cinteiṁ; V.K.: cintedi; M.Ch.M.* and *V.K.Ch.: cintayet.*

161. *M.M.V.2.* and *V.K.: uvaāraṇioiṇī; M.M.: (se se) iāra-; M.Ch.M.: upacāraṁ niyojayantī; V.K.Ch.: upacāraniyojanī.*

162. *M.M.* and *V.K.: karemi; M.Ch.M.: kuryām; V.K.Ch.: karomi.*

163. *V.K.: varārohā; M.M.: (?).*

164. *V.K.: varaṁ; M.M.: paraṁ.*

165. *V.K.: acirād; M.M.: cirād.*

166. *V.K.* unnecessarily adds *keyūraka.*

167. *V.K.: bhṛṅgāra-; M.M.: bhṛṅgā(?)-.*

168. *V.K.: -kāñcana-; M.M.: -kā(?)nu-.*

169. *H.S.: na caitad; M.M.: na ced; V.K.: caitad.*

Miśraviṣkambhaka
Prelude to Act Four

[*Having entered*]

CHAMBERLAIN [*distressed at the constraint of his duties*]: Servants' work is hard[1] indeed. Especially[2] so are the duties of the superintendents of ladies' inner-citadels. For

I have to censure even respected people
Among those who come within at the wrong time,
And inflict punishment on the innocent attendants
Of the ladies' inner-citadels.
I can never even take a rest by day or night.
Fie on others' happiness!
Mine has been destroyed though not by myself. [1]

But now, enough of that talk! It's checked[3] by a matter that has taken place. Great Queen Madirā has ordered me thus: "Honorable Kṣīroda, you know very well about the attempt which started with the employment of a pair of *kinnaras* in order to set my daughter free from her vow. So please find out and let me know at once[4] whether or not Mahāśvetā is trying to bring back here the Prince of the middle world, who left to see his camp, which arrived in the vicinity of the temple of Śiva by following Indrāyudha's tracks." So[5] I'll now go to the girls' inner-citadel. [*After taking a few steps, with a glance*] Oh! here comes Irāvatī, Princess Kādambarī's chowrie bearer, with hurried steps. I'll ask[6] her. [*Approaches her.*]

[*Having entered*]

IRĀVATĪ: Good day, Honorable Kṣīroda!

CHAMBERLAIN: May you be fortunate! Why are you going in such a great hurry?

IRĀVATĪ: I have to go to the Pleasure[7] Grove.

CHAMBERLAIN: Why there?

IRĀVATĪ: Madalekhā has ordered me to prepare a snow house[8] there.

CHAMBERLAIN: What's this unexpected undertaking?

IRĀVATĪ: There's a reason for it.

CHAMBERLAIN: Tell me. There must be an important purpose.

IRĀVATĪ: Honorable one, haven't you heard[9] the Princess is suffering from a fever?[10]

CHAMBERLAIN: I've heard that much.[11] Now I want to know the cause of it.

IRĀVATĪ: Of course, the Prince of the middle world—[12] [*Her speech unfinished, apprehensively to herself*] Why! I've betrayed the secret it a single word.[13]

CHAMBERLAIN [*having discovered*]: There's no need to hide that! I can discover it from a part of it.

IRĀVATĪ [*to herself*]: He's surely sincere-hearted. Then, why shouldn't I tell[14] him? [*After smiling, aloud*] The Princess won't tell her desire even to her dear friends in order to carry out her vow in spite of her longing for the glorious one. Naturally, she's afflicted with a love fever.

CHAMBERLAIN: Is there a sign of his love, too?

IRĀVATĪ: How[15] can the moon[16] possibly neglect moonlight?

CHAMBERLAIN: Then, why did he go away without attaining his object?[17]

IRĀVATĪ: Mahāśvetā sent him together with *gandharva* youths lest his royal camp, sojourning nearby, should disturb her hermitage.

CHAMBERLAIN: Then, by what[18] ever means does Mahāśvetā intend to fetch him?

IRĀVATĪ: Since the Princess ins't feeling well, Mahāśvetā has just sent Keyūraka with a present[19] in his hand to fetch the most fortunate one here.

CHAMBERLAIN [*to himself*]: I've heard what I should hear. What's the point of going into the girls' inner-citadel after this? [*Aloud*] That's an appropriate attempt! Look!

Since she cherishes love for the man
    Tender with an abundance of virtues,
He entertains longing[20] for her
    Conformable to his own desire
And there is no obstacle between them,
    They will be united — that is certain.
The fruit of the tree of good deeds

Is indeed not common to all. [2]

You'd better go.

[*Exit* IRĀVATĪ.]

CHAMBERLAIN: Now I'll give the *gandharva* Queen the news of the return of her future son-in-law, Candrāpīḍa. [*Exit.*]

END OF THE *MIŚRAVIṢKAMBHAKA*
PRELUDE TO ACT FOUR

Notes

1. *H.S.: kaṣṭā - sevopajīvinām; M.M.: kaṣṭaṁ - saivopajīviṣu; V.K.: kaṣṭā - sevā.*
2. *V.K.: viśeṣād; M.M.: viśeṣam.*
3. *V.K.: -vipratiṣiddhenā(munā); M.M.: - - ṣiddhaṁ nā(-).*
4. *M.M.: idaṁ; V.K.: imaṁ.*
5. *V.K.* supplies *tad.*
6. *V.K.: prakṣyāmi; M.M.: prekṣā(kṣyā,* crossed)*mi.*
7. *V.K.: -mae līlā(vaṇaṁ); M.M.: - maa lekhā(-); M.Ch.M.* and *V.K.Ch.: -mayā līlā(vanam).*
8. *V.K.: (hima)ghara-; M.M.: (-)ara-; M.Ch.M.: (hima)kara-; V.K.Ch.: (-)gṛha-.*
9. *H.S.: sudaṁ; M.M.: muṇiaṁ; V.K.: suṇiaṁ; M.Ch.M.* and *V.K.Ch.: śrutam.*
10. *V.K.: saṁdāveṇa; M.M.: saṁdāreṇa; M.Ch.M.* and *V.K.Ch.: saṁtāpena.*
11. *M.M.: etāvat; V.K.: etat.*
12. *V.K.: majjhamaloarāauttaṁ; M.M.: majhaloarāavuttaṁ; M.Ch.M.: madhyamalokarājaputraḥ; V.K.Ch.: - putraṁ.*
13. *Vide supra,* n. 12.
14. *V.K.: ṇiveijjai; M.M.: ṇī-; M.Ch.M.: nivedayiṣyāmi; V.K.Ch.: nivedyate.*
15. *H.S.: kahaṁ; M.M.* and *V.K.: kahiṁ; M.Ch.M.: kutra; V.K.Ch.: kathaṁ.*
16. *V.K.: candeṇa; M.M.: careṇa; M.Ch.M.* and *V.K.Ch.: candreṇa.*
17. *V.K.: akṛtārtha (-); M.M.: -tham (-).*
18. *V.K.: kayā; M.M.: kadā.*
19. *H.S.: pāhuaa-; M.M.: lāhuḍaa-; V.K.: pāhua-; M.Ch.M.: prābhṛtaka-; V.K.Ch.: prābhṛta-.*
20. *M.M.: rucī; V.K.: rucir.*

ACT FOUR

[*Enter* CANDRĀPĪḌA, *seated on the throne, his* JESTER *and* PATRALEKHĀ.][1]

CANDRĀPĪḌA [*to himself*]:

As if she were a golden creeper yoked to a soul,
  Or lightning that has started roaming on the earth,
Or another victory banner of the flower-bowed Love,
  She has not left my heart since I saw her. [3]

Moreover,

Her face is for my eyes' pleasure,[2]
  But the moon, for their torment;
Her eyes are for my heart's joy,
  But the mind-born Love's arrows, for its bursting;
Her voice is for my ears' great delight,
  But the lute's sound, foir their exhaustion —
Even among like objects, Brahmā creates
  Inequality owing to his destructiveness. [4]

PATRALEKHĀ [*to herself*]: Surely the Crown Prince must be[3] still thinking about the incident on Hemakūṭa he has told us about.

CANDRĀPĪḌA [*to himself*]: Oh, why! I can't restrain my wretched[4] heart wayward through its passion for a person hard to acquire. [*After reflecting*] Or perhaps that's truly her love. For

Her bracelet's fall at the time of giving betel,
  Her amorous glances at the top of her mansion
And her embarrassment in her unusual talks[5] —
  Why can they not[6] betray her lovesickness?[7] [5]

JESTER: Surely such is the respect of masters for their servants![8] For this friend hasn't even talked to me, his companion, since he met the *gandharva* Princess.

PATRALEKHĀ: Silly Dramiḍadhārmika! why do you talk nonsense? Surely kings' minds are filled with thousands of duties.

CANDRĀPĪḌA: Patralekhā, you have cleverly guessed what is on my mind.

JESTER [*proudly*]:[9] What ever is beyond the power of my intelligence?[10] So friend, tell[11] me the cause of your mind's disturbance. She'll surely respect me for that.

CANDRĀPĪḌA: What else can I be thinking about?

> That incomparable sincere-heartedness of Mahāśvetā,
> Kādambarī's great respect pleasant with affection
> And my other female friends' ample courtesy and charm —
> They enchant and fascinate my heart entirely. [6]

PATRALEKHĀ: Thus again and again even in their absence, the Prince is loud in praise of their kindness surely common to no one else.

CANDRĀPĪḌA [*to himself*]:

> My heart, you were then courageous to take me away
> From the charming-browed girl's presence;
> This excitement is not becoming to you.
> How could I possibly divert you now? [7]

[*Half out of the dressing room*]

PORTRESS: Crown Prince, here's some *gandharva* youth who has arrived at the guardroom and requests thus: "How can I obtain the pleasure of seeing the Prince?"

CANDRĀPĪḌA: He's surely Keyūraka! He was introduced to me as a close attendant of the Princess. Saudāminī, show him in!

PORTRESS: As the Crown Prince commands. [*Exit.*]

[*Having entered with two others*]

KEYŪRAKA: May the Prince be victorious!

CANDRĀPĪḌA: Keyūraka, come here now.

KEYŪRAKA [*sits down.*]

CANDRĀPĪḌA: How's the Princess?

KEYŪRAKA: How can't she be well when she has shown the Crown Prince a favor like this? [*After turning around*] Friends Kiṁśuka and Kiṅkirat, show him the Princess' tokens of remembrance sent by her own hands.

JESTER: I'm sure they're sweetmeats!

CANDRĀPĪḌA: The nominal Brahmin[12] is always hungry.

TWO MEN [*after opening a lotus leaf box with a top sealed with lotus fibers*]: These are betel leaves pale as the cheeks[13] of beautiful girls afflicted with the torment of separation. This is a piece of camphor[14] twinkling as a bright star in the autumnal season. And this is the sandal paste whose unique fragrance has perfumed this place.

KEYŪRAKA [*having taken them, gently*]: Prince, please accept this gift. [*Handing it over*] And Princess Mahāśvetā told in a message . . .

CANDRĀPĪḌA: What does the Lady command?

KEYŪRAKA:

"I think you brought[15] us a delight like that
Of seeing you for a moment,
Alas! to make us feel a pain like this
Of suffering[16] separation from you. [8]

Besides, we don't know why Princess Kādambarī has been extremely ill since you departed. So glorious one, please show us a favor by coming back at once. And please forgive this improper forwardness in a message."

JESTER [*aside*]: Why! my friend will be exhausted by going to and coming back from Hemakūṭa.

CANDRĀPĪḌA [*to himself*]: Oh, Mahāśvetā has said something clearly.[17]

KEYŪRAKA: And her friends Madalekhā and others blamed the Prince.

CANDRĀPĪḌA [*eagerly*]: How so?

KEYŪRAKA:

"It is unworthy of a gentleman to seduce
An innocent maiden in this manner;
No doubt you have, as if a thief,
Taken away our friend's heart." [9]

PATRALEKHĀ: A clever reproach!

JESTER [*aside*]: Friend, are you still dissatisfied?[18]

CANDRĀPĪḌA [*to himself*]:

Cheer up, my heart! Congratulations!
Your love is appropriate;
Your wish has been requited
In the words of her attendants. [10]

[*Aloud*] Tell me, Keyūraka. What has been the pastime of the Princess after I left? Is there sometimes talk about me?

KEYŪRAKA: What do you think,[19] Prince?

After she barely sent you away
    From her mansion in that manner,[20]
She was there very long with her face pale,
    And in order to see[21] how far you had gone,
She repeatedly directed towards her window
    Her wide eyes shedding small tear drops. [11]

PATRALEKHĀ [*aside*]: The passion of the *gandharva* Princess has surely grown extreme.[22]

KEYŪRAKA: When the Prince went out of sight, she came down from there and climbed the Pleasure Mountain. And there,

"He held a musical circle in this arena;
    In this bower, he was seen again in the evening;
He received our service on this edge
    Of the white water lily pool beside my mansion,"
Thus talking, the Princess passed the whole day. [12]

JESTER [*aside to* PATRALEKHĀ]: It has turned out fine. Surely she is longing for him as he is, for her.

KEYŪRAKA: And Madalekhā told me at daybreak:

"She has neither pleasure in meals
    Nor joy in music nor delight in jokes
Nor regard for her friends as before;
    She has spent[23] the night only in bed,
Her eyes closed, mind exhausted
    And face covered with her garment's hem. [13]

And her burning fever is getting worse."

CANDRĀPĪḌA [*to himself*]: Luckily, he has told me the state of the Princess' heart in every detail. Even then, I don't feel confident because I'm not observing her for myself.[24] [*Aloud*]

Without fail, I will now attend[25]
    Upon the Princess not feeling well.

Who ever neglects a flower garland suffering
From rustlings owing to summer's heat? [14]

PATRALEKHĀ & JESTER: That's worthy of a friendship like that!

CANDRĀPĪḌA: Are you also interested[26] to see Princess Kādambarī?

BOTH: If the Prince wishes to honor us, too.

CANDRĀPĪḌA [*to a servant*]: Inform Minister Vaiśampāyana on duty that we're going to Hemakūṭa now.

SERVANT: Certainly. [*Exit.*]

CANDRĀPĪḌA [*after standing up*]: Keyūraka, please show us the way forward.

KEYŪRAKA:

Pass Acchoda along the path on its bank
Adorned with young lotus buds and pollen!
Then go into Caitraratha, where
Fatigued[27] wayfarers rest everywhere!
Then climb Mt. Hemakūṭa
By means of this flight of steps!
Then enter the city of the *gandharva* King!
Thus arrive with delight! [15]

[*All walk aournd.*]

CANDRĀPĪḌA [*to himself*]:

Sweet[28] to my heart is a sight of her
Even if it is acquired in a dream;[29]
I am going to see that very fawn-eyed girl
With my eyes once again. [16]

KEYŪRAKA: Now, here's the main gate to the girls' inner-citadel.

[*All act entering it.*]

PATRALEKHĀ [*after looking around*]:[30] The wealth of the *gandharva* King surely surpasses that of the gods and demons![31]

JESTER [*aside*]: Great King Citraratha is worthy to be a relative by marriage.

[*Off stage*]

Decorate the fence with *hrībera* flowers!

Sprinkle the ground with cold water!
Make the beds[32] fit to lie down upon
With camphor and sandal!
Spread a soft silken canopy
Over the posts of banana trees!
Tie fresh lotus buds to the lattice windows! [17]

And again,

Friend, set the moonstone slabs
Cold as the liquid in Śiva's throat!
Friend, furnish the pleasure couch
With white water lilies' fresh innermost leaves!
Friend, throw ornamental lotus fibers and sprouts
Into the rivers of misty water!
Kādambarī has arrived in the snow house,
Her fever extremely aggravated. [18]

KEYŪRAKA: That's an announcement by a servant of the Princess.

CANDRĀPĪḌA: What's[33] the cause of this fever of Kādambarī?

KEYŪRAKA: Crown Prince, now enter the snow house through the interior of the Pleasure Grove[34] and greet the Princess. I'll find out if Mahāśvetā has finished her duties, and come back. [*Exit.*][35]

PATRALEKHĀ: Crown Prince, what's this in front that looks[36] like a mass of emeralds heaped up?

CANDRĀPĪḌA: Surely it's the Princess' snow house covered[37] with fresh banana leaves.

JESTER: Then please enter it.

[*All act entering it.*]

CANDRĀPĪḌA [*after looking around*]: Oh, what skill in arranging an apparatus[38] for cooling service!

Water drops fall through the flutterings
Of the wings of sporting artificial geese;
Here puppets wave with their hands
Chowries of lotus fibers;
An imitation cloud makes peacocks
Eager to make *kekā* cries;
And deer take a walk on the grounds
Covered with synthetic grass.[39] [19]

PATRALEKHĀ: My heart seems covered with floods of spray like the snow house.

JESTER [*having acted being overcome by cold*]: Oh, dear! Oh, dear! Shivering with cold[40] in front of it, my limbs seem to be shrinking now.

CANDRĀPĪḌA: How strange! How strange! All forms of cold, though checked[41] by one another, thus get together in one place at the same time.

Here arises a stream of moonlight
Cold as a shower of nectar;
Here breathe zephyrs friendly as a flow
Of *nīpa* flowers' fragrance;
In addition, on all sides freezes
This heap of snow —
This apparatus is neither on the earth
Nor in the heaven of the gods. [20]

JESTER: Now, what ever is that throng[42] of girls? They are in garments made of soft inner banana leaves.[43] All their limbs are anointed with very cold sandal paste.[44] And they are beautiful with bracelets of withered lotus fibers, bellies with strings of trembling gems, and charming pearl necklaces tied to garlands of blown jasmine buds.

CANDRĀPĪḌA: Surely they're the Princess' servants engaged in the service of cooling her.

PATRALEKHĀ: Crown Prince, who ever is that girl? She appears to be getting her friends to prepare[45] a remedy for her fever.

CANDRĀPĪḌA [*having seen her*]: Ah! my eyes have obtained consolation. Patralekhā, she is the daughter of Citraratha.

The wide-eyed girl is rolling[46]
Upon a couch of sprouts,
Her mass of braided, adorned hair[47] fallen
And limbs moving to and fro —
It is as though Love had laid his bow
With a loosened string of bees
Upon a bench of precious stones. [21]

PATRALEKHĀ: The Crown Prince didn't say much to describe her exceptional beauty.

JESTER: How come my friend doesn't get affected by love after seeing[48] such a gem of a girl?

CANDRĀPĪḌA [*having observed her*]: Why, she looks different! In fact, her

Eyes are rivaling a pair of large black bees
    Painted in a picture;
Her face is synonymous with a lotus flower
    Not entirely closed;
Her arm-creepers are drooping languidly, much emaciated
    As lotus fibers attacked[49] by heat;
Moreover, is her body emulating a thin digit
    Of the moon on its first night? [22]

Patralekhā, I'll now hide here behind the royal column[50] and listen to her secret talk.

PATRALEKHĀ: As the Prince pleases.

[*All stay thus.*]

[*Enter* KĀDAMBARĪ *as described, and her two friends.*]

KĀDAMBARĪ: Friend, who has told this untruth that the[51] Prince has come back?

MADALEKHĀ: The servants never tell a falsehood.

CANDRĀPĪḌA: Who's that the Princess is so eager to see?

JESTER: Well, who else but me[52] can be the topic of this talk?

KĀDAMBARĪ: Then, how come he hasn't shown up yet?

TAMĀLIKĀ: I think he's delaying by meeting[53] Mahāśvetā performing her duties in the temple of Lakṣmī.

MADALEKHĀ: I heard he had entered the banana grove.

PATRALEKHĀ: The talk entirely concerns the Prince.

KĀDAMBARĪ [*acting the intensity of her fever*]:[54] My heart's fever is intense!

MADALEKHĀ: Princess, this sprout couch[55] is shaking.[56] So get up and sit down on the stone[57] covered with red *pāṭala* flowers. It's made thoroughly cold with special lotuses in a heap of snow[58] mixed with sandal sap brought instantly through violent shaking in the hollows of moonstone dolls' hands. It's beautiful with emeralds furnished with an uninterrupted series of brilliant sprinklings of rain in a stream of a mass of water drops from an artificial shower. And it resembles[59] a crystal slab on which fresh camphor and the pith of banana trees are falling down.

KĀDAMBARĪ: Why do you torment me like this again and again with futile efforts? [*Slowly gets up and sits down.*]

CANDRĀPĪḌA: Her body is extremely enfeebled. For

Leaning with one hand-sprout
Upon her friend staying together,
Lifting up[60] with the other
Her garment's loosened knot from her broad loins,
Stooping with the weight of her breasts
And taking steps very slowly,
The slender-bellied girl[61] barely moved
From one couch to another, taking a long time. [23]

MADALEKHĀ: Tamālikā, come and fan[62] our dear friend with the lotus leaf fan. It has a handle of clean lotus fibers, and sheds particles of ice perfumed with the scent of very cold *uśīra* roots. I'll sprinkle her eyes, forehead mark, hands, feet and breasts[63] with the water brought in a small moonstone pitcher.

KĀDAMBARĪ: Friends, take off[64] these gemmed gold ornaments causing me intense heat![65]

TAMĀLIKĀ: Madalekhā, do so. And dress[66] our dear friend in a garment suitable for providing coolness with sprouts, lotus fibers, camphor and barks.

MADALEKHĀ: [*acts doing so.*]

CANDRĀPĪḌA:

"Her excessively fevered limbs are covered with garlands
And bracelets of half-withered lotus fibers,
And fresh sandal paste instantly dries up[67] on them.
Is that lovesick girl[68] revealing to me
Her extremely intensified internal fever or not?"
Thus thinking, my entire heart swings. [24]

PATRALEKHĀ: There's no room for doubt about that! Otherwise, you've thoroughly described the marks of her beauty.

CADNRĀPĪḌA [*hopefully, to himself*]:

If only this lovely girl is afflicted
With a fever due to love for me,
At once I will become
The foremost of the fortunate. [25]

TWO FRIENDS [*after looking at each other*]: Oh, how stubborn our dear friend is in her vow! Even in a situation like this, she won't tell us[69] what's in her heart. So we should do[70] what's appropriate for this occasion.

[*Having entered without using a curtain*][71]

KEYŪRAKA: Why! Prince Candrāpīḍa is hiding here. [*After approaching him*] Mahāśvetā has completed her duties and arrived here. Now Prince, cheer up Princess Kādambarī!

CANDRĀPĪḌA: In fact, we've been waiting for you to come here. Now[72] show us the way.

KEYŪRAKA: This way,[73] this way, Prince.

[*All walk around.*]

MADALEKHĀ [*having looked*]: Our friend has obtained a consolation. The Crown Prince has arrived here.

KĀDAMBARĪ [*excited with joy, tries to get up to greet*[74] *him.*]

CANDRĀPĪḌA: Princess![75] *Gandharva* race's moonlight! Kādambarī!

This body delicate as a lotus petal is
Already exhausted with fever.
You should not be fatigued.[76] There is no need
To restrain[77] yourself to greet me. [26]

KEYŪRAKA: Princess, this is the Crown Prince's confidante.

PATRALEKHĀ [*bows.*]

KĀDAMBARĪ [*aside*]: She's ready to come this far with the Crown Prince.

KEYŪRAKA: And this is the Prince's Brahmin who is a connoisseur in all his confidential talks.

KĀDAMBARĪ: How do you do, sir?

JESTER: May your wishes be fulfilled!

MADALEKHĀ: Prince, please grace this camphor seat.

[*All sit down duly.*]

KĀDAMBARĪ [*to* KEYŪRAKA]: Oh, hurry up Lady Mahāśvetā to greet the Crown Prince!

KEYŪRAKA: Certainly. [*Exit.*]

CANDRĀPĪḌA [*to himself*]: Now I'll observe the deer-eyed girl's feelings through a roundabout talk. [*Aloud*] Friends Madalekhā and Tamālikā!

Tell me, what is the cause
Of this mental anguish of the maiden? [27, *pāda* 1]

MADALEKHĀ: Prince, you should investigate the cause yourself![78]

CANDRĀPĪḌA:

In that case, I, too, feel pain indeed. [27, 2]

TAMĀLIKĀ: That[79] befits your tender-heartedness.[80]

CANDRĀPĪḌA:

Then, why is she counteracting it?[81] [27, 3]

TWO FRIENDS: The dear, glorious one[82] has power over this!

CANDRĀPĪḌA:

Otherwise, Love's command would be frustrated! [27, 4]

KĀDAMBARĪ [*to herself*]: Why! my dear friends[83] have told the Prince[84] what should be told him.

[*Off stage*]

Princess, keep away this wretched bird! This ill-behaved one humiliates[85] me.

CANDRĀPĪḌA [*having observed*]: Madalekhā, what's that?

MADALEKHĀ: The Princess has given this mynah named Kālindī in marriage to this parrot named Parihāsaka.

PATRALEKHĀ: Then, what's the cause of this love quarrel?[86]

MADALEKHĀ: Since she saw him with some[87] female in a solitary place again today, she is jealous and won't take food even if we beg her to.

CANDRĀPĪḌA [*smiles at his* JESTER.]

JESTER: We hear this story in India as well. Loving[88] him like this, she's suffering the very great fire of torment.

[*Off stage*]

Hey![89] nominal Brahmin proud of being the Crown Prince's[90] favorite friend, you can't deceive her. This clever girl knows crooked speech. No one can allure Kādambarī's servants.

CANDRĀPĪḌA: Friend, stop it! Parihāsaka is angry.

TWO FRIENDS: Princess, Kālindī has given up the quarrel[91] and gone away[92] from here in anger. [*After standing up, to* PATRALEKHĀ] Friend, you come, too! We'll appease her[93] love anger.[94]

PATRALEKHĀ [*to herself*]: We know his[95] intention. [*Aloud to the* JESTER[96]] Sir, you'll talk[97] about this, too!

JESTER: I'm coming right now!

[*Exit the two friends,* PATRALEKHĀ[98] *and the* JESTER.]

KĀDAMBARĪ: Why! all[99] my friends are gone.

CANDRĀPĪḌA [*after approaching her*]: Princess, there's really no need of flurry! I'm here with you. Tell me, what shall I do?

Shall I lift up your scattered locks
And adorn them with flowers, my dear?
Shall I fan your perspiring face
Gently with my breath?
Shall I rub your afflicted body
With the lotus pollen on the couch?
Or shall I adjust your buttocks' fallen string[100]
With the girdle, my girl?[101] [28]

KĀDAMBARĪ [*extremely flurried*]: Please don't commit a breach of decorum!

CANDRĀPĪḌA: Dear Kādambarī!

When ever even for a moment
Would lightning exist without a cloud?
Oh, how would moonlight fall
If it were separated from the moon?
A river would not take repose
Except through union with the ocean!
Would a little creeper obtain a spot
On a young tree by avoiding[102] clinging to it? [29]

[*Acts embracing her.*]

KĀDAMBARĪ [*acting keeping him away, her breasts covered with crossed arms, to herself*]:[103] I will by no means break my vow! What else but death will Love bring me?

[*Off stage*]

This way, this way, Lady.

[*The two hear it and stay dissembling.*]

[*Enter* MAHĀŚVETĀ, *accompanied by her friends, and* PATRALEKHĀ *and the* JESTER.]

MAHĀŚVETĀ [*to herself*]:[104] Kādambarī with a wretched vow has barely told her friends her secret, but she stubbornly won't fulfill her desire. All right. If that's the case,

I'll remove her stubbornness myself. [*Having approached, aloud*] Welcome, Prince!

CANDRĀPĪḌA [*stands up and bows.*]

MAHĀŚVETĀ: Friend Kādambarī, has your fever gone down yet? How come there's no efficacy in spite of the remedy being taken?

TWO FRIENDS: Oh, look at the Crown Prince's friendship! He has come back to this remote place out of respect for your command without even attending to his royal duties.

CANDRĀPĪḌA: I should respect the Lady's[105] order. Besides, how[106] can I stay calm[107] after hearing of such a physical state of the Princess? Look!

A loving person should experience the same state
As his friend in sorrow as[108] in joy;
He can surely remove[109] some distress —
Such[110] is the conduct of a gentleman. [30]

[*Having entered in a flurry*]

KEYŪRAKA: Crown Prince! Valāhaka's son, Meghanāda, has come from the camp and informs in the gateway: "Couriers have arrived from the Great King's presence in Ujjayinī and wish to see the Prince."

CANDRĀPĪḌA [*looks at* MAHĀŚVETĀ.]

MAHĀŚVETĀ [*to herself*]: He can marry my friend when he returns[111] from the camp later on . . . if fate doesn't interfere.

MADALEKHĀ & TAMĀLIKĀ:[112] Our dear friend seems a little happier to see the Crown Prince.

MAHĀŚVETĀ: Kādambarī, permit him to go so that you can see him again.

KĀDAMBARĪ [*to herself*]: How can I permit him to? [*Aloud*] He should attend to his royal duties.

KEYŪRAKA [*to himself*]: The sorrow of the Princess is indeed very deep. Thus in first loves,

Couples unaware of each other's feelings
On account of their shyness,
Unable to fulfill their desires,
Grieve for a very long time. [31]

CANDRĀPĪḌA [*to himself*]: Alas! What ever among desirable things did I gain in spite of the meeting with my beloved I barely secured?

I did not smell her face-lotus,
    Nor did I even once drink her lip-*bimbas*;
My nails did not make a mark of enjoyment
    On her cheeks feeling horripilation,
Nor did my hand play with her deep navel
    On the pretext[113] of loosening her garment's knot,
Nor did my eyes obtain a feast
    In spite of their target fixed on her girdle. [32]

Or rather, my good fortune is only this much.

This sandal paste from her breasts is the sole eyewitness
    Of my good fortune of the strong embrace;
It seems to revive my heart-lotus trampled down[114]
    And abandoned by the Love-Elephant.[115] [33]

[*Aloud*] I should be remembered in the talks of the Princess' attendants. But please understand that I will not live without realizing[116] a meeting with the Princess again. [*Walks around with* PATRALEKHĀ *and the* JESTER.]

KĀDAMBARĪ [*to* PATRALEKHĀ]: Friend, you stay! I'll send you[117] later on.

CANDRĀPĪḌA: Patralekhā, you are lucky. Serve[118] the Princess on my behalf.

PATRALEKHĀ [*falls* at CANDRĀPĪḌA's *feet and returns.*]

JESTER: Oh, I'm left to be your only companion now!

MAHĀŚVETĀ: Friend Kādambarī, you have been consoled. Now go inside and take[119] your meal.

KĀDAMBARĪ: As the Lady pleases. [*After getting up,*[120] *to herself*] My good fortune to be united with the glorious one is this much.

CANDRĀPĪḌA [*walking around, to himself*]: Now surely

She is dragged by Love
    Yet held in check by her firm vow
As if a long bank of clouds, by the wind
    And the Himālaya's[121] slope. [34]

So be it. The goddess of fate alone has power.

[*Exeunt omnes.*]

END OF ACT FOUR

Notes

1. *V.K.* supplies *parijanaś ca*, but it seems unnecessary, for servants of minor importance do not always have to be mentioned in stage directions of entering and exiting.
2. *M.M.V.2.* and *VK.*: *tṛptaye; M.M.: dṛptaye.*
3. *V.K.: hodavvaṁ; M.M.: bhaviai (= bhavīadi); M.Ch.M.* and *V.K.Ch.: bhavitavyam.*
4. *V.K.: hata-; M.M.: hanta-.*
5. *V.K.: (avyāvahārika)kathāsu; M.M.: (-ka)thāsu.*
6. *V.K.: kathaṁ na; M.M.: kathan nu.*
7. *V.K.: manobhavārtim; M.M.: -ātkim.*
8. *M.M.* and *V.K.: assidajaṇesu; M.Ch.M.: utsukajane; V.K.Ch.: āśritajaneṣu.*
9. *M.M.V.2.* and *V.K.: sagarvam; M.M.: sagarham.*
10. *H.S.: kā ṇu khu abhūmī me (buddhivihavassa); M.M.: - - - (?) (-); V.K.: ṇa khu - - (-); M.Ch.M.: kā nu khalv abhūmir me (buddhivibhavasya); V.K.Ch.: na khalv - - (-).*
11. *H.S.: vākhāṇehi; M.M.: va°khāṇehi; M.Ch.M.: vyākhyānaya; V.K.: vācakkhehi; V.K.Ch.: vyācakṣva.*
12. *Dvijabandhu* (lit. a twice-born by relationship).
13. *M.M.* and *M.Ch.M.: -gaṇḍamaṇḍala-; V.K.* omits *maṇḍala.*
14. *V.K.: ghaṇasārakhaṇḍaṁ; M.M.: vaṇasāraṣaṇḍaṁ; M.Ch.M.* skips; *V.K.Ch.: ghanasārakhaṇḍam.*
15. *H.S.: ghaṭayasi hi; M.M.: ghaṭaya*(?); *V.K.: dadase sma.*
16. *(viraha)darśana(kleśam)* (lit. seeing); cf. *avalokana (sukhaṁ)* in this verse.
17. *M.M.V.2.* and *V.K.: sodbhedam; M.M.: so(?)m.*
18. *V.K.: aparitoso; M.M.: (vi)parīto so; M.Ch.M.* and *V.K.Ch.: aparitoṣaḥ.*
19. *M.M.V.2.* and *V.K.: avadhāritaṁ; M.M.: avasāditaṁ.*
20. *V.K.: tathā; M.M.: (?)thā.*
21. *V.K.: vīkṣitum; M.M.: vīkṣitam.*
22. *M.M.V.2.* and *V.K.: accārūḍho; M.M.: a°carāiniddhā; M.Ch.M.: atyantaṁ dṛḍhaḥ; V.K.Ch.: atyārūḍhaḥ.*
23. *M.M.V.2.* and *V.K.: kṣayaṁ; M.M.: svayaṁ.*
24. *M.M.V.2.* and *V.K.: svayam avimṛśato; M.M.: vimṛśato.*
25. *V.K.: avekṣaṇīyā; M.M.: apekṣaṇīyā.*
26. *V.K.: kutūhalinau; M.M.: kutra vilīnena; M.M.V.2.: kutūhalīnena.*
27. *H.S.: -khinna-; M.M.: -viddha-; V.K.: -siddha-.*
28. *V.K.: svadate; M.M.: svadato.*
29. *V.K.: svapnopalabdham; M.M.: svapnopy alabdham.*
30. *M.M.: parito valokya; V.K.: -vilokya.*
31. After this *M.M.* has the following speech assigned to Candrāpīḍa: *candrā* || *nanv ayaṁ(idaṁ, H.S.) dvitīyaṁ hṛdayaṁ sahasā nayanasya*, which means: Suddenly but certainly this is a second heart to the eyes. *V.K.* omits; *H.S.* follows.

32. *H.S.: vedikāḥ; M.M. & V.K.: vedikā.*

33. *V.K.* unnecessarily supplies *bhavet.*

34. *V.K.* supplies *(līlā)vanā(ntarāla-).*

35. *V.K.* rightly supplies the following, which is necessary for Keyūraka, who enters again later in this act (*vide* slightly after vs. 25): *yāvad aham api parisamāpitaniyamāṁ mahāśvetāṁ jñātvā āgacchāmi* | | *(iti niṣkrāntaḥ).*

36. *VK.: dīsai; M.M.: i°jai; M.Ch.M.: vilokyate; V.K.Ch.: dṛśyate.*

37. *M.M.: (-dalac)channaṁ; V.K.: (-dala)lāñchanaṁ.*

38. *M.M.: -sāmagrya(saṁvidhāna-); V.K.: -sāmagrī(- -).*

39. *V.K.: -śādvalitāsu; M.M.: -śāskhalitāsu; M.M.V.2.:- śādyalitāsu.*

40. *V.K.: himasīdālūṇi; M.M.: (purado) ñciama°jhadāluṇā; M.Ch.M.* provides no *chāyā* for this line; *V.K.Ch.: himaśītālūni.*

41. *V.K.: (itaretara)viruddhānāṁ; M.M.: (-)viruddho.*

42. *M.M. & V.K.: -saṁgho; M.Ch.M.: -sārthaḥ; V.K.Ch.: -saṅghaḥ.*

43. *V.K.: -patta-; M.M.: -aimeta-; M.Ch.M.: -jālamātra-; V.K.Ch.: -patra-.*

44. After this *M.M.* has the following, which *V.K.* omits probably because it is too corrupt to make out and *M.Ch.M.* provides only a long lacuna for it: *(-sa°vaṁgo) bālaseāipa°ipu°isirāvaa°sa sirīlajaladāja°visiṇa°ca°gopaḍiṇava ka°pūradilaa sohiramaṇaharaṇī ḍāilehosomāi (mṛ<mi, V.K.>ṇāla-).*

45. *H.S.: viracīaanta-; M.M.: virauṁjaṁta-; M.Ch.M.: viracyamāna-; V.K.: viraia-; V.K.Ch.: viracita-.*

46. *M.M.V.2.* and *V.K.: vilhṭhati; M.M.: (?).*

47. *M.M.: -dhammilla-; V.K.: dhāmmilla.*

48. *V.K.: daṭṭhūṇa: M.M.: ihiūṇa; M.Ch.M.: labdhvāpi; V.K.Ch.: dṛṣṭvā.*

49. *V.K.: -āghrāta-; M.M.: -ābrāta-.*

50. *V.K.: (rāja)stambhā(vāritena): M.M.: (-)rambhā(-).*

51. *V.K.: so; M.M.: kīriso; M.Ch.M.* and *V.K.Ch.: sa.*

52. *M.M.: hodu, maṁ viṇā ko aṇṇo; V.K.: tumaṁ viṇā - -; M.Ch.M.: bhavatu, māṁ vinā kaḥ punar; V.K.Ch.: tvāṁ vinā ko nyo.* The Jester is only trying to be funny; *V.K.*, unaware of this, changes *māṁ* into *tumaṁ.*

53. *V.K.: pekkiduṁ (= pekkhiduṁ) vilambedi tti takkemi; M.M.: peṅkhiaṁ vilaṁohoṁ, janā* | |; *M.Ch.M.* and *V.K.Ch.: prekṣituṁ vilambata iti tarkayāmi.*

54. *V.K.* unnecessarily supplies *halā; V.K.Ch.: sakhi.*

55. *V.K.: -tappao; M.M.: -saṁdhāo; M.Ch.M.: -sārthakaḥ; V.K.Ch.: -talpakaḥ.*

56. *M.M.V.2.* and *V.K.: vilulio; M.M.: vidalio; M.Ch.M.: vidalita (-); V.K.Ch.: vilulita (-).*

57. *V.K.: (-paḍala)silātalammi; M.M.: (- -)talimaṁmi; M.Ch.M.: (-paṭala)tale; V.K.Ch.: (- -)śilātale.*

58. *V.K.: -himacchaḍā-; M.M.: -hima°hī(cha, M.M.V.2.)la°hī(cha, M.M.V.2.)ḍā-; M.Ch.M.: -himacchalacchaṭā-; V.K.Ch.: -himacchaṭā-.*

59. *V.K.: sarisammi; M.M.: (-ga°bha)avi°i°ṇṇe; M.Ch.M.: (-garbha)kavilakṣeṇa; V.K.Ch.: sadṛśe.*
60. *V.K.: saṁdadhatī; M.M.: saṁdadhati.*
61. *H.S.: tanūdarī; M.M.* and *V.K.: talodarī* (a pot-bellied girl).
62. *V.K.: ehi vījaya; M.M.: ehi; M.Ch.M.: vijaya; V.K.Ch.: ehi vījaya.*
63. *V.K.: hiaammi vi; M.M.: hiaa°hi (mi, M.M.V.2.)-; M.Ch.M.: (pāṇipāde) subhage pi; V.K.Ch.: (-) hṛdaye ca.*
64. *M.M.* and *V.K.: sahīo, avaṇeha; M.Ch.M.* and *V.K.Ch.: sakhyaḥ, apanayata.* Since Kādambarī is apparently talking to her two friends: Madalekhā and Tamālikā, the correct Sanskrit *chāyā* is *sakhyau, apanayatam* (in the dual number; in Prakrit the plural is used instead because the dual does not exit in it).
65. *V.K.: adisaidasaṁdāvakāraṇāiṁ; M.M.: aisaasaṁdāṇa vala°taāla(raaṇa-); M.Ch.M.: atiśayasantāpayitṛkāni: V.K.Ch.: atiśayitasaṁtāpakāraṇāni.*
66. *H.S.: dharāvehi a; M.M.: - aṁ; V.K.: dharāvehi; M.Ch.M.: dharāpaya ca; V.K.Ch.: dhāraya.*
67. *M.M.V.2.* and *V.K.: āśyānībhavad-; M.M.: ā(?)nībhavad-.*
68. *V.K.: kāmārtā; M.M.: tāmārtā.*
69. *M.M.* and *V.K.: ṇo; M.Ch.M.* skips; *V.K.Ch.: no; H.S.Ch.: nau. Vide supra*, n. 64.
70. *M.M.* and *V.K.: amhehiṁ - -kāriṇīhi(ṁ); M.Ch.M.* and *V.K.Ch.: asmābhir - -kāriṇībhir; H.S.Ch.: āvābhyām - -kāriṇībhyām. Vide supra*, n. 64.
71. *H.S.: praviśyāpaṭākṣepeṇa; M.M.* and *V.K.: praviśya paṭākṣepeṇa. Vide* Trans., Act II, n. 93.
72. *V.K.* supplies *tan(-).*
73. *V.K.: ita (ito-); M.M.: tad (- -).*
74. *M.M.: abhyutthātum: V.K.: utthātum.*
75. *V.K.: devi; M.M.: devī devī.*
76. *V.K.: āyāsayituṁ; M.M.: āsāyituṁ.*
77. *V.K.: -niyantraṇābhir; M.M.: -nirayantrābhir.*
78. *V.K.: kumāra tumaṁ evva kāraṇaṁ ṇirūviduṁ aruhasi; M.M.: - - eva - ṇirūpidaṁ arha(ruha, M.M.V.2.)si; M.Ch.M.: tvam eva nirūpayitum arhasi; V.K.Ch.: kumāra tvam - kāraṇaṁ nirūpayitum -.* The meaning which Madalekhā really wishes to convey is: Prince, you should consider yourself to be the cause!
79. *M.M.: edaṁ; M.Ch.M.: etat; V.K.* omits.
80. *M.M.* and *V.K.: sahiaabhāvassa; M.Ch.M.: sakhitvasya; V.K.Ch.: sahṛdayabhāvasya.*
81. *- vidhatte vipratīkāram eṣā;* the really intended meaning of this is: - is the resisting me?
82. *Ahimado mahābhāo;* more explicitly: the glorious one, her beloved.
83. *M.M.* and *V.K.: piasahīhi(ṁ); M.Ch.M.* skips; *V.K.Ch.: priyasakhībhiḥ; H.S.Ch.: -sakhībhyām. Vide supra*, n. 64.
84. *M.M.: rāavutta°sa; V.K.: juvarāassa; M.Ch.M.* and *V.K.Ch.: yuvarājasya.* After this *M.M.* has *paru°kavirahi; M.Ch.M.* skips; *V.K.* omits.
85. *M.M.* and *V.K.: paribhavijjāmi; M.Ch.M.: paribhūye; V.K.Ch.: paribhāvye.*

86. *H.S.: aha kiṁṇimitto imo paṇaakalaho; M.Ch.M.: atha kinnimitto yaṁ praṇayakalahaḥ; V.K.Ch.* omits *(a)yaṁ; M.M.: kahaṁ kiṁṇimitto ja°va°raṇṇakalaho; V.K.: aha kiṁ- paṇaakalaho.*

87. *H.S.: kāe vi; M.M.: tāe -; V.K.: kae -; M.Ch.M.* and *V.K.Ch.: kayāpi.*

88. *V.K.: paṇaantīe; M.M.: vaṇaaṁti(tīe, M.M.V.2.): M.Ch.M.: praṇayānvitāyā (asyāḥ); V.K.Ch.: praṇayantyā.*

89. *V.K.* supplies *re; M.M.: (?).*

90. *M.M.V.2.* and *V.K.: nūtnarāja-; M.M.: (?)rāja-.*

91. *H.S.: kalahavādaṁ pariccaia; V.K.: - piri-; M.M.: kaivipāṇe pi pariccaai; M.Ch.M.: kalahavādena parityajya; V.K.Ch.: -daṁ -.*

92. *V.K.: gaā; M.M.: gaācarāṁraṁ; M.Ch.M.: gatavatī; V.K.Ch.: gatā.*

93. *V.K.: edāe; M.M.: (-mo)numāṇa; M.Ch.M.* and *V.K.Ch.: (-mo)syāḥ.*

94. *M.M.V.2.* and *V.K.: paaṇarosaṁ; M.M.: caarosaṁ; M.Ch.M.* and *V.K.Ch.: praṇayaroṣam.*

95. *V.K.: se; M.M.: imāa (ṇaṁ, M.M.V.2.); M.Ch.M.: (jñāto)syā (abhi-); V.K.Ch.: (jānīmo)syā(bhi-).*

96. *V.K.* supplies *vidūṣakaṁ prati.*

97. *V.K.: vādaieṇa; M.M.: vāhā(bho, M.M.V.2.)aeṇa; M.Ch.M.: vādayitṛkena; V.K.Ch.: vādayitrā.*

98. *H.S.* supplies *patralekhā ca.*

99. *M.M.: sa°vo; M.Ch.M.: eva sarvaḥ; V.K.: evva; VK.Ch.: eva.*

100. *srastaṁ - nitambāśrayam. H.S.* takes *āśraya* as a means of support such as a string.

101. *M.M.* and *V.K.: vāso.* It seems to be used here in place of *vāsu* for a metrical reason.

102. *M.M.: tyaktvā; V.K.: tyaktā.*

103. *H.S.: svagataṁ svastikapihitastanā nāṭyena pariharantī; M.M.: - smitapihita- - -harati; M.M.V.2.* and *V.K.: svastikapihita- - -harantī.*

104. *V.K.* supplies *svagatam.*

105. *M.M.V.2.* and *V.K.: āryāyā (-); M.M.: ā(?)yā (-).*

106. *V.K.: kathaṁ; M.M.* repeats.

107. *M.M.V.2.* and *V.K.: avasthātuṁ; M.M.: upasthātuṁ.*

108. *V.K.: (sukha) iva; M.M.: (-) i(?).*

109. *V.K.: apohituṁ; M.M.: -tan (nu).*

110. *V.K.: iyatī; M.M.: (prabhur) iyariyatī.*

111. *H.S.: ṇivaṭṭia sakko imiṇā sahīe pāṇiggaho kāduṁ; M.M.: ṇivā(va°, M.M.V.2.)ṭia sa°kaṁ - - - -; V.K.: ṇivaṭṭieṇa imiṇā sakkaṁ sahīe pāṇiggahaṁ kāaiduṁ; M.Ch.M.: nivartya śakyaḥ anena sakhyāḥ pāṇigrahaḥ kartum; V.K.Ch.: nivṛttena anena śakyaṁ sakhyāḥ pāṇigrahaṁ kārayituṁ.*

112. *M.M.: madalekhātamālike* ||; *V.K.: madalekhā - - tamālie; M.Ch.M.* follows *M.M.*

113. *V.K.: (nīvīviślathanac)chalān (na); M.M.: (-naṁ) balān (-).*

114. *M.M.V.2.* and *V.K.: -mardita-; M.M.: -madita-.*

115. *Madanadvipa;* it also means an elephant in rut.

116. *M.M.V.2.* and *V.K.: (na -darśanam) asaṁbhāvya sthīyata (ity); M.M.: (- - -ṁ) saṁbhāvyaṁ niyata (-).*

117. *H.S.: pesīasi; M.M.: vesīasi; M.Ch.M.: preṣyase; V.K.: pesaijjasi; V.K.Ch.: preṣiṣyase.*

118. *V.K.: sevyatām; M.M.: sevyatā.*

119. *V.K.: ṇivvaṭṭehi; M.M.: ṇiva°ṭahi; M.Ch.M.: nirvartasva; V.K.Ch.: nirvartaya.*

120. *M.M.: utthāya; V.K.* omits.

121. *M.M.V.2.* and *V.K.: cādrirājasya; M.M.: cādirājasya.*

Cūlikā
Prelude to Act Five

[*Off Stage*]

Ho! Ho! Actors of the divine land who offer the best stage, *śṛṅgāra rasa* and music![1] The Crown Prince left for Ujjayinī immediately after the order in the letter the Great King, Tārāpīḍa, sent him. You really should give the dramatic performance with unfailing[2] efforts, for the venerable Vaiśampāyana is still staying here.[3] Candrāpīḍa ordered him — his second heart, Minister Śukanāsa's son — together with General Valāhaka, to take care of the camp, which was about to depart slowly owing to its fatigue from the journey of the world conquest, from which it had long suffered.

All the royal people respect
    This man's orders as that man's;[4]
This man endlessly enjoys
    All amusements as that man[5] does;
And this man graciously shows
    Opportune favors as that man does —
Therefore, you should give him
    This[6] performance very skillfully. [1]

END OF THE CŪLIKĀ
PRELUDE TO ACT FIVE

Notes

1. *H.S.: (raṅgaśṛṅgāra)rasasaṅgīta-; M.M.: (-)rasa(?)gīta-; V.K.: (-)saṁgīta-.*
2. *V.K.: pratyamogha-; M.M.: pratimogha-.*
3. *V.K.: (-to)tra vartate(dyāpi); M.M.: (- -)nu(& tra)vartate(-).*
4. *V.K.: tasyevā (syāpi); M.M.: tasyaivā(-).*
5. *V.K.: teneva; M.M.: tenaiva.*
6. *M.M.V.2.* and *V.K.: (prayogo) py ayam; M.M.: (-)vyayam.*

ACT FIVE

[*Enter* VALĀHAKA.]

VALĀHAKA: Oh, how fortunate the Great King, Tārāpīḍa, is!

Candrāpīḍa has conquered the whole of India
By the strength of his arms;
He has bought this land of *kinnara*s as well
At the price[1] of his friendship. [2]

[*After reflecting*] Patralekhā — Kulūta's King's daughter, in whom the Prince places all his confidence — has come back from the capital of Citraratha. So I should inform the second minister, Vaiśampāyana, of this, and send her with my son Meghanāda to Ujjayinī ahead of the army[2] according to the Crown Prince's order. Vaiśampāyana is very eager to see the dramatic performance the divine land's actors are going to produce in the music hall they have built through their power. Now I'll go to him. [*Walking around*] Ah! the royal camp's vicinity has excessive beauty of eventide. For

The host of warriors stay beside a fence
Of the edges of swords held in their hands;
The patrol elephants' trunks come and go
By turns on the roads;
The tents provide brightness
With haloes of lamplight;
And these bards praise the Prince
By singing a story of his prowess. [3]

[*After looking ahead*[3]] Oh, how captivating the music hall is! For here

The songs, together with the lute's sounds,
Intoxicate the pet deer;
The drum's vigorous sounds
Excite curiosity in the peacocks;
The geese[4] constantly move their feet
In their skill of walking step by step;[5]
And the lovely girls' anklets give delight
With their charming jingles. [4]

[*After going inside*] Here's the second minister!

Now he is distressed to be separated
    Form his friend, the Crown Prince;
He should comfort himself
    In this manner[6] with amusements. [5]

[*Approaches him.*]

[*Enter* VAIŚAMPĀYANA, *seated, and his retinue.*][7]

VAIŚAMPĀYANA [*to himself*]: Oh, what is this?

As if it were the eyewitness of the moment
    Of my first meeting with my beloved one,
This place, merely glanced at, agitates my heart
    Long anxious for not having attained its object. [6]

Or rather, this is a transformation of my despondency[8] due to separation from Candrāpīḍa. [*After looking ahead*] Oh, the General is coming here! Sir, this way, this way.

VALĀHAKA: May the Minister be victorious! [*Sits down.*]

VAIŚAMPĀYANA: Honorable Valāhaka,

Now I am indeed separated
    From my only friend.
What is this?
    Oh! stupor is arising all over me
As it would surely appear
    If I were approached
By the total loss of the sight of my parents
    Or[9] the destruction of my own body. [7]

VALĀHAKA [*having stopped his ears*]: Perish the evil! Perish the evil! What will the glorious one say? This is the nature of a friendship formed a long time ago. [*To himself*] How can I possibly distract him? [*Aloud towards the dressing room*] Oh, they, actors! why are you still delaying? Now show us the invisible[10] and very wonderful!

Prologue to the *Mahāśvetāpuṇḍarīka*

[*Having entered*]

DIRECTOR [*with folded hands*]:

That[11] bodiless Love, who delights in sweetness
But is hard to uproot on account of his firmness,
Alone wins the fruit and roots
Of the tree of transmigration. [8]

VALĀHAKA: This is a passionate[12] and laudable opening benediction.

VAIŚAMPĀYANA: Oh, what great riches the art[13] of speech has!

DIRECTOR [*with great respect*]:

Its fourfold division was created
By Brahmā out of the Vedas;[14]
It can make past and future objects visible;
And when it acquires a body,
All the arts become very enjoyable[15] in it[16] —
Whose heart would not be delighted
With the nectar of the dramatic art,
The fruit of universal sovereignty? [9]

Now, let the people of taste be acquainted[17] with this play I'm going to stage! It's the *Mahāśvetāpuṇḍarīka* by name. Its plot was composed by Kādambarī. And it's very much like nectar for the eyes.

VAIŚAMPĀYANA [*as if remembering, to himself*]: What? "Mahāśvetā" by name? All right, we'll see. [*Aloud*] Let the actors enter!

DIRECTOR [*towards the dressing room*]: Hey! Now sing with reference to the fragrant season in which the matter to be acted out takes place!

[*Sung off stage*]

As soon as a young bee, to suck honey,
Clings to a cluster of mango blossoms,
A quick-carrying wind
Takes him away somewhere. [10][18]

VAIŚAMPĀYANA [*pondering*]: What's this incident hinted by a special song?

VALĀHAKA: The *dhruvā* song[19] is indeed the life of the dramatic art.

DIRECTOR: Oh! here's my lady, who has put on the costume for Mahāśvetā.[20] Well, I should also get ready[21] to perform soon.[22] [*Exit.*]

END OF THE PROLOGUE TO THE *MAHĀŚVETĀPUṆḌARĪKA*

The *Mahāśvetāpuṇḍarīka*

[*Enter* MAHĀŚVETĀ *and her friend.*]

MAHĀŚVETĀ: Friend Taralikā, let's take a walk here when Mother completes her special vow in the temple of Śiva.

TARALIKĀ: As my dear friend pleases.

[*Both walk around.*]

VAIŚAMPĀYANA [*having observed, to himself*]:

This moon-faced girl delights my heart
As if I remembered her.
Have I seen her in my previous life,
Or a painting, or a dream, or magic? [11][23]

VALĀHAKA [*acting astonishment*]: Ah! is there such whiteness as this, too?[24]

Is she covered with moonstones?
Or nailed up with ivory?
Or woven with lotus fiber threads?
Or adorned with sandal paste?
Or painted with a camphor paintbrush?
Or strung with pearls?
Or prepared with silver?
Or rather, made of moonbeams? [12]

TARALIKĀ: Princess, look at the beauty of the spring season passing in the forests of Lake Acchoda's vicinity!

MAHĀŚVETĀ: Friend, let's pick[25] flowers in this garden of red *aśoka* trees, the Hall of Love's Pleasure House.

[*Both act picking*[26] *flowers.*]

VAIŚAMPĀYANA [*to himself*]:

A beautiful girl's hand-lotus
And an *aśoka* tree's blossoms and buds
Can be subtly[27] observed to open
Only with a gemmed seal ring. [13]

MAHĀŚVETĀ [*after observing*]: Where can I find this indescribable fragrance I've never experienced before? [*After looking*] Certainly in these forests, these bees gathered in a swarm are going after this scent of a tree's blossoms.[28]

TARALIKĀ: And it's fit for a superhuman world.[29]

MAHĀŚVETĀ: We'll go after it, too.

[*Both walk around.*]

VALĀHAKA: Oh! some divine ascetic youth has descended from the sky, and is entering with[30] his friend. Now at last manifested in him[31] is the common substratum of *śānta*[32] and *śṛṅgāra*! For he —

Entirely covered with matted hair
Red as a mass of lightning,
And wearing some bark garment
Like a golden-colored china rose on an ear —[33]
Is playfully making an ear ornament
Out of a celestial tree's blossom cluster
Emitting a strong scent
And dripping drops of nectar. [14]

[*Enter a pair of ascetic youths as described.*]

FIRST: Friend Kapiñjala, the mountain that is Śiva's Pleasure Mansion is surely very close to here.

KAPIÑJALA: Then, dear friend Puṇḍarīka, please relieve your fatigue from traveling[34] in the sky here in Caitraratha for a white.

[*Both walk around.*]

VAIŚAMPĀYANA [*watching* PUṆḌARĪKA, *to himself*]: Oh, where does this partiality conformable to familiarity come from?

Why is it that this man,
Who has assumed another's body,
Looks just like myself in a mirror?

[*Giving a look at* KAPIÑJALA]

Why is it that this man, long gazed[35] upon,
Makes this body of mine eager[36] to embrace him
As if he were my childhood friend? [15]

[*Looks at them.*]

KAPIÑJALA: Friend, look at the extraordinary beauty[37] of the Caitraratha forest[38] on the days of the *caitra* month! For here

The *aśoka* tree is thick
As a heap of buds;
The young mango tree is very heavy
As a cluster of blossoms;
The top[39] of the spring creeper bower
Appears to have a swarm of bees;
Moreover, this wind is dense
As a flood of fragrance. [16]

PUṆḌARĪKA [*after looking around*]: How wonderful this is! In the spring season, even animals subtly follow the order of Rati's companion. For

A bee is sucking fragrant honey deposited in a vessel
Of a *vakula* blossom[40] his beloved has sucked and left;
Moreover, this gaggling gander is dexterously making
A delightful gesture to his naive beloved. [17]

VALĀHAKA [*observing* VAIŚAMPĀYANA *and* PUṆḌARĪKA, *to himself*]: What could possibly be the reason for this?

They appear[41] to possess the same beauty
Surpassing that of the five-arrowed Love.
What speech[42] and activity seem proper for them to take up
On account of their separateness?[43]
And this age of theirs fit for *śṛṅgāra*
Does not make them different from each other.
Oh! indeed only one garment
Makes a distinction between the two. [18]

VAIŚAMPĀYANA [*to himself*]:

I know all this to be a mere performance by actors;
Even so, oh! my heart is getting extremely restless
In an indescribable way yet with genuine[44] conviction.
Why! all of a sudden, irresistible grief is arising. [19]

MAHĀŚVETĀ [*after looking ahead*]: Oh, who's that ascetic youth possessed of special marks? He's coming, accompanied by his worthy friend[45] as if Love by Spring.

TARALIKĀ: This special scent must have arisen from that blossom cluster he's wearing as an ear ornament.

MAHĀŚVETĀ [*to herself*]: I can't possibly ask him. All right then. [*Aloud*] What ever tree can be the source of that?

TARALIKĀ: I'll now find everything out from his friend's mouth. Friend, you, too, approach[46] and honor the ascetics.

[*Both approach them.*]

PUṆḌARĪKA [*having looked, eagerly*[47]]:

Who ever is this curved-browed girl
    Whose beauty puts down all women?
Is she a goddess, a weapon of Love?
    Or is she a dryad of Caitraratha? [20]

MAHĀŚVETĀ [*to herself*]: Oh! at the mere sight of him, I'm overwhelmed with an emotion forbidden to maidens.

TARALIKĀ: Honor the son of an ascetic[48] with a handful of these red *aśoka* flowers!

MAHĀŚVETĀ [*having approached him, to herself*]: Wouldn't I get flurried now?[49] [*Strews a handful of flowers and bows gracefully.*]

PUṆḌARĪKA [*to himself*]: Oh, why! I'm overpowered with excessive love. For to me,

Her head somewhat bent,
    Hair's end slightly shaken charmingly,[50]
Neck-stalk somewhat stooped,
    Necklace slightly trembling
And very lovely back showing a little,
    The doe-eyed girl has elegantly made a bow. [21]

[*Aloud*] May you attain fruit[51] conformable to your desire!

TARALIKĀ: Thank you, sir.

VALĀHAKA [*after observing* MAHĀŚVETĀ *and* PUṆḌARĪKA]: How charming lovers' first passionate gestures are! For

Love will shortly see[52]
    A battle of archery[53] between these two
Practising as if spontaneously
    An unprecedented art of arrows[54]
By casting each other sidelong glances
    Just like the petals of sleepless blue lotuses. [22]

TARALIKĀ [*after observing the facial expression of the two, to herself*]: Brahmā's skill in creation has borne fruit,[55] for Love seems to have united these two[56] on the spot.[57] [*After approaching* KAPIÑJALA, *aloud*] Sir, we are rather curious about. . .[58]

KAPIÑJALA: About what?

TARALIKĀ: About these: Who ever is this glorious one? And what tree does this blossom cluster belong to?[59]

KAPIÑJALA: Lady, what's the use of this inquiry of yours? Even so, listen!

MAHĀŚVETĀ [*to herself*]:[60] Be attentive, my heart!

KAPIÑJALA: This is Puṇḍarīka by name, of the venerable Śvetaketu residing in a divine world, born in Lakṣmī.

VAIŚAMPĀYANA [*with excessive earnestness*]: Oh! I hear words that seem[61] to be long-familiar and to purify the three worlds.

KAPIÑJALA: Since this is the fourteenth day of a lunar fortnight,[62] he's going to Mt. Kailāsa with the desire to pay homage to Śiva.[63] And this is a *kalpa* tree's[64] blossom cluster which on the way a dryad of the Nandana forest put on his ear as an ornament.

TARALIKĀ: I see.

MAHĀŚVETĀ [*wishfully, to herself*]:

Oh, blossom cluster, you are lucky!
    Clinging to his ear, you kiss his cheek;[65]
And in the guise of a bee's honey-sweet buzz,
    You murmur a secret to him.[66] [23]

VAIŚAMPĀYANA: Oh! I seem to remember all this forgotten incident now.[67]

VALĀHAKA: This is only natural. For

He is in this state of spiritlessness.[68]
    What ever would he not feel? And what man would not?
His recollection of an intention denied[69] in his other life
    Is occasioned by the identical object. [24].

PUṆḌARĪKA [*to* MAHĀŚVETĀ]: Oh, curious girl,[70] what's the use of that inquiry alone? Take this! [*Putting his ear ornament on her, to himself*] Ah! I have accomplished my end. For

This hand of mine has touched
    Her round cheek entirely sprouting

With a mass of horripilation
And starry with drops of perspiration. [25]

[*Acts loss of self-control.*]

MAHĀŚVETĀ [*having observed him, to herself*]: Why! he doesn't even notice[71] his rosary falling down from the palm of his hand because his heart is overwhelmed with love. I'll take it, then. [*Takes it and puts it on her neck.*]

VAIŚAMPĀYANA [*After observing her*]:

Her face,[72] marked with a crystal rosary
And wearing a spray from a celestial tree,
Resembles the moon[73] with a host of stars
And a heap of fresh nectar foam. [26]

[*Having entered without using a curtain*][74]

SUNSHADE BEARER: Princess,[75] come now! Your mother has made her special vow.

MAHĀŚVETĀ [*to herself*]: How can I leave him and go away?[76] Or rather, the fruit of my eyes' merit[77] is only this much. [*Departs with difficulty.*][78]

TARALIKĀ [*to herself*]: Oh, how pale my dear friend's face[79]-lotus is now!

KAPIÑJALA [*having observed, indignantly*]: Hey, invincible-souled Puṇḍarīka!

If your restraint has been conquered by wantonness,
Truth has been conquered by falsehood;[80]
Light, by darkness; virtuous deeds,[81] by evil deeds;
And knowledge, by ignorance. [27]

PUṆḌARĪKA [*anxiously*]: Tell me, friend Kapiñjala! How am I deviating from the right course?[82]

KAPIÑJALA: Surely you don't even know this ill-mannered girl[83] has taken away your rosary. Then, enough of being your fellow *brahmacārin*![84] [*Exit.*]

PUṆḌARĪKA [*to himself*]: The rosary is happy there with the great feast of clinging to her neck. [*Acoud*] Oh, fickle girl! you stole my rosary while we were looking on. [*Acts anger.*]

VALĀHAKA: Minister Vaiśampāyana, look now!

The son of a divine sage may
Gently knit brows on his forehead,

And barely speak harsh words,
    His lips trembling;
Even so, his heart's desire can be known
    From his sidelong glances
Like bees wandering about the face-lotus
    Of his dear girl. [28]

MAHĀŚVETĀ [*having returned,*[85] *to herself*]: The change of his complexion tells me[86] his anger is extreme.[87] [*Aloud*] I took the rosary because it was falling and going to get spoiled by the dust on the ground. Take this! [*Takes her pearl necklace off her neck and gives it to him. Exit with her friend.*]

PUṆḌARĪKA [*putting on the pearl necklace*]: Alas! Alas!

Entrusting her heart to me[88] as if it were a deposit
    And receiving mine with her eyes[89]
As if it were a counter-deposit,[90]
    My darling left with difficulty. [29]

VAIŚAMPĀYANA: Oh! the lotus-eyed girl, who appeared like lightning, has disappeared somewhere. [*After reflecting*]

That deer-eyed girl's face
    Concealed by a silken veil
Is for my joy as the moon's disc
    Hidden by a piece of autumnal cloud. [30]

PUṆḌARĪKA [*acting feelings of love*]:[91]

That charming-eyed girl has an army:
    Rati[92] is her companion; Spring, her friend;
Flowers, her arrows; a row of bees, her bowstring;
    And a sugarcane[93] stalk, her bow.
Are many things headed by the moon,
    Sandal and the wind also her kinsmen?
O Love! all this of yours is praiseworthy,[94]
    If you do not torment the lovesick. [31]

Now I'll follow her, and obtain all information about her from her attendant lingering behind her. [*Walks around.*]

[*Having entered*]

TARALIKĀ: Staying within his sight like this,[95] I should follow my dear friend overpowered with love. [*Does so.*]

PUṆḌARĪKA [*having found and approached her*]:[96] Lady, which sounds does your friend make propitiating spells with her name? And whose family does she make a mine[97] of a girl-gem with her birth?

TARALIKĀ: This is Mahāśvetā, begotten by Haṁsa, a *gandharva* king, in the womb[98] of Gaurī, an *apsaras* born of the moon's beams. She is going to Mt. Hemakūṭa, which is her residence. And I am Taralikā by name, her betel box bearer and dear friend.

VALĀHAKA: Surely this Hemakūṭa the author has written[99] about must be the same that the Crown Prince has visited twice.

PUṆḌARĪKA: Then, blessed lady, please carry out this sole request of mine.[100]

TARALIKĀ: That is indeed a favor to me.

PUṆḌARĪKA [*after tearing off a hem of his upper bark garment*]: I'll now write this *āryā* verse showing[101] my ardent desire with the juice of this *tamāla* tree's buds. [*Does as described.*]

VAIŚAMPĀYANA: What ever would be the right message for a love like this? [*Reflects.*][102]

PUṆḌARĪKA [*after writing*]: Lady, please show this to the *gandharva* Princess in secret. [*Gives it to her.*]

TARALIKĀ [*acts taking*[103] *it and putting it into the betel box.*]: I'll give it to the Princess at once. [*Walks around.*]

PUṆḌARĪKA [*having returned*]: Where ever should I divert my excited self? [*After walking around*] Oh! this is the Acchoda lake filled[104] with transparent water.[105]

With lotuses comparable to her face,
    Waves charming as her eyebrows,
Ruddy geese resembling her breasts,
    Saivala weeds rivaling[106] her mass of hair,
Fish like her eyes, and
    Sandbanks emulating her broad buttocks,
It seems to show outside me
    The girl[107] confined to sitting in my heart. [32]

[*After looking around*]

Here I saw that maiden like this Caitraratha forest:
    She had a bee[108] honored as her forehead mark,[109]

And her body was beautiful[110]
As the blossoms and buds of a creeper. [33]

[*Walks around.*]

VALĀHAKA [*having observed him*]: Why! Puṇḍarīka like a full moon seems as if he were eclipsed by intense passion.[111] [*With a glance given sideways*] I feel everything Minister Vaiśampāyana feels, but this firmness checks me.[112]

PUṆḌARĪKA:[113]

Longing for the wrong person,
My heart seems[114] to split into two;
Their desire's object gone,[115]
All my senseorgans seem[116] strange;
My body is getting heavier and
Becoming a burden as if it were another's;
Moreover, is this life of mine departing,
Perhaps in a moment? [34]

Now I'll take a rest right here in an arbor of red *aśoka*s growing on the bank of this lake. [*Exit.*]

TARALIKĀ: Here's the gateway to the girls' inner-citadel. And[117] here at the top of the mansion is my dear friend, who appears to be absent-mindedly[118] gazing[119] in that very direction. I'll do her a favor now. [*Acts ascending the mansion.*]

VAIŚAMPĀYANA [*having looked at her*]: Why! this is that same wide-eyed girl.

Holding in one hand her face, where her lashes' tips
Are tied to her eyes with large tears,
Making her *bimba*-lips otherwise
With deep, hot sigh-winds,
And drawing[120] something after giving up actions
Dependent on her outer senseorgans,
She appears as if she were in a painting,
Her limbs totally[121] motionless. [35]

[*Enter* MAHĀŚVETĀ *as described.*]

MAHĀŚVETĀ [*to herself*]: Oh! I'm an unfortunate girl who has lost maidenhood. I even showed my milk-white body in that manner. What ever would be the consolation[122] for me infatuated solely with union with a man hard to obtain?

TARALIKĀ [*after approaching her*]: This! [*Gives her the letter.*]

MAHĀŚVETĀ: Who ever sent it to me?

TARALIKĀ: He who stole your heart!

MAHĀŚVETĀ [*opens it and reads it.*]:

> Enticing[123] my[124] love[125] with your pearl necklace[126]
> White as a lotus stalk,
> You have shown it hope and taken it far away
> As if it were a wild goose. [36][127]

[*Acts extreme joy, reading*[128] *it again and again.*]

VAIŚAMPĀYANA: Honorable Valāhaka, what is this? This arrangement of words[129] has moved my heart, too.

VALĀHAKA: Agreement[130] certainly takes place in different speeches by poets of taste. For

> The same object manifests itself in all their hearts
> Owing to the universality of genius;
> Even the sameness in composition is easily obtained
> Through their arrangement[131] of suitable words. [37]

TARALIKĀ: Did he make his heart clear[132] enough?

MAHĀŚVETĀ: His feelings are expressed through a poetic fancy; in other words, his arrangement of words is only half-open in an *āryā* verse.[133] And his grief due to separation is manifested through uneven lines.[134]

[*Enter halfway from the dressing room.*]

PORTRESS: Princess, an ascetic youth called Kapiñjala has arrived at the guardroom.

MAHĀŚVETĀ: Show him in at once,[135] Prabhañjanikā!

PORTRESS: Certainly. [*Exit.*]

[*Having entered*]

KAPIÑJALA: Hail to the *gandharva* Princess!

MAHĀŚVETĀ [*after standing up and greeting him with folded hands*]: Please take a seat here.

[*All sit down.*]

MAHĀŚVETĀ [*looks at* TARALIKĀ.]

TARALIKĀ: How's your friend, sir?

KAPIÑJALA: In fact, this effort is intended for himself.[136]

MAHĀŚVETĀ: How so?

VAIŚAMPĀYANA: Oh! overwhelmed with friendship, the ascetic has undertaken even a messenger's task quite unfit for himself.

VALĀHAKA: The virtuous shouldn't give this up.[137] Look!

Good people cleverly restrain beforehand[138]
Their friend gone along the wrong path;
But if he is unrestrainable,
They do what is favorable to himself.
Why should not friendship[139] make one do
What is unfit for oneself? [38]

KAPIÑJALA: How could I explain this extremely shameful thing?

On one hand we are, calmness-predominant ascetics,
And on the other is Love desired by the vulgar;
But now the wind can uproot even mountains[140]
Immovable at a time of universal destruction. [39]

MAHĀŚVETĀ: Tell me clearly, sir!

KAPĪÑJALA [*after sighing*]: Puṇḍarīka's conduct at that time was quite clear to both of you as well.

TARALIKĀ: Yes, indeed.

MAHĀŚVETĀ: What happened after we returned here?[141]

KAPIÑJALA: Quite unable to endure such a dishonorable change in him, I went away somewhere else.[142]

TARALIKĀ: Of course.[143]

KAPIÑJALA: And then, when I looked for my friend because I shouldn't stay away from him though he was engaged in the wrong path . . . In some arbor on Acchoda . . .[144]

Alas! There I found[145] Puṇḍarīka
With a strange appearance:
His eyes' corners were extremely red
Owing to incessant weeping;
His lip-*bimba*s were exceedingly gray and dry
On account of sighing;

And he was rolling over
Upon the grounds of crystals. [40]

MAHĀŚVETĀ [*aside*]: Why! the glorious one is so much afflicted with love.

TARALIKĀ: We saw him in such a state. What wonder is it he's so distressed now?

KAPIÑJALA: And repeatedly admonished, he told me thus:

"Friend, it is proper to listen with my mind
To what you advise[146] me, but
My mind is gone to her for fear of Love's arrows.
What is the use of advice?" [41]

MAHĀŚVETĀ [*to herself*]: I disregarded[147] my friend's words in the same way.

VAIŚAMPĀYANA:

He should follow his friend by understanding[148]
The intoxicating nature[149] of youth,
The irresistible nature of Love's arrows
And the exciting nature of spring's beauty. [42]

KAPIÑJALA: And for the venerable one,[150]

Lying down upon fresh sprouts,
Fanning his body[151] with banana leaves,
Anointing it with sandal paste,
Decorating it with lotus fibers
And sprinkling it with water drops
Whose touch was cold as nectar —
Everything[152] was fruitless;
That Love[153] alone flourished. [43]

So I concluded I couldn't remove his agony except through his union with you, and came here under the pretext of bringing[154] lotus leaves.

VALĀHAKA: This expedient of his is appropriate.

What good could other remedies do
To a violent love fever?
A passion that does not attain its object
Even leads to death. [44]

MAHĀŚVETĀ: Taralikā, what shall we do[155] about this?

[*In the second dressing room, the sound of anklets and the voice of panegyrics.*]

KAPIÑJALA [*having given ear*]: What's this uproar?

TARALIKĀ: Since the Princess is feeling ill, her mother must have come.

MAHĀŚVETĀ[156] [*having turned around towards* KAPIÑJALA]: Sir, please understand that I will by all means fulfill[157] your friend's desire, and go ahead.

KAPIÑJALA: I have nothing more to say. You know what's right for such a love between you two and for this visit of mine. [*Stands up and walks around.*]

MAHĀŚVETĀ: Now I'll get up and greet Mother, and when I send her off, I'll get ready for my own business. [*Exit with* TARALIKĀ.]

KAPIÑJALA: Oh, no! Something like sprinkling salt on a wound has happened now. For

Separation from the dear girl
 Has now befallen my friend;[158]
Love's attack is irresistible to him;
 In addition, the moon is now rising,
Its splendor upward,
 Kindling with its beams
The minds of those
 Longing for their beloveds.[159] [45]

[*After walking around*] This is surely the arbor where Puṇḍarīka was staying.

[*In the second dressing room*]

Oh, ill-natured, wretched moon!

What ever has become[160] of the fierceness
 Of your rays upon that Rāhu?[161]
Now you are discourteously showing it
 Upon me separated from my beloved.
Oh, extremely sinful one,[162]
 Give up your vain cruelty![163]
Do you not know such a result
 Of the separation[164] of stars? [46]

You, too, suffer separation from your beloved life after life, wailing like this![165]

KAPIÑJALA [*having heard this, in a flurry*]: Why! that sounds like my friend's wailing. And Mahāśvetā, who was the cause of this calamity, is delaying.

[*Enter* MAHĀŚVETĀ *in a sportive garment, and* TARALIKĀ.]

MAHĀŚVETĀ: Friend, I[166] was right to disregard[167] the bold frivolity of going to see him by myself. Otherwise, my life[168] surely wouldn't survive[169] Love and the moon.

TARALIKĀ: What are you talking about? Indeed,[170] the entrance to the fifth stage of the almighty love is called Moonrise.[171]

KAPIÑJALA: I'll cheer up my friend with the very[172] hope of getting united with his dearest girl. [*Exit.*]

MAHĀŚVETĀ: Luckily, no one saw us[173] coming out of the side door of the Pleasure Grove.

TARALIKĀ: When the preceptor of youth,[174] Love, is pleased with innocent girls' boldness to go to meet their lovers for the first time, he surely arranges them a "street-stove" suitable[175] for the time and the place.

[*Both walk around.*]

VAIŚAMPĀYANA: Honorable Valāhaka, now to me,

The tortures of hell seem to be happening all at once;
    I feel as if I had sunk into darkness hard to cross;
Alas! my heart is discomposed as if it had long
    Not accomplished its end — What can I do? [47]

VALĀHAKA: Take courage, glorious one! Getting thus totally absorbed in the experiences of *rasa*s and *bhāva*s is certainly the nature of those of poetic taste.[176] Likewise, those who have established the truth of the *dhvani* system think:

By scrutinizing the text of a drama,
    One obtains in one's perception
A *bhāva* concealed[177] by other *bhāvas*
    Yet incessantly lasting because of its subtle nature. [48]

You're experiencing feelings of separation from a person[178] close to you. And because of that separation, you're overcome[179] by excessive grief.

MAHĀŚVETĀ [*gesticulating*[180] *an omen*]: What ever could this be? My right eye is about to throb.

TARALIKĀ: [*to herself*]: Could it be some calamity to Puṇḍarīka? Maddening[181] torment by Love can indeed deprive[182] separated people even of their lives.

[*Both walk around.*]

[*In the second dressing room*]

Wretched flower-arrowed Love!
    Your attempt has borne fruit now!
Moon! Why do you commit this grave sin
    Of murdering an ascetic?
Friend! Where ever are you going away,
    Mercilessly leaving me masterless?
Mahāśvetā! For my friend,
    You are certainly Death! [49]

MAHĀŚVETĀ [*having heard this, in a flurry*]: Taralikā, what's that? Oh, I'm destroyed! I'm ill-fated!

TARALIKĀ: Come quickly! We'll see[183] the actions of fate![184]

[*Both go with hurried steps.*]

[*Enter* KAPIÑJALA, *wailing,* PUṆḌARĪKA's *body placed on his lap.*]

KAPIÑJALA:

Oh, Mother! Lakṣmī! You are destroyed!
    The wicked fate has taken away your son!
Oh, Father! Sage Śvetaketu!
    Where would your affection for your son be?
Oh, Puṇḍarīka! Why do you not
    Answer me, your wailing friend?
Where ever would the knowledge,
    Austerities and friendship of yours be? [50]

[*Keeps wailing.*][185]

VALĀHAKA: Oh, how unrestrained poets are! Even those they elevate[186] have an end to their lives.

KAPIÑJALA [*having seen*]: Lady! *Gandharva* Princess! Beloved of Puṇḍarīka's desire! Mahāśvetā!

Come and soothe him! He respects your words,[187]
    For you are his beloved.
Oh, look! He has been keeping silence[188] all this time,
    For you have delayed. [51]

MAHĀŚVETĀ: Taralikā! Oh, I'm destroyed! I'm ill-fated! Here's the venerable Kapiñjkala, holding on his lap[189] my lord, Puṇḍarīka, as if he were an uprooted[190] young coral tree. [*Swoons.*]

TARALIKĀ: Princess, take heart! Take heart![191] The glorious one must be closing his eyes only because he's sleeping.[192] So don't imagine anything inauspicious!

MAHĀŚVETĀ [*after plucking up courage with difficulty*]: Oh, my lord! I swear the truth by touching your foot-lotus. I have passed the day with the misery of not being united with you. Oh, please, break this silence![193] I'm folding my hands to you like this. [*After falling at his feet*][194] Or rather, what's the use of these[195] futile chatterings? Taralikā, light a fire! I must follow my lord.

TARALIKĀ [*in tears*]: Why! the wicked fate[196] has made a tool out of my friendship in an action like this. All right, I'll do so and give up[197] my life as well.

VALĀHAKA [*after looking sideways*]: Why! Vaiśampāyana is still unconscious. Perhaps[198] it's better because he's not seeing this great tragedy, his heart becoming so delicate. [*After looking upward*] Why is this light extremely bright but cold to the touch descending from the sky?[199] [*After observing it*]

Oh, who is this divine-looking youth
    Descending to the earth from the sky?
He is wearing a garland,
    A beautiful crown studded with gems,
A pearl necklace glittering
    As a row of bright stars on his chest,
A garment white as snow
    And a forehead mark of camphor. [52]

[*Having entered*]

DIVINE MAN: Dear Mahāśvetā! you mustn't give up your life. Without fail, you'll have the great joy of getting reunited with him. [*Acts lifting up* PUṆḌARĪKA *and flying up into the sky.*]

MAHĀŚVETĀ [*with fear, sorrow and astonishment*]: Venerable Kapiñjala, what's this, like magic?

KAPIÑJALA [*after tying his mass of matted hair angrily and flurriedly*]: Hey, wretch! Stop! Stop! Where[200] are you taking my friend? [*After turning back while flying up*] Dear *gandharva* Princess! Now I

Will endeavor to reunite you[201] with my friend,
    Though he has departed to another world,
As daybreak reunites a lotus
    With the set sun. [53]

[*Exit with the* DIVINE MAN.][202]

VALĀHAKA: Oh! this is extremely painful to Haṁsa's daughter.

Such being the case with her dear man,
　　It quite befits her
To give up her life in this manner[203] —
　　It will lead her to rest.
This strange arrangement of fate
　　Is strengthening[204] her bond of desire;
Or rather, has a series of deep sorrows
　　Approached her again now? [54]

TARALIKĀ [*after falling sorrowfully at* MAHĀŚVETĀ's *feet*]: Princess, please give up that resolution! No doubt,[205] overwhelmed with pity, the moon himself came out of his disc and carried away the glorious Puṇḍarīka afflicted with a love fever to his own world in order to console him because of his kinship with you.

MAHĀŚVETĀ: Friend, your life is hard to obtain. Go away! Enough of your series of unaccomplishable[206] wishes!

TARALIKĀ: Friend, don't talk like that! Know yourself to have obtained a birth in the family of *apsarases* arisen from the moon's beams.

MAHĀŚVETĀ: I have no hope. How can I sustain[207] my life when the glorious one has gone out of sight[208] like that?

TARALIKĀ: But again, what[209] if that divine man himself or the venerable Kapiñjala should bring back your beloved here with his life restored?

VALĀHAKA: Oh! even though her friend has shown[210] her scope for hope, the *gandharva* Princess is very much afflicted with the unbearableness of her long suffering[211] from separation. For

A female ruddy goose will certainly be reunited
　　With her beloved at daybreak; yet she is distressed.
Oh! she does not know why she is grief-stricken.
　　The nature of love is indeed the absence of firmness. [55]

MAHĀŚVETĀ: What can I do? My good fortune is destroyed. I can't[212] even follow my beloved at my own will[213]. All right, until Kapiñjala comes back, I'll stay here practising asceticism for the sake of reunion with my departed[214] lord with this paraphernalia of his for asceticism and this rosary I obtained before. Taralikā,[215] neither you nor my kinsmen nor elders can ever stop me.[216]

TARALIKĀ: I'll bring everything here to Acchoda.[217] So maintain your life.

MAHĀŚVETĀ: Then show me the way to Acchoda. There right now I must make a vow, take an ablution and put on the *kalpa* tree bark garments my husband was wearing before. [*Exit with* TARALIKĀ.]

VALĀHAKA: Minister Vaiśampāyana, come to your senses![218] [*Shakes him with his hand.*]

[*The sound of a conch in the first dressing room.*]

VALĀHAKA: Oh, how time goes by!

Shaking off the seal of sleep
From soldiers and deer-eyed girls
Relishing[219] the pleasure of love-making,
Surely being heard by people[220] here
With half-opened, half-closed eyes, and
Mixed with drums' sounds simultaneously produced,
The sound of a conch, an incarnation of a star,
Indicates the youth of night near the watchmen. [56]

VAIŚAMPĀYANA [*as if he had regained consciousness with difficulty*]: Oh dear! I've gotten into a big trouble. For

My mind seems to remember
Something it has forgotten;
I regard the unfamiliar departed boy
As if[221] he were familiar;
I am afflicted with remorse
Lika a secret sinner —
There is nothing more to say:
Myself as I am, I do not seem myself. [57]

VALĀHAKA [*towards the dressing room*]: Ho! Ho! Actors dwelling in *Kimpuruṣa* Land!

We have certainly seen before[222]
Dramas such as the *Śākuntala*;
Yet the poetic charm of this performance
Seems to move[223] our hearts even more than theirs. [58]

Stop acting! We'll see the rest of your performance tomorrow.

[*In the dressing room*]

Then we'll do what the gentlemen please.

VALĀHAKA: Minister, please go inside and take a rest now. I'll honor the troupe of divine actors with the help of the treasurer.[224]

VAIŚAMPĀYANA [*after standing up, to himself*]: Surely agitation like this ins't due to watching the play alone.

Is the cause of my mind's perturbation
The excitement of everyone?[225]
Or my series of desires?
Or my memory[226] of another life? [59]

[*Walks around slowly owing to musing.*]

VALĀHAKA [*to himself*]: Tomorrow morning, when his mind is sound,[227] I'll tell him and send[228] Patralekhā with Meghanāda to the presence of the Crown Prince.

[*Exeunt omnes.*]

END OF ACT FIVE

Notes

1. *M.M.V.1.* and *V.K.: -śulkena; M.M.: -śuṣkeṇa.*
2. *V.K.: daṇḍacakrasya; M.M.: maṇḍalakasya.*
3. *M.M.: agre (valokya); V.K.: agrato (-).*
4. *V.K.: haṁsā (-); M.M.: haṁsān (-).*
5. *Cārīcaṅkramacāturīṣu.*
6. *V.K.: evam; M.M.: evā(tmānam).*
7. *M.M.: parijanaś ca; V.K.* omits it, probably because they never speak.
8. *V.K.: nirvedasyaiva; M.M.: nirvedasyai(?)nimayata (vivarto yaṁ).*
9. *H.S.: yad vā; M.M.: yava; V.K.: yac ca.*
10. *M.M.: adṛśyam; V.K.: dṛśyam* (lit. visible; beautiful). *Vide infra*, vs. 9.
11. *H.S.: (jayati) sa (saṁsāra-); M.M.V.1.: (-) saṁ (- -).*
12. *M.M.V.2.: samadā; M.M.: saṁvadā; V.K.: samapadā.*
13. *V.K.: -śilpasya: M.M.: -śīlasya.*
14. *Vide* Bharata, *Nāṭyaśāstra*, eds. M.R. Kavi *et al.*, chap. I, vs. 17:
    jagrāha pāṭhyam ṛgvedāt sāmabhyo gītam eva ca |
    yajurvedād abhinayān rasān ātharvaṇād api ||
15. *V.K.: svadante; M.M.: sadatte.*
16. *V.K.: cāsya; M.M.: yāsya.*
17. *V.K.: avadhārayatu; M.M.: avadhārayituṁ.*

18. *H.S.: jāvakkhu mahu nipāuṁ bhamarajuā cūamajjarīṁ lagai | oharai kahiṁ vi imaṁ dāvakkhukkhippahārako pavaṇo* ||; *V.K.: - | - kahi - - tāvaccippahāriṇo* - ||; *M.M.: jāpañcia aṁghāiṁ bhamarajuā cūamañjarīṁ mahai | oaharai kahiṁ - - ta°ciadāhiṇo* - ||; *M.Ch.M.* skips the whole verse; *H.S.Ch.: yāvat khalu madhu nipātuṁ bhramarayuvā cūtamañjarīṁ lagati | apaharati kutrāpy enaṁ tāvat khalu kṣiprahārakaḥ pavanaḥ* ||; *V.K.Ch.: - | - - - tāvat kṣiprahārī* - ||
19. *V.K.: dhruvā; M.M.: dhradavā.*
20. *V.K.: - parigṛhītavatī varṇikāṁ mahāśvetāyāṇ; M.M.: - parigṛhītavarṇikāmahāśvetāyāḥ.*
21. *M.M.: sajjībhaveyam; V.K.: -bhavāmi.*
22. *V.K.: anantara-; M.M.: ananta-.*
23. *V.K.* needlessly switches the two half verses.
24. *V.K.* supplies (*kiṁ īdṛśam*) *api.*
25. *V.K.: ociṇumo; M.M.: o°ci-; M.Ch.M.: vicinumaḥ; V.K.Ch.: avacinuvaḥ.*
26. *V.K.: -avacayaṁ; M.M.: -apacayaṁ.*
27. *H.S.: nipuṇaṁ (nirūpaṇīyo); V.K.: nipuṇa(-); M.M.: -ṇa(-pi-).*
28. *H.S.: saccaṁ edesu vaṇesu jutthoccidā ede pāavapasūṇaparimalaṁ imaṁ aṇusaranti mahuarā; M.Ch.M.: satyam eteṣu vaṇeṣu yūthoccitā ete pādapa(prasūna,* supplied by *H.S.)parimalam imam anusaranti madhukarāḥ; M.M.: saccaṁ edesu khuñjauṁsiāe sesapāavapasūṇaparimalā aṇusaranti imaṁ mahuarā;V.K.: - ede khu jutthiāe sepāliāpasūṇaparimalaṁ aṇusaranti mahuarā; V.K.Ch.: satyam ete khalu yūthikāyāḥ śephālikāprasūnaparimala(m,* supplied by *H.S.) (a,* supplied by *H.S.)nusaranti madhukarāḥ.*
29. *M.Ch.M.* has *amānuṣalokocitaṁ ca.*, which should be assigned to Taralikā; *H.S.Ch.: amāṇusalooidaṁ ca. M.M.* has no Prakrit corresponding to this *chāyā*; as a result, the preceding speech of Mahāśvetā is followed by another of her own. *V.K.* fails to notice *M.Ch.M.*
30. *V.K.: saha; M.M.: mama.*
31. *M.M.: aparokṣitaitasmin (= -kṣitā + etasmin); V.K.: -kṣite tasmin.*
32. *M.M.: śānta-; V.K.: śānti-. Vide* Intro., chap. IX.
33. *Kanakavarṇakarṇejapam.*
34. *V.K.: (ambara)gamana(khedam); M.M.: (-)patha(-).*
35. *V.K.: dṛṣṭaś; M.M.: dṛṣṭiś.*
36. *V.K.: (āliṅgano)tsukam ivā(ṅgam); M.M.: (-)tsukitam a(-).*
37. *V.K.: paśya saviśeṣacārutāṁ; M.M.: paśyasi viśeṣacārutā.*
38. *M.M.: vanasya; V.K.* omits.
39. *V.K.: -agram; M.M.: -agre.*
40. *M.M.V.2.* and *V.K.: vakulakusumapātrīsambhṛtaṁ; M.M.: vakulamukulapātīsambhṛtaś.*
41. *V.K.: lakṣyate; M.M.: vakṣyate.*
42. *V.K.: vyāhāra (ceṣṭākramaḥ); M.M.: vyāpāra(-).*
43. *V.K.: pārthakyād; M.M.: vārdhakyād.*

44. *H.S.: sāttvika-; M.M.: sā(tā, M.M.V.2)tvika-; V.K.: tāttvika-.*

45. *V.K.: sakhiṇā; M.M.: sa°khiṇā; M.Ch.M.* and *V.K.Ch.: saha; H.S.Ch.: sakhyā.*

46. *V.K.: uvasappia; M.M.: upasa°via; M.Ch.M.: upasarpyatām; V.K.Ch.: upasṛtya; H.S.Ch.: upasṛpya.*

47. *M.M.V.2.* and *V.K.: saspṛham; M.M.: (?).*

48. *M.M.: muṇiṇaṁdaṇa°sa; M.Ch.M.: muninandanasya; V.K.: muṇijaṇassa; V.K.Ch.: munijanasya.*

49. *V.K.: dāṇiṁ; M.M.: la(i, M.M.V.2.)mojāṇi; M.Ch.M.* and *V.K.Ch.: idānīm.*

50. *V.K.: ānamramauli rucirā(lulitālakāntam); M.M.: āndolilā kalayatā (-).*

51. *V.K.* supplies *-(pha) la-.*

52. *V.K.: draṣṭā(ciraṁ); M.M.: dṛṣtā (-).*

53. *M.M.V.2.*, and *V.K.: khurali(janyam); M.M.: (?) (-).*

54. *M.M.V.2.* and *V.K.: astra(kalām); M.M.: asu(-).*

55. *M.M.: phalidaṁ; V.K.: palidaṁ; M.Ch.M.* and *V.K.Ch.: phalitaṁ.*

56. *H.S.: duve vi ede; M.M.: (?)ve vi ede; V.K.: duve vi; M.Ch.M.* and *V.K.Ch.: dvāv apy etau.*

57. *M.M.: e°kapae; V.K.: ekkapaa evva; M.Ch.M.* and *V.K.Ch.: ekapada eva.*

58. *M.M.V.2.: atthi ṇo kiṁ vi koūhalaṇi; M.M.: a°(?)toūhaiṁ; V.K.: atthi kiṁ vi koūlaṁ; M.Ch.M.: asti me kim api kautūhalam; H.S.Ch.: - nau - - -; V.K.Ch.* omits *me.*

59. *H.S.: kassa vā taruṇo mañjarī iaṁ tti etti evva; M.M.: ka°sa vā ta(?)e°va; M.M.V.2.: - - taruṇo mañjarī ye matti etti e°va; V.K.: kassa vā tavassiṇo tti etti eva; M.Ch.M.* and *V.K.Ch.: kasya vā tapasvina ity etāvati eva; H.S.Ch.: - - taror mañjarīyam ity - -*

60. *M.M.: svagatam; V.K.* omits.

61. *M.M.V.2.: iva cā(kṣarāṇy); M.M.: (?) (-); V.K.* omits *iva.*

62. *V.K.* supplies *(caturdaśī)ti (kṛtvā).*

63. *V.K.* omits *(kṛtti)kā(vāsasaṁ).*

64. *Kalpadruma-.*In the novel *Kādambarī* of Bāṇa, however, this is a *pārijāta* tree; *vide Kādambarī (Pūrvārddha)*, ed. by M. Pant, p. 494: *iyaṁ . . . pārijātanāmā pādapa . . . Kalpa* is only a generic term for any of the five kinds of trees in the *Nandana* forest of Indra; *pārijāta*, the specific name of one of them.

65. *M.M.V.2.: dhaṇṇāsi kaṇṇalaggā mañjari se cumbasi kavolaṁ; M.M.: - -bhṛṅgā -rī - -sikapolaṁ; V.K.: - - laggā cumbasyassettha mañjari kavolaṁ; M.Ch.M.* and *V.K.Ch.: dhanyāsi karṇalaggā cumbasy asyātra mañjari kapolam.*

66. *H.S.: maarandamahuramahuaraṇiṇaaṇiheṇa a jappasi vi rahassaṁ; V.K.:* identical with *H.S.* except that it does not give *vi*, which is metrically necessary; *M.M.: -maira-ṇihāhiṁ ca ja°pasi raha°saṁ; M.Ch.M.* and *V.K.Ch.: makarandamadhuramadhukaraninadanibhena ca jalpasi rahasyam.*

67. *V.K.: aye! vismṛtaḥ sarvo py eṣa vṛttānto dya mayā smaryata iva; M.M.: aye vismṛta ivaiṣa vṛttānta smaryate mayā sarvaḥ.*

68. *M.M.: anādare(smin); V.K.: anādira(-).*

69. *V.K.: -nihnutā(nubandham); M.M.: -nihnuto(-).*
70. *V.K.: kutūhalini; M.M.: kutrahalinī(ni, M.M.V.1.).*
71. *M.M.* and *V.K.: muṇedi; M.Ch.M.: jānāti; V.K.Ch.: manyate.*
72. *V.K.: vadanaṁ; M.M.: yad idaṁ.*
73. *V.K.: (-puñja)m indum; M.M.: (- -)bindum.*
74. *M.M.: praviśyāpaṭākṣepeṇa; V.K.: praviśya paṭākṣepeṇa. Vide* Trans., Act II, n. 93.
75. *H.S.: bhaṭṭidārie; M.M.* and *V.K.: -dārīe; M.Ch.M.: bhaṭṭini; V.K.Ch.: bhartṛdārike.*
76. *M.M.: gamissaṁ; V.K.: gamississaṁ; M.Ch.M.* and *V.K.Ch.: gamiṣyāmi.*
77. *M.M.* and *V.K.: -puṇṇa-; M.Ch.M.: -pūrṇa-; V.K.Ch.: -puṇya-.*
78. *M.M.: iti kathañ cit prasthitā; V.K.: - - - kati cit padāni gacchati.*
79. *M.M.* and *V.K.: vaaṇa-; M.Ch.M.: ānana-; V.K.Ch.: vadana-.*
80. *M.M.V.2.* and *V.K.: satyam anṛtena; M.M.: tasyamanūkena.*
81. *M.M.V.2.* and *V.K.: sukṛtam; M.M.: (-ā)nukṛtam.*
82. *V.K.: skhalitam; M.M.: svalitam.*
83. *V.K.* omits (*anayā durvinītakanyayā*) *ca.*
84. *M.M.V.2.* and *V.K.: sabrahmacāritayā; M.M.: -cārikayā.*
85. *V.K.* supplies *nivṛtya; vide supra,* n. 78.
86. *M.M.: me; M.Ch.M.: me; V.K.* omits.
87. *V.K.: ahiaaro (se amarissotti bhiṇṇa-); M.M.: ahiao(-amariso°ti a°hiṇṇa-); M.Ch.M.: adhi(gato,* crossed) *kataro(marṣa iti asyābhinna-); V.K.Ch.: adhikataro (syāmarṣa iti bhinna-).*
88. *M.M.V.2.* and *V.K.: mayi; M.M.: (?).*
89. *V.K.: dṛṣṭyā; M.M.: diṣṭyā.*
90. *Pratinyāsam.*
91. *M.M.: madanākūtam abhinayan; V.K.* assigns it to Vaiśampāyana immediately after the preceding verse (30).
92. *V.K.: ratiḥ; M.M.: rahas.*
93. *V.K.: puṇḍrekṣu-; M.M.: puṇḍrakṣa-.*
94. *V.K.: ślāghyaṁ; M.M.: ślākhyaṁ.*
95. *V.K.* omits (*evaṁ mae) pu°haitiraoceduṁ (imāsa-; imassa-, M.M.V.2.); M.Ch.M.* provides no *chāyā* for it.
96. *M.M.: dṛṣṭvā, upasṛtya ca; V.K.: taralikāṁ dṛṣṭvā upasṛtya.*
97. *M.M.V.2.* and *V.K.: -khanitām; M.M.: -vanitām.*
98. *V.K.: gabbhe; M.M.: bīa; M.Ch.M.: bījaṁ; V.K.Ch.: garbhe.*
99. *V.K.: nibaddhaḥ; M.M.: nibadhya.*
100. *M.M.: - karaṇīyā tvayeyam ekā mamābhyarthanā; V.K.: - karaṇīyaṁ tvayedaṁ yan mayābhyarthyase.*

101. *V.K.: -sūcanīm imām; M.M.: -sūcanīyamim.*

102. *M.M.: iti vicārayati; V.K.: - cintayati.*

103. *V.K.* supplies *ādāya.*

104. *V.K.: -pūritam; M.M.: -pūram.*

105. After this *V.K.* needlessly supplies *idaṁ hi.*

106. *V.K.: praspardhibhiḥ; M.M.: spardhālubhiś.*

107. *V.K.: bālāṁ; M.M.: phālaṁ.*

108. *V.K.: -dvirephā; M.M.: -(?); M.M.V.1.: -bhramā.*

109. *M.M.V.2.* and *V.K.: tilaka-; M.M.: kilaka-.*

110. *V.K.: lalita-; M.M.: (?)-; M.M.V.2.: lalitā-.*

111. *M.M.: valā || nirūpya, katham unmādoparāga iva puṇḍarīkapūrṇacandrasya; V.K.* assigns it to Vaiśampāyana.

112. *M.M.: pārśvato dattadṛṣṭiḥ, amātyavaiśampāyana(no, H.S.) yad yad vimṛśati ca tathā tathāham api kiṁ nu(tu, M.M.V.2.) dhṛtir iyaṁ rundhe. V.K.*, however, keeps only the stage direction and assigns it together with another stage direction by himself to Puṇḍarīka: *pārśvato dattadṛṣṭiḥ, madanavegaṁ rūpayan.*

113. *V.K.* rightly assigns to Puṇḍarīka the following verse and prose, which *M.M.* assigns to Valāhaka. Judging from their contents and the stage direction *iti niṣkrāntaḥ* immediately after them, they clearly belong to Puṇḍarīka. *Vide* also the preceding note.

114. *M.M.V.2.* and *V.K.: iva; M.M.: iti.*

115. *V.K.: vigataviṣayautsukyaṁ; M.M.: nijanijas*(or *su)yāvṛttaṁ.*

116. *V.K.:* supplies *iva* in *cānyad ivendriya-.*

117. *M.M.: a; M.Ch.M.: ca; V.K.* omits.

118. *V.K.: suṇṇahiaā; M.M.: saṁsia; M.Ch.M.* and *V.K.Ch.: śūnyahṛdayā.*

119. *V.K.: āloaantī; M.M.: puloaṁkī(tī, M.M.V.2.); M.Ch.M.* and *V.K.Ch.: ālokayantī.*

120. *V.K.: ālikhanty(antaś-); M.M.: ālikhaty(- -).*

121. *(Niścala)tarair.*

122. *M.M. and V.K.: āsāsaṇaṁ; M.Ch.M.: āśaṁsayā; V.K.Ch.: āśvāsanam.*

123. *V.K.: vipralobhyamāno; M.M.: -labhya-.*

124. *V.K.: me; M.M.: haṁ (haṁsa).*

125. *Mānasajanmā* means both love (lit. born in the mind) and a goose (lit. born in Lake *Mānasa = haṁsa).* This is a pun (*śleṣa*).

126. *V.K.* supplies (*muktāla)ta(yā*).

127. Narasiṁha borrows this *āryā* verse directly from Bāṇa's novel *Kādambarī; vide Kādambarī (Pūrvārddham)*, ed. by M. Pant, p. 508.

128. *M.M.V.2.* and *V.K.: vācayantī; M.M.: vācaya(tī,* inserted later) *ti.*

129. *H.S.: gato yam eva vāggumphaḥ; M.M.: gate - - -gumbhaḥ; V.K.: gato - - -gumbhaḥ.*

130. *M.M.V.2.* and *V.K.: saṁvādaḥ; M.M.: asaṁvādaḥ.*

131. *V.K.: -saṁniveśāt; M.M.: -pāriśeṣyāt.*

132. *V.K.: cittāvikkaraṇaṁ.; M.M.: ci°taṇi°pu°raṇṇaṁ; M.Ch.M.: cittavispu(or phu)raṇam; V.K.Ch.: cittāviṣkaraṇaṁ.*

133. *H.S: gāhāe; M.M.: vāha°thevehi; M.Ch.M.: gāthārthepihi; H.S.Ch.: gāthāyām; V.K.* omits.

134. *V.K.: visarisarehadāe; M.M.: visarīsarohadāe; M.Ch.M.* and *V.K.Ch.: visadṛśarekhatayā.* By this Mahāśvetā seems to mean that the unevenness of the two lines (30 morae in the first and 27 in the second) of the *āryā* verse by Puṇḍarīka (36) clearly indicates his grief.

135. *H.S.: jhatti eṇaṁ; M.M.: jha°ki(ti, M.M.V.2.)ṇaṁ; V.K.: ettha eṇaṁ; M.Ch.M.: jhaṭiti; V.K.Ch.: atrainaṁ.*

136. *M.M.V.2.* and *V.K.: tadartha (eva); M.M.: kad- (-).*

137. *H.S.: apohyaṁ; M.M.: avodyaṁ; V.K.: apodyaṁ.*

138. *Pūrvam:* before anything disastrous happens.

139. *M.M.V.2.* and *V.K.: maitri; M.M.: maiti.*

140. *Girīn;* it also means respectable ones. True sages are said to survive even a time of universal destruction (*pralaya*).

141. *M.M.: ito (= ido); M.Ch.M.: itaḥ; V.K.* omits.

142. *M.M.: kapi || nanv aham asambhāvitām asyedṛśīṁ vikṛtim amṛṣyamāṇaḥ kuto py avakrānto smi; V.K.* omits this, probably because it happened while Mahāśvetā was still around, not after she returned home.

143. *M.M.: addhi edaṁ (= atthi -); M.Ch.M.: asty etat; V.K.* omits. *Vide* the preceding note.

144. *M.M.V.1.: kasmin(ś,* supplied by *H.S.)cid acchodalatāmaṇḍape; M.M.: kasmin vidacchedalatā-; V.K.: -ś cid acchodabisacchedalatā-.*

145. *V.K.: avaikṣi; M.M.: avekṣi.*

146. *V.K.: upadiśasi; M.M.: -ti.*

147. *H.S.: mae vi avahīridāi; M.M.: - pi avahīdāi; M.Ch.M.: mayāpy avadhīritāni; V.K.: mae piavirahidāe; V.K.Ch.: mama priyavirahitāyāḥ.*

148. *V.K.: (vayaso)vadhārya; M.M.: (-)(?)dhāryaṁ.*

149. *V.K.* supplies (*unmādaka)tva(ṁ).*

150. *M.M.: āryasya; V.K.: asya.*

151. *V.K.: gātre; M.M.: gātrair.*

152. *V.K.: sarvaṁ; M.M.: sarvaḥ.*

153. *V.K.: kāmaḥ sa; M.M.: kāmasya.*

154. *M.M.V.2.* and *V.K.: -ānayanāpadeśād; M.M.: -menā(?)d.*

155. *M.M.* and *V.K.: paḍivajjhāmo; M.Ch.M.: pratipadyāmahe; V.K.Ch.: pratipatsyāmahe; H.S.Ch.: pratipadyāvahe.*

156. *V.K.* omits (*mahā ||)huṁ, (kapiñjalā-).*

157. *M.M.: -saṁvādai°taaṁ; M.Ch.M.: -sampādayitṛkam; V.K.: -saṁpādaaṁ; V.K.Ch.: -sampādakam.*

158. *H.S.: suhṛdor; M.M.: suhṛdād; V.K.: suhṛdā.*

159. *M.M.: unmanasām; V.K.: unmasām* (misprint).

160. *V.K.: (kva nu) tava gatas; M.M.: (- -) gatavatas.*

161. *V.K.: rāhāv; M.M.: nāthā(hā, M.M.V.2.)v.*

162. *M.M.: tvam apy atipātakin; V.K.: mayi tvam ayi pātakin.*

163. *M.M.V.1.: vṛthānistriṁśatvaṁ; M.M.: vṛdhāni-; V.K.: vṛthā ni-.*

164. *V.K.: -viyoga-; M.M.: -adhiyoga-; M.M.V.1.: -abhiyoga-.*

165. *H.S.: evam anukrośaṁs tvam apy anubhava janmani janmani priyāviraham; V.K.: evam evām anukrośaṁs - - - - - priyāvirahakhedam; M.M.: evam anukrośas tvam anubhava - - priyāvirahaḥ.*

166. *V.K.* omits (*mae*) *sae* (wrong repetition of *mae*); *M.Ch.M.* has no *chāyā*.

167. *VK.: aṇavekkhantīe; M.M.: aṇuveṅkha (kkha, M.M.V.2.)tīe; M.Ch.M.: anapekṣantyā; V.K.Ch.: anavekṣantyā.*

168. *M.M.V.2.* and *V.K.: jīviaṁ; M.M.: viaṁ; M.Ch.M.: priyaḥ; V.K.Ch.: jīvitaṁ.*

169. *V.K.: nāvasesijjai; M.M.: na(nā, M.M.V.2.)vasesiala(i, M.M.V.1.); M.Ch.M.: khalu avaśiṣyeta; V.K.Ch.: nāvaśiṣyeta; H.S.Ch.: nāvaśiṣyate.*

170. *M.M.: khu; M.Ch.M.: khalu; V.K.* omits.

171. *V.K.: candodayo; M.M.: -daye; M.Ch.M.: candrodaye; V.K.Ch.: -dayo.* It is clear from this speech that Taralikā did not hear correctly what Mahāśvetā said.

172. *M.M.: (-pratyāśayā) vā; V.K.* omits.

173. *H.S.: ṇa pekkhiāo; M.M.: pe°khio mhi; V.K.: ṇa pekkhio; M.Ch.M.* and *V.K.Ch.: na prekṣite.*

174. *H.S.: jovvaṇagurū; M.M.: jo°vaṇavirū; M.Ch.M.: yauvanagurur; V.K.* omits.

175. *H.S.: -samuiaṁ ratthāhasantikaṁ; M.M.: -samulaāiṁ ra°thahaṁsatī°kāiṁ; M.Ch.M.: -samucitāṁ rathyāhasantikām; V.K.: - samuiaṁ kajjajādaṁ; V.K.Ch.: -samucitaṁ kāryajātam.* By this, perhaps Narasiṁha figuratively means a warm heart provided by Love.

176. *M.M.: bhāvakānām; V.K.: bhāvukānām.*

177. *V.K.: -channaḥ (sthāsnuḥ); M.M.: -channa(-).*

178. *H.S.: (pratyāsanna) jano (palabdha-); M.M.* and *V.K.: (-)janano(- -).*

179. *M.M.V.2.* and *V.K.: abhibhūyase; M.M.: anu-.*

180. *V.K.: sūcayantī; M.M.: -yanti.*

181. *H.S.: unmādaittao; M.M.* and *V.K.: ummattao; M.Ch.M.: unmādayitṛkaḥ; V.K.Ch.: unmastakaḥ (unmattakaḥ?).*

182. *V.K.: (jīviaṁ) vi harai; M.M.: (-) a viharai; M.Ch.M.: (jīvitaṁ) ca virahayati; V.K.Ch.: (-) api harati.*

183. *H.S.: pekkhāmo; M.M.: peṅkhā(kkhā, M.M.V.2.)mi; V.K.: pekkhamha; M.Ch.M.: prekṣāvaḥ; V.K.Ch.; paśyāmo.*

184. *M.M.V.2.* and *V.K.: vihivilasiāiṁ; M.M.: vihilasiāiṁ; M.Ch.M.: kim etad iti; V.K.Ch.: vidhivilasitāni.*

185. *M.M.: iti muhur muhuḥ pralapati; V.K.* omits.

186. *V.K.* supplies *(āropya)te (teṣv).*

187. *V.K.: vacas (tavaiṣa); M.M.: svaṁs(-).*

188. *M.M.V.2.* and *V.K.: (baddha)maunaḥ; M.M.: (-)mānas.*

189. *V.K.: aṅke dhārīadi; M.M.: ako(ke, M.M.V.2.) pā(dhā, M.M.V.2.)rīai; M.Ch.M.: aṅkam āropyate; V.K.Ch.: aṅke dhāryate.*

190. *V.K.: unmmūlio; M.M.: u°miliami(mī, M.M.V.2.)laṇo; M.Ch.M.: unmīlitamīlana (iva); V.K.Ch.: unmūlita (-).*

191. *H.S.: āssasidu āssasidu bhaṭṭidāriā; M.M.: āsāsidu nna(2, M.M.V.2.) bha°ṭidāriā; M.Ch.M.: bhartṛdārike āśvasihi āśvasihi; V.K.: āssasidu bhaṭṭidāriā; V.K.Ch.: āśvasitu bhartṛdārikā.*

192. *V.K.: niddāmettaṇimīliaṇaaṇeṇa; M.M.: mu°pā(cā, M.M.V.2.) mettaṇimi°lakalaṇeṇa; M.Ch.M.* and *V.K.Ch.: nidrāmātranimīlitanayanena.*

193. *H.S.: appehi avaaṇattaṇaṁ edaṁ; M.M.: a°pasu avaaṇapadaṁ -; M.Ch.M.: alpayāvacanatvam etat; V.K.: muñcehi suaṇavaaṇittaṇappadaṁ edaṁ; V.K.Ch.: muñca sujanavacanīyatāspadam etat.*

194. *H.S.: iti pādayor nipatya; M.M.: - -ḥ pātya; V.K.: pādayor nipatya.*

195. *V.K.: edehi; M.M.: ra°evia; M.Ch.M.* and *V.K.Ch.: etair.*

196. *V.K.: devvahaaeṇa; M.M.: ḍa°deveṇaṁ; M.M.V.2.: tha°devveṇaṁ; M.Ch.M.* and *V.K.Ch.: daivahatakena.*

197. *V.K.: pariccajjai; M.M.: pari°calai(iu, M.M.V.2.)°vāriaiṁ; M.Ch.M.* and *V.K.Ch.: parityajyata (eva).*

198. *V.K.* supplies *athavā.*

199. *V.K.: (jyoti)r divo (vatarati); M.M.: (-)dīpo(-).*

200. *V.K.: kva; M.M.: || ka ||.*

201. *(Ayam aham) bhavatīṁ*, a deictic reference in the prose immediately before the verse.

202. *M.M.: iti divyapuruṣeṇa saha niṣkrāntaḥ; V.K.: - -puruṣam anusaran niṣkrāntaḥ.*

203. *V.K.: ayaṁ; M.M.: idaṁ.*

204. *M.M.: dṛḍhayati; V.K.: draḍhayati.* Both are correct.

205. *V.K.* omits *(asaṁsaaṁ) jeṇa; M.Ch.M.: (asaṁśayaṁ) yena.*

206. *V.K.: aghaḍidāhiṁ; M.M.: abhaṭṭidāhiṁ; M.Ch.M.* and *V.K.Ch.: aghaṭitābhir.*

207. *M.M.* and *V.K.: dhārīai; M.Ch.M.: dhriyate; V.K.Ch.: dhāryate.*

208. *V.K.: diṭṭhiagoaraṁ gamide vi; M.M.: di°di(ṭhi, M.M.V.2.) goaraṁ ala(i, M.M.V.2.)gae vi; M.Ch.M.: dṛṣṭyagocaraṁ gamite; V.K.Ch.: - - pi.*

209. *H.S.: kahaṁ; M.M.* and *V.K.: kahiṁ; M.Ch.M.* and *V.K.Ch.: katham.*

210. *V.K.* omits *pradarśite (pradarśite pi).*

211. *V.K.: cirānubhavaduḥsahatayā; M.M.: (-śe) cirānubhavinīm asahatayā.*

212. *M.M.: dullaho hoi; V.K.: - jādo; M.Ch.M.: durlabho bhavat; V.K.Ch.: -jātaḥ; H.S.Ch.: -bhavati.*

213. *V.K.: jāe sacchandado; M.M.: - sasa°ha(cha, M.M.V.2.)ṁdado; M.Ch.M.: yat tādṛśasaṁrambhād api; V.K.Ch.: yasyāḥ svacchandato.*

214. *H.S.: mudassa tassa bhūassaṁgamaṇimittaṁ; M.Ch.M.: mṛtasyāsya bhūyassaṅgamanimittaṁ; M.M.: ta°sa ciasi°ghaṁ saṁgamiṇimittaṁ; V.K.: tassa saṁgamaṇimittaṁ; V.K.Ch.: tasya saṁgamanimittaṁ.*

215. *V.K.* supplies *taralie; V.K.Ch.: taralike.*

216. *V.K.* supplies *ahaṁ; V.K.Ch.: ahaṁ.*

217. *V.K.: imassiṁ acchoammi evva savvaṁ vi āṇaissaṁ; M.M.: ima°sī a°bhe ahaṁ eva sa°ve vi aṇumāṇai°saṁ; M.Ch.M.: asminn acchoda evāhaṁ sarvam apy ānayiṣyāmi; V.K.Ch.:* omits *ahaṁ.*

218. *V.K.: sattvasaṁstho bhava; M.M.: sasatvaśandho (saṁstho, M.M.V.2.) -.*

219. *V.K.: (bhogalīlā)rasānām; M.M.: (-)lasānām.*

220. *V.K.: janair; M.M.: kulair.*

221. *Iva* is understood though it is not in this *pāda* for a metrical reason as in the other three of the verse.

222. *V.K.: purāpi tāvan (ni-); M.M.: purā purāvan (- -).*

223. *V.K.: nartayatīva; M.M.: nartanavatīva.*

224. M.M.V.1. and *V.K.: bhaurika-; M.M.: bhautika-.*

225. M.M.V.2. and *V.K.: sarva(vibhramaḥ); M.M.: sva(-).*

226. *V.K.: (janmāntara)smṛtiḥ; M.M.: (-)sthitiḥ.*

227. *V.K.: svastha(hṛdayāya); M.M.: svasya(-).*

228. *V.K.: preṣaṇīyā tāvan (megha-); M.M.: peṣaṇīyā yāvan (- -).*

Aṅkamukha
Prelude[1] to Act Six

[*Having entered*]

JESTER: Oh, dear! Oh, dear! I'm not happy although my friend has now returned after enjoying traveling for conquest[2] for a long time. Night and day longing for Kādambarī dwelling in a divine land as if he were Purūravas longing for Urvaśī, he bothers me unseasonably even during meals.[3] But it's awfully strange that though he's shaking[4] like that, he won't even accept[5] a cooling service for fear of his elders. He's sustaining his life solely by listening to Kādambarī's message repeatedly read by his betel box bearer, who has come back from the city[6] of *Kimpuruṣa* Land. So, whom should I ask where he is now? [*After looking in the direction of the dressing room*][7] Surely that's the chief maid called Makarikā, closest to Mother, Queen Vilāsavatī. She's coming out of the Prince's mansion. I'll ask her.[8] [*Towards the dressing room*] Makarikā, where's my dear friend? [*After acting listening*][9] Are you saying it's been some time since he went out for a walk?[10] All right, I'll go there, too. [*After turning around*] I'm sure he wants[11] to divert himself in the isolated Pleasure Grove[12] bordered by seats of beautiful fibrous roots. I'll attend on him now. [*Exit.*]

END OF THE *AṄKAMUKHA*
PRELUDE TO ACT SIX

Notes

1. This is obviously an *aṅkamukha,* though *M.M.* and *V.K.* call it a *viṣkambhaka; vide* Intro., chap. VII.
2. *V.K: (ciraālāṇuhūda)viaasaṁcāro; M.M.: (-nubhūdā)vai°sāpiasīcaro(sahacāro, M.M.V.1); M.Ch.M.: (cirakālānubhūta) (?) yasya vijayasañcārasya; V.K.Ch.: (-)vijayasaṁcāra (-).*
3. *V.K.: abbhavahāresu vi; M.M.: a°bhavahāra(?); M.Ch.M.: abhyavahārakāryeṣv api; V.K.Ch.: abhyavahāreṣv api.*

4. *V.K.: taha vipphuranto vi; M.M.: - visūranto; M.Ch.M.: tathāvidhāntaraṅgo pi; V.K.Ch.: tathā viṣphurann api.*
5. *V.K.: geṇhai; M.M.: aṇukaṇṇai; M.Ch.M.: anukampate; V.K.Ch.: gṛhṇāti.*
6. *H.S.: -purādo; M.M.: -va(ca, M.M.V.1.)rāhiṁ; V.K.: -purehiṁ; M.Ch.M.* and *V.K.Ch.: -purāt.*
7. *V.K.* supplies *nepathyābhimukhaṁ (dṛṣṭvā).*
8. *V.K.* supplies *taṁ pucchissaṁ; V.K.Ch.: tāṁ prakṣyāmi.*
9. *V.K.* supplies *śravaṇam abhinīya.*
10. *V.K.: bahivviha (hā, H.S.)ratthaṁ; M.M.: bāhirālīvivihāra°thaṁ; M.Ch.M.* and *V.K.Ch.: bahir vihārārthaṁ.*
11. *V.K.: icchadi; M.M.: imo ima°hīdi; M.Ch.M.: icchāmi; V.K.Ch.: icchati.*
12. *V.K.: -vaṇammi; M.M.: -vaṇesu; M.Ch.M.* and *V.K.Ch.: -vane.*

ACT SIX

[*Enter* CANDRĀPĪḌA, *accompanied by* PATRALEKHĀ *and his* JESTER.]

CANDRĀPĪḌA [*to himself*]:

I returned as the conqueror[1] of the entire earth,
Long beheld Father's feet,
Created in Mother's mind the joy
"I am the hero's mother,"
And made my intimate, worthy people wealthy;[2]
Yet this heart[3] of mine is agitated:
It is afflicted with separation
From the daughter of Citraratha. [1]

JESTER: Friend, you've conquered the four quarters. And you're staying in the middle of your kinsmen in your country's capital. How come you look depressed?

PATRALEKHĀ: Oh, fool, you seem deaf! Day after day the Crown Prince has been telling you the cause of his heart's anguish. Even then, you ask him again and again.

JESTER: Friend, tell that to me once again. I'll listen to it this time and wipe out the fault of deafness.

CANDRĀPĪḌA: Friend, why do you act as if you didn't know about the incident?

Owing to the importance of Father's order,[4]
I came back without telling the Princess.
How could my heart possibly be
Free from regrets now? [2]

JESTER: The *gandharva* Princess has certainly[5] captivated your heart.

PATRALEKHĀ: Oh, I don't know how the condition of this mutually extreme passion[6] beween you two will turn out.

CANDRĀPĪḌA [*after sighing*]:

Even a wish charming with quick union
With a dear one[7] in a very remote land[8]
Could bear fruit[9] for some people
Owing to the results of their merit. [3][10]

Well, where should I divert my mind now?[11]

PATRALEKHĀ: Why![12] the honorable Kailāsa is still[13] tarrying.

JESTER: Did you order him to clear the garden?

CANDRĀPĪḌA: Yes, I did.

[*Having entered*]

CHAMBERLAIN: Now I'll inform the Crown Prince I've carried out his order. [*After approaching him*] Prince, I've inspected these grounds of the garden on Śiprā's bank,[14] where swarms[15] of bees fly up from the filaments of *śirīṣa* flowers slightly shaken by cool breezes from waves, and the quarters are darkened by woods of trees, mainly mountain ebonies, *aśoka*s, pines and mangos.

CANDRĀPĪḌA: Honorable Kailāsa,

I surely see the grounds[16] of the shore,
  Where water is sent everywhere[17]
Into young gardens through canals,
  Fences are formed[18]
With rows of *ketaka* shoots,
  And in a lovely reed arbor
Half seen are townsfolk smiling at pigeons
  Playing and cooing sweetly. [4]

Now keep all these servants out of the garden until we[19] come out.

CHAMBERLAIN: As the Crown Prince commands. [*Exit.*]

CANDRĀPĪḌA [*With a gesture of going inside*]:

With a flock of flamingos taking delight in a walk[20]
  On swings of shaking[21] waves purifying their bodies,
And with full-blown lotuses and water lilies,
  This water of the river gives us pleasure. [5]

PATRALEKHĀ: Crown Prince, here's[22] a crystal slab inside *pāṭala* creepers. Please sit down here.[23]

[*All sit down.*]

CANDRĀPĪḌA [*after staying only for a moment, to himself*]: Oh, my dissatisfied heart,[24] why are you so unhappy like myself?

You enjoy a bee's good fortune in her feet,

Eagerly receive[25] a goose's delight in her buttocks,
Secure bliss attainable only to a *cakora* in her face,
And take a *cātaka*'s joy in her mass of hair;
What ever wish other than these do you have to speak of? [6]

JESTER: Surely he's still overpowered by the flood of a river of longing. So how can[26] he compose himself?

PATRALEKHĀ: You say that again and again.[27] Except the incident of the Princess, what else could ever be the cause of his heart's anguish?

CANDRĀPĪḌA: Patralekhā, you have observed well. For

Loving each other yet separated by lands,
A young couple enjoy
Talking to each other through messages
And looking at each other through pictures. [7]

So bring[28] me the canvas I haven't finished painting and the paintbrushes.

PATRALEKHĀ: [*takes them out of a box and hands them over to him.*]

CANDRĀPĪḌA [*after receiving them*]: Freinds, look[29] here!

Here painted is the very respectable temple of Lakṣmī;
Here painted[30] is Kādambarī with her friends;
And here painted[31] I am, tied with sidelong glances,
As if with cords, by her checked by shyness' force.[32] [8]

PATRALEKHĀ: We're both delighted the Prince has shown skill in creating art with his own fingers.[33]

CANDRĀPĪḌA: I feel[34] the same way as you said. However,

First a lotus stalk like her beautiful shank,
Then a banana tree like her buttocks' support,
Then water with hairy creepers,
Then a pair of jars graced by her arms,
Then[35] a *bimba* fruit like her pouted lips,[36]
Then[37] a bow[38] marked with her eyes
And then the graceful moon —
Like this, I can paint more.[39] [9]

JESTER: But friend,[40] I'm sure Citraratha's daughter dwelling in your heart[41] has indeed[42] come out of your heart-lotus tormented[43] with the fire of love by way[44] of your arm-stalk under the guise of a painting. So, what ever[45] beyond this remains to be painted?[46]

CANDRĀPĪḌA: I'll paint and show you now. [*After doing so,*[47] *showing with his hand*]

This here is the Pleasure Mountain;
  This is the mansion;[48]
This is the charming water lily pool;
  This beside me[49] is she;
This is the enjoyable snow house;
  And these two unrestrained ones are we,
To whom by fate was born a love
  Rich[50] in affection but fruitless. [10]

[*To his beloved in the painting as if she were really there*]

Agony indeed set foot in you
  By embracing[51] you forcefully;
But[52] it has been transferred into my body,
  And is growing very intense.[53]
So, lovely girl! allow me to enjoy
  The nectar of your *bimba*-lips.
Love, if unchecked in attracting passion cleverly,
  Will calm down, not otherwise. [11]

PATRALEKHĀ [*to herself*]: Why! the Prince imagines all this so vividly. [*After receiving the painting board, aloud*] Prince, enough of this Princess in the painting! Here's the message the Princess wrote with her own hand. Look at it![54]

CANDRĀPĪḌA: Then . . . My eyes are filled with tears born of my beloved's memory. You, sprinkle nectar on my ears.

JESTER: You have certainly read this message before. Why are you going to read it now with great respect as if it had been sent recently?

CANDRĀPĪḌA: Fool![55] Anything connected with my[56] beloved one is always captivating to me. Look!

I beheld her face;
  Yet my eyes' desire has doubled.
I certainly touched her body;
  Yet how can these arms be satisfied?[57]
I repeatedly drank her speech-honey;

Yet these ears are not free from thirst.
My heart deeply in love with her
Does not delight in momentary enjoyments. [12]

PATRALEKHĀ [*acts taking a birch bark*[58] *letter and oepning it.*]

JESTER: If my eyes were'nt blinded by darkness, I'd read it and subdue her pride of being clever.[59]

PATRALEKHĀ [*reads it with a smile*]:

My misery gets fresher every moment
Even while I am suffering it.
How much more of it must I endure?
Hope alone sustains my life. [13][60]

Surely it is easy for women in separation
To obtain their beloveds in a drawing;
Yet even that is difficult for me,
Whose eyes are full of tears coming out. [14][61]

I know we are not going to be united
In this life of mine.
So, glorious one! attain with ease
The joy of union with me in my next life. [15][62]

CANDRĀPĪḌA:

If that deer-eyed girl has given up shyness
And told thus in her message,
Let the earth be truly flooded at once
With an ocean of passion!
Let moonlight, sandal, wine, cuckoos and others
Shine without restraint!
And let Love, an archer of powerful[63] commands,
Be long victorious everywhere! [16]

PATRALEKHĀ: I, too, must ask the Prince. Is it proper for the compassionate Prince to neglect the Princess in a state like that?

CANDRĀPĪḌA: You have rightly advised[64] me. For

Were the lovely-browed girl's frequent amorous gestures
Not intent on making me sense her emotion?

Doubting if even they were only spontaneous,
I have been deprived of my desires by fate. [17]

Besides, the incident in the snow house[65] was quite obvious to both of you as well.[66]

Her friends sensed our hearts and barely left us alone
With words full[67] of intended ambiguity.
Deeply in love, I desired some amorous play; yet
The water-lily-eyed one only resisted me stubbornly. [18][68]

PATRALEKHĀ: Her body was wasting away every day; she had only beauty left. Mahāśvetā barely made her give up persistence in her vow with conciliatory words and by falling at her feet. So she wrote this message herself, handed it to me and sent me to get you back from the camp.[69]

CANDRĀPĪḌA: Alas! the fruit of my good fortune was in my hand but dropped because of a storm of fate.

JESTER: What's the use of regretting bygones?

CANDRĀPĪḌA: All right.

I will endeavor to fulfill this desire[70]
By all means[71] with all my strength;
Yet when I remember her delicate body,
My heart throbs. [19]

JESTER: Then you shouldn't think of anything[72] else. He who longs for union with his beloved surely sustains[73] his life.[74]

CANDRĀPĪḌA [*after looking elsewhere*]: Patralekhā, do you see what has arrived[75] from a remote coconut forest to the vicinity of the Mahākāla temple's main gate? To my great surprise, it's approaching here.

JESTER: Surely it must be a host of soldiers[76] arriving from the camp!

PATRALEKHĀ [*after observing it*]: Crown Prince, I think the horsemen's[77] leader approaching[78] here with the heat warded off by a sunshade is Keyūraka, an attendant of the Princess.

CANDRĀPĪḌA: There is indeed no object impossible to attain among those desired. [*Towards the dressing room*] Hello! Who's[79] there?

[*Having entered*]

CHAMBERLAIN: Please command me, Crown Prince.[80]

CANDRĀPĪḌA: Some people are arriving here.[81] Please tell their leader we're staying here, and bring[82] him here.

CHAMBERLAIN: Certainly. [*Exit.*]

[*Having entered*]

KEYŪRAKA [*approaching*]: Oh, why! Prince Candrāpīḍa is staying here in private with two others. He — who

Is wearing on his chest
    That very necklace his beloved gave him,
The state of whose heart is betrayed
    By his wasted, pale limbs,
And who is extremely[83] bright
    With his special splendor
As if he were an elephant in rut —
    Is giving a gracious look at me approaching him. [20]

CANDRĀPĪḌA: Oh![84] Keyūraka has arrived.

KEYŪRAKA: May the Prince be victorious! [*Bows.*]

CANDRĀPĪḌA: [85]Welcome!

KEYŪRAKA: Now with the great joy of seeing the Prince's feet! [*Turns around and duly greets*[86] PATRALEKHĀ *and the* JESTER.]

CANDRĀPĪḌA: How are the Princess and her friends?

KEYŪRAKA: The inquiry after the well-being of the Princess befits the Prince, who departed without telling her so.

CANDRĀPĪḌA [*hopefully*]: There hasn't been any misfortune, I hope.

KEYŪRAKA: Nothing serious. The Princess is sustaining[87] her life now. And I believe she's tearfully searching for you.[88]

PATRALEKHĀ & JESTER: He has given the right reply.[89]

CANDRĀPĪḌA: What did my disinterested friend Mahāśvetā do?

KEYŪRAKA: Prince, after I had escorted Patralekhā to the camp and returned, I told[90] Mahāśvetā this unexpected[91] news that the Prince had gone to Ujjayinī. Then she looked at the Princess, whose face was languid with despair, and left for her hermitage all by herself, her mind perplexed about what to do.

CANDRĀPĪḌA: Oh,[92] accursed, wretched Candrāpīḍa! Just like this you can drop a stroke of thunderbolt on those who rely on you in the name of friendship.

JESTER: Tell us, sir! How did Citraratha's daughter[93] behave after that?[94]

KEYŪRAKA: After that — I swear by the Prince's foot-lotus —

She would neither hear when called
Nor see even her dear friends eagerly;
She would get embarrassed
With strange words in her talks,
Make an effort to go somewhere
But reach elsewhere,
Or resort[95] to long indifference
In order to sustain her life. [21]

Moreover,

She would stay in the Lakṣmī temple,
Her hope grown for a while,
Walk very impatiently
Around the Pleasure Mountain,
Give a somewhat blurred look
At the bank of her mansion's water lily pool,
Or go[96] to the snow house
And simply sigh and weep. [22]

CANDRĀPĪḌA [*after sighing*]:

On one hand is the lovely-browed girl's body
Tender as a fresh lotus fiber;
On the other are Love's arrows
Exerting themselves violently like thunderbolts.
Alas! I am merciless![97]
What is the use of my lamenting now?
I have long neglected a jasmine flower
Made to fall in a forest fire. [23]

[*Sheds tears.*]

JESTER [*wipes them off with a hem of his garment.*]

CANDRĀPĪḌA: Oh, no! Why do you wipe off the beneficent[98] tears? Look!

Owing to the constancy of my sole desire
To see Kādambarī's face-lotus,
I have reached a firm state of heart
Which shows no interest in others;[99]
A flood of tears prevents my eyes

From throbbing at any other form of beauty.[100] [24]

JESTER [*to* KEYŪRAKA]: Sir, tell us now!

KEYŪRAKA:

She would throw her body onto a flower couch
With a violent love fever,
Get her agony bearable for a while
With a hint that you might come,
And spend her night
Without ever winking her eyes,
Asking us "Tell me
How much time has passed?"[101] [25]
And sometimes, when she arose from sleep at daybreak,
"Candrāpīḍa, show mercy upon me![102]
Give me the joy of seeing you!
Dwelling in my heart, you know
I am in love with you,"[103]
Thus her mynahs would repeat
What she had uttered in a dream;
Trembling with embarrassment,[104]
She would explain to people it was about Śiva.[105] [26]

PATRALEKHĀ: Alas! That happened when I was[106] there, too.

KEYŪRAKA:

She would go out of her bedchamber
Without even Magadha women's songs;
She would not even let her maidservants
Ornament her at daybreak;
Longing for you, she rejected ball sports,
Gave up dancing,
Abandoned her desire for pleasure groves
And dropped her taste for wine. [27]

CANDRĀPĪḌA [*acting defeat by Love*]:[107]

Rati's husband, do me a favor!
Destroy my body already emaciated
And sustained by breaths like thunderbolts
With your arrows of terrible power!

Take away my beloved dwelling in my heart!
Thus I beg you now with folded hands.[108] [28]

KEYŪRAKA: Oh, Prince, such talks of longing of the Princess are reported.

"This beloved of mine is indeed
A feast for my eyes.
Friends, I am talking fruitlessly[109]
To him devoid of mercy,"
Thus speaking aimlessly for a moment,
She would seem infatuated[110] —
Waking her up would not make her happy. [29]

CANDRĀPĪḌA: Then, did the Princess give you a message and get you to pursue[111] me?

KEYŪRAKA: The Princess didn't give me any message. But since she was in such a state, the Great Queen, Madirā, sent me to Mahāśvetā's hermitage. And then Mahāśvetā sent me to the presence of the Prince's feet.

CANDRĀPĪḌA: Then tell me Mahāśvetā's message.

KEYŪRAKA:

"Fruitless is this skill of Brahmā in creating women;[112]
Untrue is his reputation of being benevolent.
Now, friend, I consider it quite improper for you
To make my request a vain effort." [30]

These are the lady's words.

CANDRĀPĪḌA: She has told[113] me what I should be told. What can I do? It's not right to go without telling my elders. Besides, my second heart, Vaiśampāyana, who speaks acceptable words,[114] isn't at hand.

[*Off stage*]

Ho, ho, couriers! How far[115] has the army returned?

JESTER [*having heard it*]: Luckily, Minister Vaiśampāyana has arrived.

CANDRĀPĪḌA: Wait! We'll listen.

[*Off stage again*]

As far as Daśapura!

CANDRĀPĪḌA [*joyfully*]: Friend Patralekhā! Friend Keyūraka!

I have known[116] such a bond of love
    Since our exchange of passionate glances, and
The Princess' vow contrary to her emotion is gone;
    Hemakūṭa will never be in a wilderness for me
Departing after infroming my elders of this
    And obtaining an order from their mouths. [31]

But you two, please go ahead and try[117] to sustain the life of the Princess.

KEYŪRAKA: My effort has borne fruit[118] now.

JESTER: Luckily, I'll get a wedding feast before long because I'm a Brahmin.

CANDRĀPĪḌA [*towards the dressing room*]: Is the honorable Kailāsa there?

[*Having entered*]

CHAMBERLAIN: Here I am!

CANDRĀPĪḌA: Bring Meghanāda here.

CHAMBERLAIN: As the Prince commands. [*Exits and reenters with* MEGHANĀDA.]

MEGHANĀDA [*to himself*]: This is usually[119] the way of servants.

My lord has a tender heart towards his dependents,
    And my devotion to my master is invariable;
Nevertheless, I am now feeling nervous
    Of meeting him face to face. [32]

[*After approaching him, aloud*] May my master be victorious!

CANDRĀPĪḌA: Meghanāda, please take this girl once again to the place where you brought her from.

MEGHANĀDA: Your favor is accepted.

CANDRĀPĪḌA [*to* PATRALEKHĀ *and* KEYŪRAKA]: Go and tell the Princess thus:

I know[120] you are tormented by Love
    Just as I am afflicted by him,
But you must take courage to sustain[121] your life.
    Darling! I will come there right now
To serve the presence of your feet,
    Unless the goddess of fate hinders us. [33]

THE TWO[122] [*fall at* CANDRĀPĪḌA's *feet and exit.*]

CANDRĀPĪḌA:[123] Now I'd like to go to greet Vaiśampāyana with Father's permission. [*To the* JESTER][124] Friend, please hurry up the host of princes[125] for the journey.

JESTER: I'll be the general! [*Exit.*]

CANDRĀPĪḌA: Kailāsa, show me the way leading to Father's presence.

CHAMBERLAIN: This way, this way, Crown Prince.

CANDRĀPĪḌA [*after going out of the garden, walking around*]:

Father with a heart full of affection
    Fondles me with sweet[126] words and great respect,
And I myself make an effort to be obedient to him;
    Even so, I still cannot forget the Princess. [34]

CHAMBERLAIN: Here's the Great King. He's staying in a pavilion named Desire's Dwelling with Queen Vilāsavatī and the venerable Śukanāsa. Please approach him.[127]

CANDRĀPĪḌA: Honorable one, remain on your duty.

CHAMBERLAIN: Certainly.[128] [*Exit.*]

CANDRĀPĪḌA [*walks around.*][129]

[*Enter* TĀRĀPĪḌA *as described, and his*[130] *retinue.*]

TĀRĀPĪḌA [*having seen him*]: Here comes our son to delight us with the news of Vaiśampāyana's arrival![131]

CANDRĀPĪḌA [*approaches decorously*[132] *and bows in due form.*]

TĀRĀPĪḌA: My son,[133] this way, this way! [*Shows his lap.*]

CANDRĀPĪḌA [*approaches affectionately and sits down on the ground, putting aside a seat brought by a servant.*]

ŚUKANĀSA:

He has an unrestrained understanding[134]
    Of the four Vedas;
The strength of his arms has been examined
    In the eight regions;
His respect for the elders is such as this —
    What else among wishes remains to be fulfilled?
Only his marriage conformable to the householder's laws
    To a wife of suitable family and birth! [35]

VILĀSAVATĪ: That is indeed my sole unfulfilled wish.

CANDRĀPĪḌA [*after bending his face a little down, to himself*]: Oh, my elders are talking about their wishes.[135] I see my wish concealed for now by meeting my friend. Well, but why is his news still delayed[136] though he has come near?

[*Having entered*]

VALĀHAKA [*to himself*]: How can I possibly tell them the news about Vaiśampāyana terrible as a cloudless thunderstorm?[137] [*Approaches and duly bows.*]

TĀRĀPĪḌA: General, when is our son Vaiśampāyana going to delight[138] us?

VALĀHAKA [*after sighing*]: On the very beautiful day of the Crown Prince's departure, he looked somewhat dispirited as a result of his feelings. On the following day, eager to pay homage[139] to the moon-crested Śiva dwelling in Caitraratha, he visited Acchoda with us . . . Then,[140]

Fixing his eyes on some red *aśoka* arbor
    Situated on its bank
And adorned with rows of gathering bees
    As if on something familiar to him,
He long stayed as if thrown into a painting,
    His senseorgans inwardly turned;[141]
He spent the day right there is tears
    As if remembering something. [36]

ŚUKANĀSA [*to himself*]:

Ineffably fit for sport are such places as those;
    Easily attainable great excitement is youth's nature;
And, alas! a very long absence from the elders' presence
    Loosens even the bond of composure of the firm-minded. [37]

VILĀSAVATĪ: Then what did you do?

VALĀHAKA: Then after we, all his followers, repeatedly engaged in a fruitless effort[142] to request him to start for Ujjayinī, we departed from there.[143] Now it rests with the Great King to decide.

CANDRĀPĪḌA [*to himself*]: Even in a dream he doesn't make a careless mistake[144] about our mutual freindship. Why does he, who hasn't acquired life's four ends, have this sudden mind of indifference to the world?

Performing sacrifices and charitable deeds,
    One does not attain merit, to say nothing of love.
What is the use of unrighteous wealth?
    Then, what could he have done? [38]

Or rather, my friend has done me a favor by hinting an expedient of meeting Kādambarī again.

TĀRĀPĪḌA: There's no need to speak more. I regard this as my son Candrāpīḍa's fault.

If he had not thus left the boy
  Alone in that remote place,[145]
The agony of our hearts would not be
  Thus extremely unbearable now. [39]

ŚUKANĀSA: Great King, please don't judge things unfairly like that! Although we nourished[146] and taught him well, he like an ill-natured parrot didn't show us familiarity. So, may he fall into that very animal species[147] and suffer hundreds of miseries in some desolate forest![148] [*Sheds tears.*]

TĀRĀPĪḌA: Venerable one, you really shouldn't say that! For the harshness of the unforgiving elders towards their youngsters can indeed take the form of a curse on them.

CANDRĀPĪḌA [*to himself*]: Oh, alas! That thrust with a spear of censure seems to break my heart. [*After standing up, aloud*] Father, please permit me to fetch my freind!

ŚUKANĀSA: What ever sensible person would permit throwing a gold ornament into the water[149] in order to save a tin ornament sunk in a deep lake?[150]

TĀRĀPĪḌA: Venerable one, I don't approve of your words in this matter. [*To* VILĀSAVATĪ] As the Queen wishes.

VILĀSAVATĪ: I could somehow[151] endure the misery of not seeing my son for a few days, but couldn't possibly see his face tormented[152] with separation from his friend.

TĀRĀPĪḌA: Though afflicted with sorrow, the Queen has spoken rightly.

CANDRĀPĪḌA: [*acting zeal to depart, bows, his diadem removed.*][153]

TĀRĀPĪḌA: [*after hugging him, choked with tears*]:

I wish to be happy by placing the burden of the earth
  Upon you wedded to a suitable wife —
To those desires springing up in me,
  This great obstacle has thus arisen. [40][154]

VALĀHAKA: King, you shouldn't shed tears at a time of departure.

VILĀSAVATĪ: Will I see my sons' face-lotuses again by a favor of Avanti's tutelary deities?

VILĀHAKA [*after sighing, to himself*]: I don't know about Candrāpīḍa's, but she surely won't see Vaiśampāyana's again.

CANDRĀPĪḌA [*with folded hands to his elders*]: You have granted me leave to depart.[155] [*Walks around.*]

ŚUKANĀSA: What can I do? Our son[156] has a great attachment for an unworthy thing. All right. General, go and send the Crown Prince the host of horsemen exhausted with the long journey but familiar with the region.

VALĀHAKA: As the Minister commands. [*Walks around.*]

CANDRĀPĪDA [*after coming out of the royal court*]: Here's Indrāyudha all ready. Why does he look somewhat[157] sad, his neighing of joy ceased? Or rather, the hearts of living beings get afflicted very easily. [*To himself*] And now.

Dejected since I heard the news about my friend
    But delighted because I am going to see the Princess,
My heart is in the state of a *cakora* bird
    Staying between hot and cold rays of light.[158] [41]

VALĀHAKA [*after approaching him*]: Crown Prince, please understand that the Minister has sent you the army.

CANDRĀPĪḌA: All right. You can return. And[159] cheer up Father, the venerable Śukanāsa, Mother and Manoramā. [*Having acted mounting* INDRĀYUDHA]

I will soon come back here
    With my friend
Through great efforts,[160]
    Unless fate's hostilities assail me.[161] [42]

[*Exeunt omnes.*]

END OF ACT SIX

Notes

1. *V.K.: -jayinā; M.M.: -jayitā.*
2. *V.K.: aiśvaryaṁ (praṇayī janaḥ); M.M.: aiśvarya(- -).*
3. *M.M.V.2.* and *V.K.: cetaś; M.M.: śvetaś.*
4. *V.K.: tātājñā-; M.M.: tatrajñā-.*
5. *V.K.: ṇaṁ; M.M.: ṇa; M.Ch.M.: na; V.K.Ch.: nanu.*
6. *V.K.: - aṇṇoṇṇādisāiṇī aṇurāasamavatthā; M.M.: - aṇoṇaṁ osāiṇī aṇurāasamava°dhā; M.Ch.M.: - anyonyānurāgadaśā; V.K.Ch.: - anyonyātiśāyinī anurāgasamavasthā.*

7. *V.K.: praṇayijanatvarita-; M.M.: -janas tvarita-.*
8. *V.K.: deśād; M.M.: daśād.*
9. *V.K.: hi phalen (manorathaḥ); M.M.: viphalo (-).*
10. Cf. Harṣa's *Ratnāvalī*, ed. by R. Mishra (Varanasi: Chaukhamba Amarabharati Prakashan, 1982), Prologue, vs. 6:

    dvīpād anyasmād api madhyād api, jalanidher diśo py antāt |
    ānīya jhaṭiti ghaṭayati vidhir, abhimatam abhimukhobhūtaḥ ||
11. *V.K.: kvedāniṁ; M.M.: (?)dāniṁ.*
12. *H.S.: kahaṁ; M.M.* and *V.K.: kahiṁ; M.Ch.M.* and *V.K.Ch.: katham.*
13. *M.M.: dāṇiṁ vi; M.Ch.M.: idānīm apy; V.K.: dāṇiṁ; V.K.Ch.: idānīṁ.*
14. *M.M.V.2.: śiprātaṭo-; M.M.: suprāṭo-; V.K.: siprātaṭo-.*
15. *V.K.: -kulāḥ; M.M.: -kulyāḥ.*
16. *V.K.: (taṭa)bhuvaḥ; M.M.: (-)bhuvi.*
17. *V.K.: (-salilā)ḥ sarvataḥ; M.M.: (- -) (?)s.*
18. *V.K.: vihita-; M.M.: vahata-.*
19. *M.M.V.2.* and *V.K.: yāvad asmaṇ(niṣkramaṇam); M.M.: vā(?) (-).*
20. *M.M.V.2.* and *V.K.: viharaṇa-; M.M.: viraha-.*
21. *V.K.: -calat-; M.M.: -taradat-.*
22. *V.K.: edaṁ; M.M.: edaṁ taṁ; M.Ch.M.: etat tat; V.K.Ch.: etat.*
23. *V.K.: ettha nisīau bhavaṁ; M.M.: kahiṁ ci°ṭhasu; M.Ch.M.: tat tatra tiṣṭhatu; V.K.Ch.: atra niṣīdatu bhavān.*
24. *V.K.: ayi asantuṣṭa hṛdaya; M.M.: api asantuṣṭahṛdayaḥ.*
25. *M.M.V.2.* and *V.K.: ādriyase; M.M.: ādiyase.*
26. *M.M.V.2.* and *V.K.: karīai; M.M.: -ala; M.Ch.M.* and *V.K.Ch.: kriyeta; H.S.Ch.: kriyate.*
27. *H.S.: puṇo puṇo vaṇṇesi jaṁ taṁ; M.M.: - - va°ṇṇasiṁ ja(jaṁ, M.M.V.2.) -; M.Ch.M.: punaḥ punar varṇayasi yat tad; V.K.* omits.
28. *V.K.: tad ānaya; M.M.: tarhi pradarśaya.*
29. *V.K.: paśyatam; M.M.: -tām.*
30. *M.M.V.2.* and *V.K.: vilikhitā; M.M.: vilasitā.*
31. *V.K.: cālikhito; M.M.: pālita(?).*
32. *V.K.: hrīyantraṇāniyatayāpi; M.M.: hrīyantanā niyatayāci(pi, M.M.V.2.).*
33. *H.S.: saaggahatthena hassāvo daṁsiaṁ deveṇa ṇeuṇṇaṁ sippaviraanāe tti; M.M.: sara°gaha°theṇa pibailāmo daṁsiaṇeuṇaṁ si°paviraaṇo(ṇā, M.M.V.2.)e; M.Ch.M.: svāgrahastena hṛṣyāvo darśitaṁ devena naipuṇyaṁ śilpaviracanena; H.S.Ch.: - - - - - -viracanāyā iti; V.K.: deveṇa daṁsiaṁ sipparaaṇāṇeuṇaṁ deṭṭhūṇa takkemi deveṇa vi ṇa puṇo evvaṁ lehiduṁ pārīyadi tti; V.K.Ch.: devena darśitaṁ śilparacanānaipuṇyaṁ dṛṣṭvā tarkayāmi devenāpi na punar evaṁ lekhituṁ pāryeteti. V.K.* means: After observing the skill in creating art the Prince has shown, I believe even the Prince (himself) wouldn't be able to paint like this again.

34. *M.M.: bhāvavṛttiḥ; V.K.: niṣkarṣaḥ.*

35. *V.K.: anvag; M.M.: (?); M.M.V.2.: anyad.*

36. *V.K.: -adharam(-); M.M.: -(?)m(-).*

37. *V.K.: adho; M.M.: atho.*

38. *V.K.: kārmukaṁ; M.M.: kāmyakaṁ.*

39. *V.K.: punar lekhitum; M.M.: (?)lepi(khi, M.M.V.2.)tum.*

40. *V.K.* supplies *vaassa; V.K.Ch.: vayasya.*

41. *V.K.: cittavaṭṭiṇī; M.M.: cintavva°ṭiṇī; M.Ch.M.: cakravartinī; V.K.Ch.: cittavartinī.*

42. *H.S.: saccaṁ; M.M.: sa°cia; M.Ch.M.: satyāya; H.S.Ch.: satyaṁ; V.K.* omits.

43. *V.K.: -saṁdāvidādo; M.M.: -saṁdāvavidādo; M.Ch.M.: -santāpavidagdhāt; V.K.Ch.: -santāpitāt.*

44. *V.K.: -maggado; M.M.: -maṅga(gga, M.M.V.2.)to; M.Ch.M.: -agrato; V.K.Ch.: -mārgato.*

45. *M.M.: uṇa; M.Ch.M.* omits; *V.K.* omits; *H.S.Ch.: punar.*

46. *M.Ch.M.* breaks off here.

47. *Iti tathā kṛtvā = ity ālikhya* (after painting).

48. *V. K.: so yaṁ krīḍāgirir iha tathā sā ca saudhāśrayeyaṁ; M.M.: (?); M.M.V.2.: - - -girir aha sā - -.*

49. *M.M.V.2.* and *V.K.: mame(yam); M.M.: maye(-).*

50. *V.K.: (prema)sāndro pi; M.M.: (-)sāme vi(pi, M.M.V.2.).*

51. *V.K.: parirambhaṇān (mama); M.M.: -rambhaṇam (-).*

52. *V.K.* supplies *tu.*

53. *V.K.: sudṛḍhaṁ; MM.: kṛto.*

54. *V.K.: esa devīe sahatthalihio saṁdeso | taṁ ṇirūvehi; M.M.: edaṁ devīe saha°dhalihiasaṁbhe (de, M.M.V.2.)saṁ bhaavaṁ taṁ ṇirūvehi; V.K.Ch.: eṣa devyā svahastalikhitaḥ saṁdeśaḥ | taṁ nirūpaya.*

55. *M.M.V.2.* and *V.K.: mūrkha; M.M.: (?).*

56. *H.S.: (prasaṅgo) mama (praṇayijanasya); M.M.: mat(prasaṅgaḥ) (-); V.K.: (-) (-).*

57. *V.K.: tṛpyataḥ; M.M.: (kathaṁ) nū(tṛ, M.M.V.2.)pyata.*

58. *V.K.: bhūrja-; M.M.: bhuja-.*

59. *H.S.: jai mae timirandhadiṭṭhiṇā ṇa bhavijjai tadā ahaṁ evva vāaanto edāe viaḍḍhattaṇagavvaṁ avaharissaṁ; V.K.: - - - - hoijjai - - - - - - avaharississaṁ; M.M.: - - ki(ti, M.M.V.2.) miraṁdhadi° (ṭhi,* inserted by *M.M.V.2.)ṇo(ṇā, M.M.V.2.) - bhavi°jai - - - vāe(aṁ, M.M.V.2.)to edāe°vaḍi°caṅga°vaṁ ahari°ja°saṁ; V.K.Ch.: yadā mayā timirāndhadṛṣṭinā nābhaviṣyata tadā aham eva vācayan etasyā vidagdhatāgarvam apāhariṣyam; H.S.Ch.: yadi - - na bhūyate - - - - - - apahariṣyāmi.*

60. *V.K.:*

kettiamettaṁ sahiau paccāśādhariapāṇae dukkhaṁ |
jaṁ aṇuhojjantaṁ avi khaṇe khaṇe ṇavaṇavaṁ hoi ||

M.M.:

ke°tiama°taṁ kīranulaṁ(tīraḍalaṁ, M.M.V.2.) maalehe (hiallehe, M.M.V.2.) mae virahadukkhaṁ |
jaṁ aṇuho°jaṁtaṁ avi khaṇṇe viuhiaṁ (ṇiuṇiaṁ, M.M.V.2.) hoi ||

V.K.Ch.:

kiyanmātraṁ sahyatāṁ pratyāśādhṛtaprāṇayā duḥkham |
yad anubhūyamānaṁ api kṣaṇe kṣaṇe navanavaṁ bhavati ||

61. *V.K.*:

sulaho khu itthiāṇaṁ virahe ālekkhavallaho hoi |
mama uṇa so vi ṇa sulaho bappuggamapuṇṇaṇaaṇāe ||

M.M.:

bahuā i°dhiāṇaṁ viraho āle°khava°lahe hi°vi |
maha uṇa taṁ pi ṇa suiṇa°ḍelihii°viṇapārioja°si ||

V.K.Ch.:

sulabhaḥ khalu strīṇāṁ virahe ālekhyavallabho bhavati |
mama punaḥ so pi na sulabho bāṣpodgamapūrṇanayanāyāḥ ||

62. *M.M.*:

jāṇe ahaṁ ima°si(siṁ, M.M.V.2.) ja°me maha ṇa°dhi āsaṁgho(go, H.S.) |
tā suhaa sulahasaṁgamaso°kho ja°ma (man, M.M.V.2.)tara(tare, H.S.) hohi ||

H.S.Ch.:

jāne ham asmin janme mama nāsty āsaṅgaḥ |
tat subhaga sulabhasaṅgamasaukhyo janmāntare bhava ||

V.K. omits this verse, probably because it is too pessimistic and does not fit in very well with his edition of verse 13, in which Kādambarī's life is still sustained by hope, or because it is contrary to what is actually going to happen later on in the play: Candrāpīḍa's death, not Kādambarī's, though, of course, it is only what she is feeling now. As a result of the inclusion of this verse into the Translation, the numbering of the following verses of this act in it differs from that in *V.K.*

63. *M.M.V.2.* and *V.K.*: *(-tro)rjita-*; *M.M*: *(- -)jjhita-*.

64. *V.K.*: *anuśiṣṭo*; *M.M.*: *-viṣṭo*; *M.M.V.2.*: *-diṣṭo*.

65. *V.K.*: *himagṛhavṛttāntaḥ*; *M.M.*: *hi(?)gṛhodantaḥ*.

66. After this *M.M.* has *bata balavatī tasyās sandhyā manorathabodhinī*, which means: Oh! the powerful twilight indicates (or awakens) her desire. *V.K.* omits this because it is obviously out of place here. Though it scans perfectly in the *hariṇī* meter, used in the following verse, it is not part of it.

67. *M.M.V.2.* and *V.K.*: *-garbhitaiḥ*; *M.M.*: *-garhitaiḥ*.

68. After this *M.M.* has the following speeches assigned to Patralekhā and Candrāpīḍa: *patra || taṁ vi mae pu°hia(chiā, M.M.V.2.)e devīe ava°sa°bharauraraṁ sarojiaṁ ala°khedi a°taṇo paḍiṇṇaṁ u°taraṁ*, and *candrā || atha kathaṁ devyāyam abhyupagatas sandeśaḥ*. *V.K.* omits

these because they both seem out of place here. Patralekhā's speech is a little too corrupt to make any good sense of, but Candrāpīḍa's approximately means: Why! then, this is the message that has arrived from the Princess.

69. *V.K.: diṇe diṇe parihijjamāṇagattā lāvaṇṇamettasesā iaṁ mā(mahā, H.S.)sedāe sapāapaaṇaṁ santavaaṇehiṁ kahaṁ vi moiapaḍiṇṇāṇibbandhā saaṁ evva imaṁ saṁdesaṁ vilihia mama hatthammi dattūṇa māṁ(maṁ, H.S.) pesidavadī tumaṁ khandhāvārādo evva paḍiṇivaṭṭeduṁ; M.M.: - - lāaṇṇasesā iaṁ māseāe savā(pā, M.M.V.2.)apaḍaṇaṁ svahasaha°sehi moiapaḍiṇṇo āsitaṁ si°ceakhaṇe pesidamhi khaṁdāvārado e°va devaṁ paḍiṇivvaṭṭeda (du, M.M.V.2.)ṁ; V.K.Ch.: dine dine parihīyamānagātrā lāvaṇyamātraśeṣeyam mahāśvetayā sapādapatanaṁ sāntvavacanaiḥ katham api mocitapratijñānirbandhā svayam eva vilikhyemaṁ sandeśaṁ mama haste dat(tt, H.S.Ch.)vā (māṁ,* supplied by *H.S.Ch.) preṣitavatī tvāṁ skandhāvārād eva pratinivartayitum.*

70. *V.K.: (prayate) bhivāñchitam; M.M.: (-)bhivāhitam.*

71. *V.K.: sarvathaiva; M.M.: sarvathaiṣa.*

72. *V.K.* supplies *kiṁ vi; V.K.Ch.: kim api.*

73. *H.S.: rundhedi; M.M.: ruhai; V.K.: dhāraai (= dhāredi, H.S.); V.K.Ch.: dhārayati; H.S.Ch.: ruṇaddhi.*

74. *V.K.* omits *aṅga(aṇa, M.M.V.2.)aṁvi (jīviaṁ).* After this speech *M.M.* has the following assigned to Patralekhā, which *V.K.* omits: *patra || a°cāhidaṁ jai mahāsedāe ve(pe, M.M.V.2.)si°jai e°va ko vi āṇa°tihārao |*

75. *V.K.* omits *(āgatam i) ve (to).*

76. *V.K. : bhaḍaṇikurumbeṇa; M.M.: (keṇa, M.M.V.2.) vi bhaḍakusu°bhaeṇa; V.K.Ch.: bhaṭanikurumbeṇa.*

77. *V.K.: turaasāiāṇaṁ; M.M.: turaṁgasāraṁ(ī, M.M.V.2.) esipehuṇa; V.K.Ch.: turagasādināṁ.*

78. *V.K.: parāpatai; M.M.: i°(la, M.M.V.2.)khi°jai; V.K.Ch.: parāpatati.*

79. *M.M.: ko (tra bhoḥ); M.M.V.2.* and *V.K.: kaḥ ko (- -).*

80. *V.K.: ājñāpayatu yuvarājaḥ; M.M.: ājñāpaya.*

81. *V.K.: ke py atra samāgacchanti; M.M.: tad anv iyam upagate.*

82. *V.K.: prāpayatu; M.M.: prapetu.*

83. *M.M.V.2.* and *V.K.: (śobhāviśeṣa)bhṛśo(j; jj, V.K.) (valo); M.M.: (-)hṛto(-) (-).*

84. *M.M.: aho; V.K.: aye.*

85. *V.K.* needlessly adds *bhadra.*

86. *M.M.: samudācāraṁ karoti; V.K.: samudācarati.*

87. *V.K.: vidhāryate; M.M.: (?)pidhāryate.*

88. *H.S.: tathā ca manye tasyā bāṣpāmbhobhiḥ tvadanveṣaṇam udīyate; M.M.: - - tasyāḥ bāṣpāmbhobhir udīyate śayituṁ (manye, M.M.V.2.) tvadanveṣaṇam; V.K.* omits.

89. *M.M.: patralekhāvidūṣakau || sāhu diṇṇaṁ u°taraṁ; H.S.Ch.: sādhu dattam uttaram; V.K.* omits.

90. *V.K.* supplies *(mayā) yadā (nivedito).*

91. *M.M.: atarkito; V.K.: atarkitopagato.*
92. *H.S.: haṁho (hatātman); M.M.: haṁ (-); V.K.: hā (-).*
93. *M.M.: -pu°tie; H.S.Ch.: -putryāḥ V.K.: -ṇandiṇīe; V.K.Ch.: -nandinyāḥ.*
94. *V.K.: tado (pahudi); M.M.: taha (-); V.K.Ch.: tataḥ (prabhṛti).*
95. *V.K.: bhajate; M.M.: bhajane.*
96. *M.M.: anuprāptā; V.K.: anu prāptā.*
97. *M.M.V.2.* and *V.K.: gata(ghṛṇena); M.M.: bata (-).*
98. *M.M.: upakāribhūtam; V.K.: upakāri.*
99. *V.K.: para(nirvyapekṣām); M.M.: pari(-).*
100. *V.K.: rūpāntara-; M.M.: kūpā- -.*
101. *V.K.: vadata (kiyatī yātā) veleti (naḥ paripṛcchatī); M.M.: vadati (- -) lokhela (- -).*
102. This verse is quoted by Vemabhūpāla in his *Sāhityacintāmaṇi* (hereafter cited as *S.C.*); *vide* Intro., chap. V. *S.C.* and *V.K.: candrāpīḍa prakaṭaya dayāṁ; M.M.: candrāpīḍaḥ* || *prakaṭaya(?)dayā.*
103. *M.M.V.2.: jānīṣe mām manasi nivasan baddhabhāvāṁ tvam eva; M.M.: - - - - bandhabhāvaṁ - eve(tthaṁ); S.C.: - - - -baṁdhabhāvā tvam eva; V.K.: - tvam - - baddhabhāvāṁ tvayīmām.*
104. *V.K.: vrīḍālolā; M.M.: nīlālobhaḥ; M.M.V.2.: vrīḍā-; S.C.: vrīlālola.*
105. *Śūlapāṇau.* Śūlapāṇi and Candrāpīḍa are both epithets of Śiva.
106. *V.K.* omits (*diāe; ṭṭhiāe, V.K.*) *kaivi* (*e°vaṁ*).
107. *M.M.V.2.* and *V.K.: kāmābhiṣaṅgam abhinayan; M.M.: - -nayann uvāca.*
108. *V.K.: - priyām manasi vartinīm pariharaiṣa baddhoñjaliḥ; M.M.: - priyā - vartate - baddhā(dho, M.M.V.2.)ñjaliḥ.*
109. *V.K.: mithyaiva; M.M.: mithyeva.*
110. *V.K.: pramoha (iva); M.M.: pramoda (-).*
111. *V.K.: anupātito; M.M.: anupatito.*
112. *M.M.V.2.*, and *V.K.: strī-; M.M.: (?)-.*
113. *V.K.: saṁdiṣṭaṁ; M.M.: sandṛṣṭaṁ.*
114. *H.S.: (na sannihito) grāhyavāgnivedayitā; M.M.: (- -) grāhyavā(?) (k, M.M.V.2.)nivedatāyitā; V.K.* omits.
115. *V.K.* omits *kiyatanaḥ (kiyaty antare).*
116. *V.K.: vidito; M.M.: vito.*
117. *H.S.: gantavyam prayatitavyañ ca; M.M.: prayatitavyam; V.K.: gantavyam.*
118. *V.K.* supplies *sa(phalaprayāso).*
119. *V.K.: sāmānyataḥ (sevakānām); M.M.: sāmānya(-).*
120. *M.M.V.2.* and *V.K.: jāne; M.M.: jāte.*
121. *V.K.: sthairyāya; M.M.: sthairyāva(dhairyan tvayā).*
122. *M.M.: tau* ||; *V.K.: patralekhākeyūrakau.*

123. *V.K.* supplies *candrāpīḍaḥ.*
124. *V.K.* supplies *vidūṣakam prati.*
125. *V.K.: rājakaṁ (yātrāyai); M.M.: rāja(-).*
126. *M.M.V.2.* and *V.K.: cāṭu-; M.M.: cārdra-.*
127. *V.K.* supplies *upasarpatu bhavān.*
128. *V.K.* supplies *tathā, iti (niṣkrāntaḥ).*
129. *V.K.: parikrāmati; M.M.: savinayam upasarpati.*
130. *H.S.: bhavataś; M.M.: (?)bhavataś; M.M.V.2.* and *V.K.: vibhavataś.*
131. *V.K.: (vaiśampāyanasy)āgamana-; M.M.: (-sya)gamana-.*
132. *V.K.* supplies *savinayam (upasṛtya yathākramam praṇamati); vide supra,* n. 129.
133. *M.M.: vatsa (ita itaḥ); V.K.* repeats.
134. *H.S.: prajñaiva; M.M.: prājñeva; V.K.: prajñeva.*
135. *V.K.: manoratha(saṁvādo); M.M.: buddhi(-).*
136. *V.K.: vilambyate; M.M.: vilambate.*
137. *M.M.V.2.* and *V.K.: anabhranirghātadāruṇaṁ; M.M.: ana(?)dāruṇaṁ.*
138. *M.M.: ānandayati; V.K.: ānandayiṣyati.*
139. *M.M.V.2.* and *V.K.: ninaṁsur; M.M.: (?)nāṁsur.*
140. *V.K.* omits *(yadā - tadā) ca.*
141. *M.M.V.2.* and *V.K.: (antar)mukhair; M.M.: (-)bhavair.*
142. *M.M.: -prayatne; V.K.: -prayatnaiḥ*
143. *V.K.: tato; M.M.: ito.*
144. *V.K.: prāmādikaṁ skhalitam; M.M.: prātharṣaka(laṁ, M.M.V.2.) skhalitaḥ(taṁ, M.M.V.2.)* (blurred).
145. *V.K.: (tatra) dūre; M.M.: (-) pūre.*
146. *M.M.: poṣitena; V.K.: supoṣitena.*
147. *V.K.: -jātau; M.M.: -jātena.*
148. *V.K.: -araṇye (duḥkha-); M.M.: -araṇya(duḥkha-).*
149. *V.K.: jāmbūnadasya jale vikṣepam; M.M.: jāmbūnadajala-.*
150. *M.M.* and *V.K.: hradāvamagnasya; M.M.V.2.: hṛdayāva-.*
151. *V.K.: kahaṁ vi (sakkaṁ mae); M.M.: kahaṁ mae (- -); V.K.Ch.: katham api (śakyam mayā).*
152. *M.M.: -dūmiaṁ; H.S.Ch.: -dūnam; V.K.: -dūamāṇaṁ; V.K.Ch.- dūyamānam.*
153. *V.K.: apasārita-; M.M.: apasāsāta-.*
154. This verse is repeated after Act VIII, vs. 8.
155. *V.K.: abhyanujñātaḥ; M.M.: (yuṣmābhir) apy anujñātaḥ.*
156. *V.K.* supplies *vatsasya.*
157. *M.M.: kiñ cit; V.K.* omits.

158. *H.S.: -bhāsāṁ; M.M.: -bhāsaś; V.K.: -bhāsoś* (the sun).

159. *M.M.: api ca; V.K.* omits.

160. *V.K.: bahubhir yatnair; M.M.: (?) yatnai.*

161. *H.S.: niyateḥ prātikūlyāni yadi māṁ nābhiyuñjate; M.M.: niyataḥ pratikūlyāni - - -; V.K.: niyatīḥ prātikūlyena - - nābhiyujyate.*

Miśraviṣkambhaka
Prelude to Act Seven

[*Having entered*]

TARALIKĀ: The Princess has ordered me to obtain from the sylvan deity's presence[1] an offering for the Lord Śiva's worship performed for many days on account of Kādambarī's unhappiness.[2] I'll go to her now. [*Walks around.*]

[*Enter Caitraratha's* SYLVAN DEITY.][3]

SYLVAN DEITY[4] [*after looking around*]: Oh, how ingeniously the rainy season's Fortune carries out my order![5] For

This forest has *kuṭaja* trees blossoming,
Nicula reeds blooming, jasmine flowers[6] opening,
Priyaka blossoms coming out, *kakubha* blossoms expanding,
Ketaka flowers growing tall, peacocks crying,
Bees flying about intoxicated, *cātaka* birds trembling,
Rivers flowing and fireflies[7] flying out. [1]

[*Having seen*] Oh! here's my friend[8] Taralikā seen after a long time.

TARALIKĀ [*approaches and bows.*]

SYLVAN DEITY: Good girl, may you live long! Has our friend Mahāśvetā, who made Kādambarī give up her vow, come back from Hemakūṭa?[9]

TARALIKĀ: Yes, she has.

SYLVAN DEITY: Taralikā,[10] please tell me the truth. I heard from the mouths of a pair of *kinnaras* sporting in moonlight this news:[11] Keyūraka, dispatched with the hope of bringing back Candrāpīḍa, who left unexpectedly,[12] has returned with Patralekhā, saying[13] "He will come with his elders' permission."

TARALIKĀ: That's right.

SYLVAN DEITY: Then,[14] I'm very glad.

TARALIKĀ: Now bring flowers, fruit and sprigs.

SYLVAN DEITY [*acts taking and giving them.*]

TARALIKĀ: Friend, I'm going. [*Returns.*]

SYLVAN DEITY [[15]*casting a glance*]: Oh, who is that?

His limbs are white as pollen in *ketaka* flowers,
    And have only beauty left;
He is wearing disheveled locks
    Variegated with wild flowers,
And looking around aimlessly
    With a pair of tearful eyes —
He is probably engaged[16] in searching
    For some kinsman of his here.[17] [2]

Why! he has entered Mahāśvetā's hermitage.

[*Off stage*]

Oh, beautiful girl![18]

If you, frowning thus,[19] give up your desire for enjoyment,
    And alas! try to practise[20] asceticism,
Let the mind-born Love, endowed with vain heroic fame
    Spread in the three worlds, put down his bow-creeper! [3]

TARALIKĀ [*after giving ear and turning around*]: Navamālikā, who ever[21] is saying this extremely unpleasant thing?

SYLVAN DEITY: Wait! We'll listen.[22]

[*Off stage again*[23]]

Lovely girl! if you mercilessly ignore me[24]
    Repeatedly pierced by Love's arrows,
What ever virtue[25] will you have in this world?
    On the contrary, you will have sin!
The formost religious merit, the wise say,
    Is indeed to deliver the afflicted. [4]

TARALIKĀ: Alas! Alas![26] Mahāśvetā, devoted to Puṇḍarīka, can never endure tortures like this. She'll surely destroy either him or[27] herself. I'll go with hurried steps now.

SYLVAN DEITY: Friend Taralikā, she mustn't bring a calamity to him! I know from his voice that he's Candrāpīḍa's friend Vaiśampāyana.

TARALIKĀ: Why! he's staying alone even after the army has departed.[28] What good would he do?[29] Now I'll keep away my friend from anger, and him[30] from this improper action. [*Exit.*]

[*Off stage again*[31]]

God Śiva![32] if I have succeeded in remaining faithful to my lord, Puṇḍarīka, since I met him, let this man, enamored of the wrong girl and showing love with his mouth like a parrot, fall into that very species for the reason of those wanton words of his![33]

SYLVAN DEITY: Oh! a great disaster has happened now. The position of the virtue of wives who regard their husbands as gods certainly wouldn't be otherwise. [*Anxiously*] He has the signs of a great man. Then why has he done this improper thing? There must be a good reason for it. I'll find it out through deep meditation now. [*After doing so*] Oh! what intense passion the divine ascetic's son has,[34] even though he has moved into another body! And it's appropriate that Haṁsa's daughter, partial only to his appearance she saw before, is harsh and cruel[35] to him, although he's quite attractive. All right, I shouldn't disclose this information, for it's about to become clear all by itself. Even so, she should compose her agitated mind now. [*Exit.*]

END OF THE *MIŚRAVIṢKAMBHAKA*
PRELUDE TO ACT SEVEN

Notes

1. *V.K.: vaṇadevadāsaāsādo; M.M.: vaṇadeva(yā,* inserted by *M.M.V.2.)saāsāhi: V.K.Ch.: vanadevatāsakāśāt.*
2. *H.S.: kāambarīdukkhaṇimittaṁ; M.M.: kāambarīṇimi°te duḥkhe; V.K.: kāambarīṇimittaṁ; V.K.Ch.: kādambarīnimittam; H.S.Ch.; kādambarīduḥkhanimittam.*
3. *V.K.: tataḥ praviśati caitrarathavanadevatā; M.M.: praviṣṭā caitrarathadevatā.*
4. *V.K.* supplies *vanadevatā.*
5. *V.K.: aho asmannideśānuvṛtticaturatā vāridasamayaśriyaḥ; M.M.: nanv ayam asmadviśle(viśe, M.M.V.2.)ṣānuvṛttivāro vāridasamaśriyam.*
6. *V.K.: (ucchvasan)mālati; M.M.: (-)mālatī.*
7. *V.K.: (niṣpatat)tridaśagopam; M.M.: (-)tidaśakopam.*

8. *M.M.: sakhī; V.K.: priyasakhī.*
9. *V.K.: tyājitakādambarīpratijñā hemakūṭān nivṛttā; M.M.: tyājitā kādambarī- hemakūṭan -*
10. *M.M.: taralike; V.K.* omits.
11. *V.K.* supplies (*- pravṛttiś -) yathā.*
12. *M.M.V.2.* and *V.K.: atarkita-; M.M.: atakṣita-.*
13. *V.K.* supplies *kathayan.*
14. *V.K.* supplies *tarhi.*
15. *V.K.* needlessly adds *vilokya (sadṛṣṭikṣepam).*
16. *V.K.: -vyāpṛtaḥ; M.M.: -vyāvṛtaḥ.*
17. *V.K.: (chāyāvaśeṣai)r ito; M.M.: (-)(?)to.*
18. *(Vara)varṇini;* it also means a female ascetic. Cf. Bhāravi, *Kirātārjunīya,* ed. with Mallinātha's comm. *Ghaṇṭāpatha* by N.R. Ācārya (Bombay: Nirṇaya Sāgar Press, 1954), canto I, vs. 1 and comm.: - *varṇi(liṅgī) - || varṇaḥ praśastir asyāstīti varṇī brahmacārī |*
19. *H.S.: itthaṁnatabhru (bhavatī); M.M.: itthaṁnatabhrū (-); V.K.: itthaṁ natabhru (-).*
20. *V.K.* supplies *(yatate) carituṁ (tapasyāṁ).*
21. *V.K.: ko uṇa; M.M.: keṇa; V.K.Ch.: kaḥ punar.*
22. *M.M. vanade || tiṣtha śṛṇumaḥ(-vaḥ, H.S.); V.K.* omits.
23. *V.K.* supplies *punar.*
24. *V.K.: niranukrośayā mayy upekṣā; M.M.: (?)krośayāmabhyupekṣā.*
25. *H.S.: ko vā dharmas; M.M.* and *V.K.: ko yaṁ -.*
26. *M.M.: haddhi 2; V.K.: haddhi; V.K.Ch.: hā dhik.*
27. *V.K.: vā; M.M.: pāpa; V.K.Ch.: vā.*
28. *M.M.: kahaṁ gae vi khaṁdhāvāre eko(ekko, M.M.V.2.) imo ciṭhai (ciṭṭhai, M.M.V.2.): V.K.: kahiaṁ khandhāvārammi ekko evva imo ciṭṭhai tti; V.K.Ch.: kathitaṁ skandhāvāre eka evāyaṁ tiṣṭhatīti; H.S.Ch.: kathaṁ gate pi skandhāvāre eko yaṁ tiṣṭhati.*
29. *M.M.: bhodu kiṁ imiṇā; V.K.: hodu; V.K.Ch.: bhavatu; H.S.Ch.: bhavatu kim anena.*
30. *V.K.: taṁ; M.M.: kaṁ; V.K.Ch.: tam.*
31. *V.K.* supplies *punar.*
32. *V.K.: paramesara; M.M.: paramesare; V.K.Ch.: parameśvara.*
33. *V.K.: tadā eso atthāṇakāmuo suo via daṁsiamuharāo ediṇā soccandavaaṇattaṇeṇa tassiṁ evva jādīe ṇivaḍio hodu; M.M.: - - a°dhāṇaṁ kāmudai suā via daṁsiaṁ mahārāo hidiṇṇā sa°haṁ(chaṁ, M.M.V.2.) davaaṇa°taṇeṇa tāe°tia jāīe ṇiveḍio hoi(u, M.M.V.2.); V.K.Ch.: tadā eṣo sthānakāmukaḥ śuka iva darśitamukharāga etena svacchandavacanatvena tasyām eva jātau nipatito bhavatu.*
34. *M.M.V.2.* and *V.K.: divyarṣinandanasya; M.M.: divya(?)sya.*
35. *H.S.: prātikūlyapāruṣyam; M.M.: prātikūlapāruṣyam; V.K.: pratikūlapārūṣyam.*

ACT SEVEN

[*Enter* CANDRĀPĪḌA, *mounted on* INDRĀYUDHA *and his* JESTER.]

CANDRĀPĪḌA [*after looking around*]: It is indeed miserable to be a traveler, especially in the rainy season.

Carried by horses with faces bent down
Through the force of the rainfall
And legs soaked in the mud up to the knees,
And exhausted[1] with their armor
Wet[2] with the rain and so hard to keep on,
The horsemen are following me with difficulty. [5]

JESTER: Alas! Alas![3] I've never experienced[4] a life like this[5] exposed to danger and the full development of a disaster.

CANDRĀPĪḌA: This is a great set of simultaneous calamities.[6] For[7]

I cannot stay calm even for a moment,
For I have not obtained that[8] deer-eyed girl;
My friend has committed a blunder like this
At the wrong time;
The season[9] has clouds' ear-piercing noise;
Moreover, Love is thus merciless —
The nature[10] of fate is a path thoroughly crooked
For those afflicted with unhappiness. [6]

JESTER: This rainy season is unbearable[11] even to us; how much more to you longing for your beloved?[12]

CANDRĀPĪḌA: You have spoken the truth.

This Fortune of the rainy season is assuming
The lovely girl's frown with a rainbow,
Her hair's luster with peacoks' tail feathers,
Her body's splendor with lightning,
Her *bimba*-lips' color with swarms of ladybugs[13]
And her eyes' beauty with fresh sprouts;
Even so, this is not good enough
For the satisfaction of my heart. [7]

JESTER: Don't worry about union with your beloved just now.[14]

CANDRĀPĪḌA: Friend, my joy of meeting the Princess surely must be[15] near now.

In no time I will see my two friends there,
 Haṁsa's daughter and Śukanāsa's son;
Even so,[16] this heart is darkened.[17]
 Why is that? [8]

Friend, tell me. How far are we from the Caitraratha forest?

JESTER: Why do you still ask that? Haven't we already arrived in it?

CANDRĀPĪḌA [*after observing*]: Indeed these are the forests, abodes of hunters dwelling[18] on Hemakūṭa, which are the eyewitnesses[19] of my[20] pursuit of a pair of *kinnaras*. And here,

Infatuating my heart with the fragrance
 Of young opening jasmine flowers,
Dense with drops of honey wine
 From *nīpa* trees' fresh expanding[21] buds,
Turning the quarters[22] white
 With *ketaka* flowers' pollen,
These breezes, sprinkling a shower,
 Seem to kindle the fire of my love. [9]

[*After going a little inside*] Is this lake Acchoda?

It appears as if it were another
 With a flock of geese flying up,
Lotuses and white and blue water lilies submerged
 And muddy water overflowing its bank. [10]

Now I'll look for my friend in the arbors on its verge. So surround the entire forest with the horsemen, for he may really go elsewhere, embarrassed[23] by our arrival.

JESTER: That's impossible as long as I'm awake! [*Exit with the attendants.*]

CANDRĀPĪḌA [*walking around*]:

O that fate could be so gracious as to let
 Someone, sometime and somehow,

See his friend doing well
Again after a long time,
Tell him by himself
About his own heart's torment
And sport with him joyously
After his wish has been well-accomplished! [11]

[*After looking around*] Why! there's no sign of my dear friend's staying here.[24] Did he go away somewhere on hearing from Patralekhā's mouth I was coming?[25] [*After reflecting*] Meghanāda, who escorted her[26] to Hemakūṭa and returned, surely told me he didn't find Vaiśampāyana, who had remained behind. [*Anxiously*] Where ever could he have gone? [*With a sigh*] May it be well with my friend Vaiśampāyana by all means!

[*In the sky*]

Where could Vaiśampāyana's well-being be now?

CANDRĀPĪḌA [*after stopping his ears*]: Oh, why! I hear this voice from the sky weeping.[27] Then I'm sure[28] it's not easy to see my friend again. [*Sorrowfully*] Where is that precious friend of mine[29] now? In any case, a calamity has befallen him.[30]

My friend is no longer seen on this[31] earth.
Where ever[32] can I look for him[33] now?
Besides, the desire to see my beloved urges me.
Since my afflicted heart is divided into two,[34]
It is hard to attain either[35] of them. [12]

Perhaps Mahāśvetā knows Vaiśampāyana's whereabouts because she's staying nearby. [*Making* INDRĀYUDHA *move*[36] *towards*[37] *her hermitage*] But now,

"What ever will she say when I ask her?"
Thus thinking, I am filled with misgivings.
I wish to ask her;
Yet I am afraid as well. [13]

Oh, where does this large crowd of people, mostly noble[38] women, come from? [*Reflecting*] Is this intended to be the day of our arrival? Then I'm sure Princess Kādambarī will be here with her attendants. [*Apprehensively and then hopefully*][39]

"False one, you went away
Without telling me before.
Now what ever must you do?"

With these words,
She may even resort to silence.
Or possibly the lovely girl may
Delightedly honor with embraces
Me arrived on the appointed day. [14]

[*Eagerly urges* INDRĀYUDHA *on.*][40]

[*Enter* KĀDAMBARĪ *with her two friends, leaning on* PATRALEKHĀ[41] *and being shown the way by* KEYŪRAKA.]

KĀDAMBARĪ [*after looking at* PATRALEKHĀ]: Is the Prince really going to grace this place today?

PATRALEKHĀ: Princess, I swear[42] by your pair of foot-lotuses that the Crown Prince is going to give you the joy of seeing him right now.

TWO FRIENDS: Friend, don't be impatient! The tutelary deities of the *gandharva* race will fulfill your wish in a moment.

KEYŪRAKA: This way, this way, Princess.

[*All walk around.*]

CANDRĀPĪḌA [*hopefully*]: Perhaps with my friend Vaiśampāyana's consent,

Some day I will be happy[43]
To take the lovely girl in my hands
Covered with hosts of horripilation-sprouts
Instantly arisen out of their roots,
Possessed of copper-red finger-leaves
Pervaded with perspiration,
Encircled by an auspicious woolen cloth[44]
And tremulous with excitement. [15]

All right, I'll look for him in Mahāśvetā's presence now.[45] [*Exit.*]

KEYŪRAKA [*after looking ahead*]: Friends, that horseman's body is hard to see because of the great distance, but I recognize him as Prince Candrāpīḍa.

PATRALEKHĀ [*after observing him*]: He is really the Crown Prince mounted on Indrāyudha.

KĀDAMBARĪ [*delightedly to herself*]: Ah! I feel as if I were immersed[46] in a great lake[47] of joy now.

TAMĀLIKĀ: Why does he look as if he were alone?[48]

MADALEKHĀ:He's approaching Lady Mahāśvetā, his retinue probably dismissed[49] lest there should be any disturbance to her hermitage.

KĀDAMBARĪ: That's proper. That's proper.[50] Now, where's the Lady's[51] hermitage?

KEYŪRAKA: Here's the entrance to her hermitage. Please enter, Princess.

[*All act entering.*]

KEYŪRAKA [*after looking around*]: Why! those grounds of the vicinity of the Śiva temple do not look beautiful as before. For

Deprived of their birds' tumults, the trees
Appear to be meditating;
Their blossoming ceased, the little creepers
Are undergoing languor suited to summer;
Their eyes[52] filled with tears, the deer
Are not taking the fresh blades of *durvā* grass —
Its riches thus lamentable,
The great Caitraratha forest[53] is empty and strange. [16]

KĀDAMBARĪ [*to herself*]:[54] Wouldn't the Lady get emaciated,[55] her heart exhausted[56] by supporting the burden of missing her beloved for long? Besides, I don't know[57] how, but I'm sure it only remains[58] for me[59] to break my vow, since the Crown Prince has arrived.[60]

PATRALEKHĀ [*having looked*]: Princess, look there! That's surely the Lady, accompanied by Taralikā, staying at the foot of a *kadamba* tree.[61]

KĀDAMBARĪ [*after observing her*]: Alas! my friend's face appears distressed.[62]

TWO FRIENDS: Surely now is the time for the actions of the poison of the Love-Snake![63]

KEYŪRAKA:

With bright moonlight, very long night watches,
Full-blown[64] jasmine flowers,
Breezes fragrant with sandal trees, lovely evenings
And peacocks' cries
Sweet and delightful[65] as the *ṣadja* note,
Love has tormented her many days here.
Alas! how many more days from now
Is he going to torment her?[66] [17]

[*Approaches her.*][67]
[*Enter* MAHĀŚVETĀ, *accompanied by* TARALIKĀ.][68]

MAHĀŚVETĀ: Taralikā, did you really hear from the sylvan deity's mouth this is the Crown Prince's friend Vaiśampāyana?

TARALIKĀ: I surely heard so.

MAHĀŚVETĀ: Alas! Alas![69] I[70] am ill-fated. Even my good fortune has thus turned out dreadful like a poisonous creeper's.[71] What answer can I give the Prince asking where his friend is now? [*Weeps.*]

TARALIKĀ: What should my friend do in this case? In the entire world of living beings, their weals and woes are indeed governed by their own actions.

KĀDAMBARĪ [*having approached*]: Friend Mahāśvetā, why are you distressed like this?

MAHĀŚVETĀ [*having seen her*]: Friend Kādambarī, please don't talk to me. I'm an evil-natured *rākṣasī*.[72] I brought the Crown Prince's friend Vaiśampāyana to a state like that.[73]

PATRALEKHĀ [*agitatedly*]: I heard on Hemakūṭa from the mouths of a pair of *kinnaras* that the honorable Vaiśampāyana, his mind depressed for some reason, remained behind even after the host of princes had departed, and then[74] wandered into Mahāśvetā's hermitage as if he were mad. [75]What ever has happened to him, who[76] annoyed the Lady?

MAHĀŚVETĀ [*stands still in tears, her face down.*]

KEYŪRAKA: Taralikā, tell us. What misfortune has befallen him?[77] For he

Is the Crown Prince's friend
　　In meetings for amusements,
His leader in battles, and
　　His minister in assisting him in politics. [18]

TARALIKĀ [*tells what has happened.*]

[*All act grief.*]

KEYŪRAKA: Oh, alas! Now indeed

The Prince is separated from his worthy friend
　　As if Youth from Love,
Or Love from Spring
　　Or Spring from Gentle Breeze. [19][78]

PATRALEKHĀ: How is it possible for my master's heart not to break when he hears[79] this news like the fall of a horrendous thunderbolt?

KĀDAMBARĪ: Such are our fates. For my right eye is throbbing, indicating a misfortune.

TWO FRIENDS: We saw[80] the Crown Prince entering the hermitage. Why is he still delaying?

[*Having entered in a flurry*]

JESTER: Lady Mahāśvetā, save the Prince! Save him from this danger to his life!

ALL: What about him?

JESTER: I don't know . . .[81] Later on I started looking for Vaiśampāyana. Then I was told[82] what had happened by his servants I found.[83] As soon as I came here,[84] I saw right in front[85] my friend, who had entered the hermitage, remaining still on Indrāyudha, all his limbs motionless.[86]

ALL: Oh, fate,[87] why do you destroy everybody?

KĀDAMBARĪ [*swoons.*]

KEYŪRAKA:

> Alas, let Rāhu arrived from somewhere
> Swallow the full moon
> Obtained at last with difficulty!
> Then, what ever state would this hen *cakora*,
> Hindered[88] from quaffing nectar from it,
> Not attain to now on account of grief? [20]

MAHĀŚVETĀ [*after taking courage*]: Oh,[89] I'm unfortunate.[90] But I'm not suffering miseries alone.[91] I see my friend with an unfulfilled[92] desire sinking[93] into an ocean of sorrow.[94]

PATRALEKHĀ [*to the* JESTER]: Sir, take me where my master is.[95]

MADALEKHĀ and TAMĀLIKĀ [*in tears, fanning with their garments' hems*]: Princess, take heart! Take heart! Come and look[96] at the lord of your life!

KĀDAMBARĪ [*after waking up*]: Friends, show[97] me where the lord of my life is.

JESTER: Come this way.

[*All stand up and walk around.*]

KĀDAMBARĪ [*having looked, agitatedly*]: Oh, I'm unfortunate! I'm destroyed! Friends, can't you see? The glorious one looks[98] just as the honorable one told us. [*Swoons.*]

[*All cry out and fall down onto the ground.*]

MAHĀŚVETĀ: Oh, how cruel we are! For we are sustaining our lives even[99] while watching the Crown Prince in such a state.

KĀDAMBARĪ [*having stood up, plucking up courage*]: Or rather, I should rejoice[100] at this occasion, when union is unhindered for me following him to the other world.

PATRALEKHĀ: Oh, Great King's family ornament! Oh, India's good fortune! Oh, Mālava people's well-produced fruition! Oh, Ujjayinī's adornment! Oh, full moon for Vilāsavatī's eyes! Where[101] are you [*Swoons.*][102]

KĀDAMBARĪ [*Having resorted to Sanskrit, choked with tears*]: Oh, Madalekhā, I'm going to follow the lord of my life now.

Please set my parrots and mynahs free!
  Take care of my pet deer tenderly!
Hold a wedding ceremony
  For my young *aśoka* tree and *priyaṅgu* creeper!
Paint me on the canvas
  Where I have painted my beloved!
And give us in your folded hands, my friend,[103]
  A libation of water from the Pleasure Pool! [21]

KEYŪRAKA [*after sighing*]: Lady,[104] we really don't see[105] any cause of the Crown Prince's state.

If he had not heard
  The news about Vaiśampāyana,
This surely would not be his state;[106]
  Hope would sustain his life. [22]

MAHĀŚVETĀ [*after reflecting, remorsefully*]: Now I remember! I have no hope! When Vaiśampāyana disturbed me, I took a certain oath so that such an incident wouldn't happen again.

ALL: What oath?

MAHĀŚVETĀ: The oath that any lover of a woman who enters this place again[107] must instantly become equal to an immobile object.

JESTER: That's what happened to this lover of Kādambarī. Alas! Alas![108]

MAHĀŚVETĀ: What's the use of talking more? I am[109] the cause of the whole disaster.

KĀDAMBARĪ: Whatever may be the case, I must abandon my body. Keyūraka, bring down the glorious one from his horse now.

KEYŪRAKA [*having acted touching him while doing so*]: Oh, why! Prince Candrāpīḍa has become like a jeweled[110] doll. Princess, where shall I put the Prince down?

KĀDAMBARĪ [*after sitting down*]: Give him here. I'll hold him with my body for a while and then follow him. [*Takes*[111] *him and holds him with her body.*]

KEYŪRAKA [*casting a glance*]:

Light is arising from his body;
It seems to anoint our bodies[112] with nectar,
And is ineffably soothing[113]
To our tearful eyes. [23]

[*All act resisting looking at it.*]

[*In the sky*]

Dear Mahāśvetā!
Previously[114] when I was taking away Puṇḍarīka,
I prevented you from following him in death;[115]
It is appropriate you have sustained your life, for[116]
You are going to be[117] united with your beloved. [24]

Now observe some wonderful nature of fate!

His body has attained the state of moonstones[118]
Owing to the position of your virtue.
Candrāpīḍa's must not be thought to be otherwise
Than being preserved through a power of such nature:
Kādambarī is comforting it
With the special touch[119] of her hand-lotuses.
They shall soon regain consciousness
In order to convince you two of this matter. [25]

KEYŪRAKA: What a wonder!

Immediately after uttering words about what it is,
The light is disappearing[120] beyond our eyes' power,
Arousing astonishment in our hearts
By flashing as if it were ascending lightning.[121] [26]

PATRALEKHĀ [*after waking up*,[122] *extremely agitatedly*[123]]: [124]Hey, Indrāyudha, come now! Separated from your master, you're not happy, either. Friends, you're now going to dispatch me for the service of my master. [*Exit with* INDRĀYUDHA.][125]

JESTER: Oh, alas! I don't know what she has decided to do.

MADALEKHĀ & OTHERS: Why! our friend has started[126] for Acchoda.

MAHĀŚVETĀ: Oh! they have both[127] sunk[128] into the lake.

KĀDAMBARĪ: She's very[129] fortunate, for she has remedied the burden of her misery[130] without any delay.[131]

KEYŪRAKA: Now another[132] great wonder has happened[133] here.

Indrāyudha,[134] sunk into the water,
Has later[135] risen as some divine ascetic.
But Patralekhā herself is not coming up[136] at all.
Alas! she has really[137] sunk into the lake.[138] [27]

JESTER: Who's that ascetic? His bark garment and tied matted hair are covered with moss[139] because of his long stay in the water.

MADALEKHĀ & TAMĀLIKĀ: Surely we've seen him before.[140]

MAHĀŚVETĀ [*having observed him, as if recognizing him*]: Taralikā, look at him! Surely you remember him, too. He's certainly the venerable Kapiñjala.

TARALIKĀ [*having seen him*]: He really is[141] the companion of your lord, Puṇḍarīka.

KĀDAMBARĪ: Why! the Lady is repeatedly saying "He's that Kapiñjala! He's that Kapiñjala!"

[*Having entered*]

KAPIÑJALA: Luckily, my curse has been completed, but

I am indeed[142] afflicted with separation from Puṇḍarīka,
A reservoir of friendship since our births,
In the same way that[143] I am afflicted with separation
From my long-familiar Candrāpīḍa. [28]

I made a promise in that manner. How can I possibly see Mahāśvetā without my friend? Even so, I should now console Kādambarī, for despair has newly arisen in her on account of a sudden disaster to her most beloved. [*After approaching them*] Dear ladies, may you not become widows!

BOTH [*having folded their hands, tearfully*]: Why! something contrary to the reality has come out[144] of your mouth.

KAPIÑJALA: [145]Please don't think like that! Hear what those two, Puṇḍarīka and Candrāpīḍa, did[146] in private. This is what happened.[147] [*Tells in their*[148] *ears exactly so and so.*]

MAHĀŚVETĀ [*after cheering up a little*]: Father, who restored my lord to life at another time, has quite[149] opportunely taken pity on me. My lord, Puṇḍarīka!

understand[150] that I myself was Death to you, who continued[151] to love me though you were in another body.

KĀDAMBARĪ [*having sighed*]: Now stop[152] your series of strange wishes! It's not inconsistent that the Prince appears[153] to be the moon. Otherwise, how can he possibly[154] be extremely beautiful like this?

MAHĀŚVETĀ: But sir, why couldn't you even show yourself all this time?

KAPIÑJALA: What can I do about things impossible to counteract?[155]

I stayed several days at the side of my preceptor,
Who was prolonging my friend's life by means of rites;[156]
Then, on account of someone's[157] curse, I entered into
Indrāyudha and assumed his[158] body until today. [29]

KEYŪRAKA: In that case,[159] it must be you[160] who brought the Crown Prince here,[161] who was pursuing a pair of *kinnaras*.

KAPIÑJALA: Of course.

KEYŪRAKA [*with his hands folded*]:

Then, where is Patralekhā gone?
Where are the two friends[162] of yours now?
They must be both living in other bodies
Owing to their curses[163] — this much I can tell. [30]

KAPIÑJALA: I, too, wish to find[164] everything out from the venerable Śvetaketu. I repeatedly request[165] you two ladies to follow the moon's word. [*Exit.*]

ALL[166] [*astonished*]: We're experiencing both what we've never seen and what we've never heard at the same time.

KĀDAMBARĪ: Friend, since such is the case, you tell me what to do.

MAHĀŚVETĀ: Now the story of your[167] lord has also[168] been[169] manifested to me. Say,[170] I have prevented you from following him in death,[171] though merely with consolatory words. What can you do now? Your beloved's body is right in front of you as a sign of trust.

KĀDAMBARĪ: Why does the Lady talk like this?[172]

TWO FRIENDS[173] [*having fallen at her feet*]: Princess, follow the Lady's advice! For[174]

Any kind of image would do a favor,
If worshiped;
How much more, the visible moon god,

When propitiated and pleased? [31][175]

KEYŪRAKA: Princess, why do you still think otherwise? Look!

Was not Rati indeed united once again
    With her beloved, the mind-born Love,
Even though he had attained the state of a moth
    In the flames from Śiva's eye on his forehead?[176] [32]

KĀDAMBARĪ [*to herself*]: I can't resist the desire to get united with my beloved.[177] [*Aloud*] As you think. [*To* KEYŪRAKA] Now tell[178] this incident to Father, Mother and the whole *gandharva* family in such a way that they may not feel despair because of me.

KEYŪRAKA [*to himself*]: Fortunately, the Princess is positively supporting[179] her body. [*Aloud*] As the Princess has ordered. [*Exit.*]

KĀDAMBARĪ: Friends, bring[180] me flowers and cosmetics! I must adorn my lord with them.

TWO FRIENDS [*do so.*]

KĀDAMBARĪ [*to the* JESTER]: Honorable one, you have witnessed[181] the whole incident. Cheer up the host of princes and sons of good family headed by Meghanāda. And tell what has happened[182] to the elders in Ujjayinī as well.

JESTER [*after standing up, despondently*]: How can I calm down[183] the host of princes? And how can I tell the elders? [*Walks around.*]

KĀDAMBARĪ: Friends, come[184] this way. We'll do what we've been told to do. [*Exeunt omnes.*]

END OF ACT SEVEN

Notes

1. *V.K.: -khedāḥ; M.M.: -bhedāḥ.*
2. *V.K.: (varṣ)ārdra-; M.M.: (-)ādi-.*
3. *M.M.: haddhi 2; V.K.: haddhi; V.K.Ch.: hā dhik.*
4. *V.K.: ṇāṇuhūdo kadā vi; M.M.: ṇāṇubhūdo cairantara°javiaavaiṇara°mivi; V.K.Ch.: nānubhūtaḥ kadāpi.*
5. *V.K.: eāriso; M.M.: aaṁ; V.K.Ch.: etādṛśo.*
6. *M.M.: yugapadāpatparamparā; V.K.: yugapadāpatitā apatparamparā.*
7. *V.K.* supplies *tathāhi.*

8. *V.K.: tām aprāpya; M.M.: tāṁ(?) (saṁ,* inserted afterwards; *ma, M.M.V.2.)prāpya.*
9. *V.K.: kālaḥ (karṇa-); M.M.: kālā (-).*
10. *V.K.: nisarga (eva); M.M.: anisarga (-).*
11. *H.S.: dussaho eso pāussamao; M.M.: dūsaho esa pāasosamayo; V.K.: dussahaaro eso pāussamao; V.K.Ch.: duḥsahatara eṣa prāvṛṭsamayo; H.S.Ch.: duḥsaha - -.*
12. *V.K.: ukkaṇṭhiassa; M.M.: u°(?)ka°di(ṭhi, M.M.V.2.)a°sa; V.K.Ch.: utkaṇṭhitasya.*
13. *V.K.: indragopa-; M.M.: indrakopa-.*
14. *V.K.* omits *(mā dāva) uṭhie (uṭṭhie, M.M.V.2.) (dāṇiṁ).*
15. *V.K.: (anantarāvaśyaṁ)bhāvī (devīsaṁdarśanotsavaḥ); M.M.: (-) bhāvi(-).*
16. *H.S.: bhavitā tathāpi; M.M.* and *V.K.: bhavatād athāpi.*
17. *M.M.V.2.* and *V.K.: dhūmāyate cittam; M.M.: rūmāyate vittam.*
18. *V.K.: (hemakūṭa)dhāmnāṁ (kirātānām) āvāsabhūtāni (kānanāni); M.M.: (-)nāmnā (-) āvāsabhūtā(?) purośalya (-).*
19. *M.M.: -sākṣiṇi; V.K.: -sākṣibhūtāni.*
20. *M.M.: (yāni) me (kinnara-); V.K.* omits.
21. *V.K.: (pratyagra)smayamānanīpa-; M.M.: (-)svayamāni (na, M.M.V.1.)nīva(pa, M.M.V.1.)-.*
22. *V.K.: (dhavalatāṁ) āpādayanto diśo; M.M.: (-) āpātayanto diśān.*
23. *M.M.V.2.* and *V.K.: vailakṣyān nūnam; M.M.: vailakṣyāsūnam.*
24. *M.M.V.2.: katham iha(api, M.M.) na kiñ cid upalakṣaṇam apy avasthātuḥ priyasakhasya; V.K.: - iha - - - upalakṣyate vasthānalakṣma priyasakhasya.*
25. *V.K.: kiṁ nu (khalu -); M.M.: na (- -).*
26. *M.M.: imāṁ; M.M.V.2.* and *V.K.: māṁ.*
27. *V.K.: kruśatī; M.M.: (?)śatī; M.M.V.2.: uśatī.*
28. *M.M.: avaśyaṁ (- manye); V.K.:* omits.
29. *M.M.: me tādṛśaṁ; V.K.: ma etādṛśaṁ.*
30. *H.S.: janasya tasya; M.M.: janasyāsya; V.K.* omits.
31. *V.K.: (naivā)syām (bhuvi); M.M.: (naiva) syāt (-).*
32. *H.S.: kva nu hi; M.M.: (?); V.K.: kva nu khalu.*
33. *M.M.V.2.* and *V.K.: etasya; M.M.: ekasya.*
34. *V.K.: dvaidhībhāvān (mama); M.M.: -bhāvaṁ (-).*
35. *Ubhayaṁ* (lit. both).
36. *V.K.: upasarpayan; M.M.: upasarpan.*
37. *M.M.: (āśrama)mukham; V.K.: (-)samīpam.*
38. *M.M.: udāra(varṇinī-); V.K.: udāravara (- -).*
39. *H.S.: sāśaṅkaṁ tataḥ sāśaṁsam; M.M.: sāśaṁṅka* later corrected as *sāśaṁsam; V.K.: sāśaṁsam. Sāśaṅkaṁ* is for the first half of the following verse (14); *sāśaṁsam,* for its second half.

40. *M.M.V.1.* and *V.K.: pravartayati; M.M.: pravartayan.*

41. *M.M.: patralekhālambinī; V.K.: patralekhāṁsāvalambinī.*

42. *V.K.: savāmi devīe; M.M.: savāmi(sāmi, M.M.V.2.) devīeṇa; V.K.Ch.: śapāmi devyāḥ.*

43. *M.M.V.2.* and *V.K.: dhanyaḥ; M.M.: sanya.*

44. *Maṅgalyorṇāvalayini.*

45. *M.M.: tāvan (mahā-); V.K.* omits.

46. *V.K.: majjidā via; M.M.: (?)a; M.M.V.2.: majjā viā; V.K.Ch.: majjiteva.*

47. *V.K.: mahaddhadammi; M.M.: maha^{o}daṇiha^{o}mi; V.K.Ch.: mahāhrade.*

48. *V.K.: devadādudīo (via); M.M.: (-o^{o})cia; V.K.Ch.: devatādvitīya (iva).* It literally means "accompanied by a divinity".

49. *V.K.: visajjia-; M.M.: a^{o}ho(cho, M.M.V.2.)dasavarasaviha^{o}via-; V.K.Ch.: visarjita-.*

50. *M.M.: jujjai 2; V.K.: jujjai; V.K.Ch.: yujyate.*

51. *V.K.* needlessly supplies *mahāsedāe; V.K.Ch.: mahāśvetāyā (āśrama-).*

52. *V.K.: -dṛṣṭayo (na); M.M.: -dṛṣṭayā (-).*

53. *V.K.: vanyā; M.M.: varṇā.*

54. *V.K.* supplies *svagatam.*

55. *V.K.: kisadā; M.M.: kūsai^{o}tipi; V.K.Ch.: kṛśatā.*

56. *V.K.: -kilamenta-; M.M.: -tii^{o} (khila^{o}, M.M.V.2.)ma^{o}ta-; V.K.Ch.: -klānta-.*

57. *M.M.: ṇa āṇe; V.K.: - jāṇemi; V.K.Ch.: na jāne.*

58. *H.S.: evva avasisīadi tti; M.M.: - avasesiai^{o}ti; V.K.: avasesiaṁ bhavissadi tti; V.K.Ch.: avaśeṣitaṁ bhaviṣyatīti; H.S.Ch.: evāvaśiṣyata iti.*

59. *V.K.* supplies *me; V.K.Ch.: me.*

60. *V.K.: uvaṭṭhie; M.M.: i^{o}di(puṭṭhi, M.M.V.2.)e; V.K.Ch.: upasthite.*

61. *V.K.: kaambataru-; M.M.: kaiṁbaa(ta,* inserted later by *M.M.V.2.)rada-; V.K.Ch.: kadambataru-.*

62. *V.K.: haddhi pajjāulavadaṇā sahī me lakkhīadi; M.M.: ha^{o}dhavahai^{o}dhagaṁḍamaṇḍalāparuṇṇavaaṇā a(ā, M.M.V.2.)la^{o}khiadi; V.K.Ch.: hā dhik paryākulavadanā sakhī me lakṣyate.*

63. *V.K.: samao khu eso manmahaphaṇivisavijaṁhiāṇaṁ; M.M.: - - so eso vaṁmahaha(pha, M.M.V.2.)ṇivisavisa(thya, M.M.V.1.,* unclear) *aṁhiṁ(a,* inserted by *M.M.V.2.)āṇaṁ; V.K.Ch.: samayaḥ khalv eṣa manmathaphaṇiviṣavijṛmbhitānām.*

64. *V.K.: sphuṭaiḥ; M.M.: sphuṭo.*

65. *V.K.: -kalaiś; M.M.: -sakhaiś.*

66. *H.S.: kiyato bādhiṣyate taḥ param; M.M.: - bādhiṣyato(te, M.M.V.2.) vāṁ param; V.K.: kim ato bādhiṣyate sāṁpratam.*

67. *M.M.: utsarpati; V.K.: upasarpati.*

68. *M.M.: taralikāsahitā; V.K.: taralikayā saha.*

69. *M.M.: haddhi 2; V.K.* omits; *H.S.Ch.: hā dhik hā dhik.*

70. *V.K.* supplies *me; V.K.Ch.: mama.*

71. *V.K.: visaladāe; M.M.: vilasaṁ(visala, M.M.V.2.)āe; V.K.Ch.: viṣalatāyā (iva).*

72. *V.K.: rakkhasīe; M.M.: raṅgha(ggha, M.M.V.2.)sīe; V.K.Ch.: rākṣasyā.*

73. *V.K.: tārisiṁ dasaṁ; M.M.: tārisī; V.K.Ch.: tādṛśīṁ daśāṁ.*

74. *H.S.: (mahāsedāsamaṁ) tado; M.M.: (-) tato; V.K.: (-) samantado; V.K.Ch.: (mahāśvetāśramaṁ) samantataḥ; H.S.Ch.: (-) tataḥ.*

75. *V.K.* needlessly adds *kahehi; V.K.Ch.: kathaya.*

76. *V.K.* needlessly adds *evvaṁ; V.K.Ch.* drops.

77. *V.K.: asya saṁvṛttaṁ; M.M.: asannivṛttam.*

78. More literally: As if from Gentle Breeze, Spring; or from Spring, Love; or from Love, Youth, the Prince is separated from his worthy friend. This verse is quoted by Vemabhūpāla in his *Sāhityacintāmaṇi* (hereafter cited as *S.C.*).

M.M.V.2. and V.K.:

mandānilena madhur iva madhuneva viyuktavān madanaḥ ।
madaneneva taruṇi(ṇī, MM.)mā devaḥ suhṛdānukūlena ।।

S.C.:

maṁdānilena madhunīva madhuneva viyuktapān madanaḥ ।
madananaiva taruṇīva nāṁtare vihaṁgahastā suhṛdānurūpeṇa ।।

Vide Intro., chap. V.

79. *V.K.: suṇia; M.M.: āṇanta°sa; V.K.Ch.: śrutvā.*

80. *V.K.: avaloio; M.M.: dūrohi puloio; V.K.Ch.: avalokitaḥ.*

81. *V.K.* needlessly adds *kālaṇaṁ; V.K.Ch.: kāraṇam.*

82. *V.K.: sāvida-; M.M.: suda-; V.K.Ch.: śrāvita-.*

83. *V.K.: diṭṭhehiṁ tassa; M.M.: diṭhevi ima°sa; V.K.Ch.: dṛṣṭais tasya.*

84. *V.K.: ettha; M.M.: ido; V.K.Ch.: atra.*

85. *H.S.: purado evva; M.M.: purado°cia; V.K.: purada evva; V.K.Ch.: purata eva.*

86. *V.K.: ṇippanda-; M.M.: ṇi°ha°(cha°, M.M.V.2.)da-; V.K.Ch.: niḥspanda-.*

87. *M.M.: de°va; V.K.: hadavidhe; V.K.Ch.: hatavidhe; H.S.Ch.: daiva.*

88. *M.M.: -vyāvṛtā; V.K.: -vyāpṛtā.*

89. *M.M.: ā; M.M.V.1.: kahaṁ; V.K.: amho; V.K.Ch.: aho.*

90. *V.K.: mandabhāadheā; M.M.: mandabhāāeṇavara; V.K.Ch.: mandabhāgadheyā.*

91. *V.K.* supplies *kevalaṁ; V.K.Ch.: kevalaṁ.*

92. *V.K.* supplies *a(puṇṇa-); V.K.Ch.: a(pūrṇa-).*

93. *V.K.: majjantiṁ; M.M.: ma°jatiṇṇaṇo; V.K.Ch.: majjantīṁ.*

94. *V.K.: soasāare; M.M.: soasāarama°jha°mi; V.K.Ch.: śokasāgare.*

95. *V.K.* omits (- *sāmī) eso apu°ṇakammāda°somi.*

96. *V.K.: pekkha; M.M.: puloehi; V.K.Ch.: paśya.*
97. *V.K.: daṁseha (sahīo); M.M.: daṁsehi (-); V.K.Ch.: darśayataṁ (sakhyau).*
98. *V.K.: dīsai; M.M.: dīsahi; V.K.Ch.: dṛṣyate.*
99. *V.K.* supplies *(poi°tio; pekkhantio, M.M.V.2.) vi; V.K.Ch.: (paśyantyo) pi.*
100. *V.K.: paharisevvo (samao); M.M.: paharisa°se°va(-); V.K.Ch.: praharṣitavyaḥ (samayaḥ).*
101. *V.K.: kahiṁ; M.M.: kahaṁ; V.K.Ch.: kutra.*
102. *M.M.: iti moham upagacchati; V.K.* omits.
103. *M.M.: sakhi; V.K.; saha.*
104. *M.M.V.2.: ārye; M.M.* and *V.K.: ārya.*
105. *M.M.: paśyāmo vayam; V.K.: paśyāmy evaṁ.*
106. *H.S.: daśeyaṁ na bhaved eva; V.K.: - - bhavaty -; M.M.: daśacedadaśastye(ntye, M.M.V.2.)va. V.K.* switches the two lines of this verse.
107. *V.K.: (jo uṇa) ettha itthiākāmuo (pavisai); M.M.: (- -) imaṁ jaṁ kiṁ vi vā i°dhiṁ tāmeṁto (-); V.K.Ch.: (yaḥ punar) atra strīkāmukaḥ (praviśati). H.S.Ch.* for *M.M.* is: *(- -) imām yat kim api vā strīṁ tamayan (atra,* supplied; *ettha, H.S.) (-),* and roughly means: any man who enters here again, tormenting this woman in any manner. But Candrāpīḍa did not enter her hermitage, tormenting her in any manner.
108. *M.M: haddhi haddhi; V.K.* places this at the beginning of the speech. After this *M.M.* has *duhiā rovidavi°padīva°dhalido* as part of the Jester's speech, and also the following for Taralikā: *tarali || a°dhi eso jo holahaparisāṇubhavaṇi°jo kao vaṇadevadāe; V.K.* omits both.
109. *M.M.: mi; V.K.: saṁvuttā; V.K.Ch.: saṁvṛttā; H.S.Ch.: asmi.*
110. *M.M.V.2.* and *V.K.: maṇi-; M.M.: muni-.*
111. *V.K.* supplies *ādāya.*
112. *M.M.V.2.* and *V.K.: dehaṁ naḥ; M.M.: dehinaḥ.*
113. *H.S.: (kim api) prāsādikaṁ; M.M.: (- -) prasādanaṁ; V.K.: (- -) tu prasādanaṁ.*
114. *H.S.: prāg asi; M.M.: pra(prā, M.M.V.2.) (?) nu(?)si; V.K.: prathamam asi.*
115. *V.K.* supplies *(anumaraṇā)n (nivāritā).*
116. *V.K.: yat; M.M.: yāvat.*
117. *V.K.: bhavitā; M.M.: bhavatā.*
118. *V.K.* supplies *(śa)śi(maṇimayatāṁ).*
119. *M.M.V.2.* and *V.K.: (karasarasiruha)sparśato; M.M.: (-)ssargato.*
120. *V.K.: layam (upayāty); M.M.: (?)m (-).*
121. *M.M.: taḍid; V.K.: taṭid.*
122. *H.S.* supplies *prabudhya; vide supra,* n. 102.
123. *V.K.* supplies *sodvegātiśayam.*
124. *V.K.* omits *tāvāuva°khia°pāvediva°sakālaṁtarabhāviṇīvedanāpadiva°tiṁ | (bho)*
125. After this *V.K.* omits the [illegible]owing speech, which seems to be a scribal error: *vi || haddhi 2 || kiṁ esahiāesamhi sāmis[illegible]vā [illegible]visañjidaṁ mhi tumhahiṁ.*

126. *M.M.V.2.* and *V.K.: patthidā; M.M.: va°phiyā; V.K.Ch.: prasthitā.*
127. *V.K.: duve vi; M.M.: parāī or paraṇaī; V.K.Ch.: dvāv api.*
128. *V.K.: ṇimaggā; M.M.: ṇimaṅga(gga, M.M.V.2.); V.K.Ch.: nimagnāv.*
129. *H.S.: sā evva paraṁ; M.M.: sa°cia paraṁ; V.K.: esā evva; V.K.Ch.: eṣaiva; H.S.Ch.: saiva paraṁ.*
130. *V.K.: dukkhabharo; M.M.: du°vaharo; V.K.Ch.: duḥkhabharaḥ.*
131. *V.K.: avilambiaṁ evva; M.M.: vilaṁbiaṁ; V.K.Ch.: avilambitam eva.*
132. *V.K.: aparam; M.M.: avaram.*
133. *M.M.: udbhūtam; V.K.: utthitam.*
134. *V.K.: (indrāyudho yo -) sa; M.M.: (- - -) san.*
135. *H.S.: param; M.M. and V.K.: (-muninā) samam.*
136. *V.K.: unmajjati; M.M.: unmajjatī.*
137. *M.M.V.2.* and *V.K.: nūnam; M.M.: nītam.*
138. *V.K.: antarhradaṁ; M.M.: antahṛdan (ni-).*
139. *V.K.: -sevālia-; M.M.: -se, ālio°la-; V.K.Ch.: -śaivālita-.*
140. *H.S.: ṇaṁ eso diṭṭhapuvvo evva; V.K.: - - - via; M.M.: ṇa - diṭṭhapuvvesu; V.K.Ch.: nanv eṣa dṛṣṭapūrva iva; H.S.Ch.: - - - eva.*
141. *V.K.: (saccaṁ) so evva; M.M.: (-) so°cea (= sa caiva, H.S.Ch.); V.K.Ch.: (satyaṁ) sa eva.*
142. *H.S.: nu; M.M.* and *V.K.: na.*
143. *V.K.* supplies *yathā.*
144. *H.S.: ṇiggaaṁ paccakkhavivarīaṁ āsi; M.M.: ṇi°gaa pa°ca°khavipariāi -; V.K.: ṇiggaia vaaṇaṁ paccakkhavivariaṁ -; V.K.Ch.: nirgatya vacanaṁ pratyakṣaviparītam āsīt; H.S.Ch.: nirgataṁ pratyakṣaviparītam -.*
145. *V.K.* needlessly adds *bhadre.*
146. *V.K.: nirvṛttam; M.M.: nivṛttaṁ.*
147. *M.M.: eṣa vṛttāntaḥ; V.K.* omits.
148. *M.M.: iti tayoḥ; V.K.* omits.
149. *M.M.: khu; V.K.* omits; *H.S.Ch.: khalu.*
150. *H.S.: jāṇāhi ayya; M.M.: - aa; V.K.: hā ṇāha; V.K.Ch.: hā nātha; H.S.Ch.: jānīhy ārya.*
151. *V.K.: aṇubaddha-; M.M.: aṇubandha-; V.K.CH.: anubaddha-.*
152. *V.K.: ciṭṭhau; M.M.: ciṭṭhai; V.K.Ch.: tiṣṭhatu.*
153. *V.K.: saṁdiṭṭho; M.M.: sāndravadiṇṇo; V.K.Ch.: saṁdṛṣṭaś.*
154. *H.S.: kahaṁ vā assa; M.M.: - va; V.K.: kahiṁ vā se; V.K.Ch.: kathaṁ vā tasya; H.S.Ch.: - vāsya.*
155. *V.K.: (aśakya)pratikriyeṣu; M.M.: (-)parikriyeṣu.*
156. *V.K.: vidhānaiḥ: M.M.: (abhivardhayato) pi yānaiḥ.*
157. *V.K.: kasya cid; M.M.: tasya -.*
158. *V.K.: indrāyudhasya (vapur); M.M.: indrāyudhaṁ sva(-).*

159. *V.K.* supplies *tarhi.*

160. *V.K.: bhavataiva; M.M.: bhagavataiva tāvad.*

161. *M.M.: idaṁ; V.K.: imaṁ pradeśam.*

162. *V.K.: tau (bhavat)suhṛdau; M.M.: tena(tau, M.M.V.2.) (-) suhṛdena.*

163. *H.S.: śāpād anyaśarīre vartiṣyete; M.M.: śāpavaśā(da,* inserted by *M.M.V.2.)nyaśarīre nuvartiṣyete; V.K.: śāpavaśād anyaśarīre vartiṣyete.*

164. *M.M.: vijñātuṁ; V.K.: jñātum.*

165. *VK.: abhyarthaye; M.M.: abhyarthayāmi.*

166. *V.K.: sarvāḥ* (all the female characters present, who speak Prakrit); *M.M.: sarve.*

167. *H.S.* supplies *(ṇāhassa) te; H.S.Ch.: (nāthasya) te.*

168. *M.M.: (kahā)vi; V.K. omits; H.S.Ch.: (kathā)pi.*

169. *V.K.* wrongly adds *ṇa; V.K.Ch.: na.*

170. *H.S.: he; M.M.; kādaṁ || he; V.K.* omits.

171. *V.K.: vāriāsi aṇumaraṇādo; M.M.: avapāria°āsi aṇumariduṁ; V.K.Ch.: vāritāsi anumaraṇāt.*

172. *V.K.* supplies *evvaṁ; V.K.Ch.: evaṁ.*

173. *M.M.: sakhyau* (Madalekhā and Tamālikā); *V.K.: sakhyaḥ.*

174. *H.S.: tathā hi; M.M.: kiṁ ca; V.K.* omits.

175. *H.S.:*

ko vi paḍimāviseso paricarijanto aṇuggahaṁ kuṇai |
paccakkhacandadevo kiṁ uṇa ārāhidappasaṇṇotti ||

M.M.:

jo ko vi paḍimāriseso vi paricari°jaṁto aṇu°gahaṁ kuṇai |
kiṁ uṇa pa°ca°khadevo bhaavaṁ caṁdo ārāhida°pasa°ṇo°ti ||

V.K.:

- - - paḍimāviseso paricarijjanto aṇuggahaṁ - |
- - ppaccakkhadevo cando ārāhidappasaṇṇotti ||

H.S.Ch.:

ko pi pratimāviśeṣaḥ paricaryamāṇo nugrahaṁ karoti |
pratyakṣacandradevaḥ kiṁ punar ārādhitaprasanna iti ||

V.K.Ch.:

yaḥ ko pi - - - - |
kiṁ punaḥ pratyakṣadevaś candra ārādhitaprasanna- ||

176. *M.M.: puraharalalāṭanayanajvalane śalabhatvam upagatenāpi; V.K.: puraharalalāṭanayane śalabhatvam upāgatenāpi.*

177. *V.K.Ch.* needlessly adds *(vallabha) jana-.*

178. *V.K.: ṇiveehi; M.M.: uvaṇṇasehi; V.K.Ch.: nivedaya.*

179. *V.K.: niścita(śarīra)dhāraṇā; M.M.: niśvasita(-)sāraṇā.*

180. *V.K.* omits (*uvaṇeha) (?)ubhoāṇidāi (pu°phāṇulevaṇāiṁ*).

181. *V.K.: paccakkhia-; M.M.: pa°ca°kha-; V.K.Ch.: pratyakṣita-.*

182. *V.K.: jahauttaṁ; M.M.: jahauttaṁtaṁ; V.K.Ch.: yathāvṛttam.*

183. *M.M.: pariava°thāvemi; V.K.: pariatthāvemi (va* missing); *V.K.Ch.: paryavasthāpayāmi.*

184. *H.S.: sahīo (ido) eha; M.M.* and *V.K.: sahio (-) -; V.K.Ch.: sakhyaḥ, (ita) eta; H.S.Ch.: sakhyāv (-) etam.*

Miśraviṣkambhaka
Prelude to Act Eight

[*Enter* MĀTAṄGA[1] *with a cage*[2] *in his hand.*]

MĀTAṄGA: Luckily, here's a parrot in an arbor of rose apple trees.[3] I'll spread a net, then.[4] [*Does so.*][5]

[*Having entered in the form of a parrot*][6]

VAIŚAMPĀYANA[7] [*talks in his sleep*]: Dear *gandharva* Princess Mahāśvetā, please accept me devoted[8] to your feet!

I am not feeling this bond of love for the first time;
My heart remembers intimacy with you in another life;
And I have found you repenting —
How can I bear this misery of separation? [1]

MĀTAṄGA [*after laughing*]: Why! he remembers incidents in his previous lives as sages do. Exhausted with remorse, he's calling Mahāśvetā[9] [*Shakes the net with his finger.*][10]

VAIŚAMPĀYANA [*after waking up, with a glance given in front, to himself*]: Who's this? I can guess he's from a savage class. He's catching me with a net as if he were a servant[11] of Death. [*Despairingly*] Or rather,[12]

Why should not regrettable disasters
Frequently befall people like me
Who disregard the words of the good and
Repeatedly undergo transformations into beasts. [2]

[*Aloud*] Who are you, my dear? What did you capture me here for? If you had a desire for meat, why didn't you kill me while I was asleep? If it was merely for sport, release me longing to see my beloved!

MĀTAṄGA: Listen! Our master's daughter living in a *caṇḍāla* village[13] sent[14] hundreds of men here to catch[15] you. First I also hunted[16] and looked for you in the Vindhya forest, but didn't get you. But today I found you thanks to our good luck.[17] Now I'm going to give you to our mistress.[18] Ask her either to keep you or to set you free.[19]

VAIŚAMPĀYANA [*disgustedly, to himself*[20]]: Oh.[21] you're ruined! Wicked one! Wretched sage! Miserable Puṇḍarīka!

Formerly you lived on cooked food and
Oblations' remainder with pleasant fragrance
In a divine world's hermitages with beautiful vicinities;
But now you are going to a *mātaṅga* village
Shunned even by fools from a distance
To eat impure, fetid carrion[22] left for dogs. [3]

[*Aloud*] My dear, I'm a sage who remembers his births. You'll surely acquire virtue if you save me from this danger of evil. So set me free! And since nobody is watching this, you have no fear of offending.

MĀTAṄGA [*after laughing*]: Listen, fool![23]

Why ever and when on earth
Would a man carry out a fearless action?
All the five elements dwelling in his body
Are watching everything. [4][24]

VAIŚAMPĀYANA [*after sighing, to himself*]: I can't possibly avoid this except by abandoning my life.[25]

I certainly did not make[26]
My nurturer Hārita's toil fruitful,
Nor did I listen to the advice[27]
Of my friend Kapiñjala though I saw[28] him,
Nor did I go to the Caitraratha forest
And see Mahāśvetā's face —
What did I of evil nature accomplish
Even in the memories of my previous lives? [5]

MĀTAṄGA [*after taking him*]: I'm going to giv· him to my mistress and get a reward from her.[29] [*Walks towards the caṇḍāla village.*]

VAIŚAMPĀYANA [*after observing in front*]: Oh, why! I know that this place, whose vicinity is covered with a spurge[30] forest, is the location of the *caṇḍāla* village, though he doesn't say so. For

Solely eager[31] to obtain a morsel
　　Of a hanging cow's or buffalo's skull,
Dogs are making ear-piercing loud noises;
　　Smoke offensive to the nose[32] is arising
From the blood,[33] fat, meat, marrows and bones
　　Savage girls are roasting[34] everywhere. [6]

Alas! Alas![35] Because I've been in a state like this, I haven't even obtained the glorious deed of staying at the feet[36] of my fathers, Śukanāsa and Tārāpīḍa, who have been practising asceticism in Caitraratha since they abandoned their kingdom owing to grief for their sons. In any case, abandoning my body will surely lead[37] me to ease.

[*Exeunt ambo.*]

END OF THE *MIŚRAVIṢKAMBHAKA*
PRELUDE TO ACT EIGHT

Notes

1. *H.S.: mātaṅgaḥ; M.M.: mātaṅgavakraḥ; M.M.V.2.* and *V.K.: mātaṅgakaḥ.* After this *M.M.* gives only *mātaṅga* or *mātaṁ* for short. *V.K.* gives *mātaṅgakaḥ* throughout this prelude. In the novel *Kādambarī,* Mātaṅga is the name of the leader of an army of hunters; *vide* Bāṇa, *Kādambarī (Pūrvārddha),* ed. by M. Pant, p. 110: *-mātaṅganāmānaṁ śabarasenāpatim apaśyam.*
2. *V.K.: vītaṁsa-; M.M.: vitaṁsa-.*
3. *H.S.: diśṭiā eśe khu yaṁbūṇiuñjammi śue;M.M.: diṭṭhaśiā - - aṁbūṇiuaṁmi śute śu(e,* inserted by *M.M.V.2.); V.K.: diṭṭhaśiā (diṭṭhiā, H.S.* Śaurasenī) *- - jambuṇiuñjammi śue; V.K.Ch.: diṣṭyā eṣa khalu jambūnikuñje śukaḥ.* This character speaks Māgadhī Prakrit.
4. *H.S.: yāva; M.M.* and *V.K.: āva; V.K.Ch.: yāvat.*
5. *H.S.: tathā karoti; M.M.: yathā -; V.K.* omits.
6. *H.S.: praviśya śukarūpaḥ; M.M.: - -rūpo; V.K.: tataḥ praviśati śukarūpo vaiśampāyanaḥ.*
7. *M.M.: vaiśampāyanaḥ; V.K.: śukaḥ. V.K.* unnecessarily allots all the speeches of Vaiśampāyana in this prelude to the parrot, who is, in fact, Vaiśampāyana (originally Puṇḍarīka), reborn as a result of Mahāśvetā's curse.
8. *V.K.: (ayaṁ pāda)praṇayī (janaḥ); M.M.: (- -)praṇayi(-).*
9. *H.S.: kahaṁ eśe iśiṇo via śumaridapulavayammavuttante paccādāveṇa kilante mahāśedaṁ āhūedi; V.K.: - - - - śumariapuvvajaṇṇauttanto - kilando ayyamahāśedaṁ -; M.M.: - hi śe iśiṇo idapulavaa°mavuttaṁte a°aviādapañcādāveṇa vilade mahāśedāṇulāāhi; V.K.Ch.: katham eṣa ṛṣir

iva smṛtapūrvajanmavṛttāntaḥ paścāttāpena klānta āryamahāśvetām āhvayati; H.S.Ch.: - - ṛṣaya - - - - mahāśvetām -.

10. *V.K.: iti aṅgulyā vāgurāṁ cālayati; M.M.: aṅgulyā vācayati.*

11. *V.K.: kiṁkara iva; M.M.: kiṁtara lava.*

12. *V.K.: atha vā; M.M.: yathā vā.*

13. *V.K.: pakkaṇaṇivāsiṇie; M.M.: va^{o}(pak, M.M.V.2.)kaṇāhiesidhiṇie; V.K.Ch.: pakkaṇanivāsinyā (a-).*

14. *H.S.: aṇuppeśidā; M.M.: aṇu^{o}ve(pe, M.M.V.2.) śidā; V.K.: aṇuppesidā; V.K.Ch.: anupreṣitāḥ.*

15. *V.K.: gahaṇaṇimittaṁ; M.M.: (ga,* inserted afterwards) *haṇāvimālisāra^{o}devi; V.K.Ch.: grahaṇanimittaṁ.*

16. After this *V.K.* omits *(vilaiiākheḍeṇa) paṁpāśaivali śala(?) duṣkaṁmi (a^{o}ṇeśide).*

17. *V.K.: ayya uṇa amhae śukidavaśeṇa tumaṁ diṭṭho(diśṭe, H.S.); M.M.:a^{o}a - eidekeṇaviāvālinoāśamāhiuḍiṇe disṭe amae śukīdavaśeṇa; V.K.Ch.: adya punar asmākaṁ sukṛtavaśena tvaṁ dṛṣṭaḥ.*

18. *H.S.: tā hage śamappemi śāmiṇie; M.M.: tāṁ hage śama^{o}pemiṁ -; V.K.: tā hagge śamappemi śāmiśudāe; V.K.Ch.: tasmāt haste samarpayāmi svāmisutāyāḥ; H.S.Ch.: tasmād ahaṁ - svāminyāḥ.*

19. *H.S.: taṁ evva abbhatthehi bandhāha mokkhāha vā; M.M.: - - a^{o}bhandhehi vaṁdhāha mokoha -; V.K.: - - abbhatthehi | śāmiṇi evva pahavai tujjha bandhāha mokkhāha vā; V.K.Ch.: tāṁ evābhyarthaya | svāminyeva prabhavati tava bandhāya mokṣāya vā; H.S.Ch.: - - bandhāya mokṣāya vā.*

20. *H.S.* supplies *ātmagatam.*

21. *M.M.: ā; V.K.: hā.*

22. *H.S.: kravyaṁ (yad aśuci -); M.M.: kavyaṁ (tad - -); V.K.: kravyaṁ (tad - -). Havya* in the first *pāda* of this verse means an oblation to a god, while *kavya* means on oblation to a deceased ancestor. The correct reading here, however, is *kravya.*

23. *V.K.: muddha; M.M.: mu^{o}dhe; V.K.Ch.: mugdha.*

24. *H.S.:*

kiṁ vā kadā uṇa kalīadi a puliśeṇa aśaṅkide kamme |
śalīlagoalabhūdāi evva pañca vi savvaṁ pekkhanti ||

V.K.:

- - kaā - kiladi puliśeṇa aśaṅkidaṁ kammo |
śālīlagoalāi pañca vi bhūdāi pekkhaī savvaṁ ||

M.M.:

kiñ ca kadā uṇa kīidi puliśeṇa aśaḥkie kaṁme |
śaśalīlagoaleśuṁ pañcale bhūdeśu āalūeśuṁ ||

V.K.Ch.:

kiṁ vā kadā punaḥ kriyate puruṣeṇāśaṅkitaṁ karma |
śarīragocarāṇi pañcāpi bhūtāni paśyanti sarvam ||

H.S.Ch.:
- - - - kriyate ca puruṣeṇā - - |
śarīragocarabhūtānyeva pañcāpi sarvaṁ paśyanti ||

Cf. Bāṇa, *Kādambarī*, ed. by P. Peterson, Part I, p. 355; *(re mohāndha) yasya śubhāśubhakarmasākṣibhūtāḥ pañca lokapālās tavaivātmaśarīrasthitā na paśyanti so nyasya bhayād akāryaṁ nācarati.*

25. *V.K.: prāṇatyāgaṁ vinā; M.M.: prāṇatyāgam e(kaṁ,* inserted by *M.M.V.2.)(?) vinā.*
26. *V.K.: nīto; M.M.: nito.*
27. *M.M.V.2.* and *V.K.: uaadeśaḥ; M.M.: apadeśaś.*
28. *M.M.V.2.* and *V.K.: dṛṣṭasya; M.M.: duṣṭasya.*
29. *V.K.: imaṁ khu śamappia śāmiṇīśaāśādo pālitośiaṁ geṇhāmi; M.M.: aaṁ khu mośohaṇe pālitośie śāmiṇīe phaśādiādi; V.K.Ch.: imaṁ khalu samarpya svāminīsakāśāt pāritoṣikaṁ gṛhṇāmi (gṛhṇāmi, H.S.Ch.).*
30. *V.K.: (adhigamyate) snug(vana-); M.M.: (-)stu(- -).*
31. *V.K.: (-kabalīkārai)kahevākinaḥ; M.M.: (- -)(?)kapotinaḥ; M.M.V.2.: (- -)(?)kahevākinaḥ.*
32. *V.K.: ghrāṇendriya-; M.M.: prāṇendriya-.*
33. *V.K.: asṛṅ(medo-); M.M.: asūn(- -).*
34. *V.K.: saṁbhṛjjyamāneṣv; M.M.: saṁbha(bhu, M.M.V.1.)jyamāneṣv.*
35. *M.M.: hanta 2; V.K.: hanta.*
36. *M.M.: pādamūlayor; V.K.: -mūle.*
37. *M.M.V.2.* and *V.K.: kalpate; M.M.: kampate.*

ACT EIGHT

[*Enter* TĀRĀPĪḌA, VILĀSAVATĪ, *and* ŚUKANĀSA.]

TĀRĀPĪḌA: Averse to the world and devoted[1] to our vow to be forest dwellers, we have indeed long forgotten the numerous pleasures of the senses to be enjoyed by *nāgarikas*.[2] For

Even in forests as if in gardens,
  Even in stone slabs as if in couches,
Even in bark garments as if in cloaks,
  Even in birds' cries as if in songs,
Even in streams of mountain water[3]
  As if in sporting lotus pools
And even in mountain caves as if in palaces,
  These hearts of ours rejoice immensely. [7]

Nevertheless, for sixteen years
  I have been afflicted with grief for my son;
And even so, particularly at this moment
  My life is painful. [8]

Oh, my son Candrāpīḍa!

I wish to be happy by placing the burden of the earth
  Upon you wedded to a suitable wife —
To those desires springing up in me,
  This great obstacle has thus arisen. [6.39 repeated][4]

[*Weeps, reciting on.*]

VILĀSAVATĪ [*in tears*]:[5] My lord, our daughter-in-law[6] Kādambarī has disregarded the order of fate, saying, "How long[7] am I going to live with my desire unfulfilled?" and resolved to go into Lake Acchoda.

ŚUKANĀSA: I've heard that, too. For that very reason, she[8] has prohibited even the festival of moonlight. King, just look! The absence of her consent[9] has hindered even the appearance of the autumn season. For

Even with their blossoms sleepless,
  Saptacchada trees do not send forth their fragrance;

Even in the vicinity of lotus pools,
Geese are afraid to gabble[10] sweetly;
Even with Agastya arisen,
Water does not attain its usual clearness[11] —
Perhaps, even with a fresh sugarcane bow in his hand,
Love does not give a glance. [9]

TĀRĀPĪḌA: Queen, what has Mahāśvetā done about this?

VILĀSAVATĪ [*tearfully*]: They say[12] she has decided[13] likewise with a picture board with a portrait of Puṇḍarīka on it.

TĀRĀPĪḌA [*after reflecting*]:[14]

Surely in a dream before
The moon's orb entered your mouth,[15]
And a white lotus flower entered your friend's;[16]
Then our sons were born in those very forms.[17]
The happiness the divine[18] voice spoke of
Will come to our sons;[19]
Queen,[20] we should await the time
With faith[21] in this. [10]

ŚUKANĀSA: As the King says.

We should watch the fruit about to ripen
Without getting agitated.
Women are rash —
What should we do about that? [11]

ALL [*act alarm.*]

[*Having entered in a flurry without using a curtain*][22]

KEYŪRAKA [*after prostrating himself*]: Great King, we have obtained a very great and desirable[23] wonder now.

TĀRĀPĪḌA: Then tell me.

KEYŪRAKA: Patralekhā, who plunged herself and sank into Acchoda since the calamity was such[24] then, was, in fact, Rohiṇī, who had descended for the service of her lord.

ŚUKANĀSA: Otherwise, we wouldn't find such an excellent disposition.

KEYŪRAKA: She was kept from being born as her lord's companion[25] and made to remain[26] in the world of the moon. But now she has come here in her own person[27] in order to prevent the two *gandharva* Princesses from this[28] rash act, which she learnt through meditation.[29]

VILĀSAVATĪ: How wonderful! Indeed innate is the virtue of divine women.[30]

KEYŪRAKA: Moreover, she says that[31] Candrāpīḍa and Puṇḍarīka are going to regain consciousness on this very day.

VILĀSAVATĪ [*tearfully*]: That is only consolation. Where is such merit of ours?[32]

KEYŪRAKA: Please don't think like that! In fact, Rohiṇī is going to show[33] the two assuming different bodies in a different land in order to convince us right here through her supernatural power.

ŚUKANĀSA: That's appropriate. For that very reason, the Princess requests her elders to be present there.

TĀRĀPĪḌA: What other than that should we do?

ALL [*stand up and walk around.*]

VILĀSAVATĪ: Keyūraka, tell this incident to my friend Manoramā as well and bring[34] her.

KEYŪRAKA [*after exiting and reentering*]: Queen, they are all keeping away[35] from the Great King's presence. So[36] take your seats.

ALL [*do so.*]

KEYŪRAKA: Now I'll get Rohiṇī to prepare for the desired end.[37] [*Exit.*]

[*In the sky*]

Pay attention to this![38]

ŚUKANĀSA: Rohiṇī is really about to show us her supernatural power.

TĀRĀPĪḌA: [*after looking*]:[39] Oh, what a great wonder this is! For here I see Vidiśā, the capital[40] of the Daśārṇa country, which I saw before during my world conquest.

Here[41] are those market streets[42]
With heaps of glittering invaluable gems;
Here are those residential districts
With abundant wealth;
And here is that Vetravatī[43] River,
Which gives me delight with its water
Abounding in sandal juice
From the breast-banks of women.[44] [12]

ŚUKANĀSA: [*showing with his hand*]:

In this extremely luxurious[45] assembly hall,
Mounted on the throne, attended by princes,
Some king is holding a conversation
On a suitable topic;
He reminds us[46] of Candrāpīḍa
Consecrated as the Crown Prince[47]
On account of their likeness
In age and appearance. [13]

TĀRĀPĪḌA: I do believe he's really my body. For

This boy's face like a full moon,[48]
His eyes resembling lotuses,
His pair of extremely long arms
Protecting remote regions, and
His chest-slope surpassing[49] a bamboo mountain's slope
Look exactly like those of my boy —
The two are an object and its reflection
Explanatory of each other.[50] [14]

VILĀSAVATĪ: Oh, my boy, why is this? Show[51] affection to your elders.

ŚUKANĀSA: Why, this portress holding[52] a golden staff in her folded hands seems to want to speak[53] to the Great King of Vidiśā.

[*Off stage*]

Your Majesty, here's some *caṇḍāla* girl from the South, standing at the gate in order to make you a present of some gem of a parrot.

[*Off stage again*][54]

What harm is there? Bid her enter.

VILĀSAVATĪ: Who ever is this girl with the good fortune of extraordinary beauty? She has opened a gemmed cage held on a *mātaṅga* boy's[55] head, and is taking out a parrot with her hand.

[*Off stage*]

Oh! Brahmā's effort to create beauty is misplaced. For this

Slender-waisted girl dark as aloe leaves,
Wearing a garment beautiful as buds' color
And holding a parrot on her lovely forearm
Full of rays from her gemmed bracelets,

Resembles the Yamunā River with little creepers[56]
Adorned with a mass of *śaivāla* weeds
And with water like twilight
On account of forests growing[57] fresh gems. [15]

ŚUKANĀSA: The Lord of the Daśārṇa country has spoken rightly.

[*Off stage again*]

O Great King! This is a parrot[58] named Vaiśampāyana who has thoroughly mastered all[59] the arts and become a gem in the three worlds. I have brought him to your feet, for you alone are worthy to receive all gems.

ŚUKANĀSA: [*remembering*]: Oh,[60] my son! you have attained[61] a state like this because of my[62] anger. I am indeed wicked.

TĀRĀPĪḌA: Venerable one, please take courage! What can we do about this irremediably[63] terrible torment of fate?

[*Off stage*]

Great King! Glorious Śūdraka! Listen to these sweet words!

Located very close to the fire of their hearts' grief,
Bathed in tears and devoid of pearl necklaces,[64]
The pairs of breasts of your enemies' wives
Seem to be observing a vow. [16][65]

VILĀSAVATĪ: Alas! Alas! He resembles my son not only by name but also by voice. Oh,[66] fate! why do you deprive him of his body like that?

[*Off stage*]

We[67] have never in this life observed[68] a speech activity accompanied by scholarship like this.

TĀRĀPĪḌA: As the host of princes said, he indeed[69]

Properly turned his face,
Gracefully raised[70] his right foot, and recited[71]
With correct manners and places of articulation,
Accents, phonemes, words and grammatical purity. [17]

[*Off stage*]

You are such a special bird. Who are you?

[*Off stage again*][72]

King, listen attentively[73] for a moment!

There is the Vindhya forest,
  That is,[74] the abode of Agastya,
Where lived[75] Rāma,
  Who destroyed demons with arrows.[76] [18]

TĀRĀPĪḌA: He's probably talking about the past beginnings[77] of his own present life.

ŚUKANĀSA [*choked with tears*]: Oh, my son Vaiśampāyana, you have fallen into such a creature's life. [*Swoons.*]

VILĀSAVATĪ: Why! the venerable Śukanāsa is closing his eyes.[78]

TĀRĀPĪḌA: Venerable one, compose yourself!

Munificence shines in affluence;
  Disinterest, in wisdom; prowess, in battle;
Lack of envy at others, in erudition;
  Likewise, firmness shines in adversity. [19]

ŚUKANĀSA [*after taking courage with difficulty*]: Where is my son?

TĀRĀPĪḌA: The time is near at hand when we can see our sons again. But[79] now listen to the story he's telling.

ŚUKANĀSA: Has he started telling his own story yet?

TĀRĀPĪḌA: Yes, he has. While consoling[80] the swooned venerable one, I heard[81] this much content of his speech.

ŚUKANĀSA: What is it?

TĀRĀPĪḌA:[82]

There he became[83] a parrot;
  Then[84] Hārīta took him away for fear of a hunter;
Then from Jābāli our son learnt[85]
  His past deeds in previous lives;
While going to the *gandharva* girl's presence,
  He fell into a *caṇḍāla* daughter's[86] power
By the force of fate again,
  And spent several days in her *caṇḍāla* village.[87] [20]

  This is all.

VILĀSAVATĪ: Now we'll listen again to the story he's telling.[88]

[*Off stage*]

Thus time went by. And when I opened my eyes this morning,

I found myself confined in a golden cage
By this girl of beautiful appearance,
And beheld her *caṇḍāla* village[89]
Showing like a city in heaven.
Hardly had I surrendered my vow of silence
In order to say,[90] "What is this?"
When she arrived in the presence of your feet. [21]

ALL [*act astonishment.*]

[*Off stage again*]

We wish to know[91] why she acted thus first repulsively[92] and then charmingly.

TĀRĀPĪḌA: Our hearts are also full of curiosity to hear that.[93]

[*Off stage*]

As regards that matter, I am not without[94] curiosity as the King is not.

ŚUKANĀSA: The *caṇḍāla*[95] girl seems to want to say[96] something[97] herself.

[*Off stage*]

Oh, ornament of the earth! Rohiṇī's husband! Joy to Kādambarī's eyes! Moon![98] Why don't you still realize[99] you're in another body[100] acquired through supernatural power?

VILĀSAVATĪ: Luckily, my son has been reminded of his previous lives.

[*Off stage*]

I here am your uterine sister![101] this Puṇḍarīka's mother! the great Lakṣmī! But in order to avoid contact with people, I manifested myself as belonging to the *mātaṅga* class.

ŚUKANĀSA: Otherwise, how[102] can there be this appearance surpassing all women's[103] beauty?

[*Off stage again*]

Owing to his own misconduct, this son of mine was reduced from the state[104] of a divine ascetic to that of a human being, and then to that of a bird. So I captured him so that he would repent and not enter a state even lower than that.[105]

TĀRĀPĪḌA: What ever wouldn't[106] love for a son make one do?[107]

[*Off stage*]

I have brought him to your presence because you two must end your curses simultaneously.[108] So assume[109] your old body and enjoy with your friend the happiness of being united with your beloved one. Permit me to enter my own abode.

ŚUKANĀSA [*with astonishment*]:

Why! After speaking thus,
This daughter of the milky ocean
Is going into the midst of the sky,
Making remote regions resound
With the jingles of her gemmed bracelets,
And her glory being extolled
By *siddhas*, *vidyādhara*s and others
Filling heavenly carriages. [22]

[*Off stage*]

Without knowing all these years
The incidents in my previous births,
I lived[110] in joys and sorrows
As if my mind were stupefied.
Now her words[111] have wakened me;
I remember everything
As if I had been awakened from sleep.[112] [23]

Friend Vaiśampāyana, or rather Puṇḍarīka, do you long for Mahāśvetā?

[*Off stage again*][113]

Friend Candrāpīḍa,

Even now, my former devotion to my parents
Is naturally easy to regain;
So is my friendship
Formed before with my friend;
And so is my passion
Previously arisen towards my beloved;
Yet unable to endure the delay,
Love urges me greatly. [24]

TĀRĀPĪḌA:[114]

Why! he[115] has remembered the calamitous incidents

In his past births;
He is loosening[116] the digits of his consciousness,
His senseorgans gradually closing. [25]

Having found his dear old body by the power of his merit,
He wishes to suffer[117] no more calamities,
And loathes to stay in that body even for a moment
As a gentleman does in the house of another. [26]

VILĀSAVATĪ: Oh, why! My son is unconscious!

ŚUKANĀSA [*to himself*]:[118] Oh! Because of their likeness in appearance, the Queen believes this is he though he's only staying in another body. [*Aloud*][119] Queen, please do not grieve! Rohiṇī is showing[120] all this beyond our senses through her supernatural power.

TĀRĀPĪḌA: Whatever may be the case, I can't bear to see any more of what's happening to my son.

ŚUKANĀSA [*towards the dressing room*]: Goddess Rohiṇī, please stop this painful thing!

[*In the sky*]

You two will have[121] a feast for your eyes[122] when you embrace your beloveds' bodies[123] with their friend.[124] I'm leaving for the world of the moon in order to send back Puṇḍarīka, who has secured the happiness he deserves.

VILĀSAVATĪ: Oh, how great her power is! For now we no longer see that[125] city, but only the hermitage as before.

[*Off stage*]

BARD:

With its riches of digits come forth from the disc of the sun
Set through the whim of fate,
The full moon can delight a water lily[126] afflicted with separation
Without difficulty by means of its beams' help. [27]

The third time for the observance has approached now.

TĀRĀPĪḌA: Come, venerable one. We'll go t Acchoda now. [*Exeunt ambo.*][127]

VILĀSAVATĪ: [*towards the dressing room*]: Dear Kādambarī! Now cease attempting the rash act, and put on my son a costume fit for the special happiness. Dear Mahāśvetā! Discard your garment for austerities,[128] and put on auspicious ornaments.

[*Off stage*]

We have received your instructions.

VILĀSAVATĪ [*towards the dressing room*]: Friend Kulavardhanā, come! Show me the way to the hermitage.

[*Having entered*]

KULAVARDHANĀ: This way, this way, Queen.

[*Both walk around.*]

[*Enter* KĀDAMBARĪ, *watching* CANDRĀPĪḌA'S *ornamented body.*]

KĀDAMBARĪ: I have performed an ablutionary rite for my lord with pure,[129] cold water from Acchoda. I have anointed his limbs wearing a silken garment[130] with sandal paste. I have placed fragrant wreaths[131] on his head brilliant[132] with a glittering gemmed crown. And I have hung[133] on his neck the *śeṣahāra*, which has been an eyewitness of my first[134] love. [*Looks at him longingly.*]

VILĀSAVATĪ: Now I'll[135] prepare the materials for my lord eager to worship the Brahmins. [*Exit with*[136] KULAVARDHANĀ.]

KĀDAMBARĪ: Oh, I'm unfortunate![137] I don't know when ever the glorious one is going to actualize[138] Rohiṇī's words. [*Indicating an omen*] Why is this left eye[139] of mine throbbing unprecedentedly? [*after sighing*] Or rather,[140] good omens surely yield fruit to those who have performed meritorious deeds. All right. Since my friends[141] aren't closeby, I'll cool[142] my love fever by embracing him. I have long desired this. [*Acting embracing him, with horripilation*] Immersed in an ocean of joy, I can't really describe what this is.[143] Why! I'm getting again now the same kind of special sensation as the horripilation I felt on my chest in the snow house.[144]

[*Having entered, consciousness regained*]

CANDRĀPĪḌA: Beloved Kādambarī, enough of grief and[145] fear! That nectar-like embrace of yours around my neck has revived me.

That darkness of a curse which suddenly caused[146]
    This separation to us as if to a couple of ruddy geese
Has been removed[147] with great difficulty
    By my merit as if by the sun.[148] [28]

KĀDAMBARĪ [*with astonishment and joy*]: Since I'm not sure[149] of my good fortune, I can't really open my eyes and see him. [*After opening her eyes*] Why! my lord has regained all his previous beauty as if he had awaked from sleep. He's beautiful just as the moon set free by Rāhu.

CANDRĀPĪḌA: Beloved daughter of Citraratha!

I was long ignorant of what had happened before
As if my mind were stupefied;[150]
Then I recognized such a state as this
In my other life,
And spent even a few moments
As if a hundred ages.
Oh, tell me!
How did you spend your long separation? [29]

KĀDAMBARĪ: Even for a moment I can't leave my lord obtained with great difficulty, and go elsewhere. Now, who ever is going to get[151] my dear friend Mahāśvetā to share my experience of the joy for the eyes? And my friends who went to prepare my costume[152] are delaying.

[*Enter* MAHĀŚVETĀ *with her friends, being shown the way*[153] *by* KEYŪRAKA.]

KEYŪRAKA: This way, this way, Princess.

MAHĀŚVETĀ [*after giving ear*]: What do you think, friends? My heart seems consoled without cause. I hear[154] the Prince's voice like nectar for the ears,[155] which I have enjoyed before.

TARALIKĀ: Today Rohiṇī's words[156] have indeed assured the arrival of your complete happiness.

MADALEKHĀ and TAMĀLIKĀ [*after seeing him*]: Princess! here we see the Crown Prince accompanied by the Princess with his physical beauty[157] even greater than before.

KEYŪRAKA: Her two friends have observed well.

His face appears brilliant like the moon's disc
Concealed and released by a cloud; moreover,
Charming with pupils moving like bees, his eyes enjoy[158]
The luster of full-blown lotuses at dawn.[159] [30]

MAHĀŚVETĀ: Fortunately, my friend Kādambarī is rejoiced by the Prince, who has regained his life. [*Walking around, excited with joy, to herself*] I hope the rest of Rohiṇī's words will also come true like this.[160]

KEYŪRAKA [*after looking elsewhere*]:

Given the support of a hand by his friend,
Some handsome divine youth is
Gracefully descending here
To the surface of the earth

From the nectar-beamed moon's disc
By way of the sky —
Surely this[161] must be that Puṇḍarīka. [31]

TARALIKĀ [*after observing him*]: He really is the lord of my friend's life!

MAHĀŚVETĀ [*joyfully*]: Now sustaining my life is fruitful.

[*Enter* PUṆḌARĪKA, *leaning*[162] on KAPIÑJALA's *arm.*]

KAPIÑJALA: Friend Puṇḍarīka,[163]

Rohiṇī has taken off[164] your pair of bark garments
And dressed[165] you in a pair of heavenly silken ones;
She has loosened your tied unkempt hair
And placed a gemmed crown on your head —
According to your father's order,
She has prepared you this bright appearance
Suitable for your future status as a householder
And that as a *gandharva* king. [32]

PUṆḌARĪKA: She is indeed the greatest cause[166] of all our good fortune as you are.

KAPIÑJALA [*showing* MAHĀŚVETĀ *with his hand*]:

Here she is! She was determined to follow you
Though you were gone to another world.
Since she heard of her subsequent happiness
In the moon's and my words,
She has been long sustaining her spear of a life
Hopefully but with difficulty.
Console her, a respectable lady
Whose primary concern is fidelity to her lord! [33]

PUṆḌARĪKA [*after approaching* MAHĀŚVETĀ]:

Lovely girl! come and embrace my intensely fevered body
With your fevered body;[167]
I will conquer your fever with my fever
As if a missile with missiles.[168] [34]

[*The two embrace.*]

CANDRĀPĪḌA: Princess Kādambarī, the saying that a blessing follows[169] a blessing is true. For

This dear friend of yours, Mahāśvetā,
    Has long pined for Puṇḍarīka;
Haṁsa's daughter is united with her beloved
As if a goose[170] with hers. [35]

KĀDAMBARĪ: Oh! I see my dear friend happy to be united with her beloved.

CANDRĀPĪḌA & PUṆḌARĪKA [*approach and touch each other with their hands.*]

CANDRĀPĪḌA: Thus our mutual curse has indeed done us the greatest favor by bringing us friendship.

PUṆḌARĪKA: Glorious moon! Protector of the world! Gem adorning Śiva's head!

If you, merciful to me cruel with a previous offense,
    Had not taken this body to your own abode
And nourished it with your beams tender with nectar,
    How could I feel happy like this today?[171] [36]

KAPIÑJALA: Friends Candrāpīḍa and Puṇḍarīka,

May the friendship between you two,
    Tender with the existence of affection
Thus arisen to each other,
    Prosper like that between Mitra and Varuṇa! [37]

MAHĀŚVETĀ: Prince, I have seen[172] you come to yourself thanks to your merit.

KĀDAMBARĪ [*after embracing* MAHĀŚVETĀ]: Friend, now you have completed and released[173] my[174] vow.

KAPIÑJALA: May the *gandharva* Princesses be victorious!

FRIENDS [*with a bow*]: Are our friends both happy to be united with their beloveds at the same time?

KĀDAMBARĪ: Friends, inform the elders practising austerities of this good fortune.

FRIENDS: Certainly! [*Walk around, dancing for joy.*]

MAHĀŚVETĀ: Keyūraka, go to Hemakūṭa and speak pleasant words[175] to the elders.

KEYŪRAKA: Certainly! [*Exit.*]

MADALEKHĀ: That is surely the Great King. He has heard the good news somewhere, and is coming here[176] with the venerable Śukanāsa.

TAMĀLIKĀ: Dramiḍadhārmika is showing Vilāsavatī and Manoramā the way here.[177]

ALL:[178] Great King, your wishes[179] have been fulfilled by the Crown Prince's and his friend's recovery of consciousness.[180]

[*Enter* TĀRĀPĪḌA *and* ŚUKANĀSA, VILĀSAVATĪ *and* MANORAMĀ, *and the* JESTER.]

TĀRĀPĪḌA & ŚUKANĀSA[181] [*to* VILĀSAVATĪ *and* MANORAMĀ]: Have you both heard the nectar-like news?

VILĀSAVATĪ & MANORAMĀ:[182] What's the point of hearing it now? Right here our sons, together with their brides,[183] are sprinkling[184] wonderful moonlight on our eyes.[185]

CANDRĀPĪḌA & PUṆḌARĪKA [*to themselves*]:

Considering whatever misfortune fate has brought them
To have been caused by their own misconduct,
Modest people of ready repentance become ashamed
To show their faces in front of the worthy. [38]

[*Both approach and duly salute all.*][186]

MANORAMĀ: Vaiśampāyana no longer[187] has his characteristics!

ŚUKANĀSA: Of course not.

KAPIÑJALA [*after approaching these two*]: Venerable ones, please listen!

You are the sage Śvetaketu's partial incarnation;
This lady is Lakṣmī's;
And Puṇḍarīka here is the son of you two —
Do not ever think otherwise. [39]

ŚUKANĀSA [*recollecting*]: Kapiñjala has spoken the truth!

MANORAMĀ: Now I remember! Surely Lakṣmī granted me a boon, when she was taking a walk in the lotus beds of the celestial Ganges, with the words "While I practise austerities in the world of mortals, I will become a human and have a special experience with you."[188]

ŚUKANĀSA: Well done! Now our hearts are attached to Puṇḍarīka alone.[189]

TĀRĀPĪḌA: Then, we should respect the venerable couple especially from now on. [*After looking elsewhere*]

Why! *Kinnara*s singing,
*Apsarase*s engaged in dancing on all sides,

A host of *cāraṇa*s frolicking,
Siddha women trembling, intoxicated with wine,
*Yakṣa*s increasingly delighted,
And *vidyādharas* filled[190] with joyful feelings,
Both *gandharva* Kings have arrived here,
Together with their Queens. [40]

[*Enter* CITRARATHA, HAṀSA, MADIRĀ *and* GAURĪ, *being shown the way by* KEYŪRAKA.]

CITRARATHA & HAṀSA[191] [*to each other*]:

This task of the elders
Of giving away their daughters
Properly[192] to meritorious suitors
Has not been easy to accomplish;
In spite of the ineffable calamity
That happened on the way,
Fortunately today your happiness has arisen
From that very sam[193] [41]

MADIRĀ & GAURĪ[194] [*to each other*]: Friend, congratulations on your acquisition of a worthy son-in-law!

TĀRĀPĪḌA & ŚUKANĀSA: Oh,[195] *gandharva* Emperors! Friends, this way, this way!

VILĀSAVATĪ & MANORAMĀ: This way, this way,[196] *gandharva* Empresses! [*Embrace one another.*]

MADIRĀ & GAURĪ: Dear Kādambarī! Dear Mahāśvetā! Come here! [*Embrace them.*][197]

HAṀSA: Why are we still procrastinating? On this very[198] auspicious occasion — though it has sprung[199] from our children's[200] mutual love — we should hold their wedding ceremonies[201] for the sake of the custom of the world.

TĀRĀPĪḌA & ŚUKANĀSA: As our friends please.

CITRARATHA [*giving* KĀDAMBARĪ *into* CANDRĀPĪḌA's *hand*]: Oh, my son-in-law! Candrāpīḍa! Moon reborn on the earth! Honorable one, please receive[202] the *gandharva* Kingdom as well as her dowry.

HAṀSA [*after giving* MAHĀŚVETĀ *into* PUṆḌARĪKA's *hand*]: I have given the respectable one my sovereignty as her dowry.[203]

TĀRĀPĪḌA: Prince Candrāpīḍa!

You of divine nature were born as my son[204]
Owing to my religious merit;
You acquired great scholarship in the arts;
Good fortune was brought to you[205]
Under the guise of your crown princedom;
And we observed your prowess,
Conqueror of the eight regions!
Now you are accompanied by a virtuous wife.
Congratulations! What other fruit could there be
In the expedition of mundane existence? [42]

From now on, we, who have taken a vow to be hermits, are going to dwell in this very Caitraratha forest. Please accept[206] with your friend the sovereignty of India as well.

CANDRĀPĪḌA: Why is Father ordering me like this?[207]

ŚUKANĀSA: Crown Prince, please accede to the Great King's order. Still,

Performing the three,[208] acting by the three,[209]
Attaining success in the four,[210]
Protecting the four,[211] restraining[212] your five,[213]
Shunning the six,[214] able to employ the six,[215]
Free from the seven,[216] and
Bringing and nourishing the seven,[217]
May you alone bravely protect the whole earth
As long as the sun and the moon exist here![218] [43]

[*Empties over* CANDRĀPĪḌA's *and* PUṆḌARĪKA's *heads a gold jar filled with Acchoda's water and brought by a servant.*]

[*Off stage, the sound of a celestial kettle drum, and a shower of flowers.*]

KAPIÑJALA: Friends, what further service beyond this should these two gentlemen offer you two?

CANDRĀPĪḌA & PUṆḌARĪKA: Friend, what further service can there be beyond this? Look!

Oh, long unhappy themselves
When we were unhappy,
All our elders have become happy today,
When we have become happy. [44]

Yet may it be thus: [*speech of the actors*][219]

May the victorious kings make the earth
Intent upon right![220]
May the glorious Indra grant a desired rain
From time to time!
May all the virtuous attain happiness with ease
And feel content![221]
Furthermore, may these minds of ours reflect
Upon devotion to Śiva alone! [45]

[*Exeunt omnes.*]

END OF ACT EIGHT
AND OF THE *KĀDAMBARĪNĀṬAKA*
OF NARASIṀHA[222]

Notes

1. *M.M.: -niratair; V.K.: -niyatair.*
2. *V.K.: nāgarikopabhogyo; M.M.: nnāṭavikopabhogyā (viṣaya-).*
3. *M.M.V.2.* supplies *(acala)jala(syandeṣu); V.K.* adopts.
4. *M.M.* and *V.K.* give only the first *pāda.*
5. *V.K.* supplies *sāsram.*
6. *V.K.* omits *(a°autta) ja (soṇṇā).*
7. *V.K.: kettiaṁ kālaṁ; M.M.: ke°tiaṁ va kāla; V.K.Ch.: kiyantaṁ kālam.*
8. *V.K.: tayā; M.M.: mayā.*
9. *V.K.: tasyā anumatyabhāvena; M.M.: tasyānupratyābhavena.*
10. *V.K.: kūjitum; M.M.: kūjitam.*
11. *V.K.: prasādam; M.M.: prasā(?)m; M.M.V.2.: prasādarām.* Water is supposed to become clear with the rise of the star Agastya, or Canopus.
12. *H.S.: (sā vi) kila; M.M.: (- -) kira; V.K.* omits.
13. *V.K.: vavasiā; M.M.: virala(i, M.M.V.2.)u°mahai; V.K.Ch.: vyavasitā.*
14. *V.K.* adds *devi,* but it seems unnecessary because the following verse contains *devi (devī* emended).
15. *V.K.: ānane tava nanu; M.M.: ānanaṁ nanu tava.*
16. In the novel *Kādambarī,* Śukanāsa saw in a dream a Brahmin place a white lotus flower on his wife Manoramā's lap; *vide* Bāṇa, *Kādambarī (Pūrvārddha),* ed. by M. Pant, p. 230: *adya khalu mayāpi niśi svapne - śāntamūrtinā divyākṛtinā dvijena - - - - puṇḍarīkam utsaṅge devyā manoramāyā nihitaṁ dṛṣṭam.*

17. *Tathaiva:* lit. exactly so, precisely in that manner, &c.
18. *V.K.: daivyā (kiloktaṁ girā); M.M.: devyā (khiloktaṁ -).*
19. *H.S.: (yac cā)smattanayos; M.M.* and *V.K.: (- ca) hrādanayos.*
20. *V.K.: devi; M.M.: devī(pratyayavatīr; -vadbhir, M.M.V.2.).*
21. *M.M.V.2.* and *V.K.: pratyayavadbhir (atra); M.M.: (devī) pratyayavatīr (-).*
22. *H.S.: praviśyāpaṭākṣepeṇa sasaṁbhramam; M.M.: praviśya paṭākṣepeṇa sasaṁbhramaṁ(maḥ, M.M.V.2.) keyūrakaḥ; V.K.: - - sasaṁbhramaḥ.* For *apaṭākṣepeṇa, vide* Trans., Act II, n. 93.
23. *V.K.: abhimataṁ; M.M.: ahitañ.*
24. *V.K.: tādṛśi (vyatikare); M.M.: tādṛśī (-).*
25. *H.S.: bhartṛdvitīyajananāvaruddhā; M.M.: bhartā dvitīyajananā (?) (ṣi, M.M.V.2.)ddha; V.K.: bhartrā saha.*
26. *V.K.: (bhuvane) vasthāpitāpi; M.M.: (-)na sthāpitā(?) sauhārdavidehṛdayā.*
27. *M.M.: sākṣād eveyaṁ āyātā; V.K.: sākṣād ihāgatā.*
28. *M.M.: (sāhasād) asmāt; V.K.* omits.
29. *V.K.: dhyānādhigatāt; M.M.: dhyānādigadhigatāt.*
30. *V.K.: paudisiddhaṁ khu sāhuttaṇaṁ divvanārīṇaṁ; M.M.: sava°tīsuviaṇī sādu°taṇaṁ -; V.K.Ch.: prakṛtisiddhaṁ khalu sādhutvaṁ divyanārīṇām.*
31. *V.K.* supplies *iti.*
32. *V.K.: kudo amhāṇaṁ tārisaṁ sukaaṁ; M.M.: kuto bramhāṇataraṁ suta(ka, M.M.V.2.)aṁ; V.K.Ch.: kuto smākaṁ tādṛśaṁ sukṛtam.*
33. *V.K.: āvirbhāvayati; M.M.: -yanti.*
34. *V.K.: āṇehi - maṇoramaṁ vi; M.M.: āārehi - maṇoraham api; V.K.Ch.: ānaya - manoramām api.*
35. *V.K.* adds *(pariharantyas) tiṣṭhanti.*
36. *V.K.* omits *(tataḥ) kila.*
37. *H.S.: yathābhimatanirvahaṇam; M.M.: -nirvāhanā(ṇā, M.M.V.2.)ya; V.K.: -nirvahaṇāya.*
38. *V.K.: avaheharin edaṁ; M.M.: avārehaṇadaṁ; V.K.Ch.: avadhatta idam.*
39. *V.K.* supplies *dṛṣṭvā.*
40. *H.S.: vidiśā rājadhānī; M.M.* and *V.K.: vidiśārājadhānī.*
41. *V.K.: (yad) iha (vetravaty-); M.M.: (yad)i bha(ved ravaty-).*
42. *M.M.V.2.* and *V.K.: vipaṇīpathāḥ; M.M.: vivarṇitā.*
43. *V.K.: (yad iha) vetravaty(āpagā); M.M.: (yadi bha)vedra(da, M.M.V.2.)vaty(āpagāḥ).*
44. *M.M.V.2.* and *V.K.: (-stana)taṭī-; M.M.: (--)kaṭī-.*
45. *V.K.: mahitavibhave; M.M.: mahati vibhave.*
46. *M.M.: no; V.K.: nau.*
47. *M.M.V.2.* and *V.K.: candrāpīḍaṁ - yauvarājyābhiṣiktaṁ; M.M.: -ḍas - -ṣiktaḥ.*
48. *V.K.* omits *(pūrṇendu)bimba(pratimaṁ).*
49. *V.K.: pratyākhyāyi (suparvaparvatataṭaṁ) vakṣastaṭaṁ; M.M.: pratyākhyāya (-) vakṣastaṭe.*

50. *M.M.: nigamau (bimbānubimbāv ubhau); V.K.: nikamau (- -).*
51. *V.K.: daṁsehi; M.M.: (kahaṁ edaṁ)sesi; V.K.Ch.: darśaya.*
52. *M.M.: -gṛhīta-; V.K.: -garbhita-.*
53. *V.K.: vijijñāpayiṣatīva; M.M.: vijijñapiṣatīti(tīva, M.M.V.2.).*
54. *V.K.: punar nepathye; M.M.: punas tatraiva.*
55. *V.K.: -dāraa-; M.M.: -dāriā-; V.K.Ch.: -dāraka-.*
56. *V.K.: -upalatikāṁ; M.M.: -upi-.*
57. *V.K.: -vardhakavanī-; M.M.: -baddhaka(?; ma, M.M.V.2.)nī.*
58. *V.K.* supplies *suo; V.K.Ch.: śukaḥ.*
59. *V.K.: saala(kalāpāraṁ*); *M.M.: posa*°*di(-); V.K.Ch.: sakala(kalāpāraṁ).*
60. *V.K.: hā; M.M.: yā.*
61. *M.M.: upāgato; V.K.: upagato.*
62. *V.K.: mamaiva; M.M.: mameva.*
63. *V.K.: apratīkāra(dāruṇe); M.M.: pratīkāraṁ(-).*
64. *Vimuktāhāraṁ [vi + (muktā + hāra)]*; it also means "having given up food" (*vimukta + āhāra*).
65. Narasiṁha borrows this *āryā* verse directly from the *Kādambarī* of Bāṇa; *vide Kādambarī (Pūrvārddha),* ed. by M. Pant, p. 44.
66. *V.K.* supplies *hā*; *V.K.Ch.: hā.*
67. *V.K.* supplies *asmābhir.*
68. *V.K.: lakṣitā; M.M.: rakṣitā.*
69. *M.M.: yathābhihitaṁ rājacakreṇa tathā hy eṣaḥ; V.K.: tathaivaitat yathābhihitaṁ rājacakreṇa* | *tathā hy eṣaḥ.*
70. *M.M.: unnamya* (used for a metrical reason in place of a more appropriate *unnamayya*); *V.K.: unmucya.*
71. *V.K.: paṭhati; M.M.: paṅkti(sphuṭa-).*
72. *V.K.: punar nepathye; M.M.: punas tatraiva.*
73. *M.M.: avahitaś; V.K.: avahitamanāḥ.*
74. *V.K.: nāma; M.M.: yatra.*
75. *V.K.: vasan (yatraiva); M.M.: vasaty (atraiva).*
76. *M.M.V.2.* and *V.K.: śaraiḥ; M.M.: śanaiḥ.*
77. *V.K.: (vyatīta)kathāmukham; M.M.: (-)kathāyā mukham.*
78. *V.K.: ṇimillialoaṇo; M.M.: ṇimi*°*i(la, M.M.V.2.)kalakiṇaṁ e*°*va; V.K.Ch.: nimīlitalocana (ārya-).*
79. *M.M.: tu; V.K.* omits.
80. *V.K.: āśvāsayataiva; M.M.: -yateva.*
81. *V.K.: avadhṛto; M.M.: avasaraḥ dhṛto.*

82. *V.K.* supplies *tārāpīḍaḥ.*
83. *V.K.: āyātaḥ; M.M.: āyātā.*
84. *V.K.: (-bhayāj)jātu; M.M.: (- -)jāta(hārītanito).*
85. *V.K.: jñāta-; M.M.: jāta-.*
86. *M.M.: (mātaṅga)putryāḥ (kṣapayati); V.K.: (-)putryā* (-).
87. *M.M.V.2.* and *V.K.: pakkaṇe; M.M.: pattaṇe.*
88. *V.K.: kahijjantaṁ; M.M.: kahi°ja°ti e°va; V.K.Ch.: kathyamānaṁ.*
89. *M.M.V.2.* and *V.K.: pakkaṇam; M.M.: pattanam.*
90. *Vedituṁ* seems to be used here for a metrical reason in place of the correct *vedayituṁ.*
91. *V.K.: vividiṣāmaḥ; M.M.: vivadiṣāma.*
92. *M.M.: -jugupsanīyam; V.K.: -jugupsitam.*
93. *V.K.: etat; M.M.: etāvat.*
94. *V.K.: aṇapagata-; M.M.: anupagata-.*
95. *M.M.: mātaṅga-; V.K.: māgaṅga-* (misprint).
96. *M.M.V.2.* and *V.K.: vyājihīrṣur iva; M.M.: vyājihīrṣatīti.*
97. *V.K.: kim api; M.M.: katham iva.*
98. *H.S.: kāambarīloaṇāṇanda canda; V.K.: -āṇandacanda; M.M.:-āṇa* (. . ., blurred); *V.K.: kādambarīlocanānandacandra; H.S.Ch.: -ānanda candra.*
99. *V.K.: ṇa paḍibujjhasi; M.M.: paḍibundhasu; V.K.Ch.: na pratibudhyase.*
100. *V.K.: (-deha)ntaraṁ; M.M.: (- -)ṁtaro; V.K.Ch.: (-dehā)ntaram.*
101. *M.M.: sahoarī; VK.: -rā; V.K.Ch.: sahodarā; H.S.Ch.: -rī.* Lakṣmī considers himself to be a uterine sister of Śūdraka, or the moon, because both the moon and she were churned out of the ocean; she does not mention this in Bhūṣaṇa's sequel to Bāṇa's novel *Kādambarī.*
102. *M.M.V.2.* and *V.K.: kuta (idam); M.M.: kṛta* (-).
103. *M.M.V.2.* and *V.K.: -aśeṣaramaṇī; M.M.: -aśeṣāramaṇī-.*
104. *M.M.: -bhāvado; V.K.: -bhāvādo; V.K.Ch.: -bhāvāt; H.S.Ch.: -bhāvato.*
105. *V.K.: tā ido vi ṇikaṭṭhaaraṁ dasaṁ mā pavisadutti; M.M.: - e°tho - ka°ṭhadaraṁ - - pavajadu°ti; V.K.Ch.: tad ito pi nikṛṣṭatarāṁ daśām mā praviśatv iti.*
106. *V.K.: na; M.M.: (nāmā,* later corrected as *nāma)nu (kārayet).*
107. After this *M.M.* has the following verse in the *śārdūlavikrīḍita* meter: *anyāny eva tapāṁsi tāni labhate yair nāma putraṁ janaḥ, kṛcchreṇāsya bahuprayatnaviṣamaṁ vārtena saṁvardhanam | (?) ka(?) ivāvadhiś śrutasamutkṛṣṭāṁ vidhātur dhiyaṁ, saṁskārānuvidhāyi vṛttam anaghīkartuñ ca jāgartyate |* *V.K.* omits this because it seems rather irrelevant and partly incomprehensible. It seems to mean approximately: There are indeed different austerities by which a man begets a son. Raising him requires a great effort and is painful, for the skill of doing so is very difficult. The authority . . . the excellent thought of the Creator . . . And his conduct, obedient to an impression in his mind, is woken up to make itself without sin.

108. *V.K.: duvehiṁ vi tujjhehiṁ samasāvāvasāṇehiṁ hodavvaṁ ti; M.M.: doṇṇa - tu°jhāṇa - vasāṇeṇa - -; V.K.Ch.: dvābhyām api yuvābhyāṁ samaśāpāvasānābhyāṁ bhavitavyam iti.*
109. *V.K.: parigahia-; M.M.: sarigahia-; V.K.Ch.: parigṛhīta-.*
110. *V.K.: abhūvam; M.M.: abhūvan.*
111. *M.M.V.2.* and *V.K.: vacobhir; M.M.: vayobhir.*
112. *V.K.: suptaprabuddha iva; M.M.: suptaḥ prabuddha iva.*
113. *V.K.: punar nepathye; M.M.: punas tatraiva.*
114. *M.M.V.2.* supplies *tārā* |; *V.K.* follows.
115. *V.K.* supplies *ayam.*
116. *M.M.: ślathayati; V.K.: kathayati.*
117. *V.K.: prapitsuḥ; M.M.: pravitsuḥ.*
118. *V.K.* supplies *svagatam.*
119. *V.K.* supplies *prakāśam.*
120. *V.K.: sākṣātkāryate; M.M.: -kriyate.*
121. *H.S.: bhavissadi; M.M.: hoi; V.K.: hodu; V.K.Ch.: bhavatu; H.S.Ch.: bhaviṣyati.*
122. *V.K.: ṇaaṇuccavo; M.M.: ṇaāāsavo; V.K.Ch.: nayanotsavaḥ.*
123. *V.K.: -viggahāṇaṁ; M.M.: -vi°gahokalāṇi; V.K.Ch.:- vigrahayor.*
124. *Kapiñjala.*
125. *H.S.: sā (ṇaarī): M.M.: taṁ (-); V.K.: so (-); V.K.Ch.: sā (nagarī).*
126. *V.K.: śaknoty eva niśāpatiḥ kumudinīṁ - nirmātum āmodinīm; M.M.: - aiva niśāpateḥ kumudinī - nirmādam -.*
127. *H.S.: ubhau niṣkrāntau; M.M.: ubhau* || *kau, tau(M.M.V.2.) niṣkrāntau; V.K.: tārāpīḍaśukanāsau niṣkrāntau.*
128. *H.S.: pariccattaṇiamavesā; V.K.: pariccaiaṇiamavesā; M.M.: (tumaṁ vi)ri°calaapadesa(maṁgalā-); V.K.Ch.: parityaktaniyamaveṣā.*
129. *V.K.: amala-; M.M.: amaa-; V.K.Ch.: amala-.*
130. *V.K.: dhāriapaṭṭaṁsuassa; M.M.: pariva°ta°sua°sa; V.K.Ch.: dhāritapaṭṭāṁśukasya.*
131. *V.K.: sugandhio māliāo; M.M.: suvaṇṇaa°dhiamālaāo; V.K.Ch.: sugandhayo mālikāḥ.*
132. *V.K.: -bhāsure (sīsammi); M.M.: -bhāsu(-); V.K.Ch.:-bhāsvare (śirasi); H.S.Ch.: -bhāsure (-).*
133. *V.K.: ālambio (kaṇṭhe); M.M.: ālaṁvidoa(-); V.K.Ch.: ālambitaḥ (kaṇṭhe).*
134. *V.K.: puḍama-; M.M.: pudama-; V.K.Ch.: prathama-.*
135. *H.S.: (jāva ahaṁ) vi; M.M.: (- -) mi; V.K.* omits; *H.S.Ch. (yāvad aham) api.*
136. *M.M.: samaṁ; V.K.: saha.*
137. *M.M.: maṁdabhāā; V.K.: manja-; V.K.Ch.: mandabhāgyā.*
138. *V.K.: (saccavaaṇā) karijjissai; M.M.: (-) kari°jai; V.K.Ch.: (satyavacanā) kariṣyate.*
139. *V.K.: vāmaṇaaṇaṁ; M.M.: vāmaaṇṇaṁ; V.K.Ch.: vāmanayanam.*

140. *V.K.* supplies *aha vā; V.K.Ch.: atha vā.*

141. *H.S.: sahīo; M.M.: hio; V.K.: sahio; V.K.Ch.: sakhyaḥ.*

142. *V.K.: ṇivvāvemi; M.M.: vāṇi*° (*vā*, inserted by *M.M.V.2.)vemi; V.K.Ch.: nirvāpayāmy.*

143. *V.K.: ṇa khu mae āṇandasāaraṇimaggāe pārīadi kiṁ edaṁ ti vaṇṇeduṁ; M.M.: - - - āṇī(ṇaṁ, M.M.V.2.)daṇīsaṁdiaṁhi(chī, M.M.V.2.)e pārīai puloeduṁ; V.K.Ch.: na khalu mayā ānandasāgara-nimagnayā pāryate kim idam iti varṇayitum.*

144. *V.K.: kahaṁ pulaiavakkhatthalo jāriso himagharammi aṇuhūdo tāriso evva dāṇiṁ vi passaviseso bhāviai; M.M.: - va°mhalapulauho*(later corrected as *he)avaia(rimaava°cha°talo jāriso himaghara°mi aṇuhūdo tāriso se dāṇi vi*, partly very faint, inserted by *M.M.V.2.)sā vi bhāviai pa(pa°. . . seso*, very faint, inserted by *M.M.V.2.)sara°ti a°bhuāgādaṁ | saaṁ e°va; V.K.Ch.: kathaṁ pulakitavakṣaḥsthalo yādṛśo himagṛhe nubhūtas tādṛśa evedānīm api sparśaviśeṣo bhāvyate.*

145. *V.K.: ca; M.M.: api.*

146. *V.K.: pratipādito; M.M.: -pātito.*

147. *V.K.: apanītaḥ; M.M.: (mama) api nītā(taḥ, M.M.V.2.).*

148. *V.K.: pūṣṇeva; M.M.: pūṣeva.*

149. *V.K.: avissasantī; M.M.: avisasaṁtī; V.K.Ch.: aviśvasatī.*

150. *V.K.: saṁmūḍhacitta (iva); M.M.: saṁmūdacinta* (-).

151. *VK.: karissadi; M.M.: karedi; V.K.Ch.: kariṣyati.*

152. *V.K.* omits (*karedi*) | *etāe°cia* (*ṇeva°hī-; -chī-, M.M.V.2.*).

153. *M.M.V.1.* and *V.K.: -mārgā; M.M.: -va(r*, inserted by *M.M.V.2.)tmā.*

154. *V.K.: suṇijjai; M.M.: su°vai; V.K.Ch.: śrūyate.*

155. *V.K.: kaṇṇāmiaanto; M.M.: kaṇṇāmrāaṁto; V.K.Ch.: karṇāmṛtāyamāno.*

156. *H.S.: ajja rohiṇīvaaṇeṇa; M.M.: a°ca(ja, M.M.V.2.) rohiṇī | aṇeṇa; V.K.: rohiṇīvaaṇeṇa; V.K.Ch.: rohiṇīvacanena; H.S.Ch.: adya rohiṇī-.*

157. *V.K.: -kāntī; M.M.: -pāḍalo; V.K.Ch.: -kāntir.*

158. *V.K.: aśnuvāte; M.M.: āśubhāte.*

159. *M.M.: prātaḥprabuddhakamaladyutiṁ; V.K.: prātaḥ prabuddhakamalaśriyam.*

160. *M.M.: e°vaṁ; V.K.* omits.

161. *V.K.: ayaṁ; M.M.: idaṁ.*

162. *V.K.: -avalambī puṇḍarīkaḥ; M.M.: -avalaṁbipuṇḍarīkaḥ.*

163. *M.M.V.2.: kapiṁ, sakhe puṇḍarīka; V.K.* follows.

164. *M.M.: hṛtvā; M.M.V.1.: bhṛtvā; V.K.: hitvā.*

165. *V.K.: paridhṛtaṁ; M.M.: parihṛtan (divyaṁ).*

166. *M.M.: paranidānam; V.K.: paraṁ nidānam.*

167. *H.S.: ehy āliṅga vilāsini taptena sutaptam aṅgam aṅgena; M.M.: - - vilāsinas - - - -; V.K.: - - vilāsini tava taptena sutaptam aṅgena.*

168. *V.K.: (astram ivā)strair vijaye (tava tāpaṁ madabhitāpena); M.M.: (- -)streṇa jaye (- - -).*

169. *M.M.: anubadhnāti; V.K.: anudhāvati.*

170. *Haṁsī.*

171. *M.M.V.2.* and *V.K.: adyedṛśī; M.M.: anye-.*

172. *V.K.* omits *(mae) puṇoṁ (diṭṭho).*

173. *V.K.: moiā ṇivvūḍhā; M.M.: - vi ṇī°vūdā(vūḍhā* and *caḍā, M.M.V.2.); V.K.Ch.: mīcitā* (misprint for *mocitā) nirvyūḍhā.*

174. *V.K.: maha; M.M.: mae; V.K.Ch.: mama.*

175. *M.M.: piavao; V.K.: -vaaṇo; V.K.Ch.: priyavacano; H.S.Ch.: - vacā (bhava).*

176. *M.M.: ido; V.K.: idomuhaṁ; V.K.Ch.: itomukham; H.S.Ch.: ito.*

177. *V.K.* omits *(ido) avaharisavaṇaṁ cireṇa (damila-).*

178. *Sarvāḥ,* all the female characters present.

179. *M.M.: maṇorahā; V.K.: -rahāo; V.K.Ch.: manorathāḥ.*

180. *M.M.: cea°ṇa(lāheṇa); V.K.: ceaṇa(-); V.K.Ch.: caitanya(lābhena).*

181. *V.K.: tārāpīḍaśukanāsau; M.M.: tau.*

182. *V.K.: vilāsavatīmanorame; M.M.: te.*

183. *V.K.: vacce(ā, H.S.) vahūhiṁ samaṁ; M.M.: va(?)samaṁ; V.K.Ch.: vatsau vadhūbhyāṁ samaṁ.*

184. *V.K.: siñcanti; M.M.: siṁcitiṁ; V.K.Ch.: siñcata (āścarya-).*

185. *V.K.: amhāṇaṁ ṇaaṇesu; M.M.: aṁhāṇa(a,* inserted by *M.M.V.2.) ṇāṇaṁ; V.K.Ch.: asmākaṁ nayaneṣu.*

186. *H.S.: ubhāv upasṛtya yathocitaṁ sarvān namaskurutaḥ; V.K.: upasṛtya - - -; M.M.: upasṛtya, candrāpīḍapuṇḍarīkau yathocitaṁnamaskurvataḥ.*

187. *M.M.: (ṇa khu) - dāṇiṁ; V.K.* omits; *H.S.Ch.: (na khalu)-idānīṁ.*

188. *V.K.: dāṇiṁ mae sumarīadi | diṇṇo khu me varo mandāiṇīkamalavaṇavihāriṇie lacchīe maccaloe ṇiamaṭṭhiā tumhehiṁ samaṁ māṇusī hoūṇa savisesāṇuhavaṁ karemitti; M.M.: - - sumariadi - - - va°ro -vihāriṇie saṁcaloae ṇiama°di(ṭhi, M.M.V. 2)e tumhehi māṇusāsavasesāṇubhavaṁ karomo°ti; V.K.Ch.: idānīṁ mayā smaryate | dattaḥ khalu me varo mandākinīkamalavanavihāriṇyā lakṣmyā martyaloke niyamasthitā yuṣmābhiḥ saha mānuṣī bhūtvā saviśeṣānubhavaṁ karomīti.*

189. *M.M.: adya hi naḥ pakṣapāti puṇḍarīka eva manaḥ; V.K.: - - no manaḥ puṇḍarīke pakṣapāti.*

190. *V.K.: -vyāpṛkta-; M.M.: -vyāvṛtta-.*

191. *V.K.: citrarathahaṁsau; M.M.: tāv.*

192. *H.S.: yuktyety ayaṁ; M.M: yu(?)ty ayat; M.M.V.2.* and *V.K.: yuktety ayaṁ.*

193. *H.S.: diṣṭyā tadāyati sukhaṁ -; M.M.V.2.* and *V.K.: - tadāyatisukhaṁ -; M.M.: (?)tisukhaṁ -.*

194. *V.K.: madirāgauryau; M.M.: keyū* (later corrected as *te*).

195. *M.M.: aye; V.K.: āye.*

196. *V.K.* supplies *ido ido; V.K.Ch.: ita ito.*

197. *M.M.V.2.: madirāgauryau va°che kādaṁbari va°che mahāsede ido eha ity āliṅgataḥ; M.M.: madirā(?)ity āliṅgataḥ; V.K.* omits; *H.S.Ch.: madirāgauryau || vatsye kādambari vatsye mahāśvete ita etam || ity āliṅgataḥ.*

198. *M.M.: ati(śubhaṁyuni); V.K.* omits.

199. *M.M.: -niṣpanne pi; V.K.: -niṣpanno pi.*

200. *V.K.: vatsayor (anyonya-); M.M.: (?) (- -); M.M.V.2.: vatsayoḥ (- -).*

201. *M.M.: -vidhiḥ; V.K.: -mahotsavaḥ.*

202. *V.K.: pratipadyatāṁ; M.M.V.2.: -pādya-; M.M.: vādyatāṁ.*

203. *V.K.: yautakīkṛtaṁ; M.M.: hariṇīkṛtaṁ.*

204. *M.M.*'s first hand breaks off here with *udabhūḥ putraṁ kalāsu;* then on the same page its second hand starts with *putraḥ kalāsu tvayā. Vide* Intro., chap. II.

205. *M.M.: tvayi kṛtā (ca vikṛtā,* later corrected); *V.K.* follows.

206. *H.S.: (bhavān) pratipadyatām; M.M.: (-) -padyatam; V.K.: (-) -padyasva.*

207. *V.K.: katham evam -; M.M.: - iva -.*

208. This is Narasiṁha's own riddle verse: *dhīraḥ pañca nirudhya ṣaṭ pariharan ṣaṇṇāṁ prayogakṣamas, tisraḥ saṁjanayaṁs tribhir vyavaharan siddhiṁ caturṇāṁ śritaḥ | saṁrakṣaṁś caturo pi saptarahitaḥ saptāvahan bṛṁhayann,* (for the fourth *pāda, vide infra,* n. 218). *Tisraḥ* here seems to refer to the three means of livelihood (*vṛttis*): sacrifice (*yajña*), study (*adhyayana*) and alms (*dāna*).

209. *Tribhir* here probably refers to the three Vedas: *Ṛgveda, Yajurveda* and *Sāmaveda.*

210. *Caturṇāṁ* here probably refers to the four aims of man in life (*puruṣārthas*): religious merit (*dharma*), wealth (*artha*), love (*kāma*) and liberation (*mokṣa*). Or it may refer to the four means of success against a political enemy (*upāyas*): conciliation or negotiation (*sāman*), gift (*dāna*), causing dissension (*bheda*), and punishment or attack (*daṇḍa*).

211. *Caturo* here probably refers to the four classes (*vargas*) of *brāhmaṇas, kṣatriyas, vaiśyas* and *śūdras*.

212. *Nirudhya,* used for a metrical reason in place of a more appropriate *nirundhan.*

213. *Pañca* here undoubtedly refers to five organs (*indriyas*). Most probably it refers to the five organs of perception (*jñānendriyas*): ears (*śrotras*), skin (*tvac*), eyes (*cakṣuses*), tongue (*jihvā*) and nose (*nāsikā*); or possibly to the five of action (*karmendriyas*): hands (*hastas*), feet (*pādas*), anus (*pāyu*), genital organ (*upastha*) and that of speech (*vāc*).

214. *Ṣaṭ* here probably refers to the six internal enemies of man (*ripus*): carnal desire (*kāma*), anger (*krodha*), greed (*lobha*), arrogance (*mada*), infatuation (*moha*) and jealousy (*matsara*).

215. *Ṣaṇṇāṁ* here seems to refer to the six foreign policies (*guṇas*): peace or alliance (*sandhi*), war (*vigraha*), expedition (*yāna*), halt (*sthāna* or *āsana*), taking refuge (*saṁśraya*) and duplicity (*dvaidha* or *dvaidhībhāva*). Or it may refer to the six parts of the body (*aṅgas*): head (*śiras*), stomach (*madhya*), both arms (*bāhus*) and both legs (*jaṅghās*); or possibly to the six works auxiliary to the Vedas (*vedāṅgas*): rituals (*kalpa*), pronunciation (*śikṣā*), grammar (*vyākaraṇa*), glossary (*nirukta*), prosody (*chandas*) and astronomy (*jyotiṣa*).

216. *Sapta* here is quite unclear; it might refer to the seven constituents of a kingdom (*prakṛtis*), from which Candrāpīḍa should be carefree: king (*svāmin*), minister (*amātya*), allies (*suhṛds*), treasure (*kośa*), territory (*rāṣṭra*), fortress (*durga*) and army (*bala*).

217. *Sapta* here is also quite unclear; it might refer to the seven sages; Marīci, Atri, Aṅgiras, Pulastya, Pulaha, Kratu and Vasiṣṭha.

218. *V.K.: dhīraḥ* (in the first *pāda*) - *| ācandrārkam ihaika eva vasudhāṁ kṛtsnāṁ tvam avyāś ciram; M.M.: - - | dehitvād atha te da(?)hakam eva vasudhām ekas tvam avyāś ciram.*

219. *Bharatavākyam; vide* Intro., chap. VII.

220. *H.S.: dharmaikāgrāṁ; M.M.: -graṁ; V.K.: -gryaṁ.*

221. *M.M.: santoṣabhājaḥ; V.K.: -ṣaṁbhā-.*

222. *M.M.: samāptaṁ caitat kādambarīkalyāṇaṁ nāma nāṭakam; V.K.: kādambarīkalyāṇaṁ nāṭakaṁ samāptam.Vide* Intro., chaps. II and V.

Bibliography

Abhinanda. *The Kādambarīkathāsāra of Abhinanda.* Ed. by M.P. Durgāprasād and K.P. Parab; rev. by W.L. Ś. Paṇśīkar. Kāvyamālā, 11. 3rd rev. edn. Bombay: Nirṇaya Sāgar Press, 1925.

Abhinavagupta. *Vide* Ānandavardhana and Bharata.

Agastya. *The Kṛṣṇacarita of Agastyapaṇḍita (A Gadyakāvya).* Ed. with Intro. &c. by T. Venkatacharya. Tanjore Sarasvati Mahal Series, vol. 155. Thanjavur: Tanjore Maharaja Serfoji's Sarasvati Mahal Library, 1975.

———. *The Nalakīrtikaumudī of Agastyapaṇḍita.* (2nd and 4th cantos only.) Ed. with intro. &c. by T. Venkatacharya. Delhi: D.K. Publishing House, 1975.

Amarasiṁha. *The Nāmaliṅgānuśāsana (Amarakoṣa) of Amarasiṁha.* Ed. with Kṣīrasvāmin's comm. *Amarakośodghāṭana* by K.G. Oka. Poona: Law Printing Press, 1913.

Amaru. *Amaruśatakam.* Ed. with Vemabhūpāla's comm. *Śṛṅgāradīpikā*, intro., trans., &c. by C.R. Devadhar. Poona Oriental Series, No. 101. Poona: Oriental Book Agency, 1959.

Ānandavardhana. *Dhvanyāloka.* Ed. with Abhinavagupta's comm. *Locana* by M.P. Durgāprasād and K.P. Parab; rev. by W.L. Ś. Paṇśīkar. (Kāvyamālā, No. 25; Nirṇaya Sāgar Press, 1935). Repr. Delhi: Munshiram Manoharlal, 1983.

Bāṇa. *Caṇḍīśataka.* Ed. by M.P. Durgāprasād and K.P. Parab. Kāvyamālā, pt. 4, pp. 1-46. 3rd edn. Bombay: Nirṇaya Sāgar Press, 1937. *Vide* also Quackenbos, G.P.

———. *The Harshacarita of Bāṇabhaṭṭa.* Ed. with intro. and nn. by P.V. Kane. Repr. Delhi: Motilal Banarsidass, 1986.

———. *Harṣacarita.* Trans. by E.B. Cowell and F.W. Thomas. Delhi: Motilal Banarsidass, 1961.

———. *Kādambarī (Pūrvabhāga).* Ed. with editor's Skt. comm., Eng. trans., &c by M.R. Kale. 4th rev. edn. Delhi: Motilal Banarsidass, 1968.

——— and His Son Bhūṣaṇabhaṭṭa. *Kādambarī by Bāṇa and His Son.* Ed. by P. Peterson. Bombay Sanskrit Series, No. XXIV. Pt. 1: Skt. text; pt. 2: intro. and nn. Bombay: Government Central Book Depot, 1885.

———. *Kādambarī*. Ed. with Bhānucandra's and Siddhacandra's comm. for *Pūrvārddha*, editor's Skt. comm. for *Uttarārddha,* Hindi trans., &c. by M. Pant. 2 vols. Delhi: Motilal Banarsidass, 1976 (vol. I, repr.) and 1977 (vol. II).

———. *The Kādambarī of Bāṇa*. Trans. into Eng. with occasional omissions by C.M. Ridding. Oriental Translation Fund, New Series, II. London: The Royal Asiatic Society, 1896.

Bharata. *Nāṭyaśāstra*. Ed. with Abhinavagupta's comm. *Abhinavabhāratī* by M.R. Kavi, K.S. Rāmaswāmin and J.S. Pade. 4 vols. Gaekwad's Oriental Series. Baroda: Oriental Institute, 1926-64.

———. *Nāṭyaśāstra*. Ed. by B. Śarman and B. Upādhyāya. Kāshī Sanskrit Series, 60. Benares: Chowkhamba Sanskrit Series Office, 1929.

———. *The Nāṭyaśāstra*. Ed. and trans. by M. Ghosh. 4 vols. Calcutta: Granthalaya Private Ltd., 1967.

Bhāravi. *Kirātārjunīya*. Ed. with Mallinātha's comm. *Ghaṇṭāpatha* by N.R. Ācārya. 14th edn. Bombay: Nirṇaya Sāgar Press, 1954.

Bhāsa. *Bhāsanāṭakacakram: Plays Ascribed to Bhāsa (Original Thirteen Texts in Devanāgarī)*. Ed. by C.R. Devadhar. Poona Oriental Series, No. 54. Poona: Oriental Book Agency, 1962.

———. *Thirteen Plays of Bhāsa*. Trans. into Eng. by A.C. Woolner and Lakshman Sarup. 1st MLBD repr.; 2 vols. in one. Delhi: Motilal Banarsidass, 1985.

Bhat, G.K. *The Vidūṣaka*. Ahmedabad: The New Order Book Co., 1959.

Bhaṭṭanārāyaṇa. *Veṇīsaṁhāra*. Ed. with Jagaddhara's comm., Eng. trans., &c. by M.R. Kale. Delhi: Motilal Banarsidass, 1977.

Bhavabhūti. *Mahāvīracarita*. Ed. with Vīrarāghava's comm. by T.R.R. Aiyar, S. Rangachariar and K.P. Parab. 2nd rev. edn. Bombay: Nirṇaya Sāgar Press, 1901.

———. *Mahāvīracarita*. Trans. by John Pickford. London: Trubner and Co., 1871.

———. *Bhavabhūti's Mālatīmādhava*. Ed. with Jagaddhara's comm., Eng. trans., &c. by M.R. Kale. 3rd edn. Delhi: Motilal Banarsidass, 1967.

———. *Uttararāmacarita of Bhavabhūti*. Ed. with Ghanaśyāma's comm. by P.V. Kane; Eng. trans. by C.N. Joshi. 5th edn. Delhi: Motilal Banarsidass, 1971.

———. *The Uttararāmacharita of Bhavabhūti*. Ed. with Vīrarāghava's comm., Eng. trans., &c. by M.R. Kale. Bombay: Gopal Narayan and Co., 1911.

Bhoja. *Maharaja Bhojaraja's Shringara Prakasha: The Great Tenth Century Work on Samskrit and Prakrit Rhetoric*. Ed. by G.R. Josyer. 4 vols. Mysore: Coronation Press, 1955 (vol. 1), 1963 (vols. 2 and 3), n.d. (vol. 4).

Budhasvāmin. *Bṛhatkathāślokasaṅgraha*. Ed. and trans. into French by F. Lacote. Paris: Ernest Leroux, 1908-29.

Chattopadhyaya, S. *Nāṭakalakṣaṇaratnakośa in the Perspective of Ancient Indian Drama and Dramaturgy*. Calcutta: Punthi Pustak, 1974.

Coulson, M. *Three Sanskrit Plays.* Harmondsworth (Middlesex, England): Penguin Books Ltd., 1981.

Daṇḍin. *Avantisundarī.* (Incomplete.) Ed. with intro. by S.K. Pilla. Trivandrum Sanskrit Series, 172. Trivandrum: Bhāskaramudrālaya, 1954. *Vide* also Sastri, G. Harihara.

———. *Daśakumāracarita of Daṇḍin.* Ed. with intro., Eng. trans. &c by M.R. Kale. 4th edn.; repr. Delhi: Motilal Banarsidass, 1979.

Dasgupta, S.N. and S.K. De. *A History of Sanskrit Literature: Classical Period.* Calcutta: University of Calcutta, 1947.

Dhanañjaya. *The Daśarūpaka of Dhanañjaya with the Commentary Avaloka by Dhanika and the Sub-Commentary Laghuṭīkā by Bhaṭṭanṛsiṁha.* Ed. with intro. &c. by T. Venkatacharya. The Adyar Library Series, vol. 97. Madras: The Adyar Library and Research Centre, 1969.

Dhanapāla. The *Tilakamañjarī of Dhanapāla.* Ed. by P.B. Śastrī and K.P. Parab. 2nd edn. Kāvyamālā, 85. Bombay: Nirṇaya Sāgar Press, 1938.

Diṅnāga. *Kundamālā.* Ed. by K.K. D. Sastri. Calcutta Sanskrit College Research Series, No. XXVIII; Texts, No. 15. Calcutta: Sanskrit College, 1964.

Dutta, K.K. "*Garbhāṅka:* Its Genesis and Development in Sanskrit," *Our Heritage*, vol. VII, pt. 1, pp. 37-58. Calcutta: Calcutta Sanskrit College, 1959.

Edgerton, F. *The Panchatantra Reconstructed.* American Oriental Series, vols. 2-3. New Haven: American Oriental Society, 1924.

Gaṅgādevī. *Madhurāvijaya.* Ed. with intro. by S. Thiruvenkatachari. Annamalainagar: Annamalai University, 1957.

Gerow, E. "Plot Structure and the Development of *Rasa* in the Śakuntalā," 2 pts., *Journal of the American Oriental Society*, vol. 99, No. 4, pp. 559-72 (pt. 1); vol. 100, No. 3, pp. 267-82 (pt. 2). New Haven: The American Oriental Society, 1979 and 1980.

Gnoli, R. *The Aesthetic Experience According to Abhinavagupta.* 2nd edn.: rev. and enl. The Chowkhamba Sanskrit Studies, vol. LXII. Varanasi: The Chowkhamba Sanskrit Series Office, 1968.

Gray, L.H. "Literary Studies on the Sanskrit Novel," *Wiener Zeitschrift fur die Kunde des Morgenlandes*, vol. XIII, pp. 39-58. Vienna: Oriental Institute of the University of Vienna, 1904.

Hanumant. *Hanumannāṭaka of Śrī Hanumān.* Ed. with Skt. and Hindi comms. by J. Mishra. 2nd. edn. Haridas Sanskrit Series, 271. Varanasi: Chowkhamba Sanskrit Series Office, 1978.

Harṣa. *Nāgānanda Nāṭaka.* Ed. with Hindi trans. & c. by S. Candra. 2nd edn. Delhi: Motilal Banarsidass, 1980.

———. *Priyadarśikā: A Sanskrit Drama by Harsha.* Trans. by G. K. Nariman, A.V. Williams Jackson, and C.J. Ogden; intro., nn., and text by the latter two. Columbia University Indo-Iranian Series, vol. X. Repr. New York: Ams Press Inc., 1965.

———. *Ratnāvalī Nāṭikā.* Ed. with Hindi trans. &c. by R. Mishra. 5th edn. Haridas Sanskrit Series, 232. Varanasi: Chowkhamba Amarabharati Prakashan, 1982.

Jacob, G.A. *Laukikanyāyāñjaliḥ: A Handful of Popular Maxims Current in Sanskrit Literature.* Pt. I. 2nd edn., rev. and enl. Bombay: Tukārām Jāvajī, 1907.

Jain, J. *The Vasudevahiṇḍi: An Authentic Jain Version of the Bṛhatkathā.* (Contains intro., sel. trans., &c.) L.D. Series, 59. Ahmedabad: L.D. Institute of Indology, 1977.

Jāya. *Nṛttaratnāvalī of Jāya Senāpati.* Ed. with intro. &c. by V. Raghavan. Madras Government Oriental Series, No. CVII. Madras: Government Oriental Manuscripts Library, 1965.

Kāḷidāsa. *The Abhijñānaśākuntalam of Kālidāsa.* Ed. with Rāghavabhaṭṭa's comm., Eng. trans., &c. by M.R. Kale. 10th edn.; repr. Delhi: Motilal Banarsidass, 1977.

———. *The Abhijñānaśākuntalam of Kālidāsa.* Ed. by S.K. Belvalkar. New Delhi: Sahitya Akademi, 1965.

———. *Abhijñānaśākuntalam.* Ed. with Skt. comm., Hindi trans., &c. by K. Śāstrī *et al.* Haridas Sanskrit Series, No. 41. Varanasi: Chowkhamba Sanskrit Series Office, 1960.

———. *Mālavikāgnimitram of Kālidāsa.* Ed. with Eng. trans. &c. by C.R. Devadhar. 3rd edn.; repr. Delhi: Motilal Banarsidass, 1977.

———. *Vikramorvaśīya.* Ed. with Hindi trans. &c. by R. Tripāṭhī. Delhi: Motilal Banarsidass, 1980.

Kedārabhaṭṭa. *Vṛttaratnākaram.* Ed. with 3 Skt. comms., Hindi trans., &c. by M. Shastri. Krishnadas Sanskrit Series, No. 26. Varanasi: Krishnadas Academy, 1982.

Keith, A.B. *A History of Sanskrit Literature.* Delhi: Oxford University Press, 1973.

———. *The Sanskrit Drama: In its Origin, Development, Theory and Practice.* Oxford: Clarendon Press, 1924.

Konow, S. *The Indian Drama.* Trans. from German into Eng. by S. N. Ghosal. Calcutta: General Printers, 1969.

Krishnamachariar, M. *History of Classical Sanskrit Literature.* 3rd edn. Delhi: Motilal Banarsidass, 1974.

Krishnamacharya, V. *Vide* Narasiṁha.

Kṣemendra. *Aucityavicāracarcā.* Ed. by M.P. Durgāprasād and K.P. Pāṇḍurang. Kāvyamālā, pt. 1, pp. 115-60. 3rd edn. Bombay: Nirṇaya Sāgar Press, 1929.

———. *The Brihatkathāmañjarī of Kshemendra.* Ed. by M.P. Śivadatta and K.P. Parab. 2nd edn. Kāvyamālā, 69. Bombay: Nirṇaya Sāgar Press, 1931.

Kṣemendra. *Kavikaṇṭhābharaṇa*. Ed. by M.P. Durgāprasād and K.P. Pāṇḍurang. Kāvyamālā, pt. 4, pp. 149-69. 3rd edn. Bombay: Nirṇaya Sāgar Press, 1937.

———. *Suvṛttatilaka*. Ed. by M.P. Durgāprasād, K.P. Parab and W.L. Ś. Paṇśīkar. Kāvyamālā, pt. 2, pp. 29-54. Bombay: Nirṇaya Sāgar Press, 1932.

Kṣemīśvara. *The Caṇḍa-Kauśika of Ārya Kṣemīśvara*. Ed. with Eng. trans. &c. by S.D. Gupta. Calcutta: The Asiatic Society, 1962.

———. *Naiṣadhānanda of Kṣemīśvara*. Ed. by A.K. Warder and K.K. Raja. Madras: The Adyar Library and Research Centre, 1986.

Kuntaka. *The Vakrokti-Jīvita of Kuntaka*. Ed. with Eng. trans. &c. by K. Krishnamoorthy. Dharwad: Karnatak University, 1977.

Lacote, F. *Essai sur Guṇāḍhya et la Bṛhatkathā (Suivi du Texte Inédit des Chapitres XXVII a XXX du Nepāla-Māhātmya)*. Paris: Ernest Leroux, 1908. *Vide* also Budhasvāmin.

Mahādeva. *The Adbhutadarpaṇa of Mahādeva*. Ed. by P.B. Śāstrī and K.P. Parab. 2nd edn. Kāvyamālā, 55. Bombay: Nirṇaya Sāgar Press, 1938.

Mainkar, T. G. *Studies in Sanskrit Dramatic Criticism*. Delhi: Motilal Banarsidass, 1951.

———. *The Theory of the Saṁdhis and the Saṁdhyaṅgas*. Poona: M/S Joshi and Lokhande, 1960.

Majumdar, R.C., gen. ed. *The History and Culture of the Indian People: The Delhi Sultanate*. Vol. 6. Bombay: Bharatiya Vidya Bhavan, 1960.

Mankowski, L.V. "Bāṇa's Kādambarī und die Geschichte vom Konig Sumanas in der Bṛhatkathā," 2 pts., *Wiener Zietschrift fur die Kunde des Morgenlandes*, vol. XV, pp. 213-50 (pt. 1); vol. XVI, pp. 147-82 (pt. 2). Vienna: Oriental Institute of the University of Vienna, 1901-2.

Mārkaṇḍeya. *Prākṛtasarvasva*. Ed. with intro. &c. by K.C. Acharya. Prakrit Text Society Series, No. XI: Prakrit Grammar Series, No. 1. Ahmedabad: Prakrit Text Society, 1968.

Mirashi, V.V. *Bhavabhūti*. Delhi: Motilal Banarsidass, 1974.

Mukherji, A. *Sanskrit Prosody: Its Evolution*. Calcutta: Saraswat Library, 1976.

Narahari, H.G., ed. *Descriptive Catalogue of Sanskrit Manuscripts in the Adyar Library*, vol. V. The Adyar Library Series, No. 80. Madras: The Adyar Library, 1951.

Narasiṁha. "The Devanāgarī Transcript *Chāyā* Manuscript of the *Kādambarīnāṭaka* of Narasiṁha Preserved in the Government Oriental Manuscripts Library, Madras (Reference No. 4423)."

———. "The Devanāgarī Transcript Manuscript of the *Kādambarīnāṭaka* of Narasiṁha Preserved in the Government Oriental Manuscripts Library, Madras (Reference No. 2484)."

———. *The Kādambarīkalyāṇaṁ Nāṭakam: A Drama by Narasiṁhakavi*. Ed. with Skt. intro. by V. Krishnamacharya. Madras: The Educational Publishing Co., 1936.

Nitti-Dolci, L. *The Prākṛita Grammarians.* Trans. from French into Eng. by P. Jhā. Delhi: Motilal Banarsidass, 1972.

Nṛsimha. (*Siddhodvāha*) *of Nṛisiṁha.* Ed. with intro. by P.V. Parabrahma Sastri. Andhra Pradesh Government Epigraphy Series, No. 2. Hyderabad: The Government of Andhra Pradesh, 1968.

Pischel, R. *A Grammar of the Prākrit Language.* Trans. from German by S. Jhā. 2nd rev. edn. Delhi: Motilal Banarsidass, 1981.

Quackenbos, G.P., ed. and trans. *The Sanskrit Poems of Mayūra (Sūryaśataka and Mayūrāṣṭaka) with the Caṇḍīśataka of Bāṇa.* Columbia University Indo-Iranian Series, vol. 9. New York: Ams Press Inc., 1965.

Rāghavan, V. *Bhoja's Śṛṅgāra Prakāśa.* 3rd rev. and enl. edn. Madras: Punarvasu, 1978.

———., ed. *New Catalogus Catalogorum: An Alphabetical Register of Sanskrit and Allied Works and Authors,* vols. I and III. Madras: University of Madras, 1949 and 1967.

———. *The Number of Rasa-s.* 3rd rev. edn. The Adyar Library Series, vol. 23. Madras: The Adyar Library and Research Centre, 1975.

———. *The Social Play in Sanskrit.* Transaction No. 11. Bangalore: The Indian Institute of World Culture, 1966.

———. *Some Old Lost Rāma Plays* (*Lectures Delivered in the Annamalai University*). Annamalainagar: Annamalai University, 1961.

Raja, K. Kunjunni. *Kutiyattam: An Introduction.* Delhi: Sangeet Natak Akademi, 1964.

Rājaśekhara. *The Bālarāmāyaṇa: A Drama by Rājaśekhara.* Ed. by G.D. Śāstrī. Benares: The Medical Hall Press, 1869.

———. *Rājaśekhara's Karpūramañjarī: A Drama by the Indian Poet Rājaśekhara (About 900 AD)* Ed. by S. Konow; trans. intro Eng. by C.R. Lanman. Harvard Oriental Series, Vol. IV. Delhi: Motilal Banarsidass, 1963.

Rāmacandra & Guṇacandra. *Nāṭyadarpaṇa of Rāmacandra and Guṇacandra with Their Own Commentary.* Ed. by G.K. Shrigondekar and L.B. Gandhi. Rev. 2nd edn. Baroda: Oriental Institute, 1959.

Rāma Pāṇivāda. *Kaṁsavaho (A Prākrit Poem in Classical Style*). Ed. with intro., trans., &c. by A.N. Upadhye. Delhi: Motilal Banarsidass, 1966.

Rudradāsa. *Rudradāsa's Candralekhā (A Drama in Prakrit*). Ed. with intro. &c. by A.N. Upadhye. Rev. 2nd edn. Bombay: Bharatiya Vidya Bhavan, 1967.

Rudraṭa. *The Kāvyālaṅkāra of Rudraṭa.* Ed. with Namisādhin's comm. by M.P. Durgāprasād and W.L.Ś. Paṇśīkar. Kāvyamālā, 2. 3rd edn. Bombay: Nirṇaya Sāgar Press, 1928.

Sāgaranandin. *The Nāṭakalakṣaṇaratnakośa of Sāgaranandin.* Ed. by M. Dillon. Vol. I, Text. London: Oxford University Press, 1937.

———. *The Nāṭakalakṣaṇaratnakośa of Sāgaranandin: A Thirteenth-Century Treatise on the Hindu Theater.* Trans. by M. Dillon, M. Fowler and V. Raghavan; intro. and nn. by

V. Raghavan. Transactions of the American Philosophical Society, New Series, vol. 50, pt. 9. Philadelphia: The American Philosophical Society, 1960.

Śaktibhadra. *Āścaryacūḍāmaṇi*. Bk. ed. by C.R. Jones; text and trans. by V. Raghavan. Delhi: Oxford University Press, 1984.

Saṅghadāsa. *Vide* Jain, J.

Śāradātanaya. *Bhāvaprakāśana of Śāradātanaya*. Ed. with intro. &c. by Yadugiri Yatiraja Swami and K.S. Ramaswami Sastri Siromani. Gaekwad's Oriental Series, No. XLV. Baroda: Oriental Institute, 1930.

Sastri, G. Harihara, ed. *Avantisundarī Kathāsāra*. (Anon.) (Contains detailed intro.) Madras: Kuppuswami Sastri Research Institute, 1957.

Sastri, K.A. Nilakanta. *A History of South India: From Prehistoric Times to the Fall of Vijayanagar*. 2nd edn. London: Oxford University Press, 1958.

Sastri, S. Kuppuswami, ed. *A Triennial Catalogue of Manuscripts (Collected During the Triennium 1916-17 to 1918-19 for the Government Oriental Manuscripts Library, Madras)*. Vol. III, pt. 1, Sanskrit B. and . . . (. . . *1922-23* to *1924-25* . . .). Vol. 1, pt. 1, Sanskrit C. Madras: Government Press, 1922 and 1932 resp.

Sharma, N. *Bāṇabhaṭṭa: A Literary Study*. Delhi: Munshiram Manoharlal, 1968.

Shastri, S.N. *The Laws and Practice of Sanskrit Drama*. Vol. I. The Chowkhamba Sanskrit Studies, vol. XIV. Vārāṇasī: The Chowkhamba Sanskrit Series Office, 1961.

Shekhar, I. *Sanskrit Drama: Its Origin and Decline*. Leiden: E. J. Brill, 1960.

Siṁhabhūpāla. *The Rasārṇavasudhākara of Siṁhabhūpāla*. Ed. with intro. &c. by T. Venkatacharya. The Adyar Library Series, vol. 110. Madras: The Adyar Library and Research Centre, 1979.

Somadeva. *Kathāsaritsāgara*. Ed. by J. Śāstrī. Delhi: Motilal Banarsidass, 1977.

———. *The Ocean of Story* [*Being C.H. Tawney's Translation of Somadeva's Kathāsaritsāgara (or Ocean of Streams of Story)*]. Ed. with intro., nn., &c. by N.M. Penzer. 10 vols. 2nd rev. and enl. edn.; Indian repr. Delhi: Motilal Banarsidass, 1968.

Sriramamurti, P. *Contribution of Andhra to Sanskrit Literature*. Andhra University Series, No. 105. Waltair: Andhra University Press and Publications, 1972.

———. "The Letter from P. Sriramamurti to H. Sato, the Author of This Book, Dated August 14, 1986." *Vide* also Vāmanabhaṭṭabāṇa.

Srivastava, U. "An Edition of Arjunapaṇḍita's Commentary on the *Kādambarī* (*Uttarabhāga*) (with Indroduction and Notes in English)." Ph.D. Dissertation. Toronto: University of Toronto, 1979.

Subandhu. *Vāsavadattā: A Sanskrit Romance by Subandhu*. Ed. with intro., Eng. trans., &c. by L.H. Gray. Delhi: Motilal Banarsidass, 1962.

Śūdraka. *The Mṛichchhakaṭika of Śūdraka*. Ed. with Pṛthvīdhara's comm., Eng. trans., &c. by M.R. Kale. 3rd rev. edn. Delhi: Motilal Banarsidass, 1972.

Sūryakānta. *Kṣemendra Studies (Together with an English Translation of His Kavikaṇṭhābharaṇa, Aucityavicāracarcā and Suvṛttatilaka)*. Poona Oriental Series, No. 91. Poona: Oriental Book Agency, 1954.

Trivedi, K.H. *The Nāṭyadarpaṇa of Rāmacandra and Guṇacandra: A Critical Study*. Lalbhai Dalpatbhai Series, No. 9. Ahmedabad: L.D. Institute of Indology, 1966.

Upadhye, A.N. *Vide* Rāma Pāṇivāda and Rudradāsa.

Vāmanabhaṭṭabāṇa. *Kanakalekhākalyāṇa*. Ed. by P. Sriramamurti. Andhra Sanskrit Series, No. I. Waltair: Andhra University Press, 1978.

Vātsyāyana. *The Kāmasūtra of Śrī Vātsyāyana Muni with the Jayamaṅgalā Sanskrit Commentary of Śrī Yaśodhara*. Ed. with Hindi comm. by Śrī Devduṭṭa Śāstrī. 3rd edn. The Kashi Sanskrit Series, 29. Varanasi: Chaukhamba Sanskrit Sansthan, 1982.

Vemabhūpāla. "The Devanāgarī Transcript Manuscript of the *Sāhityacintāmaṇi* of Vemabhūpāla Preserved in the Adyar Library, Madras (Adyar Ms. Fol. 175)." *Vide* also Amaru.

Vidyānātha. *Pratāparudrīya of Vidyānātha with Ratnāpaṇa of Kumārasvāmin*. Ed. by V. Raghavan. 2nd rev. and enl. edn. Madras: The Saṁskrit Education Society, 1978.

———. *Le Pratāparudrīya de Vidyānātha avec le Commentaire Ratnāpaṇa de Kumārasvāmin*. Trans. with intro. &c. into French by P; Filliozat. Publications de L'institut Francais D'indologie, No. 26. Pondichéry: Institut Francais D'indologie, 1963.

Viśākhadatta. *Mudrārākshasa of Viśākhadatta*. Ed. with Ḍhuṇḍirāja's comm., intro., Eng. trans., &c. by M. R. Kale. 6th edn. Delhi: Motilal Banarsidass, 1976.

Viśvanātha (1). *The Saugandhikāharaṇa of Viśvanāthakavi*. Ed. by M.P. Śivadatta, K.P. Parab, and W.L.Ś. Paṇśīkar. 2nd edn. Kāvyamālā, 74. Bombay: Nirṇaya Sāgar Press, 1934.

Viśvanātha (2). *Sāhityadarpaṇa*. Ed. with Hindi comm. by Ś. Śāstrī. 9th edn.; repr. Delhi: Motilal Banarsidass, 1982.

———. *The Chandrakalā Nātikā by Viśvanāth Kavirāja*. Ed. by S.N. Rajaguru and S. Das. Bhubaneswar: Government of Orissa, 1958.

Warder, A.K. *Indian Kāvya Literature*. Delhi: Motilal Banarsidass, 1972 (vol. I), 1974 (vol. II), 1977 (vol. III), 1983 (vol. IV), 1988 (vol. V) and 1992 (vol. VI).

———. *The Science of Criticism in India*. The Adyar Library General Series, 7. Madras: The Adyar Library and Research Centre, 1978.

Williams Jackson, A.V. "Time Analysis of Sanskrit Plays," 2 pts., *Journal of the American Oriental Society*, vol. 20, pt. 2, pp. 341-59 (pt. 1); vol. 21, pt. 2, pp. 88-108. (pt. 2). New Haven: The American Oriental Society, 1899 and 1900.

Woolner, A.C. *Introduction to Prakrit*. Lahore: University of the Panjab, 1917.